SUNDAY
MISSAL

2019-2020

Living with Christ
1 Montauk Avenue, Suite 200
New London, CT 06320
1-800-321-0411
www.livingwithchrist.us

 A DIVISION OF
BAYARD, INC.

Design and Layout: Jessica Llewellyn

Illustrations and photo credits: page 8, Michael Connors

ISBN 978-1-62785-449-8

Printed in Canada

To order more copies:
Tel: 1-800-321-0411
Website: www.livingwithchrist.us

CONTENTS

How to Use
This Missal

YOUR COMPANION FOR PRAYING AND LIVING THE EUCHARIST

Over the years, the use of personal missals has changed. Before Vatican Council II (1962-65), when the Mass was said in Latin, most people needed a missal during the Mass to understand the priest's words.

Vatican II made important changes in the Mass because it recognized that the celebration of Mass was lacking several important things. First, it needed to be in language the people could understand. Second, the people were to be truly involved as "full, conscious, and active" participants in the many prayers, songs, and ritual actions of the celebration.

The Mass is not to be something that just the priest does, but something that the whole community or assembly does together—singing, listening to God's word, praying for the needs of the Church and world, thanking God, sharing the consecrated bread and wine, and finally being sent back to their homes, schools, and workplaces to live what they celebrated: God present with us to change our lives and gather us into God's own community of justice, love, and peace.

As a result, after Vatican II many parishes encouraged more participation and discouraged using missals during Mass, except perhaps by those who could not hear the readings. The focus was on listening when the Scriptures were proclaimed aloud—a reminder that God was present and speaking to us in that word.

USING THE MISSAL TO PREPARE FOR SUNDAY

So, if we are not encouraged to use our missal at Mass, is there still a use for a Sunday missal? The answer is yes. But we should now use our missal at home to help us prepare to celebrate the Sunday Eucharist more fully.

The Mass celebrates God's presence with us in word and sacrament. Through Scripture we learn how God has been present with us and what we must do to live rightly in relation to God and others. But making Scripture's message our own is not always easy. In order to get more out of our Sunday listening, we should preview the readings at home during the week.

This Sunday Missal offers resources for you, your family, and your friends to prepare for a richer celebration each Sunday. Different from other Sunday missals, this missal includes not only all the prayers and Scripture readings for the Sunday Masses, but also a variety of other helps to use at home so you can participate at Mass more "fully, consciously, actively, and as befits a community," as Vatican II desired.

WEEKLY RESOURCES FOR PREPARING FOR SUNDAY

This Sunday Missal helps you to pray and live the Eucharist by preparing each week for a richer celebration of Mass. For each Sunday throughout the year, you will find:

- **A brief reflection** inspired by the readings to consider how God's message might resonate with everyday life
- **The complete text of all of the Mass prayers and Scripture readings** chosen by the Church. Also included are these other major feast days: Mary's Immaculate Conception, Ash Wednesday, the sacred three days of Holy Week, i.e., the Triduum (Holy Thursday, Good Friday, and Holy Saturday), Mary's Assumption into Heaven, and All Saints
- At the end of each Sunday, there are helps for deepening your appreciation of both the Scripture readings and the Mass prayers from the Roman Missal:

- **Responding to the word**: questions that help you pray about and discuss the meaning and application of the Scripture readings
- **Taking a closer look**: information and reflections on biblical words and themes from the Scripture texts (indicated in bold and followed by a + in the text)

GENERAL HELPS FOR PRAYING AND LIVING THE EUCHARIST

In addition to the weekly helps, this missal contains several features that you will find helpful for deepening both your understanding of the Church's liturgical year and your prayer, including:

- **Seasonal backgrounds** at the start of each liturgical season, together with suggestions for praying and living each liturgical season (e.g., pages 65-66)
- **Basic questions for exploring Scripture** (see page 573) that you can use to discover the meaning and application to your life of any Scripture reading
- **Explanations of the Church's liturgical year**, including the Church's liturgical calendar (see page 576) and the lectionary (see page 578)
- **A brief overview of Matthew's gospel** (see page 580), the primary gospel proclaimed on Sundays this year
- **The differences between liturgical and devotional prayer** (see page 584), both of which help us grow in our life as disciples
- **A treasury of prayers** (see page 587) taken from Scripture, the saints, and the Christian tradition; and also a simple ritual for receiving Communion outside of Mass
- **A pronunciation guide for biblical words** (see page 616) for words indicated by an asterisk (*) in the Scripture readings

Our Eucharistic

Liturgy *The Order of Mass*

WE ARE A EUCHARISTIC PEOPLE

The celebration of the Eucharist or Mass is the central action that defines us as Catholics and directs our efforts to realize God's kingdom community today.

Our celebration is a ritual action that is repeated over and over so that by participating in it we can bring to consciousness, through word and sacrament, the deepest meaning of our lives.

Our celebration is *eucharist*, Greek for "thanksgiving," to remind us that our basic human relationship to God is a response to God's gifts. Everything that we have is God's gift. In our ritual, we celebrate the gift of God's own presence in the assembly that gathers, in God's word that we hear, in the consecrated bread and wine that are Christ's body and blood, and in the person of the priest who presides during the celebration.

Our celebration is also Mass, from the final Latin words of sending, *Ite missa est*, meaning "Go, you are sent." As we finish our prayer, we are reminded that we are sent to discover and proclaim God's presence in all the situations of our daily lives.

As Christians, we not only *pray* the Eucharist, but we are also called upon to *live* "eucharistic" lives. Just as Jesus took the bread, his body, and blessed and broke it to share with others, so we ask God to *take* us, *bless* us, *break* us, and *share* us with others so that "through him, and with him, and in him" we may also become sources of God's new life for the world.

INTRODUCTORY RITES

ENTRANCE ANTIPHON (Turn to the appropriate day)

GREETING

In the name of the Father, and of the Son,
  and of the Holy Spirit. *Amen.*

❶ The grace of our Lord Jesus Christ,
  and the love of God,
  and the communion of the Holy Spirit
  be with you all.
  And with your spirit.

❷ Grace to you and peace from God our Father
  and the Lord Jesus Christ.
  And with your spirit.

❸ The Lord be with you.
  And with your spirit.

PENITENTIAL ACT

Brethren (brothers and sisters), let us acknowledge our sins,
and so prepare ourselves to celebrate the sacred mysteries.

After a brief pause for silence, one of the following forms is used:

❶ *I confess to almighty God*
  and to you, my brothers and sisters,
  that I have greatly sinned,
  in my thoughts and in my words,
  in what I have done and in what I have failed to do,
    (And, striking their breast, they say:)

through my fault, through my fault,
through my most grievous fault;
therefore I ask blessed Mary ever-Virgin,
all the Angels and Saints,
and you, my brothers and sisters,
to pray for me to the Lord our God.

May almighty God have mercy on us,
forgive us our sins,
and bring us to everlasting life.
Amen.

❷ Have mercy on us, O Lord.
For we have sinned against you.

Show us, O Lord, your mercy.
And grant us your salvation.

May almighty God have mercy on us,
forgive us our sins,
and bring us to everlasting life.
Amen.

❸ The celebrant makes the following or other invocations:

You were sent to heal the contrite of heart:
Lord, have mercy. Or Kyrie, eleison.
Lord, have mercy. Or *Kyrie, eleison.*

You came to call sinners:
Christ, have mercy. Or Christe, eleison.
Christ, have mercy. Or *Christe, eleison.*

You are seated at the right hand of the Father
    to intercede for us:

Lord, have mercy. Or Kyrie, eleison.
Lord, have mercy. Or **Kyrie, eleison.**

May almighty God have mercy on us,
forgive us our sins,
and bring us to everlasting life.
Amen.

The following invocations in either English or the ancient Greek
are said, unless they have just occurred in a formula of the
Penitential Act:

Lord, have mercy.   Or   Kyrie, eleison.
   Lord, have mercy.   **Kyrie, eleison.**
Christ, have mercy.   Christe, eleison.
   Christ, have mercy.   **Christe, eleison.**
Lord, have mercy.   Kyrie, eleison.
   Lord, have mercy.   **Kyrie, eleison.**

GLORY TO GOD
Glory to God in the highest,
and on earth peace to people of good will.

We praise you,
we bless you,
we adore you,
we glorify you,
we give you thanks for your great glory,
Lord God, heavenly King,
O God, almighty Father.

Lord Jesus Christ, Only Begotten Son,
Lord God, Lamb of God, Son of the Father,
you take away the sins of the world,
   have mercy on us;
you take away the sins of the world,
   receive our prayer;
you are seated at the right hand of the Father:
   have mercy on us.

For you alone are the Holy One,
you alone are the Lord,
you alone are the Most High,
Jesus Christ,
with the Holy Spirit,
in the glory of God the Father. Amen.

COLLECT (Turn to the appropriate day)

LITURGY OF THE WORD

READINGS (Turn to the appropriate day)

HOMILY

PROFESSION OF FAITH: NICENE CREED
I believe in one God,
the Father almighty,
maker of heaven and earth,
of all things visible and invisible.
I believe in one Lord Jesus Christ,

the Only Begotten Son of God,
born of the Father before all ages.
God from God, Light from Light,
true God from true God,
begotten, not made, consubstantial with the Father;
through him all things were made.
For us men and for our salvation
he came down from heaven,

> (At the words that follow, up to and including
> and became man, all bow.)

and by the Holy Spirit was incarnate of the Virgin Mary,
and became man.

For our sake he was crucified under Pontius Pilate,
he suffered death and was buried,
and rose again on the third day
in accordance with the Scriptures.
He ascended into heaven
and is seated at the right hand of the Father.
He will come again in glory
to judge the living and the dead
and his kingdom will have no end.

I believe in the Holy Spirit, the Lord, the giver of life,
who proceeds from the Father and the Son,
who with the Father and the Son is adored and glorified,
who has spoken through the prophets.

I believe in one, holy, catholic and apostolic Church.
I confess one Baptism for the forgiveness of sins
and I look forward to the resurrection of the dead
and the life of the world to come. Amen.

OR

APOSTLES' CREED

The baptismal Symbol of the Roman Church, known as the Apostles' Creed, may be used instead of the Nicene Creed, especially during Lent and Easter Time:

I believe in God,
the Father almighty,
Creator of heaven and earth,
and in Jesus Christ, his only Son, our Lord,
> (At the words that follow, up to and including
> the Virgin Mary, all bow.)

who was conceived by the Holy Spirit,
born of the Virgin Mary,
suffered under Pontius Pilate,
was crucified, died and was buried;
he descended into hell;
on the third day he rose again from the dead;
he ascended into heaven,
and is seated at the right hand of God the Father almighty;
from there he will come to judge the living and the dead.

I believe in the Holy Spirit,
the holy catholic Church,
the communion of saints,
the forgiveness of sins,
the resurrection of the body,
and life everlasting. Amen.

PRAYER OF THE FAITHFUL

LITURGY OF THE EUCHARIST

PREPARATION OF GIFTS

Blessed are you, Lord God of all creation,
for through your goodness we have received
the bread we offer you:
fruit of the earth and work of human hands,
it will become for us the bread of life.
Blessed be God for ever.

By the mystery of this water and wine
may we come to share in the divinity of Christ
who humbled himself to share in our humanity.

Blessed are you, Lord God of all creation,
for through your goodness we have received
the wine we offer you:
fruit of the vine and work of human hands,
it will become our spiritual drink.
Blessed be God for ever.

With humble spirit and contrite heart
may we be accepted by you, O Lord,
and may our sacrifice in your sight this day
be pleasing to you, Lord God.

Wash me, O Lord, from my iniquity
and cleanse me from my sin.

Pray, brethren (brothers and sisters),
that my sacrifice and yours
may be acceptable to God,
the almighty Father.

May the Lord accept the sacrifice at your hands
for the praise and glory of his name,
for our good
and the good of all his holy Church.

PRAYER OVER THE OFFERINGS (Turn to the appropriate day)

EUCHARISTIC PRAYER
The Lord be with you.
And with your spirit.
Lift up your hearts.
We lift them up to the Lord.
Let us give thanks to the Lord our God.
It is right and just.

PREFACE
The celebrant chooses from among the possible prefaces corresponding to liturgical seasons and feasts. These prefaces are for use with Eucharistic Prayers 1-3. Eucharistic Prayer 4 has its own fixed preface.

PREFACE 1 OF ADVENT
It is truly right and just, our duty and our salvation,
always and everywhere to give you thanks,
Lord, holy Father, almighty and eternal God,
through Christ our Lord.

For he assumed at his first coming
the lowliness of human flesh,
and so fulfilled the design you formed long ago,
and opened for us the way to eternal salvation,
that, when he comes again in glory and majesty
and all is at last made manifest,
we who watch for that day

may inherit the great promise
in which now we dare to hope.

And so, with Angels and Archangels,
with Thrones and Dominions,
and with all the hosts and Powers of heaven,
we sing the hymn of your glory,
as without end we acclaim:
Holy, Holy, Holy Lord God of hosts... *(page 35)*

PREFACE 2 OF ADVENT

It is truly right and just, our duty and our salvation,
always and everywhere to give you thanks,
Lord, holy Father, almighty and eternal God,
through Christ our Lord.

For all the oracles of the prophets foretold him,
the Virgin Mother longed for him
with love beyond all telling,
John the Baptist sang of his coming
and proclaimed his presence when he came.

It is by his gift that already we rejoice
at the mystery of his Nativity,
so that he may find us watchful in prayer
and exultant in his praise.

And so, with Angels and Archangels,
with Thrones and Dominions,
and with all the hosts and Powers of heaven,
we sing the hymn of your glory,
as without end we acclaim:
Holy, Holy, Holy Lord God of hosts... *(page 35)*

PREFACE 1 OF THE NATIVITY OF THE LORD

It is truly right and just, our duty and our salvation,
always and everywhere to give you thanks,
Lord, holy Father, almighty and eternal God.

For in the mystery of the Word made flesh
a new light of your glory has shone upon the eyes of our mind,
so that, as we recognize in him God made visible,
we may be caught up through him in love of things invisible.

And so, with Angels and Archangels,
with Thrones and Dominions,
and with all the hosts and Powers of heaven,
we sing the hymn of your glory,
as without end we acclaim:

Holy, Holy, Holy Lord God of hosts... *(page 35)*

PREFACE 2 OF THE NATIVITY OF THE LORD

It is truly right and just, our duty and our salvation,
always and everywhere to give you thanks,
Lord, holy Father, almighty and eternal God,
through Christ our Lord.

For on the feast of this awe-filled mystery,
though invisible in his own divine nature,
he has appeared visibly in ours;
and begotten before all ages,
he has begun to exist in time;
so that, raising up in himself all that was cast down,
he might restore unity to all creation
and call straying humanity back to the heavenly Kingdom.

And so, with all the Angels, we praise you,
as in joyful celebration we acclaim:
Holy, Holy, Holy Lord God of hosts... (page 35)

PREFACE 3 OF THE NATIVITY OF THE LORD

It is truly right and just, our duty and our salvation,
always and everywhere to give you thanks,
Lord, holy Father, almighty and eternal God,
through Christ our Lord.

For through him the holy exchange that restores our life
has shone forth today in splendor:
when our frailty is assumed by your Word
not only does human mortality receive unending honor
but by this wondrous union we, too, are made eternal.

And so, in company with the choirs of Angels,
we praise you, and with joy we proclaim:
Holy, Holy, Holy Lord God of hosts... (page 35)

PREFACE OF THE EPIPHANY OF THE LORD

It is truly right and just, our duty and our salvation,
always and everywhere to give you thanks,
Lord, holy Father, almighty and eternal God.

For today you have revealed the mystery
of our salvation in Christ
as a light for the nations,
and, when he appeared in our mortal nature,
you made us new by the glory of his immortal nature.

And so, with Angels and Archangels,
with Thrones and Dominions,

and with all the hosts and Powers of heaven,
we sing the hymn of your glory,
as without end we acclaim:
Holy, Holy, Holy Lord God of hosts... *(page 35)*

PREFACE 1 OF LENT

It is truly right and just, our duty and our salvation,
always and everywhere to give you thanks,
Lord, holy Father, almighty and eternal God,
through Christ our Lord.

For by your gracious gift each year
your faithful await the sacred paschal feasts
with the joy of minds made pure,
so that, more eagerly intent on prayer
and on the works of charity,
and participating in the mysteries
by which they have been reborn,
they may be led to the fullness of grace
that you bestow on your sons and daughters.

And so, with Angels and Archangels,
with Thrones and Dominions,
and with all the hosts and Powers of heaven,
we sing the hymn of your glory,
as without end we acclaim:
Holy, Holy, Holy Lord God of hosts... *(page 35)*

PREFACE 2 OF LENT

It is truly right and just, our duty and our salvation,
always and everywhere to give you thanks,
Lord, holy Father, almighty and eternal God.

For you have given your children a sacred time
for the renewing and purifying of their hearts,
that, freed from disordered affections,
they may so deal with the things of this passing world
as to hold rather to the things that eternally endure.

And so, with all the Angels and Saints,
we praise you, as without end we acclaim:
Holy, Holy, Holy Lord God of hosts... *(page 35)*

PREFACE 3 OF LENT

It is truly right and just, our duty and our salvation,
always and everywhere to give you thanks,
Lord, holy Father, almighty and eternal God.

For you will that our self-denial should give you thanks,
humble our sinful pride,
contribute to the feeding of the poor,
and so help us imitate you in your kindness.

And so we glorify you with countless Angels,
as with one voice of praise we acclaim:
Holy, Holy, Holy Lord God of hosts... *(page 35)*

PREFACE 4 OF LENT

It is truly right and just, our duty and our salvation,
always and everywhere to give you thanks,
Lord, holy Father, almighty and eternal God.

For through bodily fasting you restrain our faults,
raise up our minds,
and bestow both virtue and its rewards,
through Christ our Lord.

Through him the Angels praise your majesty,
Dominions adore and Powers tremble before you.
Heaven and the Virtues of heaven and the blessed Seraphim
worship together with exultation.
May our voices, we pray, join with theirs
in humble praise, as we acclaim:
Holy, Holy, Holy Lord God of hosts... *(page 35)*

PREFACE 1 OF THE PASSION OF THE LORD
It is truly right and just, our duty and our salvation,
always and everywhere to give you thanks,
Lord, holy Father, almighty and eternal God.

For through the saving Passion of your Son
the whole world has received a heart
to confess the infinite power of your majesty,
since by the wondrous power of the Cross
your judgment on the world is now revealed
and the authority of Christ crucified.

And so, Lord, with all the Angels and Saints,
we, too, give you thanks, as in exultation we acclaim:
Holy, Holy, Holy Lord God of hosts... *(page 35)*

PREFACE 2 OF THE PASSION OF THE LORD
It is truly right and just, our duty and our salvation,
always and everywhere to give you thanks,
Lord, holy Father, almighty and eternal God,
through Christ our Lord.

For the days of his saving Passion
and glorious Resurrection are approaching,

by which the pride of the ancient foe is vanquished
and the mystery of our redemption in Christ is celebrated.

Through him the host of Angels adores your majesty
and rejoices in your presence for ever.
May our voices, we pray, join with theirs
in one chorus of exultant praise, as we acclaim:
Holy, Holy, Holy Lord God of hosts... (page 35)

PREFACE 1 OF EASTER
It is truly right and just, our duty and our salvation,
at all times to acclaim you, O Lord,
but (on this night / on this day / in this time) above all
to laud you yet more gloriously,
when Christ our Passover has been sacrificed.

For he is the true Lamb
who has taken away the sins of the world;
by dying he has destroyed our death,
and by rising, restored our life.

Therefore, overcome with paschal joy,
every land, every people exults in your praise
and even the heavenly Powers, with the angelic hosts,
sing together the unending hymn of your glory,
as they acclaim: *Holy, Holy, Holy Lord God of hosts... (page 35)*

PREFACE 2 OF EASTER
It is truly right and just, our duty and our salvation,
at all times to acclaim you, O Lord,
but in this time above all to laud you yet more gloriously,
when Christ our Passover has been sacrificed.

Through him the children of light rise to eternal life
and the halls of the heavenly Kingdom
are thrown open to the faithful;
for his Death is our ransom from death,
and in his rising the life of all has risen.

Therefore, overcome with paschal joy,
every land, every people exults in your praise
and even the heavenly Powers, with the angelic hosts,
sing together the unending hymn of your glory,
as they acclaim: ***Holy, Holy, Holy Lord God of hosts...*** *(page 35)*

PREFACE 3 OF EASTER
It is truly right and just, our duty and our salvation,
at all times to acclaim you, O Lord,
but in this time above all to laud you yet more gloriously,
when Christ our Passover has been sacrificed.

He never ceases to offer himself for us
but defends us and ever pleads our cause before you:
he is the sacrificial Victim who dies no more,
the Lamb, once slain, who lives for ever.

Therefore, overcome with paschal joy,
every land, every people exults in your praise
and even the heavenly Powers, with the angelic hosts,
sing together the unending hymn of your glory,
as they acclaim: ***Holy, Holy, Holy Lord God of hosts...*** *(page 35)*

PREFACE 4 OF EASTER
It is truly right and just, our duty and our salvation,
at all times to acclaim you, O Lord,

but in this time above all to laud you yet more gloriously,
when Christ our Passover has been sacrificed.

For, with the old order destroyed,
a universe cast down is renewed,
and integrity of life is restored to us in Christ.

Therefore, overcome with paschal joy,
every land, every people exults in your praise
and even the heavenly Powers, with the angelic hosts,
sing together the unending hymn of your glory,
as they acclaim: *Holy, Holy, Holy Lord God of hosts...* (page 35)

PREFACE 5 OF EASTER
It is truly right and just, our duty and our salvation,
at all times to acclaim you, O Lord,
but in this time above all to laud you yet more gloriously,
when Christ our Passover has been sacrificed.

By the oblation of his Body,
he brought the sacrifices of old to fulfillment
in the reality of the Cross
and, by commending himself to you for our salvation,
showed himself the Priest, the Altar, and the Lamb of sacrifice.

Therefore, overcome with paschal joy,
every land, every people exults in your praise
and even the heavenly Powers, with the angelic hosts,
sing together the unending hymn of your glory,
as they acclaim: *Holy, Holy, Holy Lord God of hosts...* (page 35)

PREFACE 1 OF THE ASCENSION OF THE LORD
It is truly right and just, our duty and our salvation,
always and everywhere to give you thanks,
Lord, holy Father, almighty and eternal God.

For the Lord Jesus, the King of glory,
conqueror of sin and death,
ascended (today) to the highest heavens,
as the Angels gazed in wonder.

Mediator between God and man,
judge of the world and Lord of hosts,
he ascended, not to distance himself from our lowly state
but that we, his members, might be confident of following
where he, our Head and Founder, has gone before.

Therefore, overcome with paschal joy,
every land, every people exults in your praise
and even the heavenly Powers, with the angelic hosts,
sing together the unending hymn of your glory,
as they acclaim: ***Holy, Holy, Holy Lord God of hosts...*** *(page 35)*

PREFACE 2 OF THE ASCENSION OF THE LORD
It is truly right and just, our duty and our salvation,
always and everywhere to give you thanks,
Lord, holy Father, almighty and eternal God,
through Christ our Lord.

For after his Resurrection
he plainly appeared to all his disciples
and was taken up to heaven in their sight,
that he might make us sharers in his divinity.

Therefore, overcome with paschal joy,
every land, every people exults in your praise
and even the heavenly Powers, with the angelic hosts,
sing together the unending hymn of your glory,
as they acclaim: *Holy, Holy, Holy Lord God of hosts...* *(page 35)*

PREFACE 1 OF THE SUNDAYS IN ORDINARY TIME

It is truly right and just, our duty and our salvation,
always and everywhere to give you thanks,
Lord, holy Father, almighty and eternal God,
through Christ our Lord.

For through his Paschal Mystery,
he accomplished the marvelous deed,
by which he has freed us from the yoke of sin and death,
summoning us to the glory of being now called
a chosen race, a royal priesthood,
a holy nation, a people for your own possession,
to proclaim everywhere your mighty works,
for you have called us out of darkness
into your own wonderful light.

And so, with Angels and Archangels,
with Thrones and Dominions,
and with all the hosts and Powers of heaven,
we sing the hymn of your glory,
as without end we acclaim:
Holy, Holy, Holy Lord God of hosts... *(page 35)*

PREFACE 2 OF THE SUNDAYS IN ORDINARY TIME

It is truly right and just, our duty and our salvation,
always and everywhere to give you thanks,

Lord, holy Father, almighty and eternal God,
through Christ our Lord.

For out of compassion for the waywardness that is ours,
he humbled himself and was born of the Virgin;
by the passion of the Cross he freed us from unending death,
and by rising from the dead he gave us life eternal.

And so, with Angels and Archangels,
with Thrones and Dominions,
and with all the hosts and Powers of heaven,
we sing the hymn of your glory,
as without end we acclaim:
Holy, Holy, Holy Lord God of hosts... *(page 35)*

PREFACE 3 OF THE SUNDAYS IN ORDINARY TIME

It is truly right and just, our duty and our salvation,
always and everywhere to give you thanks,
Lord, holy Father, almighty and eternal God.

For we know it belongs to your boundless glory,
that you came to the aid of mortal beings with your divinity
and even fashioned for us a remedy out of mortality itself,
that the cause of our downfall
might become the means of our salvation,
through Christ our Lord.

Through him the host of Angels adores your majesty
and rejoices in your presence for ever.
May our voices, we pray, join with theirs
in one chorus of exultant praise, as we acclaim:
Holy, Holy, Holy Lord God of hosts... *(page 35)*

PREFACE 4 OF THE SUNDAYS IN ORDINARY TIME
It is truly right and just, our duty and our salvation,
always and everywhere to give you thanks,
Lord, holy Father, almighty and eternal God,
through Christ our Lord.

For by his birth he brought renewal
to humanity's fallen state,
and by his suffering, canceled out our sins;
by his rising from the dead
he has opened the way to eternal life,
and by ascending to you, O Father,
he has unlocked the gates of heaven.

And so, with the company of Angels and Saints,
we sing the hymn of your praise,
as without end we acclaim:
Holy, Holy, Holy Lord God of hosts... *(page 35)*

PREFACE 5 OF THE SUNDAYS IN ORDINARY TIME
It is truly right and just, our duty and our salvation,
always and everywhere to give you thanks,
Lord, holy Father, almighty and eternal God.

For you laid the foundations of the world
and have arranged the changing of times and seasons;
you formed man in your own image
and set humanity over the whole world in all its wonder,
to rule in your name over all you have made
and for ever praise you in your mighty works,
through Christ our Lord.

And so, with all the Angels, we praise you,
as in joyful celebration we acclaim:
Holy, Holy, Holy Lord God of hosts... (page 35)

PREFACE 6 OF THE SUNDAYS IN ORDINARY TIME

It is truly right and just, our duty and our salvation,
always and everywhere to give you thanks,
Lord, holy Father, almighty and eternal God.

For in you we live and move and have our being,
and while in this body
we not only experience the daily effects of your care,
but even now possess the pledge of life eternal.

For, having received the first fruits of the Spirit,
through whom you raised up Jesus from the dead,
we hope for an everlasting share in the Paschal Mystery.

And so, with all the Angels, we praise you,
as in joyful celebration we acclaim:
Holy, Holy, Holy Lord God of hosts... (page 35)

PREFACE 7 OF THE SUNDAYS IN ORDINARY TIME

It is truly right and just, our duty and our salvation,
always and everywhere to give you thanks,
Lord, holy Father, almighty and eternal God.

For you so loved the world
that in your mercy you sent us the Redeemer,
to live like us in all things but sin,
so that you might love in us what you loved in your Son,
by whose obedience we have been restored to those gifts of yours
that, by sinning, we had lost in disobedience.

And so, Lord, with all the Angels and Saints,
we, too, give you thanks, as in exultation we acclaim:
Holy, Holy, Holy Lord God of hosts... *(page 35)*

PREFACE 8 OF THE SUNDAYS IN ORDINARY TIME

It is truly right and just, our duty and our salvation,
always and everywhere to give you thanks,
Lord, holy Father, almighty and eternal God.

For, when your children were scattered afar by sin,
through the Blood of your Son and the power of the Spirit,
you gathered them again to yourself,
that a people, formed as one by the unity of the Trinity,
made the body of Christ and the temple of the Holy Spirit,
might, to the praise of your manifold wisdom,
be manifest as the Church.

And so, in company with the choirs of Angels,
we praise you, and with joy we proclaim:
Holy, Holy, Holy Lord God of hosts... *(page 35)*

PREFACE 1 OF THE MOST HOLY EUCHARIST

It is truly right and just, our duty and our salvation,
always and everywhere to give you thanks,
Lord, holy Father, almighty and eternal God,
through Christ our Lord.

For he is the true and eternal Priest,
who instituted the pattern of an everlasting sacrifice
and was the first to offer himself as the saving Victim,
commanding us to make this offering as his memorial.
As we eat his flesh that was sacrificed for us,

we are made strong,
and, as we drink his Blood that was poured out for us,
we are washed clean.

And so, with Angels and Archangels,
with Thrones and Dominions,
and with all the hosts and Powers of heaven,
we sing the hymn of your glory,
as without end we acclaim:
Holy, Holy, Holy Lord God of hosts... *(page 35)*

PREFACE 2 OF THE MOST HOLY EUCHARIST

It is truly right and just, our duty and our salvation,
always and everywhere to give you thanks,
Lord, holy Father, almighty and eternal God,
through Christ our Lord.

For at the Last Supper with his Apostles,
establishing for the ages to come the saving memorial of the Cross,
he offered himself to you as the unblemished Lamb,
the acceptable gift of perfect praise.

Nourishing your faithful by this sacred mystery,
you make them holy, so that the human race,
bounded by one world,
may be enlightened by one faith
and united by one bond of charity.

And so, we approach the table of this wondrous Sacrament,
so that, bathed in the sweetness of your grace,
we may pass over to the heavenly realities here foreshadowed.

Therefore, all creatures of heaven and earth
sing a new song in adoration,
and we, with all the host of Angels,
cry out, and without end we acclaim:
Holy, Holy, Holy Lord God of hosts... *(page 35)*

PREFACE 1 OF THE BLESSED VIRGIN MARY

It is truly right and just, our duty and our salvation,
always and everywhere to give you thanks,
Lord, holy Father, almighty and eternal God,
and to praise, bless, and glorify your name
(on the Solemnity of the Motherhood /
on the feast day / on the Nativity / in veneration)
of the Blessed ever-Virgin Mary.

For by the overshadowing of the Holy Spirit
she conceived your Only Begotten Son,
and without losing the glory of virginity,
brought forth into the world the eternal Light,
Jesus Christ our Lord.

Through him the Angels praise your majesty,
Dominions adore and Powers tremble before you.
Heaven and the Virtues of heaven and the blessed Seraphim
worship together with exultation.
May our voices, we pray, join with theirs
in humble praise, as we acclaim:
Holy, Holy, Holy Lord God of hosts... *(page 35)*

HOLY, HOLY, HOLY

Holy, Holy, Holy Lord God of hosts.
Heaven and earth are full of your glory.
Hosanna in the highest.
Blessed is he who comes in the name of the Lord.
Hosanna in the highest.

EUCHARISTIC PRAYER 1 *(page 35)*

EUCHARISTIC PRAYER 2 *(page 42)*

EUCHARISTIC PRAYER 3 *(page 45)*

EUCHARISTIC PRAYER 4 *(page 48)*

EUCHARISTIC PRAYER 1

To you, therefore, most merciful Father,
we make humble prayer and petition
through Jesus Christ, your Son, our Lord:
that you accept
and bless these gifts, these offerings,
these holy and unblemished sacrifices,
which we offer you firstly
for your holy catholic Church.
Be pleased to grant her peace,
to guard, unite and govern her
throughout the whole world,
together with your servant N. our Pope
and N. our Bishop,
and all those who, holding to the truth,
hand on the catholic and apostolic faith.

Remember, Lord, your servants N. and N.
and all gathered here,

whose faith and devotion are known to you.
For them, we offer you this sacrifice of praise
or they offer it for themselves
and all who are dear to them:
for the redemption of their souls,
in hope of health and well-being,
and paying their homage to you,
the eternal God, living and true.

On the Nativity of the Lord and throughout the Octave add:
Celebrating the most sacred night (day)
on which blessed Mary the immaculate Virgin
brought forth the Savior for this world,
and

On the Epiphany of the Lord add:
Celebrating the most sacred day
on which your Only Begotten Son,
eternal with you in your glory,
appeared in a human body, truly sharing our flesh,
and

On Holy Thursday add:
Celebrating the most sacred day
on which our Lord Jesus Christ
was handed over for our sake,
and

From the Mass of the Easter Vigil until the Second Sunday of Easter add:
Celebrating the most sacred night (day)

of the Resurrection of our Lord Jesus Christ in the flesh,
and

On the Ascension of the Lord add:
Celebrating the most sacred day
on which your Only Begotten Son, our Lord,
placed at the right hand of your glory
our weak human nature,
which he had united to himself,
and

On Pentecost Sunday add:
Celebrating the most sacred day of Pentecost,
on which the Holy Spirit
appeared to the Apostles in tongues of fire,
and

In communion with those whose memory we venerate,
especially the glorious ever-Virgin Mary,
Mother of our God and Lord, Jesus Christ,
and blessed Joseph, her Spouse,
your blessed Apostles and Martyrs,
Peter and Paul, Andrew,
(James, John,
Thomas, James, Philip,
Bartholomew, Matthew,
Simon and Jude;
Linus, Cletus, Clement, Sixtus,
Cornelius, Cyprian,
Lawrence, Chrysogonus,
John and Paul,
Cosmas and Damian)

and all your Saints;
we ask that through their merits and prayers,
in all things we may be defended
by your protecting help.
(Through Christ our Lord. Amen.)

Therefore, Lord, we pray:
graciously accept this oblation of our service,
that of your whole family;

> **On Holy Thursday add:**
> which we make to you
> as we observe the day
> on which our Lord Jesus Christ
> handed on the mysteries of his Body and Blood
> for his disciples to celebrate;

> **From the Mass of the Easter Vigil until the Second Sunday
> of Easter add:**
> which we make to you
> also for those to whom you have been pleased to give
> the new birth of water and the Holy Spirit,
> granting them forgiveness of all their sins;

order our days in your peace,
and command that we be delivered from eternal damnation
and counted among the flock of those you have chosen.
(Through Christ our Lord. Amen.)

Be pleased, O God, we pray,
to bless, acknowledge,
and approve this offering in every respect;
make it spiritual and acceptable,

so that it may become for us
the Body and Blood of your most beloved Son,
our Lord Jesus Christ.

On the day before he was to suffer,

> **On Holy Thursday add:**
> for our salvation and the salvation of all,
> that is today,

he took bread in his holy and venerable hands,
and with eyes raised to heaven
to you, O God, his almighty Father,
giving you thanks, he said the blessing,
broke the bread
and gave it to his disciples, saying:

TAKE THIS, ALL OF YOU, AND EAT OF IT,
FOR THIS IS MY BODY,
WHICH WILL BE GIVEN UP FOR YOU.

In a similar way, when supper was ended,
he took this precious chalice
in his holy and venerable hands,
and once more giving you thanks, he said the blessing
and gave the chalice to his disciples, saying:

TAKE THIS, ALL OF YOU, AND DRINK FROM IT,
FOR THIS IS THE CHALICE OF MY BLOOD,
THE BLOOD OF THE NEW AND ETERNAL COVENANT,
WHICH WILL BE POURED OUT FOR YOU AND FOR MANY
FOR THE FORGIVENESS OF SINS.

DO THIS IN MEMORY OF ME.

The mystery of faith.

❶ *We proclaim your Death, O Lord,*
and profess your Resurrection
until you come again.

❷ *When we eat this Bread and drink this Cup,*
we proclaim your Death, O Lord,
until you come again.

❸ *Save us, Savior of the world,*
for by your Cross and Resurrection
you have set us free.

Therefore, O Lord,
as we celebrate the memorial of the blessed Passion,
the Resurrection from the dead,
and the glorious Ascension into heaven
of Christ, your Son, our Lord,
we, your servants and your holy people,
offer to your glorious majesty
from the gifts that you have given us,
this pure victim,
this holy victim,
this spotless victim,
the holy Bread of eternal life
and the Chalice of everlasting salvation.

Be pleased to look upon these offerings
with a serene and kindly countenance,
and to accept them,
as once you were pleased to accept
the gifts of your servant Abel the just,

the sacrifice of Abraham, our father in faith,
and the offering of your high priest Melchizedek,
a holy sacrifice, a spotless victim.

In humble prayer we ask you, almighty God:
command that these gifts be borne
by the hands of your holy Angel
to your altar on high
in the sight of your divine majesty,
so that all of us, who through this participation at the altar
receive the most holy Body and Blood of your Son,
may be filled with every grace and heavenly blessing.
(Through Christ our Lord. Amen.)

Remember also, Lord, your servants N. and N.,
who have gone before us with the sign of faith
and rest in the sleep of peace.
   (Pause)
Grant them, O Lord, we pray,
and all who sleep in Christ,
a place of refreshment, light and peace.
(Through Christ our Lord. Amen.)

To us, also, your servants, who, though sinners,
hope in your abundant mercies,
graciously grant some share
and fellowship with your holy Apostles and Martyrs:
with John the Baptist, Stephen,
Matthias, Barnabas,
(Ignatius, Alexander,
Marcellinus, Peter,
Felicity, Perpetua,

Agatha, Lucy,
Agnes, Cecilia, Anastasia)
and all your Saints;
admit us, we beseech you,
into their company,
not weighing our merits,
but granting us your pardon,
through Christ our Lord.

Through whom
you continue to make all these good things, O Lord;
you sanctify them, fill them with life,
bless them, and bestow them upon us.

Through him, and with him, and in him,
O God, almighty Father,
in the unity of the Holy Spirit,
all glory and honor is yours,
for ever and ever. *Amen.*

(Turn to the Lord's Prayer, page 53)

EUCHARISTIC PRAYER 2

PREFACE

It is truly right and just, our duty and our salvation,
always and everywhere to give you thanks, Father most holy,
through your beloved Son, Jesus Christ,
your Word through whom you made all things,
whom you sent as our Savior and Redeemer,
incarnate by the Holy Spirit and born of the Virgin.

Fulfilling your will and gaining for you a holy people,
he stretched out his hands as he endured his Passion,
so as to break the bonds of death and manifest the resurrection.

And so, with the Angels and all the Saints
we declare your glory,
as with one voice we acclaim:
Holy, Holy, Holy Lord God of hosts... (page 35)

You are indeed Holy, O Lord,
the fount of all holiness.

Make holy, therefore, these gifts, we pray,
by sending down your Spirit upon them like the dewfall,
so that they may become for us
the Body and Blood of our Lord Jesus Christ.

At the time he was betrayed
and entered willingly into his Passion,
he took bread and, giving thanks, broke it,
and gave it to his disciples, saying:

Take this, all of you, and eat of it,
for this is my Body,
which will be given up for you.

In a similar way, when supper was ended,
he took the chalice
and, once more giving thanks,
he gave it to his disciples, saying:

Take this, all of you, and drink from it,
for this is the chalice of my Blood,
the Blood of the new and eternal covenant,

WHICH WILL BE POURED OUT FOR YOU AND FOR MANY
FOR THE FORGIVENESS OF SINS.

DO THIS IN MEMORY OF ME.

The mystery of faith.

We proclaim your Death, O Lord,
and profess your Resurrection
until you come again.

(For other acclamations, see page 40)

Therefore, as we celebrate
the memorial of his Death and Resurrection,
we offer you, Lord,
the Bread of life and the Chalice of salvation,
giving thanks that you have held us worthy
to be in your presence and minister to you.

Humbly we pray
that, partaking of the Body and Blood of Christ,
we may be gathered into one by the Holy Spirit.

Remember, Lord, your Church,
spread throughout the world,
and bring her to the fullness of charity,
together with N. our Pope and N. our Bishop
and all the clergy.

Remember also our brothers and sisters
who have fallen asleep in the hope of the resurrection,
and all who have died in your mercy:
welcome them into the light of your face.

Have mercy on us all, we pray,
that with the Blessed Virgin Mary, Mother of God,
with blessed Joseph, her Spouse,
with the blessed Apostles,
and all the Saints who have pleased you throughout the ages,
we may merit to be coheirs to eternal life,
and may praise and glorify you
through your Son, Jesus Christ.

Through him, and with him, and in him,
O God, almighty Father,
in the unity of the Holy Spirit,
all glory and honor is yours,
for ever and ever. *Amen.*

(Turn to the Lord's Prayer, page 53)

EUCHARISTIC PRAYER 3

You are indeed Holy, O Lord,
and all you have created
rightly gives you praise,
for through your Son our Lord Jesus Christ,
by the power and working of the Holy Spirit,
you give life to all things and make them holy,
and you never cease to gather a people to yourself,
so that from the rising of the sun to its setting
a pure sacrifice may be offered to your name.

Therefore, O Lord, we humbly implore you:
by the same Spirit graciously make holy
these gifts we have brought to you for consecration,

that they may become the Body and Blood
of your Son our Lord Jesus Christ,
at whose command we celebrate these mysteries.

For on the night he was betrayed
he himself took bread,
and, giving you thanks, he said the blessing,
broke the bread and gave it to his disciples, saying:

TAKE THIS, ALL OF YOU, AND EAT OF IT,
FOR THIS IS MY BODY,
WHICH WILL BE GIVEN UP FOR YOU.

In a similar way, when supper was ended,
he took the chalice,
and, giving you thanks, he said the blessing,
and gave the chalice to his disciples, saying:

TAKE THIS, ALL OF YOU, AND DRINK FROM IT,
FOR THIS IS THE CHALICE OF MY BLOOD,
THE BLOOD OF THE NEW AND ETERNAL COVENANT,
WHICH WILL BE POURED OUT FOR YOU AND FOR MANY
FOR THE FORGIVENESS OF SINS.

DO THIS IN MEMORY OF ME.

The mystery of faith.

When we eat this Bread and drink this Cup,
we proclaim your Death, O Lord,
until you come again.

(For other acclamations, see page 40)

Therefore, O Lord, as we celebrate the memorial
of the saving Passion of your Son,
his wondrous Resurrection
and Ascension into heaven,
and as we look forward to his second coming,
we offer you in thanksgiving
this holy and living sacrifice.

Look, we pray, upon the oblation of your Church
and, recognizing the sacrificial Victim by whose death
you willed to reconcile us to yourself,
grant that we, who are nourished
by the Body and Blood of your Son
and filled with his Holy Spirit,
may become one body, one spirit in Christ.

May he make of us
an eternal offering to you,
so that we may obtain an inheritance with your elect,
especially with the most Blessed Virgin Mary, Mother of God,
with blessed Joseph, her Spouse,
with your blessed Apostles and glorious Martyrs
(with Saint N.)
and with all the Saints,
on whose constant intercession in your presence
we rely for unfailing help.

May this Sacrifice of our reconciliation,
we pray, O Lord,
advance the peace and salvation of all the world.
Be pleased to confirm in faith and charity
your pilgrim Church on earth,

with your servant N. our Pope and N. our Bishop,
the Order of Bishops, all the clergy,
and the entire people you have gained for your own.

Listen graciously to the prayers of this family,
whom you have summoned before you:
in your compassion, O merciful Father,
gather to yourself all your children
scattered throughout the world.

To our departed brothers and sisters
and to all who were pleasing to you
at their passing from this life,
give kind admittance to your kingdom.
There we hope to enjoy for ever the fullness of your glory
through Christ our Lord,
through whom you bestow on the world all that is good.

Through him, and with him, and in him,
O God, almighty Father,
in the unity of the Holy Spirit,
all glory and honor is yours,
for ever and ever. *Amen.*

(Turn to the Lord's Prayer, page 53)

EUCHARISTIC PRAYER 4
PREFACE
It is truly right to give you thanks,
truly just to give you glory, Father most holy,
for you are the one God living and true,
existing before all ages and abiding for all eternity,

dwelling in unapproachable light;
yet you, who alone are good, the source of life,
have made all that is,
so that you might fill your creatures with blessings
and bring joy to many of them by the glory of your light.

And so, in your presence are countless hosts of Angels,
who serve you day and night
and, gazing upon the glory of your face,
glorify you without ceasing.

With them we, too, confess your name in exultation,
giving voice to every creature under heaven,
as we acclaim:
Holy, Holy, Holy Lord God of hosts... *(page 35)*

We give you praise, Father most holy,
for you are great
and you have fashioned all your works
in wisdom and in love.
You formed man in your own image
and entrusted the whole world to his care,
so that in serving you alone, the Creator,
he might have dominion over all creatures.

And when through disobedience he had lost your friendship,
you did not abandon him to the domain of death.
For you came in mercy to the aid of all,
so that those who seek might find you.
Time and again you offered them covenants
and through the prophets
taught them to look forward to salvation.

And you so loved the world, Father most holy,
that in the fullness of time
you sent your Only Begotten Son to be our Savior.
Made incarnate by the Holy Spirit
and born of the Virgin Mary,
he shared our human nature
in all things but sin.
To the poor he proclaimed the good news of salvation,
to prisoners, freedom,
and to the sorrowful of heart, joy.
To accomplish your plan,
he gave himself up to death,
and, rising from the dead,
he destroyed death and restored life.

And that we might live no longer for ourselves
but for him who died and rose again for us,
he sent the Holy Spirit from you, Father,
as the first fruits for those who believe,
so that, bringing to perfection his work in the world,
he might sanctify creation to the full.

Therefore, O Lord, we pray:
may this same Holy Spirit
graciously sanctify these offerings,
that they may become
the Body and Blood of our Lord Jesus Christ
for the celebration of this great mystery,
which he himself left us
as an eternal covenant.

For when the hour had come
for him to be glorified by you, Father most holy,
having loved his own who were in the world,
he loved them to the end:
and while they were at supper,
he took bread, blessed and broke it,
and gave it to his disciples, saying:

TAKE THIS, ALL OF YOU, AND EAT OF IT,
FOR THIS IS MY BODY,
WHICH WILL BE GIVEN UP FOR YOU.

In a similar way,
taking the chalice filled with the fruit of the vine,
he gave thanks,
and gave the chalice to his disciples, saying:

TAKE THIS, ALL OF YOU, AND DRINK FROM IT,
FOR THIS IS THE CHALICE OF MY BLOOD,
THE BLOOD OF THE NEW AND ETERNAL COVENANT,
WHICH WILL BE POURED OUT FOR YOU AND FOR MANY
FOR THE FORGIVENESS OF SINS.

DO THIS IN MEMORY OF ME.

The mystery of faith.

Save us, Savior of the world,
for by your Cross and Resurrection
you have set us free.

(For other acclamations, see page 40)

Therefore, O Lord,
as we now celebrate the memorial of our redemption,
we remember Christ's Death
and his descent to the realm of the dead,
we proclaim his Resurrection
and his Ascension to your right hand,
and, as we await his coming in glory,
we offer you his Body and Blood,
the sacrifice acceptable to you
which brings salvation to the whole world.

Look, O Lord, upon the Sacrifice
which you yourself have provided for your Church,
and grant in your loving kindness
to all who partake of this one Bread and one Chalice
that, gathered into one body by the Holy Spirit,
they may truly become a living sacrifice in Christ
to the praise of your glory.

Therefore, Lord, remember now
all for whom we offer this sacrifice:
especially your servant N. our Pope,
N. our Bishop, and the whole Order of Bishops,
all the clergy,
those who take part in this offering,
those gathered here before you,
your entire people,
and all who seek you with a sincere heart.

Remember also
those who have died in the peace of your Christ
and all the dead,

whose faith you alone have known.

To all of us, your children,
grant, O merciful Father,
that we may enter into a heavenly inheritance
with the Blessed Virgin Mary, Mother of God,
with blessed Joseph, her Spouse,
and with your Apostles and Saints in your kingdom.
There, with the whole of creation,
freed from the corruption of sin and death,
may we glorify you through Christ our Lord,
through whom you bestow on the world all that is good.

Through him, and with him, and in him,
O God, almighty Father,
in the unity of the Holy Spirit,
all glory and honor is yours,
for ever and ever. *Amen.*

COMMUNION RITE

LORD'S PRAYER
At the Savior's command
and formed by divine teaching,
we dare to say:

Our Father, who art in heaven,
hallowed be thy name;
thy kingdom come,
thy will be done

on earth as it is in heaven.
Give us this day our daily bread,
and forgive us our trespasses,
as we forgive those who trespass against us;
and lead us not into temptation,
but deliver us from evil.

Deliver us, Lord, we pray, from every evil,
graciously grant peace in our days,
that, by the help of your mercy,
we may be always free from sin
and safe from all distress,
as we await the blessed hope
and the coming of our Savior, Jesus Christ.

For the kingdom,
the power and the glory are yours
now and for ever.

SIGN OF PEACE
Lord Jesus Christ,
who said to your Apostles:
Peace I leave you, my peace I give you,
look not on our sins,
but on the faith of your Church,
and graciously grant her peace and unity
in accordance with your will.
Who live and reign for ever and ever. *Amen*.

The peace of the Lord be with you always.
And with your spirit.
Let us offer each other the sign of peace.

FRACTION OF THE BREAD

May this mingling of the Body and Blood
of our Lord Jesus Christ
bring eternal life to us who receive it.

Lamb of God, you take away the sins of the world,
   have mercy on us.
Lamb of God, you take away the sins of the world,
   have mercy on us.
Lamb of God, you take away the sins of the world,
   grant us peace.

Lord Jesus Christ, Son of the living God,
who, by the will of the Father
and the work of the Holy Spirit,
through your Death gave life to the world,
free me by this, your most holy Body and Blood,
from all my sins and from every evil;
keep me always faithful to your commandments,
and never let me be parted from you.

Or

May the receiving of your Body and Blood,
Lord Jesus Christ,
not bring me to judgment and condemnation,
but through your loving mercy
be for me protection in mind and body
and a healing remedy.

COMMUNION

Behold the Lamb of God,
behold him who takes away the sins of the world.
Blessed are those called to the supper of the Lamb.

Lord, I am not worthy
that you should enter under my roof,
but only say the word
and my soul shall be healed.

May the Body (Blood) of Christ
keep me safe for eternal life.

COMMUNION ANTIPHON (Turn to the appropriate day)

PRAYER AFTER COMMUNION (Turn to the appropriate day)

CONCLUDING RITES

BLESSING

On certain days or occasions, this blessing is preceded by a solemn
formula of blessing (see page 57) or prayer over the people.

The Lord be with you.
And with your spirit.

May almighty God bless you,
the Father, and the Son, and the Holy Spirit.
Amen.

DISMISSAL

❶ Go forth, the Mass is ended.
Thanks be to God.

❷ Go and announce the Gospel of the Lord.
Thanks be to God.

❸ Go in peace, glorifying the Lord by your life.
Thanks be to God.

❹ Go in peace.
Thanks be to God.

During the Easter Octave and on Pentecost Sunday, the double alleluia is added:

❶ Go forth, the Mass is ended, alleluia, alleluia.
Thanks be to God, alleluia, alleluia.

❷ Go in peace, alleluia, alleluia.
Thanks be to God, alleluia, alleluia.

OPTIONAL SOLEMN BLESSINGS

ADVENT

May the almighty and merciful God,
by whose grace you have placed your faith
in the First Coming of his Only Begotten Son
and yearn for his coming again,
sanctify you by the radiance of Christ's Advent
and enrich you with his blessing. *Amen.*

As you run the race of this present life,
may he make you firm in faith,
joyful in hope and active in charity. *Amen.*

So that, rejoicing now with devotion
at the Redeemer's coming in the flesh,
you may be endowed with the rich reward of eternal life
when he comes again in majesty. *Amen.*

And may the blessing of almighty God,
the Father, and the Son, and the Holy Spirit,
come down on you and remain with you for ever. *Amen.*

THE NATIVITY OF THE LORD
May the God of infinite goodness,
who by the Incarnation of his Son
    has driven darkness from the world
and by that glorious Birth has illumined
    this most holy night (day),
drive far from you the darkness of vice
and illumine your hearts with the light of virtue. *Amen.*

May God, who willed that the great joy
of his Son's saving Birth
be announced to shepherds by the Angel,
fill your minds with the gladness he gives
and make you heralds of his Gospel. *Amen.*

And may God, who by the Incarnation
brought together the earthly and heavenly realm,
fill you with the gift of his peace and favor
and make you sharers with the Church in heaven. *Amen.*

And may the blessing of almighty God,
the Father, and the Son, and the Holy Spirit,
come down on you and remain with you for ever. *Amen.*

THE BEGINNING OF THE YEAR
May God, the source and origin of all blessing,
grant you grace,
pour out his blessing in abundance,
and keep you safe from harm throughout the year. *Amen.*

May he give you integrity in the faith,
endurance in hope,
and perseverance in charity
with holy patience to the end. *Amen.*

May he order your days and your deeds in his peace,
grant your prayers in this and in every place,
and lead you happily to eternal life. *Amen.*

And may the blessing of almighty God,
the Father, and the Son, and the Holy Spirit,
come down on you and remain with you for ever. *Amen.*

THE EPIPHANY OF THE LORD
May God, who has called you
out of darkness into his wonderful light,
pour out in kindness his blessing upon you
and make your hearts firm
in faith, hope and charity. *Amen.*

And since in all confidence you follow Christ,
who today appeared in the world
as a light shining in darkness,
may God make you, too,
a light for your brothers and sisters. *Amen.*

And so when your pilgrimage is ended,
may you come to him
whom the Magi sought as they followed the star
and whom they found with great joy, the Light from Light,
who is Christ the Lord. *Amen.*

And may the blessing of almighty God,
the Father, and the Son, and the Holy Spirit,
come down on you and remain with you for ever. *Amen.*

THE PASSION OF THE LORD
May God, the Father of mercies,
who has given you an example of love
in the Passion of his Only Begotten Son,
grant that, by serving God and your neighbor,
you may lay hold of the wondrous gift of his blessing. *Amen.*

So that you may receive the reward of everlasting life from him,
through whose earthly Death
you believe that you escape eternal death. *Amen.*

And by following the example of his self-abasement,
may you possess a share in his Resurrection. *Amen.*

And may the blessing of almighty God,
the Father, and the Son, and the Holy Spirit,
come down on you and remain with you for ever. *Amen.*

EASTER TIME
May God, who by the Resurrection of his Only Begotten Son
was pleased to confer on you
the gift of redemption and of adoption,

give you gladness by his blessing. *Amen*.

May he, by whose redeeming work
you have received the gift of everlasting freedom,
make you heirs to an eternal inheritance. *Amen*.

And may you, who have already risen with Christ
in Baptism through faith,
by living in a right manner on this earth,
be united with him in the homeland of heaven. *Amen*.

And may the blessing of almighty God,
the Father, and the Son, and the Holy Spirit,
come down on you and remain with you for ever. *Amen*.

THE ASCENSION OF THE LORD
May almighty God bless you,
for on this very day his Only Begotten Son
pierced the heights of heaven
and unlocked for you the way
to ascend to where he is. *Amen*.

May he grant that,
as Christ after his Resurrection
was seen plainly by his disciples,
so when he comes as Judge
he may show himself merciful to you for all eternity. *Amen*.

And may you, who believe he is seated
with the Father in his majesty,
know with joy the fulfillment of his promise
to stay with you until the end of time. *Amen*.

And may the blessing of almighty God,
the Father, and the Son, and the Holy Spirit,
come down on you and remain with you for ever. *Amen.*

THE HOLY SPIRIT

May God, the Father of lights,
who was pleased to enlighten the disciples' minds
by the outpouring of the Spirit, the Paraclete,
grant you gladness by his blessing
and make you always abound with the gifts
    of the same Spirit. *Amen.*

May the wondrous flame that appeared above the disciples,
powerfully cleanse your hearts from every evil
and pervade them with its purifying light. *Amen.*

And may God, who has been pleased to unite many tongues
in the profession of one faith,
give you perseverance in that same faith
and, by believing, may you journey from hope
    to clear vision. *Amen.*

And may the blessing of almighty God,
the Father, and the Son, and the Holy Spirit,
come down on you and remain with you for ever. *Amen.*

THE BLESSED VIRGIN MARY

May God, who through the childbearing
    of the Blessed Virgin Mary
willed in his great kindness to redeem the human race,
be pleased to enrich you with his blessing. *Amen.*

May you know always and everywhere the protection of her,
through whom you have been found worthy
　　to receive the author of life. *Amen.*

May you, who have devoutly gathered on this day,
carry away with you the gifts of spiritual joys
　　and heavenly rewards. *Amen.*

And may the blessing of almighty God,
the Father, and the Son, and the Holy Spirit,
come down on you and remain with you for ever. *Amen.*

ALL SAINTS

May God, the glory and joy of the Saints,
who has caused you to be strengthened
by means of their outstanding prayers,
bless you with unending blessings. *Amen.*

Freed through their intercession from present ills
and formed by the example of their holy way of life,
may you be ever devoted
to serving God and your neighbor. *Amen.*

So that, together with all,
you may possess the joys of the homeland,
where Holy Church rejoices
that her children are admitted in perpetual peace
to the company of the citizens of heaven. *Amen.*

And may the blessing of almighty God,
the Father, and the Son, and the Holy Spirit,
come down on you and remain with you for ever. *Amen.*

Sunday Readings
& Prayers

Christis lights our darkness!

A dvent (literally, "at the coming") prepares for the annual celebration of Jesus' birth at Christmas and his revelation to the nations at Epiphany. The Church year moves in a cycle of promise—fulfillment—proclamation, often using the images of darkness and light to accentuate the movement. With Advent we enter the first part of the cycle—promise—as, in our northern hemisphere, the dark period of the solar year begins. God's goodness gives us light, the light of the Messiah that dawns in the birth of Christ at Bethlehem and that will shine in its fullness at his coming again as King and Judge.

So in this Advent season as we begin a new Church year, we focus our attention on the demands of responding to the light of Jesus' presence. We desire to let his vision and values enlighten us and transform the darkness of our lives so that we may become a light that will lead others to God.

The lectionary focus for this year on Matthew's gospel is particularly suited to enhance our experience of enlightenment for following this way of commitment, conversion, and cooperation in the saving work of Jesus for our world today.

As we live through the seasons of the Church year, we will learn that the way of Christian discipleship always leads through the darkness of suffering to the experience of new life in Christ. Preparing the way is the first step to which our Advent experience is directed.

Praying and living the Advent season

An Advent wreath can help you and your household focus on waiting for Christ. Create a wreath from evergreen boughs and four candles (three purple and one rose or white for the joyful third week). Use the following format each week.

INVITATION TO PRAYER *As you light the candles (one for each week of Advent), invite all to share in the response.*

Leader: We look for light, and lo, darkness;
for brightness, but we walk in gloom! *(Isaiah 59:9)*

All: You, Lord, give light to my lamp;
you brighten the darkness about me. *(Psalm 18:28)*

SCRIPTURE READING *When the candles are lit, read aloud one of the Scripture readings from the day or Sunday. Either reflect quietly or invite each household member to respond to these questions:*

- How do I want Jesus to be my light this Advent (tonight)?
- How do the words of this reading help me to wait for Jesus to come?

CLOSING PRAYER *(adapted from Ephesians 5:1-2, 8-14)*
O God of light, help us be imitators of you and live in love.
For we were once darkness, but now we are light in the Lord.
Help us live as children of light,
for light produces every kind of goodness and truth.
Help us learn what is pleasing to the Lord.
We want to take no part in the works of darkness
but rather to expose them.
Christ will give us light! Amen.

December 1

DEC 1

Be awake and ready

Advent is a special time, given to us by the Church, to prepare ourselves spiritually for Christmas. As St. Paul reminds us in the second reading, this is "the hour now for you to awake from sleep." Yet there is much in our culture and daily lives that distracts us and keeps us busy. Especially in these next weeks, it is easy for us to get caught up in all the socializing, shopping, and expectations of family and friends.

Today's gospel may frighten us when it challenges us to be ready. Dare we believe in God's promise that the Son of Man is coming into our world? Can we risk trusting our desire for him and the transformation his coming will bring us, even as we wait for the fulfillment of his coming?

Yes, we can and must be awake and ready this Advent season to receive the unexpected gift of God's loving presence at any moment! Our God loves us unconditionally—C just as we are, this very day. We don't have to earn this love or prove ourselves worthy of it. Once we accept this truth, everything changes. We begin to "walk in the light" as we are called to make God's love alive through our actions. Then they too can wake up and be ready to receive God's promise through faith.

■ JOE EGAN

ENTRANCE ANTIPHON *(Cf. Psalm 25 [24]:1-3)*

To you, I lift up my soul, O my God. In you, I have trusted; let me not be put to shame. Nor let my enemies exult over me; and let none who hope in you be put to shame.

INTRODUCTORY RITES *(page 10)*

COLLECT

Grant your faithful, we pray, almighty God,
the resolve to run forth to meet your Christ
with righteous deeds at his coming,
so that, gathered at his right hand,
they may be worthy to possess the heavenly Kingdom.
Through our Lord Jesus Christ, your Son,
who lives and reigns with you in the unity of the Holy Spirit,
one God, for ever and ever. *Amen.*

FIRST READING *(Isaiah 2:1-5)*

This is what Isaiah, son of Amoz, saw concerning Judah and Jerusalem.
In days to come,
the mountain of the LORD's house
    shall be established as the highest mountain
    and raised above the hills.
All nations shall stream toward it;
    many peoples shall come and say:
"Come, let us climb the LORD's mountain,
    to the house of the God of Jacob,
that he may instruct us in his ways,
    and we may walk in his paths."
For from Zion shall go forth instruction,

and the word of the LORD from Jerusalem.
He shall judge between the nations,
  and impose terms on many peoples.
They shall beat their swords into plowshares
  and their spears into pruning hooks;
one nation shall not raise the sword against another,
  nor shall they train for war again.
O house of Jacob, come,
  let us walk in the light of the LORD!
The word of the Lord. *Thanks be to God.*

RESPONSORIAL PSALM *(Psalm 122:1-2, 3-4, 4-5, 6-7, 8-9)*
℟ Let us go rejoicing to the house of the Lord.

I rejoiced because they said to me,
  "We will go up to the house of the LORD."
And now we have set foot
  within your gates, O Jerusalem. ℟
Jerusalem, built as a city
  with compact unity.
To it the tribes go up,
  the tribes of the LORD. ℟
According to the decree for Israel,
  to give thanks to the name of the LORD.
In it are set up judgment seats,
  seats for the house of David. ℟
Pray for the peace of Jerusalem!
  May those who love you prosper!
May peace be within your walls,
  prosperity in your buildings. ℟
Because of my brothers and friends

I will say, "Peace be within you!"
Because of the house of the LORD, our God,
   I will pray for your good.
℟ **Let us go rejoicing to the house of the Lord.**

SECOND READING *(Romans 13:11-14)*

Brothers and sisters: You know the time; it is the hour now for you to awake from sleep. For our **salvation**✛ is nearer now than when we first believed; the night is advanced, the day is at hand. Let us then throw off the works of darkness and put on the armor of light; let us conduct ourselves properly as in the day, not in orgies and drunkenness, not in promiscuity and lust, not in rivalry and jealousy. But put on the Lord Jesus Christ, and make no provision for the desires of the flesh.

   The word of the Lord. *Thanks be to God.*

ALLELUIA *(Psalm 85:8)*

Alleluia, alleluia. Show us, Lord, your love; and grant us your salvation. *Alleluia, alleluia.*

GOSPEL *(Matthew 24:37-44)*

A reading from the holy Gospel according to Matthew.
Glory to you, O Lord.

Jesus said to his disciples: "As it was in the days of Noah, so it will be at the coming of the Son of Man. In those days before the flood, they were eating and drinking, marrying and giving in marriage, up to the day that Noah entered the ark. They did not know until the flood came and carried them all away. So will it be also at the coming of the Son of Man. Two men will be out in the field; one will be taken, and one will be left. Two women will be grinding at the mill; one will be taken, and one will be left. Therefore, stay awake! For you do not know on which day your Lord will come. Be sure of this: if the master of the house had known the hour of night when the thief was coming, he would have stayed awake and not let his house be broken into. So too, you also must be prepared, for at an hour you do not expect, the Son of Man will come."

The Gospel of the Lord. *Praise to you, Lord Jesus Christ.*

PROFESSION OF FAITH *(page 13)*

PRAYER OF THE FAITHFUL

PREPARATION OF GIFTS *(page 16)*

PRAYER OVER THE OFFERINGS
Accept, we pray, O Lord, these offerings we make,
gathered from among your gifts to us,
and may what you grant us to celebrate devoutly here below
gain for us the prize of eternal redemption.
Through Christ our Lord. *Amen.*

• Taking a Closer Look •

✝ **Salvation** Before it became a theological term, "salvation" described the return of a sick person to health (Latin, *salus*). Thus in a world with few medicines, it became a general term for being rescued from a difficult or life-threatening situation. Thus the agent of salvation was not only the doctor, but more generally the king or emperor or general who saved the nation by defeating their enemies. For the Jews, God was their primary agent of salvation because God rescued them from the Egyptians who threatened them with death. For Christians, Jesus is the one who rescued us from our broken relationship with God and offered us a new relationship under God's kingdom rule, which completely reorders creation and the human community.

PREFACE *(Advent 1, page 17)*

COMMUNION ANTIPHON *(Psalm 85 [84]:13)*
The Lord will bestow his bounty, and our earth shall yield its increase.

PRAYER AFTER COMMUNION
May these mysteries, O Lord,
in which we have participated,
profit us, we pray,
for even now, as we walk amid passing things,
you teach us by them to love the things of heaven
and hold fast to what endures.
Through Christ our Lord. *Amen.*

SOLEMN BLESSING: ADVENT *(Optional, page 57)*

DISMISSAL *(page 57)* ✣

• RESPONDING TO THE WORD •

Isaiah envisions a time of peace and fulfillment for the Jews.	Paul tells us to put aside godless ways and live in God's light.	Jesus reminds us that God often comes suddenly into the ordinary events of our lives.
➡ How can I encourage peace and harmony today with others?	➡ What attitude or action should I reject this Advent?	➡ What must I do to be more prepared to encounter God?

December 8

DEC 8

The kingdom comes

Compelled by visions of God's kingdom, Isaiah and John the Baptist build up and tear down.

Isaiah envisions God's peaceable kingdom. He waits for the Messiah, the "root of Jesse," who will bring righteousness and justice. His people, mired in sorrow and despair, have stopped waiting for God's kingdom. He builds them up, offering hope.

The Baptist is preparing the way for Jesus, the Messiah. His people, mired in greed and exploitation, have stopped waiting for God's kingdom. John warns: change your ways, find the right path, bear good fruit—now!

Prophets do what's necessary, so others can see reality. For John and Isaiah, God's kingdom is a compelling reality, their goal and guide. They are connected to that kingdom and long for its fullness.

We celebrate the in-breaking of God's kingdom in Jesus. How slowly that kingdom comes to fullness! But the vision is strong and compelling, as it was for Isaiah and John: God's reign of peace, justice, and healing.

We experience it in our midst and long for its fullness. Graced by the Spirit, fed by the Eucharist, we proclaim it and practice it, living in hope, love, peace, and justice. The many glimpses and tastes of God's kingdom draw us in and send us forth to share this vision with others.

■ **DINAH SIMMONS**

ENTRANCE ANTIPHON *(Cf. Isaiah 30:19, 30)*

O people of Sion, behold, the Lord will come to save the nations,
and the Lord will make the glory of his voice heard in the joy of
your heart.

INTRODUCTORY RITES *(page 10)*

COLLECT

Almighty and merciful God,
may no earthly undertaking hinder those
who set out in haste to meet your Son,
but may our learning of heavenly wisdom
gain us admittance to his company.
Who lives and reigns with you in the unity of the Holy Spirit,
one God, for ever and ever. ***Amen.***

FIRST READING *(Isaiah 11:1-10)*

On that day, a shoot shall sprout from the stump of Jesse,
and from his roots a bud shall blossom.
The spirit of the LORD shall rest upon him:
    a spirit of wisdom and of understanding,
a spirit of counsel and of strength,
    a spirit of knowledge and of fear of the LORD,
    and his delight shall be the fear of the LORD.
Not by appearance shall he judge,
    nor by hearsay shall he decide,
but he shall judge the poor with justice,
    and decide aright for the land's afflicted.
He shall strike the ruthless with the rod of his mouth,
    and with the breath of his lips he shall slay the wicked.
Justice shall be the band around his waist,
    and faithfulness a belt upon his hips.

Then the wolf shall be a guest of the lamb,
    and the leopard shall lie down with the kid;
the calf and the young lion shall browse together,
    with a little child to guide them.
The cow and the bear shall be neighbors,
    together their young shall rest;
    the lion shall eat hay like the ox.
The baby shall play by the cobra's den,
    and the child lay his hand on the adder's lair.
There shall be no harm or ruin on all my holy mountain;
    for the earth shall be filled with knowledge of the LORD,
    as water covers the sea.
On that day, the root of Jesse,
    set up as a signal for the nations,
the Gentiles shall seek out,
    for his dwelling shall be glorious.
The word of the Lord. ***Thanks be to God.***

RESPONSORIAL PSALM *(Psalm 72:1-2, 7-8, 12-13, 17)*

℟ **Justice shall flourish in his time, and fullness of
    peace for ever.**

O God, with your judgment endow the king,
    and with your justice, the king's son;
he shall govern your people with justice
    and your afflicted ones with judgment. ℟
Justice shall flower in his days,
    and profound peace, till the moon be no more.
May he rule from sea to sea,
    and from the River to the ends of the earth. ℟
For he shall rescue the poor when he cries out,

and the afflicted when he has no one to help him.
He shall have pity for the lowly and the poor;
    the lives of the poor he shall save.

℞ **Justice shall flourish in his time, and fullness of
peace forever.**

May his name be blessed forever;
    as long as the sun his name shall remain.
In him shall all the tribes of the earth be blessed;
    all the nations shall proclaim his happiness. ℞

SECOND READING *(Romans 15:4–9)*

Brothers and sisters: Whatever was written previously was written for our instruction, that by endurance and by the encouragement of the Scriptures we might have hope. May the God of endurance and encouragement grant you to think in harmony with one another, in keeping with Christ Jesus, that with one accord you may with one voice glorify the God and Father of our Lord Jesus Christ.

Welcome one another, then, as Christ welcomed you, for the glory of God. For I say that Christ became a minister of the circumcised to show God's truthfulness, to confirm the promises to the patriarchs, but so that the Gentiles might glorify God for his mercy. As it is written:

    Therefore, I will praise you among the Gentiles
        and sing praises to your name.

The word of the Lord. ***Thanks be to God.***

ALLELUIA *(Luke 3:4, 6)*

Alleluia, alleluia. Prepare the way of the Lord, make straight his paths: all flesh shall see the salvation of God. *Alleluia, alleluia.*

GOSPEL *(Matthew 3:1-12)*

A reading from the holy Gospel according to Matthew.
Glory to you, O Lord.

John the Baptist appeared, preaching in the desert of Judea and saying, "Repent, for the kingdom of heaven is at hand!" It was of him that the prophet Isaiah had spoken when he said:

> *A voice of one crying out in the desert,*
> *Prepare the way of the Lord,*
>   *make straight his paths.*

John wore clothing made of camel's hair and had a leather belt around his waist. His food was locusts and wild honey. At that time Jerusalem, all Judea, and the whole region around the Jordan were going out to him and were being baptized by him in the Jordan River as they acknowledged their sins.

When he saw many of the Pharisees and Sadducees coming to his baptism, he said to them, "You brood of vipers! Who warned you to flee from the coming wrath? Produce good fruit as evidence of your **repentance.**✝ And do not presume to say to yourselves, 'We have Abraham as our father.' For I tell you, God can raise up children to Abraham from these stones. Even now the ax lies at the root of the trees. Therefore every tree that does not bear good fruit will be cut down and thrown into the fire. I am baptizing you with water, for repentance, but the one who is coming after me is mightier than I. I am not worthy to carry his sandals. He will baptize you with the Holy Spirit and fire. His winnowing fan is in his hand. He will clear his threshing floor and gather his wheat into his barn, but the chaff he will burn with unquenchable fire."

The Gospel of the Lord. *Praise to you, Lord Jesus Christ.*

PROFESSION OF FAITH *(page 13)*

PRAYER OF THE FAITHFUL

PREPARATION OF GIFTS *(page 16)*

PRAYER OVER THE OFFERINGS
Be pleased, O Lord, with our humble prayers and offerings,
and, since we have no merits to plead our cause,
come, we pray, to our rescue
with the protection of your mercy.
Through Christ our Lord. *Amen.*

PREFACE *(Advent 1, page 17)*

COMMUNION ANTIPHON *(Baruch 5:5; 4:36)*
Jerusalem, arise and stand upon the heights,
and behold the joy which comes to you from God.

• TAKING A CLOSER LOOK •

✝ **Repentance** Because we tend to limit the meaning of repentance to being sorry for something, repentance is a somewhat inadequate translation of the Greek word *metanoia*, which describes a change of mind and heart and attitude demanded by personal conversion. It demands a re-forming of our self and our life by turning toward God and away from the evil forces that pervade our world. It is a lifelong challenge to order ourselves and our world according to the vision and values of Jesus and live out the obligations of belonging to his community of disciples.

PRAYER AFTER COMMUNION

Replenished by the food of spiritual nourishment,
we humbly beseech you, O Lord,
that, through our partaking in this mystery,
you may teach us to judge wisely the things of earth
and hold firm to the things of heaven.
Through Christ our Lord. *Amen.*

SOLEMN BLESSING: ADVENT *(Optional, page 57)*

DISMISSAL *(page 57)* ✤

✦ RESPONDING TO THE WORD ✦

The spirit-filled messiah will bring about greater justice and peace.	The Scriptures offer us encouragement.	John encourages us to change our lives to prepare for Jesus' coming.
➡ How is the Holy Spirit drawing me to create better relationships in my life now?	➡ Which Scripture readings have given me greater hope this Advent?	➡ What changes do I need to make this Advent?

December 9

Lord, deepen my faith!

Conception without original sin and an elderly woman bearing a child: both of these marvels are possible for God. That is the message for us.

God's power works in us as well, making possible what seems to be impossible. We look at our obligations and wonder how we can fulfill them, but that will be possible for us if we call upon God. We look at our weaknesses and wonder how we can overcome them, but that too will be possible for us if we call upon God.

Let us pray that our hearts may be open to all that God wants to make possible for us today.

As we celebrate Mary's Immaculate Conception, we ask for a share in the purity that was Mary's from the first moment of her life. We ask for the faith to believe that God will cleanse us where we need to be cleansed, free us where we need to be freed, and strengthen us where we need to be strong. All of this is possible for God.

🔲 FR. KENNETH GRABNER, CSC

ENTRANCE ANTIPHON *(Isaiah 61:10)*
I rejoice heartily in the Lord, in my God is the joy of my soul; for he has clothed me with a robe of salvation, and wrapped me in a mantle of justice, like a bride adorned with her jewels.

INTRODUCTORY RITES *(page 10)*

COLLECT
O God, who by the Immaculate Conception of the Blessed Virgin
prepared a worthy dwelling for your Son,
grant, we pray,
that, as you preserved her from every stain
by virtue of the Death of your Son, which you foresaw,
so, through her intercession,
we, too, may be cleansed and admitted to your presence.
Through our Lord Jesus Christ, your Son,
who lives and reigns with you in the unity of the Holy Spirit,
one God, for ever and ever. *Amen.*

FIRST READING *(Genesis 3:9-15, 20)*
After the man, Adam, had eaten of the tree, the Lord God called to the man and asked him, "Where are you?" He answered, "I heard you in the garden; but I was afraid, because I was naked, so I hid myself." Then he asked, "Who told you that you were naked? You have eaten, then, from the tree of which I had forbidden you to eat!" The man replied, "The woman whom you put here with me—she gave me fruit from the tree, and so I ate it." The Lord God then asked the woman, "Why did you do such a thing?" The woman answered, "The serpent tricked me into it, so I ate it."

Then the LORD God said to the serpent:
"Because you have done this, you shall be banned
from all the animals
and from all the wild creatures;
on your belly shall you crawl,
and dirt shall you eat
all the days of your life.
I will put enmity between you and the woman,
and between your offspring and hers;
he will strike at your head,
while you strike at his heel."

The man called his wife Eve, because she became the mother of all the living.

The word of the Lord. *Thanks be to God.*

RESPONSORIAL PSALM *(Psalm 98:1, 2–3ab, 3cd–4)*

℟ **Sing to the Lord a new song, for he has done marvelous deeds.**

Sing to the LORD a new song,
for he has done wondrous deeds;
His right hand has won victory for him,
his holy arm. ℟
The LORD has made his salvation known:
in the sight of the nations he has revealed his justice.
He has remembered his kindness and his faithfulness
toward the house of Israel. ℟
All the ends of the earth have seen
the salvation by our God.
Sing joyfully to the LORD, all you lands;
break into song; sing praise. ℟

SECOND READING *(Ephesians 1:3-6, 11-12)*

Brothers and sisters: Blessed be the God and Father of our Lord Jesus Christ, who has blessed us in Christ with every spiritual blessing in the heavens, as he chose us in him, before the foundation of the world, to be holy and without blemish before him. In love he destined us for adoption to himself through Jesus Christ, in accord with the favor of his will, for the praise of the glory of his grace that he granted us in the beloved.

In him we were also chosen, destined in accord with the purpose of the One who accomplishes all things according to the intention of his will, so that we might exist for the praise of his glory, we who first hoped in Christ.

The word of the Lord. *Thanks be to God.*

ALLELUIA *(See Luke 1:28)*

Alleluia, alleluia. Hail, Mary, full of grace, the Lord is with you; blessed are you among women. *Alleluia, alleluia.*

GOSPEL *(Luke 1:26-38)*

A reading from the holy Gospel according to Luke.

Glory to you, O Lord.

The angel Gabriel was sent from God to a town of Galilee called Nazareth, to a virgin betrothed to a man named Joseph, of the house of David, and the virgin's name was Mary. And coming to her, he said, "**Hail, full of grace!**✝ The Lord is with you." But she was greatly troubled at what was said and pondered what sort of greeting this might be. Then the angel said to her, "Do not be afraid, Mary, for you have found favor with God. Behold, you will conceive in your womb and bear a son, and you shall name him Jesus. He will be great and will be called Son of the Most High, and the Lord God will give him the throne of David his father, and he will rule over the house of Jacob forever, and of his Kingdom there will be no end." But Mary said to the angel, "How can this be, since I have no relations with a man?" And the angel said to her in reply, "The Holy Spirit will come upon you, and the power of the Most High will overshadow you. Therefore the child to be born will be called holy, the Son of God. And behold, Elizabeth, your relative, has also conceived a son in her old age, and this is the sixth month for her who was called barren; for nothing will be impossible for God." Mary said, "Behold, I am the handmaid of the Lord. May it be done to me according to your word." Then the angel departed from her.

The Gospel of the Lord. *Praise to you, Lord Jesus Christ.*

PROFESSION OF FAITH *(page 13)*

PRAYER OF THE FAITHFUL

PREPARATION OF GIFTS *(page 16)*

PRAYER OVER THE OFFERINGS
Graciously accept the saving sacrifice
which we offer you, O Lord,
on the Solemnity of the Immaculate Conception
of the Blessed Virgin Mary,
and grant that, as we profess her,
on account of your prevenient grace,
to be untouched by any stain of sin,
so, through her intercession,
we may be delivered from all our faults.
Through Christ our Lord. *Amen.*

PREFACE: THE MYSTERY OF MARY AND THE CHURCH

It is truly right and just, our duty and our salvation,
always and everywhere to give you thanks,
Lord, holy Father, almighty and eternal God.

For you preserved the most Blessed Virgin Mary
from all stain of original sin,
so that in her, endowed with the rich fullness of your grace,
you might prepare a worthy Mother for your Son
and signify the beginning of the Church,
his beautiful Bride without spot or wrinkle.

She, the most pure Virgin, was to bring forth a Son,
the innocent Lamb who would wipe away our offenses;
you placed her above all others
to be for your people an advocate of grace
and a model of holiness.

● TAKING A CLOSER LOOK ●

✢ **Hail, full of grace!** Although we tend to hear these words as overflowing with theological meaning, note that they are a greeting that Mary finds perplexing. The sense is given by Gabriel, the messenger angel: "You have found favor with God." The basic meaning of the word grace (Greek, *charis*; Latin, *gratia*) describes a free gift that is bestowed not out of merit (then it would be owed rather than a true gift) but because the giver has found some reason to single out or favor the recipient. The choice of one recipient (a favorite) from many possible ones for the gift led to the common connection of grace with honor. As the text indicates, Mary's gift is that God is with her (as God also is with us!), which is indeed both a great favor and an honor.

And so, in company with the choirs of Angels,
we praise you, and with joy we proclaim:
Holy, Holy, Holy Lord God of hosts... *(page 35)*

COMMUNION ANTIPHON

Glorious things are spoken of you, O Mary, for from you arose
the sun of justice, Christ our God.

PRAYER AFTER COMMUNION

May the Sacrament we have received,
O Lord our God,
heal in us the wounds of that fault
from which in a singular way
you preserved Blessed Mary in her Immaculate Conception.
Through Christ our Lord. *Amen.*

SOLEMN BLESSING: THE BLESSED VIRGIN MARY *(Optional, page 62)*

DISMISSAL *(page 57)* ✧

• RESPONDING TO THE WORD •

Adam and Eve shirk their responsibility for sin and blame others.	Paul reminds us that we have been chosen to participate in God's plan of salvation.	Mary's "yes" to God is unconditional and puts her completely at God's service.
➲ *Who have I blamed instead of taking responsibility for my actions?*	➲ *Where and to whom does it seem that God is directing me to serve today?*	➲ *What conditions do I try to set for what God seems to be asking me to be or do?*

December 15

**DEC
15**

Jesus is coming!

Recently a flyer arrived in our mailbox proclaiming, "Holiday Magic starts with believing." That got me thinking. What is the magic of this season? Advent is a time of waiting; we are waiting for the coming Messiah. At Christmas we will celebrate Christ's birth. God promised through the prophets that a Savior would be sent for humankind.

John the Baptist asks his followers to determine whether Jesus is the one whom God will send. Jesus points to what he himself says and does as evidence of who he is. Do I believe what I see and hear? Do I trust the words and deeds of God?

Today is also known as Gaudete (Rejoice!) Sunday, taken from the first words in today's Entrance Antiphon. Isaiah prophesies "the desert and the parched land will exult; the steppe will rejoice and bloom." Why should we rejoice? Because Jesus is coming for each one of us! He is our hope and our light. By entering our humanity he brings eternity to our reality.

With Christmas days away, may we slip away for a moment to focus on the real holiday magic of this season. May our hearts be ready to welcome Jesus as God's eternal gift to the world.

▪ **Gerry Sobie**

ENTRANCE ANTIPHON *(Philippians 4:4-5)*

Rejoice in the Lord always; again I say, rejoice. Indeed, the Lord is near.

INTRODUCTORY RITES *(page 10)*

COLLECT

O God, who see how your people
faithfully await the feast of the Lord's Nativity,
enable us, we pray,
to attain the joys of so great a salvation
and to celebrate them always
with solemn worship and glad rejoicing.
Through our Lord Jesus Christ, your Son,
who lives and reigns with you in the unity of the Holy Spirit,
one God, for ever and ever. *Amen.*

FIRST READING *(Isaiah 35:1-6a, 10)*

The desert and the parched land will exult;
    the steppe will rejoice and bloom.
They will bloom with abundant flowers,
    and rejoice with joyful song.
The glory of Lebanon will be given to them,
    the splendor of Carmel and Sharon;
they will see the glory of the LORD,
    the splendor of our God.
Strengthen the hands that are feeble,
    make firm the knees that are weak,
say to those whose hearts are frightened:
    Be strong, fear not!
Here is your God,

he comes with vindication;
with divine recompense
he comes to save you.
Then will the eyes of the blind be opened,
the ears of the deaf be cleared;
then will the lame leap like a stag,
then the tongue of the mute will sing.

Those whom the LORD has ransomed will return
and enter Zion* singing,
crowned with everlasting joy;
they will meet with joy and gladness,
sorrow and mourning will flee.
The word of the Lord. *Thanks be to God.*

RESPONSORIAL PSALM *(Psalm 146:6-7, 8-9, 9-10)*
℟ **Lord, come and save us.** *Or* **Alleluia!**

The LORD God keeps faith forever,
secures justice for the oppressed,
gives food to the hungry.
The LORD sets captives free. ℟
The LORD gives sight to the blind;
the LORD raises up those who were bowed down.
The LORD loves the just;
the LORD protects strangers. ℟
The fatherless and the widow he sustains,
but the way of the wicked he thwarts.
The LORD shall reign forever;
your God, O Zion,* through all generations. ℟

SECOND READING *(James 5:7-10)*

Be patient, brothers and sisters, until the coming of the Lord. See how the farmer waits for the precious fruit of the earth, being patient with it until it receives the early and the late rains. You too must be patient. Make your hearts firm, because the coming of the Lord is at hand. Do not complain, brothers and sisters, about one another, that you may not be judged. Behold, the Judge is standing before the gates. Take as an example of hardship and patience, brothers and sisters, the **prophets**✝ who spoke in the name of the Lord.

The word of the Lord. *Thanks be to God.*

ALLELUIA *(Isaiah 61:1)*
Alleluia, alleluia. The Spirit of the Lord is upon me, because he has anointed me to bring glad tidings to the poor. *Alleluia, alleluia.*

GOSPEL *(Matthew 11:2-11)*
A reading from the holy Gospel according to Matthew.
Glory to you, O Lord.

When John the Baptist heard in prison of the works of the Christ, he sent his disciples to Jesus with this question, "Are you the one who is to come, or should we look for another?" Jesus said to them in reply, "Go and tell John what you hear and see: the blind regain their sight, the lame walk, lepers are cleansed, the deaf hear, the dead are raised, and the poor have the good news proclaimed to them. And blessed is the one who takes no offense at me."

As they were going off, Jesus began to speak to the crowds about John, "What did you go out to the desert to see? A reed swayed by the wind? Then what did you go out to see? Someone dressed in fine clothing? Those who wear fine clothing are in royal palaces. Then why did you go out? To see a **prophet?**✢ Yes, I tell you, and more than a prophet. This is the one about whom it is written:

> Behold, I am sending my messenger ahead of you;
> he will prepare your way before you.

Amen, I say to you, among those born of women there has been none greater than John the Baptist; yet the least in the kingdom of heaven is greater than he."

The Gospel of the Lord. *Praise to you, Lord Jesus Christ.*

PROFESSION OF FAITH *(page 13)*

PRAYER OF THE FAITHFUL

PREPARATION OF GIFTS *(page 16)*

• TAKING A CLOSER LOOK •

✢ **Prophets** Biblical prophets (Greek, "to speak for or on behalf of someone") speak as God's intermediaries to the king and the covenant people. Rulers tended to forget that they were to rule according to God's covenant law and not for their own interests. The prophets spoke on behalf of God, reminding the people of God's agenda and encouraging trust in God rather than in human power and wisdom. Although their words were often taken as predicting the future, their predictive power was nothing more than a consequence of their belief that God always comes in judgment to punish evil and in mercy to reward good.

PRAYER OVER THE OFFERINGS

May the sacrifice of our worship, Lord, we pray,
be offered to you unceasingly,
to complete what was begun in sacred mystery
and powerfully accomplish for us your saving work.
Through Christ our Lord. *Amen.*

PREFACE *(Advent 1, page 17)*

COMMUNION ANTIPHON *(Cf. Isaiah 35:4)*

Say to the faint of heart: Be strong and do not fear. Behold, our
God will come, and he will save us.

PRAYER AFTER COMMUNION

We implore your mercy, Lord,
that this divine sustenance may cleanse us of our faults
and prepare us for the coming feasts.
Through Christ our Lord. *Amen.*

SOLEMN BLESSING: ADVENT *(Optional, page 57)*

DISMISSAL *(page 57)* ::

• RESPONDING TO THE WORD •

Isaiah encourages us to be strong and fear not when God comes.	James counsels patience as we wait for God.	John prepares a way for Jesus to draw near to us.
▶ What weakness and fear block my acceptance of God into my life?	▶ What makes it hard for me to be patient this Advent?	▶ What can I do today to smooth a way for God to come to others?

December 22

DEC 22

New possibilities

Imagine what it must have been like for Joseph to hear Mary's extraordinary tale of her mysterious pregnancy. He was "a righteous man." He believed in, longed for, the coming of the promised Messiah of whom Isaiah speaks in the first reading. Then he was asked to accept that God was about to fulfill that promise in such an unforeseen and scandalous way? And yet Joseph, awakening from a dream, welcomed the unexpected into his life.

Fast forward thirty years and we see the child born to Mary and Joseph spending much of his time doing the unexpected and the scandalous. Whether sitting at table with sinners and prostitutes or embracing lepers and tax collectors, Jesus would challenge people's ideas of what God was like.

Today's readings confirm that God comes to us in ways that can confuse or challenge us. At this time of year, we might expect to encounter God in cozy family gatherings and beautiful liturgical celebrations. We might not recognize him in the shivering street person or the cranky relative.

Our celebration of Christ's coming at Christmas is an invitation to open ourselves to new possibilities and new ways of seeing God. May we, like Joseph, welcome him with open and generous hearts... in whatever guise he appears.

■ TERESA WHALEN LUX

ENTRANCE ANTIPHON *(Cf. Isaiah 45:8)*

Drop down dew from above, you heavens, and let the clouds
rain down the Just One; let the earth be opened and bring
forth a Savior.

INTRODUCTORY RITES *(page 10)*

COLLECT

Pour forth, we beseech you, O Lord,
your grace into our hearts,
that we, to whom the Incarnation of Christ your Son
was made known by the message of an Angel,
may by his Passion and Cross
be brought to the glory of his Resurrection.
Who lives and reigns with you in the unity of the Holy Spirit,
one God, for ever and ever. *Amen.*

FIRST READING *(Isaiah 7:10-14)*

The Lord spoke to Ahaz,* saying: Ask for a sign from the
LORD, your God; let it be deep as the netherworld, or high
as the sky! But Ahaz answered, "I will not ask! I will not tempt
the LORD!" Then Isaiah said: Listen, O house of David! Is it not
enough for you to weary people, must you also weary my God?
Therefore the Lord himself will give you this sign: the virgin
shall conceive, and bear a son, and shall name him Emmanuel.

The word of the Lord. *Thanks be to God.*

RESPONSORIAL PSALM *(Psalm 24:1-2, 3-4, 5-6)*

R. Let the Lord enter; he is king of glory.

The LORD's are the earth and its fullness;
    the world and those who dwell in it.
For he founded it upon the seas
    and established it upon the rivers. R.
Who can ascend the mountain of the LORD?
    or who may stand in his holy place?
One whose hands are sinless, whose heart is clean,
    who desires not what is vain. R.
He shall receive a blessing from the LORD,
    a reward from God his savior.
Such is the race that seeks for him,
      that seeks the face of the God of Jacob. R.

SECOND READING *(Romans 1:1-7)*

Paul, a slave of Christ Jesus, called to be an apostle and set apart for the gospel of God, which he promised previously through his prophets in the holy Scriptures, the gospel about his Son, descended from David according to the flesh, but established as Son of God in power according to the Spirit of holiness through resurrection from the dead, Jesus Christ our Lord. Through him we have received the grace of apostleship, to bring about the obedience of faith, for the sake of his name, among all the Gentiles, among whom are you also, who are called to belong to Jesus Christ; to all the beloved of God in Rome, called to be holy. Grace to you and peace from God our Father and the Lord Jesus Christ.

    The word of the Lord. ***Thanks be to God.***

ALLELUIA *(Matthew 1:23)*
Alleluia, alleluia. The virgin shall conceive, and bear a son, and they shall name him Emmanuel. *Alleluia, alleluia.*

GOSPEL *(Matthew 1:18-24)*
A reading from the holy Gospel according to Matthew.
Glory to you, O Lord.

This is how the birth of Jesus Christ came about. When his mother Mary was betrothed to Joseph, but before they lived together, she was found with child through the Holy Spirit. Joseph her husband, since he was a righteous man, yet unwilling to expose her to shame, decided to **divorce**✢ her quietly. Such was his intention when, behold, the angel of the Lord appeared to him in a dream and said, "Joseph, son of David, do not be afraid to take Mary your wife into your home. For it is through the Holy Spirit that this child has been conceived in her. She will bear a son and you are to name him Jesus, because he will save his people from their sins." All this took place to fulfill what the Lord had said through the prophet:

Behold, the virgin shall conceive and bear a son,
    and they shall name him Emmanuel,

which means "God is with us." When Joseph awoke, he did as the angel of the Lord had commanded him and took his wife into his home.

The Gospel of the Lord. *Praise to you, Lord Jesus Christ.*

PROFESSION OF FAITH *(page 13)*

PRAYER OF THE FAITHFUL

PREPARATION OF GIFTS *(page 16)*

PRAYER OVER THE OFFERINGS
May the Holy Spirit, O Lord,
sanctify these gifts laid upon your altar,
just as he filled with his power the womb of the Blessed Virgin Mary.
Through Christ our Lord. ***Amen.***

PREFACE *(Advent 2, page 18)*

COMMUNION ANTIPHON *(Isaiah 7:14)*
Behold, a Virgin shall conceive and bear a son; and his name will
be called Emmanuel.

• TAKING A CLOSER LOOK •

✝ **Divorce** Divorce is the dissolution of a marriage. Its particular form and meaning are directly related to the cultural customs of marriage. For the ancients, marriage was primarily a compact between families without a high component of emotional attachment between husband and wife. Dissolving a marriage did not mean the untangling of years of emotional commitment but rather the untangling of family alliances. In Judaism, only the husband could initiate divorce, which entailed reversing the marriage process by sending the bride back to her family together with her personal wealth (dowry) while forfeiting any claim on whatever compensation (bride price) he might have made to her family at the time of marriage.

PRAYER AFTER COMMUNION

Having received this pledge of eternal redemption,
we pray, almighty God,
that, as the feast day of our salvation draws ever nearer,
so we may press forward all the more eagerly
to the worthy celebration of the mystery of your Son's Nativity.
Who lives and reigns for ever and ever. *Amen.*

SOLEMN BLESSING: ADVENT *(Optional, page 57)*

DISMISSAL *(page 57)* ✛

✛ RESPONDING TO THE WORD ✛

God offers to give Ahaz a sign of God's care for the people.	Paul reminds us we are called to be holy.	Joseph overcomes his fear to accept Jesus' growth in Mary's womb.
▷ *What signs of God's care have I noticed recently?*	▷ *What am I doing this Advent to draw closer to God and others?*	▷ *What fears make it hard for me to accept Jesus' growing presence in me?*

Christ's light shines in the darkness

Christmas celebrates God's becoming incarnate in time and history. The God who promised to be among us has come and continues to be with us, now and always, through Jesus and the Holy Spirit.

As the shortest days of the year end and the light of a new year begins, we celebrate Christ's presence with us to transform our world. The darkness of sin and the reign of evil now must confront the light of the nations and the reign of God. Where Christ's light is allowed to shine, the dark shadows of sin will be illumined, allowing us to live in the light. So each day, as the light intensifies, we proclaim that "Christ's light shines in the darkness, and the darkness has not overcome it" (John 1:5).

Like John the Baptist, we too are called "to testify to the light, so that all might believe through him" (John 1:7). Our testimony to Christ's light will be evident in our words and in our actions. As we are more and more enlightened by Christ, we become beacons of hope for others in a world still steeped in darkness.

Our lives are Christmas in miniature. We are invited to let God enlighten us so that we become "divinized" persons, full of the gift of the divine life and its power to change us completely. In us, God makes an appeal to all humanity to enter into this new life and live in God's light.

Praying and living the Christmas season

The twelve days between Christmas and Epiphany are a special time to celebrate Jesus as God's great gift to us and share gifts with one another. This reminds us that Eucharist (Greek for "thanksgiving") sums up our Christian lives. Let us focus our attention on God's everyday gifts to us and the gifts that we in turn receive and give. As we become more and more attentive to these gifts, we will also grow in our attitude of gratitude and be more aware of how much we have to be thankful for when we celebrate Eucharist.

Whenever your household gathers for a meal or your faith-sharing group meets, take time to thank God for being present in your daily lives. You may wish to do this as part of your grace (another word for "gift"!) before the meal.

INVITATION TO PRAYER

Leader: Jesus said, "I am the light of the world. Whoever follows me will not walk in darkness, but will have the light of life." *(John 8:12)*

All: Thanks be to God for this wonderful gift!

AROUND THE TABLE *Invite each member of the household or group to respond to these questions:*

- What gifts did I receive today from others? from God?
- How did I express my gratitude?
- What gifts did I give today to others? to God?

THINGS TO DO *Each day find one way to give a small gift of time, attention, or care for someone in the household, at work, or at school.*

December 25

**DEC
25**

God is faithful!

It is true! We have seen a great light. Throughout today's readings, we recall the fulfillment of God's promise: the birth of the long-awaited One. We remember that God keeps promises. God is faithful.

It was something of a surprise. Very few of us would have gone looking for the Savior in a stable in a remote village. Given the opportunity, Mary and Joseph would have likely chosen to be elsewhere when Jesus was born. And yet, they were in the right place at the right time.

Some saw the light in the little One born into the darkness. They hastened to honor the One who began life in that very unlikely place. Hope, peace, joy, and quiet splendor filled the air; doubt and despair disappeared into the darkness. It was still night, but a new light had been born into the world.

This tiny new life would need nurturing and support as he grew to full stature. Everything starts out small: children, families, friendships. Everything good takes time and rarely happens as planned. When life is confusing and confounding, we hold fast, grateful for the strength to endure. We are ever grateful for those who help us along the way. May this Eucharist give us the courage to trust God's greater wisdom in bringing life and love to the world.

■ BRENDA MERK HILDEBRAND

MASS DURING THE NIGHT

ENTRANCE ANTIPHON *(Psalm 2:7)*

The Lord said to me: You are my Son. It is I who have begotten you this day.

Or

Let us all rejoice in the Lord, for our Savior has been born in the world. Today true peace has come down to us from heaven.

INTRODUCTORY RITES *(page 10)*

COLLECT

O God, who have made this most sacred night
radiant with the splendor of the true light,
grant, we pray, that we, who have known the mysteries of his
    light on earth,
may also delight in his gladness in heaven.
Who lives and reigns with you in the unity of the Holy Spirit,
one God, for ever and ever. *Amen.*

FIRST READING *(Isaiah 9:1-6)*

The people who walked in darkness
    have seen a great light;
upon those who dwelt in the land of gloom
    a light has shone.
You have brought them abundant joy
    and great rejoicing,
as they rejoice before you as at the harvest,
    as people make merry when dividing spoils.
For the yoke that burdened them,
    the pole on their shoulder,

and the rod of their taskmaster
    you have smashed, as on the day of Midian.*
For every boot that tramped in battle,
    every cloak rolled in blood,
    will be burned as fuel for flames.
For a child is born to us, a son is given us;
    upon his shoulder dominion rests.
They name him Wonder-Counselor, God-Hero,
    Father-Forever, Prince of Peace.
His dominion is vast
    and forever peaceful,
from David's throne, and over his kingdom,
    which he confirms and sustains
by judgment and justice,
    both now and forever.
The zeal of the LORD of hosts will do this!
The word of the Lord. *Thanks be to God.*

RESPONSORIAL PSALM *(Psalm 96:1-2, 2-3, 11-12, 13)*
℟ **Today is born our Savior, Christ the Lord.**

Sing to the LORD a new song;
    sing to the LORD, all you lands.
Sing to the LORD; bless his name. ℟
Announce his salvation, day after day.
    Tell his glory among the nations;
    among all peoples, his wondrous deeds. ℟
Let the heavens be glad and the earth rejoice;
    let the sea and what fills it resound;
    let the plains be joyful and all that is in them!
Then shall all the trees of the forest exult. ℟

They shall exult before the LORD, for he comes;
    for he comes to rule the earth.
He shall rule the world with justice
    and the peoples with his constancy.
℟ **Today is born our Savior, Christ the Lord.**

SECOND READING *(Titus 2:11-14)*

Beloved: The grace of God has appeared, saving all and training us to reject godless ways and worldly desires and to live temperately, justly, and devoutly in this age, as we await the blessed hope, the appearance of the glory of our great God and savior Jesus Christ, who gave himself for us to deliver us from all lawlessness and to cleanse for himself a people as his own, eager to do what is good.

    The word of the Lord. *Thanks be to God.*

ALLELUIA *(Luke 2:10-11)*

Alleluia, alleluia. I proclaim to you good news of great joy: today a Savior is born for us, Christ the Lord. *Alleluia, alleluia.*

GOSPEL *(Luke 2:1-14)*

A reading from the holy Gospel according to Luke.
Glory to you, O Lord.

In those days a decree went out from Caesar* Augustus that the whole world should be enrolled. This was the first enrollment, when Quirinius* was governor of Syria. So all went to be enrolled, each to his own town. And Joseph too went up from Galilee from the town of Nazareth to Judea, to the city of David that is called Bethlehem, because he was of the house and family of David, to be enrolled with Mary, his betrothed, who was with child. While they were there, the time came for her to have her child, and she gave birth to her firstborn son. She wrapped him in swaddling clothes and laid him in a manger, because there was no room for them in the inn.

Now there were shepherds in that region living in the fields and keeping the night watch over their flock. The angel of the Lord appeared to them and the glory of the Lord shone around them, and they were struck with great fear. The angel said to them, "Do not be afraid; for behold, I proclaim to you good news of great joy that will be for all the people. For today in the city of David a savior has been born for you who is **Christ and Lord**.✝ And this will be a sign for you: you will find an infant wrapped in swaddling clothes and lying in a manger." And suddenly there was a multitude of the heavenly host with the angel, praising God and saying:

"Glory to God in the highest
    and on earth peace to those on whom his favor rests."
The Gospel of the Lord. *Praise to you, Lord Jesus Christ.*

PROFESSION OF FAITH *(page 13)*

PRAYER OF THE FAITHFUL

PREPARATION OF GIFTS *(page 16)*

PRAYER OVER THE OFFERINGS

May the oblation of this day's feast
be pleasing to you, O Lord, we pray,
that through this most holy exchange
we may be found in the likeness of Christ,
in whom our nature is united to you.
Who lives and reigns for ever and ever. *Amen.*

PREFACE *(Nativity of the Lord 1–3, pages 19–20)*

COMMUNION ANTIPHON *(John 1:14)*

The Word became flesh, and we have seen his glory.

• TAKING A CLOSER LOOK •

✚ **Christ and Lord** These two terms summarize Luke's understanding of who Jesus really is as both human and divine. The word
"Christ" (Greek for "anointed," in Hebrew, *messiah*) identifies Jesus as
the agent of salvation (savior) whom God would send to bring God's
covenant people into the right relationship with God. The word "Lord"
(Greek, *kyrios*) is the usual Greek title for a god and the circumlocution
used by Jews to avoid speaking the sacred Name of God, YHWH. This
name is now given to Jesus, and the honor due to God is now due him.

PRAYER AFTER COMMUNION

Grant us, we pray, O Lord our God,
that we, who are gladdened by participation
in the feast of our Redeemer's Nativity,
may through an honorable way of life become worthy of union
   with him.
Who lives and reigns for ever and ever. *Amen.*

SOLEMN BLESSING: THE NATIVITY OF THE LORD *(Optional, page 58)*

DISMISSAL *(page 57)* ✤

• RESPONDING TO THE WORD •

Isaiah foresees the beginning of freedom from our burdens.	We must reject godless ways to enjoy the gift of Jesus.	The child is a sign of the peace and unity God desires for all.
➡ What burdens do I want Jesus to lift from me today?	➡ What must I give up in order to live more like Jesus wants?	➡ What sign of this unity have I experienced this Advent?

MASS AT DAWN

ENTRANCE ANTIPHON *(Cf. Isaiah 9:1, 5; Luke 1:33)*
Today a light will shine upon us, for the Lord is born for us;
and he will be called Wondrous God, Prince of peace, Father of
future ages: and his reign will be without end.

INTRODUCTORY RITES *(page 10)*

COLLECT
Grant, we pray, almighty God,
that, as we are bathed in the new radiance of your incarnate Word,
the light of faith, which illumines our minds,
may also shine through in our deeds.
Through our Lord Jesus Christ, your Son,
who lives and reigns with you in the unity of the Holy Spirit,
one God, for ever and ever. *Amen.*

FIRST READING *(Isaiah 62:11-12)*

See, the LORD proclaims
to the ends of the earth:
say to daughter Zion,*
your savior comes!
Here is his reward with him,
his recompense before him.
They shall be called the holy people,
the redeemed of the LORD,
and you shall be called "Frequented,"
a city that is not forsaken.
The word of the Lord. *Thanks be to God.*

RESPONSORIAL PSALM *(Psalm 97:1, 6, 11-12)*

℟ **A light will shine on us this day: the Lord is born for us.**

The LORD is king; let the earth rejoice;
    let the many isles be glad.
The heavens proclaim his justice,
    and all peoples see his glory. ℟
Light dawns for the just;
    and gladness, for the upright of heart.
Be glad in the LORD, you just,
    and give thanks to his holy name. ℟

SECOND READING *(Titus 3:4-7)*

Beloved:
When the kindness and generous love
    of **God our savior**✝ appeared,
not because of any righteous deeds we had done
    but because of his mercy,
he saved us through the bath of rebirth
    and renewal by the Holy Spirit,
whom he richly poured out on us
    through Jesus Christ our savior,
so that we might be justified by his grace
    and become heirs in hope of eternal life.
The word of the Lord. *Thanks be to God.*

ALLELUIA *(Luke 2:14)*

Alleluia, alleluia. Glory to God in the highest, and on earth
peace to those on whom his favor rests. *Alleluia, alleluia.*

GOSPEL *(Luke 2:15-20)*
A reading from the holy Gospel according to Luke.
Glory to you, O Lord.

When the angels went away from them to heaven, the shepherds said to one another, "Let us go, then, to Bethlehem to see this thing that has taken place, which the Lord has made known to us." So they went in haste and found Mary and Joseph, and the infant lying in the manger. When they saw this, they made known the message that had been told them about this child. All who heard it were amazed by what had been told them by the shepherds. And Mary kept all these things, reflecting on them in her heart. Then the shepherds returned, glorifying and praising God for all they had heard and seen, just as it had been told to them.

The Gospel of the Lord. *Praise to you, Lord Jesus Christ.*

PROFESSION OF FAITH *(page 13)*

PRAYER OF THE FAITHFUL

PREPARATION OF GIFTS *(page 16)*

PRAYER OVER THE OFFERINGS
May our offerings be worthy, we pray, O Lord,

• TAKING A CLOSER LOOK •

✚ **God our savior** In Biblical times, wthe word "savior" meant one who rescued someone from a difficult situation. It was commonly attributed to the king, emperor, or general who saved the nation by winning a war. For the Jews, God was their primary Savior because God rescued them from their oppression in Egypt, restored them after the exile, and sustained their covenant community. For Christians, Jesus is the Savior because he saved us and offered us a new relationship under God's kingdom rule.

of the mysteries of the Nativity this day,
that, just as Christ was born a man and also shone forth as God,
so these earthly gifts may confer on us what is divine.
Through Christ our Lord. *Amen.*

PREFACE *(Nativity of the Lord 1–3, pages 19–20)*

COMMUNION ANTIPHON *(Cf. Zechariah 9:9)*
Rejoice, O Daughter Sion; lift up praise, Daughter Jerusalem:
Behold, your King will come, the Holy One and Savior of the
world.

PRAYER AFTER COMMUNION
Grant us, Lord, as we honor with joyful devotion
the Nativity of your Son,
that we may come to know with fullness of faith
the hidden depths of this mystery
and to love them ever more and more.
Through Christ our Lord. *Amen.*

SOLEMN BLESSING: THE NATIVITY OF THE LORD *(Optional, page 58)*

DISMISSAL *(page 57)*

• RESPONDING TO THE WORD •

Those who accept the Savior become God's holy people.	Jesus' presence with us is God's surprise gift.	Mary treasured all these events in her heart.
➲ *How can I help draw someone closer to Christ today?*	➲ *How can I thank God for that gift today?*	➲ *Which of these events most touches my heart today?*

MASS DURING THE DAY

ENTRANCE ANTIPHON *(Cf. Isaiah 9:5)*

A child is born for us, and a son is given to us; his scepter of power rests upon his shoulder, and his name will be called Messenger of great counsel.

INTRODUCTORY RITES *(page 10)*

COLLECT

O God, who wonderfully created the dignity of human nature and still more wonderfully restored it,
grant, we pray,
that we may share in the divinity of Christ,
who humbled himself to share in our humanity.
Who lives and reigns with you in the unity of the Holy Spirit,
one God, for ever and ever. *Amen.*

FIRST READING *(Isaiah 52:7-10)*

How beautiful upon the mountains
    are the feet of him who brings glad tidings,
announcing peace, bearing good news,
    announcing salvation, and saying to Zion,*
    "Your God is King!"

Hark! Your sentinels raise a cry,
    together they shout for joy,
for they see directly, before their eyes,
    the LORD restoring Zion.
Break out together in song,
    O ruins of Jerusalem!
For the LORD comforts his people,

he redeems Jerusalem.
The LORD has bared his holy arm
in the sight of all the nations;
all the ends of the earth will behold
the salvation of our God.
The word of the Lord. *Thanks be to God.*

RESPONSORIAL PSALM *(Psalm 98:1, 2-3, 3-4, 5-6)*

R. **All the ends of the earth have seen the saving power of God.**

Sing to the LORD a new song,
for he has done wondrous deeds;
his right hand has won victory for him,
his holy arm. R.

The LORD has made his salvation known:
in the sight of the nations he has revealed his justice.
He has remembered his kindness and his faithfulness
toward the house of Israel. R.

All the ends of the earth have seen
the salvation by our God.
Sing joyfully to the LORD, all you lands;
break into song; sing praise. R.

Sing praise to the LORD with the harp,
with the harp and melodious song.
With trumpets and the sound of the horn
sing joyfully before the King, the LORD. R.

SECOND READING *(Hebrews 1:1-6)*

Brothers and sisters: In times past, God spoke in partial and various ways to our ancestors through the prophets; in these last days, he has spoken to us through the Son, whom he made heir of all things and through whom he created the universe,

who is the refulgence of his glory, the very imprint of his being,
and who sustains all things by his mighty word.
When he had accomplished purification from sins,
he took his seat at the right hand of the Majesty on high,
as far superior to the angels
as the name he has inherited is more excellent than theirs.

For to which of the angels did God ever say:
    You are my son; this day I have begotten you?
Or again:
    I will be a father to him, and he shall be a son to me?
And again, when he leads the firstborn into the world, he says:
    Let all the angels of God worship him.
The word of the Lord. *Thanks be to God.*

ALLELUIA

Alleluia, alleluia. A holy day has dawned upon us. Come, you
nations, and adore the Lord. For today a great light has come
upon the earth. *Alleluia, alleluia.*

GOSPEL *(John 1:1–18)*
For the shorter reading, omit the indented parts in brackets.

A reading from the holy Gospel according to John.
Glory to you, O Lord.

I n the beginning was the Word,
  and the Word was with God,
  and the Word was God.
He was in the beginning with God.
All things came to be through him,
  and without him nothing came to be.

What came to be through him was life,
 and this life was the light of the human race;
the light shines in the darkness,
 and the darkness has not overcome it.
[A man named John was sent from God. He came for testimony, to testify to the light, so that all might believe through him. He was not the light, but came to testify to the light.]
The true light, which enlightens everyone, was coming into the world.
He was in the world,
 and the world came to be through him,
 but the world did not know him.
He came to what was his own,
 but his own people did not accept him.
But to those who did accept him he gave power to become children of God, to those who believe in his name, who were born not by natural generation nor by human choice nor by a man's decision but of God.
And the Word became **flesh**✝
 and made his dwelling among us,
 and we saw his glory,
 the glory as of the Father's only Son,
 full of grace and truth.
[John testified to him and cried out, saying, "This was he of whom I said, 'The one who is coming after me ranks ahead of me because he existed before me.'" From his fullness we have all received, grace in place of grace, because while the law was given through Moses, grace and truth came through Jesus Christ. No one has ever seen God. The only Son, God, who is at the Father's side, has revealed him.]
The Gospel of the Lord. *Praise to you, Lord Jesus Christ.*

PROFESSION OF FAITH *(page 13)*

PRAYER OF THE FAITHFUL

PREPARATION OF GIFTS *(page 16)*

PRAYER OVER THE OFFERINGS
Make acceptable, O Lord, our oblation on this solemn day,
when you manifested the reconciliation
that makes us wholly pleasing in your sight
and inaugurated for us the fullness of divine worship.
Through Christ our Lord. *Amen.*

PREFACE *(Nativity of the Lord 1-3, pages 19-20)*

• Taking a Closer Look •

✜ **Flesh** The word "flesh" does not just refer to the skin but is often used to describe the whole living human body (hence "flesh and blood" to describe a whole living person). But flesh also describes what is corruptible (for we all die) and prone to sin (for we are not perfect). Because "flesh" describes the reality of human existence, it is appropriate to highlight Jesus' becoming human. But because "flesh" points to that which moves us toward sin and alienation from God, it is startling to apply this to Jesus. Normally, God and flesh would not go together, but in the divine-human reality of Jesus they must.

COMMUNION ANTIPHON *(Cf. Psalm 98 [97]:3)*
All the ends of the earth have seen the salvation of our God.

PRAYER AFTER COMMUNION
Grant, O merciful God,
that, just as the Savior of the world, born this day,
is the author of divine generation for us,
so he may be the giver even of immortality.
Who lives and reigns for ever and ever. *Amen.*

SOLEMN BLESSING: THE NATIVITY OF THE LORD *(Optional, page 58)*

DISMISSAL *(page 57)* ❖

• RESPONDING TO THE WORD •

We are thankful for those who bring the good news of Jesus to us.

➡ *Who has been a special teacher of this good news in my life?*

Jesus is the human image of God.

➡ *What particular aspect of God has Jesus revealed to me during this Advent and Christmas?*

Jesus is the Word that reveals the inner thoughts and feelings of God.

➡ *What can I do to listen more carefully to God's word during the coming year?*

December 29

A lesson in parenting

When my children were young, I developed an unexpected nightly ritual. Before going to bed, I went into their rooms and checked that they were asleep in their beds. I *knew* they were there—where else could they be?—but until I could see with my own eyes that they were safe, I could not get to sleep. Such is the protective instinct of parents.

So imagine what must have gone through St. Joseph's mind when an angel came to him late one night and confirmed his worst fear—his child was in mortal danger and he had to do something. He got up instantly and, abandoning work, home, and all social connections, hastily packed and led the child and mother to safety.

To protect his child he chose to give up everything and become a refugee in a strange land. Such is the protective instinct of parents.

All parents want what St. Joseph wanted—a safe home for their children. Some are forced to flee danger and become refugees, as he did. Others are more fortunate, and can stay in their homes and protect their children by ensuring them clean air, pure water, nourishing food, good education, and a future filled with hope.

St. Joseph offers a perfect lesson in parenting—take care of your children at any cost.

■ PATRICK GALLAGHER

ENTRANCE ANTIPHON *(Luke 2:16)*

The shepherds went in haste, and found Mary and Joseph and the Infant lying in a manger.

INTRODUCTORY RITES *(page 10)*

COLLECT

O God, who were pleased to give us
the shining example of the Holy Family,
graciously grant that we may imitate them
in practicing the virtues of family life and in the bonds of charity,
and so, in the joy of your house,
delight one day in eternal rewards.
Through our Lord Jesus Christ, your Son,
who lives and reigns with you in the unity of the Holy Spirit,
one God, for ever and ever. *Amen.*

FIRST READING *(Sirach 3:2-6, 12-14)*

G od sets a father in honor over his children;
a mother's authority he confirms over her sons.
Whoever honors his father atones for sins,
    and preserves himself from them.
When he prays, he is heard;
    he stores up riches who reveres his mother.
Whoever honors his father is gladdened by children,
    and, when he prays, is heard.
Whoever reveres his father will live a long life;
    he who obeys his father brings comfort to his mother.

My son, take care of your father when he is old;
    grieve him not as long as he lives.
Even if his mind fail, be considerate of him;
    revile him not all the days of his life;

kindness to a father will not be forgotten,
　firmly planted against the debt of your sins
　—a house raised in justice to you.
The word of the Lord. ***Thanks be to God.***

RESPONSORIAL PSALM *(Psalm 128:1-2, 3, 4-5)*

℟ **Blessed are those who fear the Lord and walk in his ways.**

Blessed is everyone who fears the LORD,
　who walks in his ways!
For you shall eat the fruit of your handiwork;
　blessed shall you be, and favored. ℟

Your wife shall be like a fruitful vine
　in the recesses of your home;
your children like olive plants
　around your table. ℟

Behold, thus is the man blessed
　who fears the LORD.
The Lord bless you from Zion:*
　may you see the prosperity of Jerusalem
　all the days of your life. ℟

SECOND READING *(Colossians 3:12-21)*
For the shorter version, omit the indented part in brackets.

Brothers and sisters: Put on, as God's chosen ones, holy and
beloved, heartfelt compassion, kindness, humility, gentleness, and patience, bearing with one another and forgiving one
another, if one has a grievance against another; as the Lord has
forgiven you, so must you also do. And over all these put on
love, that is, the bond of perfection. And let the peace of Christ
control your hearts, the peace into which you were also called in

one body. And be thankful. Let the word of Christ dwell in you richly, as in all wisdom you teach and admonish one another, singing psalms, hymns, and spiritual songs with gratitude in your hearts to God. And whatever you do, in word or in deed, do everything in the name of the Lord Jesus, giving thanks to God the Father through him.

[**Wives, be subordinate to your husbands,**✝ as is proper in the Lord. **Husbands, love your wives,**✝ and avoid any bitterness toward them. Children, obey your parents in everything, for this is pleasing to the Lord. Fathers, do not provoke your children, so they may not become discouraged.]

The word of the Lord. *Thanks be to God.*

ALLELUIA *(Colossians 3:15a, 16a)*
Alleluia, alleluia. Let the peace of Christ control your hearts; let he word of Christ dwell in you richly. *Alleluia, alleluia.*

GOSPEL *(Matthew 2:13–15, 19-23)*
A reading from the holy Gospel according to Matthew.
Glory to you, O Lord.

When the magi had departed, behold, the angel of the Lord appeared to Joseph in a dream and said, "Rise, take the child and his mother, flee to Egypt, and stay there until I tell you. Herod is going to search for the child to destroy him." Joseph rose and took the child and his mother by night and departed for Egypt. He stayed there until the death of Herod, that what the Lord had said through the prophet might be fulfilled, *Out of Egypt I called my son.*

When Herod had died, behold, the angel of the Lord appeared in a dream to Joseph in Egypt and said, "Rise, take the child and his mother and go to the land of Israel, for those who sought the child's life are dead." He rose, took the child and his mother, and went to the land of Israel. But when he heard that Archelaus was ruling over Judea in place of his father Herod, he was afraid to go back there. And because he had been warned in a dream, he departed for the region of Galilee. He went and dwelt in a town called Nazareth, so that what had been spoken through the prophets might be fulfilled, *He shall be called a Nazorean.* ∗

The Gospel of the Lord. *Praise to you, Lord Jesus Christ.*

PROFESSION OF FAITH *(page 13)*

PRAYER OF THE FAITHFUL

PREPARATION OF GIFTS *(page 16)*

PRAYER OVER THE OFFERINGS
We offer you, Lord, the sacrifice of conciliation,
humbly asking that,
through the intercession of the Virgin Mother of God
and Saint Joseph,

• TAKING A CLOSER LOOK •

✚ **Wives, be subordinate to your husbands. Husbands, love your wives.** Marriage in Paul's time was very different from today. Arranged by families, its purpose was increasing the family's status or wealth and continuing the family through children. People did not marry necessarily for love. Paul's advice for women repeats what they would already know about relationships in the household: the father or husband was considered the only adult, so he thought and decided for everyone else. Women were expected merely to obey (be subordinate). For men, however, Paul's advice is shocking and challenging. He requires them to love their wives (not necessarily part of the family marriage agreement!) with the self-sacrificing love that Christ had for the Church.

you may establish our families firmly in your grace and your peace.
Through Christ our Lord. *Amen.*

PREFACE *(Nativity of the Lord 1–3, pages 19–20)*

COMMUNION ANTIPHON *(Baruch 3:38)*
Our God has appeared on the earth, and lived among us.

PRAYER AFTER COMMUNION
Bring those you refresh with this heavenly Sacrament,
most merciful Father,
to imitate constantly the example of the Holy Family,
so that, after the trials of this world,
we may share their company for ever.
Through Christ our Lord. *Amen.*

BLESSING & DISMISSAL *(page 56)* ❖

• RESPONDING TO THE WORD •

Sirach encourages us to honor our parents.	Forgiveness is an important element in family life.	Joseph must protect his vulnerable wife and child.
➡ *What can I do today to show my respect and gratitude for my parents?*	➡ *Who do I need to forgive and be forgiven by in my family?*	➡ *What can I do today to help mothers and children who need help and protection?*

January 1

May peace be with us

When the shepherds found the child Jesus lying in the manger, they glorified God for the birth of their Savior, the one who would take away their sins in his perfect love. They left rejoicing, and Mary treasured the shepherd's jubilation.

Mary's pondering was her "yes" to God. She gave birth to the Prince of Peace in a world of conflict and suffering. How would this mystery unfold? How could this needy infant, cradled in her arms, born in a dark and smelly manger, be the Son of the Most High, the King of Kings who would sit upon the throne of David?

Despite these contradictions in her life, Mary's pondering remained faithful in her total "yes" to love and serve God. Her peaceful and trusting spirit bowed freely to the will of God, as the first disciple ready to serve the Light of the World in its seeming darkness. Mary shows us how, in uncertain times, to anchor our faith and hope in a loving God.

As we honor Mary, the Holy Mother of God on this World Day of Peace, may peace be with us. Let us ponder and treasure the peace that Christ brings into our lives through the love and compassion of others. Like Mary, may we be disciples of peace faithful to Christ's "yes" to us and our "yes" to God.

■ JULIE CACHIA

ENTRANCE ANTIPHON

Hail, Holy Mother, who gave birth to the King
who rules heaven and earth for ever.

Or *(Cf. Isaiah 9:1, 5; Luke 1:33)*

Today a light will shine upon us, for the Lord is born
for us; and he will be called Wondrous God, Prince
of peace, Father of future ages: and his reign will be without end.

INTRODUCTORY RITES *(page 10)*

COLLECT

O God, who through the fruitful virginity of Blessed Mary
bestowed on the human race
the grace of eternal salvation,
grant, we pray,
that we may experience the intercession of her,
through whom we were found worthy
to receive the author of life,
our Lord Jesus Christ, your Son.
Who lives and reigns with you in the unity of the Holy Spirit,
one God, for ever and ever. *Amen.*

FIRST READING *(Numbers 6:22-27)*

The LORD said to Moses: "Speak to Aaron and his sons and tell
them: This is how you shall bless the Israelites. Say to them:
The LORD bless you and keep you!
The LORD let his face shine upon you, and be gracious to you!
The LORD look upon you kindly and give you peace!
So shall they invoke my name upon the Israelites, and I will bless them."
The word of the Lord. *Thanks be to God.*

RESPONSORIAL PSALM *(Psalm 67:2-3, 5, 6, 8)*
℟. **May God bless us in his mercy.**

May God have pity on us and bless us;
  may he let his face shine upon us.
So may your way be known upon earth;
  among all nations, your salvation. ℟.
May the nations be glad and exult
  because you rule the peoples in equity;
  the nations on the earth you guide. ℟.
May the peoples praise you, O God;
  may all the peoples praise you!
May God bless us,
  and may all the ends of the earth fear him! ℟.

SECOND READING *(Galatians 4:4-7)*

Brothers and sisters: When the fullness of time had come, God sent his Son, born of a woman, born under the law, to ransom those under the law, so that we might receive adoption as sons. As proof that you are sons, God sent the Spirit of his Son into our hearts, crying out, "**Abba,**✠ Father!" So you are no longer a slave but a son, and if a son then also an heir, through God.

The word of the Lord. ***Thanks be to God.***

ALLELUIA *(Hebrews 1:1-2)*
Alleluia, alleluia. In the past God spoke to our ancestors through the prophets; in these last days, he has spoken to us through the Son. *Alleluia, alleluia.*

GOSPEL *(Luke 2:16-21)*
A reading from the holy Gospel according to Luke.
Glory to you, O Lord.

The shepherds went in haste to Bethlehem and found Mary and Joseph, and the infant lying in the manger. When they saw this, they made known the message that had been told them about this child. All who heard it were amazed by what had been told them by the shepherds. And Mary kept all these things, reflecting on them in her heart. Then the shepherds returned, glorifying and praising God for all they had heard and seen, just as it had been told to them.

When eight days were completed for his circumcision, he was named Jesus, the name given him by the angel before he was conceived in the womb.

The Gospel of the Lord. *Praise to you, Lord Jesus Christ.*

PROFESSION OF FAITH *(page 13)*

PRAYER OF THE FAITHFUL

PREPARATION OF GIFTS *(page 16)*

PRAYER OVER THE OFFERINGS
O God, who in your kindness begin all good things
and bring them to fulfillment,

• Taking a Closer Look •

✜ **Abba** This is the Aramaic (the spoken language of Jews in the Holy Land in Jesus' time) word for "father." It is a more familiar form than the common but slightly more formal Greek word for "father," and thus represents the more intimate and close relationship that Jesus has with God. Paul does not expect the Galatians to know its meaning, so he connects the Aramaic term with its Greek translation: "Abba, Father."

grant to us, who find joy in the Solemnity of the holy
Mother of God,
that, just as we glory in the beginnings of your grace,
so one day we may rejoice in its completion.
Through Christ our Lord. *Amen.*

PREFACE *(Blessed Virgin Mary 1, page 34)*

COMMUNION ANTIPHON *(Hebrews 13:8)*
Jesus Christ is the same yesterday, today, and for ever.

PRAYER AFTER COMMUNION
We have received this heavenly Sacrament with joy, O Lord:
grant, we pray,
that it may lead us to eternal life,
for we rejoice to proclaim the blessed ever-Virgin Mary
Mother of your Son and Mother of the Church.
Through Christ our Lord. *Amen.*

SOLEMN BLESSING: THE BEGINNING OF THE YEAR *(Optional, page 59)*
   OR THE BLESSED VIRGIN MARY *(Optional, page 62)*

DISMISSAL *(page 57)* :::

• RESPONDING TO THE WORD

God reminds Moses to make blessing a regular practice.	Paul encourages us to remember that God has adopted us.	Everyone was amazed to learn about Jesus' birth.
▣ To whom can I offer a blessing today?	▣ How can I thank God for the gift of being God's child?	▣ What has most amazed me about Jesus during this Christmas season?

JAN
5

January 5

The greatest love story

Don't tell me you love me, show me! Give me a sign...

When we fall in love with someone, we look for signs that they love us too. We want to show them our love. We shower them with gifts as tokens of our love. We also want it to be reciprocal, a two-way street. That is human nature.

The ancient world placed a lot of emphasis on signs. Sometimes they trusted signs more than the written or spoken word. The scriptures contain many passages about signs. Today's gospel is full of signs and tokens of love. It is also a love story.

In it we see King Herod and astrologers, people whose job it is to interpret signs, looking for signs in the stars of the promised messiah. Herod sends the astrologers to follow a star and when they do, they find the baby Jesus. Recognizing the fulfillment of God's promise, they are filled with love and shower Jesus with signs of that love in the form of precious gifts of gold, frankincense, and myrrh.

But the greatest love story is in the baby the wise men find. This child is none other than God's only Son, the promised Messiah, the light to guide all of humankind out of darkness. What greater sign of love could God give to the world? Salvation through his own Son!

● **PATRICK M. DOYLE**

MASS DURING THE DAY

ENTRANCE ANTIPHON *(Cf. Malachi 3:1; 1 Chronicles 29:12)*

Behold, the Lord, the Mighty One, has come; and kingship is in his grasp, and power and dominion.

INTRODUCTORY RITES *(page 10)*

COLLECT

O God, who on this day
revealed your Only Begotten Son to the nations
by the guidance of a star,
grant in your mercy
that we, who know you already by faith,
may be brought to behold the beauty of your sublime glory.
Through our Lord Jesus Christ, your Son,
who lives and reigns with you in the unity of the Holy Spirit,
one God, for ever and ever. *Amen.*

FIRST READING *(Isaiah 60:1-6)*

Rise up in splendor, Jerusalem! Your light has come,
the **glory of the LORD**✝ shines upon you.
See, darkness covers the earth,
    and thick clouds cover the peoples;
but upon you the LORD shines,
    and over you appears his glory.
Nations shall walk by your light,
    and kings by your shining radiance.
Raise your eyes and look about;
    they all gather and come to you:
your sons come from afar,
    and your daughters in the arms of their nurses.

Then you shall be radiant at what you see,
   your heart shall throb and overflow,
for the riches of the sea shall be emptied out before you,
   the wealth of nations shall be brought to you.
Caravans of camels shall fill you,
   dromedaries from Midian* and Ephah;*
all from Sheba* shall come
   bearing gold and frankincense,
   and proclaiming the praises of the LORD.
The word of the Lord. *Thanks be to God.*

RESPONSORIAL PSALM *(Psalm 72:1-2, 7-8, 10-11, 12-13)*
℞ **Lord, every nation on earth will adore you.**

O God, with your judgment endow the king,
   and with your justice, the king's son;
he shall govern your people with justice
   and your afflicted ones with judgment. ℞
Justice shall flower in his days,
   and profound peace, till the moon be no more.
May he rule from sea to sea,
   and from the River to the ends of the earth. ℞
The kings of Tarshish* and the Isles shall offer gifts;
   the kings of Arabia and Seba* shall bring tribute.
All kings shall pay him homage,
   all nations shall serve him. ℞
For he shall rescue the poor when he cries out,
   and the afflicted when he has no one to help him.
He shall have pity for the lowly and the poor;
   the lives of the poor he shall save. ℞

SECOND READING *(Ephesians 3:2-3a, 5-6)*

Brothers and sisters: You have heard of the stewardship of God's grace that was given to me for your benefit, namely, that the mystery was made known to me by revelation. It was not made known to people in other generations as it has now been revealed to his holy apostles and prophets by the Spirit: that the Gentiles are coheirs, members of the same body, and copartners in the promise in Christ Jesus through the gospel.

The word of the Lord. *Thanks be to God.*

ALLELUIA *(Matthew 2:2)*

Alleluia, alleluia. We saw his star at its rising and have come to do him homage. *Alleluia, alleluia.*

GOSPEL *(Matthew 2:1-12)*

A reading from the holy Gospel according to Matthew.
Glory to you, O Lord.

When Jesus was born in Bethlehem of Judea, in the days of King Herod, behold, magi from the east arrived in Jerusalem, saying, "Where is the newborn king of the Jews? We saw his star at its rising and have come to do him homage." When King Herod heard this, he was greatly troubled, and all Jerusalem with him. Assembling all the chief priests and the scribes of the people, he inquired of them where the Christ was to be born. They said to him, "In Bethlehem of Judea, for thus it has been written through the prophet:

And you, Bethlehem, land of Judah,
    are by no means least among the rulers of Judah;
since from you shall come a ruler,
    who is to shepherd my people Israel."

Then Herod called the magi secretly and ascertained from them the time of the star's appearance. He sent them to Bethlehem and said, "Go and search diligently for the child. When you have found him, bring me word, that I too may go and do him homage." After their audience with the king they set out. And behold, the star that they had seen at its rising preceded them, until it came and stopped over the place where the child was. They were overjoyed at seeing the star, and on entering the house they saw the child with Mary his mother. They prostrated themselves and did him homage. Then they opened their treasures and offered him gifts of gold, frankincense, and myrrh.* And having been warned in a dream not to return to Herod, they departed for their country by another way.

The Gospel of the Lord. ***Praise to you, Lord Jesus Christ.***

PROFESSION OF FAITH *(page 13)*

PRAYER OF THE FAITHFUL

PREPARATION OF GIFTS *(page 16)*

PRAYER OVER THE OFFERINGS

Look with favor, Lord, we pray,
on these gifts of your Church,
in which are offered now not gold or frankincense or myrrh,
but he who by them is proclaimed,
sacrificed and received, Jesus Christ.
Who lives and reigns for ever and ever. ***Amen.***

PREFACE *(The Epiphany of the Lord, page 20)*

COMMUNION ANTIPHON *(Cf. Matthew 2:2)*

We have seen his star in the East, and have come with gifts to
adore the Lord.

• TAKING A CLOSER LOOK •

✚ **The glory of the Lord** In Hebrew, the word "glory" is related
to weight or heaviness, hence it describes someone's inner worth or
importance. When applied to humans, it can be associated with anything that gives a person dignity and commands respect, such as honor,
wealth, or wisdom. When glory is associated with God, the meaning
becomes more complex. Glory describes the essence of God's divinity
that requires us to respect and honor God, and glory also points to the
visible manifestation of God's invisible presence (for example, in the
cloud and pillar of fire leading the Hebrews during the Exodus or the
light that Isaiah sees falling on Jerusalem and God's faithful people).

PRAYER AFTER COMMUNION

Go before us with heavenly light, O Lord,
always and everywhere,
that we may perceive with clear sight
and revere with true affection
the mystery in which you have willed us to participate.
Through Christ our Lord. *Amen.*

SOLEMN BLESSING: THE EPIPHANY OF THE LORD *(Optional, page 59)*

DISMISSAL *(page 57)* ✣

● RESPONDING TO THE WORD ●

God's presence brings fullness and joy for all.	**God's love is not limited and excludes no one.**	**The magi left their familiar environment to seek and honor a Jewish king.**
➡ *When has God seemed most present to me during this Christmas season?*	➡ *How can I imitate God and include in my life someone I usually prefer to stay apart from?*	➡ *How am I being drawn to discover God in new places and situations?*

January 12

Fully human, fully divine

Our faith embraces the tension of the hypostatic union—the fully divine and fully human nature of Jesus. The Baptism of the Lord is a profound instance of the revelation of the humanity of Jesus and his desire to draw close to us.

John the Baptist baptized people "for repentance" (Matthew 3:11). If Jesus is God, why would he need to be baptized for the forgiveness of sins? One possible answer is that Jesus was baptized in order to identify totally with us. In order to identify with us, he humbled himself to undergo baptism. He even identified with the *effects* of sin that we experience: suffering and death. I draw great comfort and hope from today's episode in Matthew's gospel; Jesus is present in every experience of my life, even in my need for redemption and forgiveness. His act of humility has increased my intimacy with him.

Each time we gather for Mass, we bless ourselves with water from the baptismal font, calling to mind our baptism and Christ's. Let this week's Eucharist be an opportunity to give thanks that we have a Savior who understands our humanity and the effect that sin has on it, even as God the Father calls him "my Son, the Beloved."

■ ROSE DERKSEN

ENTRANCE ANTIPHON *(Cf. Matthew 3:16–17)*
After the Lord was baptized, the heavens were
opened, and the Spirit descended upon him like a
dove, and the voice of the Father thundered: This is
my beloved Son, with whom I am well pleased.

INTRODUCTORY RITES *(page 10)*

COLLECT
Almighty ever-living God,
who, when Christ had been baptized in the River Jordan
and as the Holy Spirit descended upon him,
solemnly declared him your beloved Son,
grant that your children by adoption,
reborn of water and the Holy Spirit,
may always be well pleasing to you.
Through our Lord Jesus Christ, your Son,
who lives and reigns with you in the unity of the Holy Spirit,
one God, for ever and ever. *Amen.*

Or
O God, whose Only Begotten Son
has appeared in our very flesh,
grant, we pray, that we may be inwardly transformed
through him whom we recognize as outwardly like ourselves.
Who lives and reigns with you in the unity of the Holy Spirit,
one God, for ever and ever. *Amen.*

FIRST READING *(Isaiah 42:1-4, 6-7)*

Thus says the LORD:
  Here is my servant whom I uphold,
    my chosen one with whom I am pleased,
  upon whom I have put my spirit;
    he shall bring forth justice to the nations,
not crying out, not shouting,
    not making his voice heard in the street.
A bruised reed he shall not break,
    and a smoldering wick he shall not quench,
until he establishes justice on the earth;
    the coastlands will wait for his teaching.

I, the LORD, have called you for the victory of justice,
    I have grasped you by the hand;
I formed you, and set you
    as a covenant of the people,
    a light for the nations,
to open the eyes of the blind,
    to bring out prisoners from confinement,
    and from the dungeon, those who live in darkness.
The word of the Lord. *Thanks be to God.*

RESPONSORIAL PSALM *(Psalm 29:1-2, 3-4, 3, 9-10)*
℟ **The Lord will bless his people with peace.**

Give to the LORD, you sons of God,
    give to the LORD glory and praise,
give to the LORD the glory due his name;
    adore the LORD in holy attire. ℟
The voice of the LORD is over the waters,
    the LORD, over vast waters.

The voice of the LORD is mighty;
  the voice of the LORD is majestic. ℟
The God of glory thunders,
  and in his temple all say, "Glory!"
The LORD is enthroned above the flood;
  the LORD is enthroned as king for ever.
℟ **The Lord will bless his people with peace.**

SECOND READING *(Acts 10:34–38)*

Peter proceeded to speak to those gathered in the house of Cornelius, saying: "In truth, I see that God shows **no partiality.**✝ Rather, in every nation whoever fears him and acts uprightly is acceptable to him. You know the word that he sent to the Israelites as he proclaimed peace through Jesus Christ, who is Lord of all, what has happened all over Judea, beginning in Galilee after the baptism that John preached, how God anointed Jesus of Nazareth with the Holy Spirit and power. He went about doing good and healing all those oppressed by the devil, for God was with him."

  The word of the Lord. *Thanks be to God.*

ALLELUIA *(Cf. Mark 9:7)*
Alleluia, alleluia. The heavens were opened and the voice of the Father thundered: This is my beloved Son, listen to him. *Alleluia, alleluia.*

GOSPEL *(Matthew 3:13–17)*

A reading from the holy Gospel according to Matthew.
Glory to you, O Lord.

Jesus came from Galilee to John at the Jordan to be baptized by him. John tried to prevent him, saying, "I need to be baptized by you, and yet you are coming to me?" Jesus said to him in reply, "Allow it now, for thus it is fitting for us to fulfill all righteousness." Then he allowed him. After Jesus was baptized, he came up from the water and behold, the heavens were opened for him, and he saw the Spirit of God descending like a dove and coming upon him. And a voice came from the heavens, saying, "This is my beloved Son, with whom I am well pleased."

The Gospel of the Lord. *Praise to you, Lord Jesus Christ.*

PROFESSION OF FAITH *(page 13)*

PRAYER OF THE FAITHFUL

PREPARATION OF GIFTS *(page 16)*

PRAYER OVER THE OFFERINGS

Accept, O Lord, the offerings
we have brought to honor the revealing of your beloved Son,
so that the oblation of your faithful
may be transformed into the sacrifice of him
who willed in his compassion
to wash away the sins of the world.
Who lives and reigns for ever and ever. *Amen.*

PREFACE: THE BAPTISM OF THE LORD

It is truly right and just, our duty and our salvation,
always and everywhere to give you thanks,
Lord, holy Father, almighty and eternal God.

For in the waters of the Jordan
you revealed with signs and wonders a new Baptism,
so that through the voice that came down from heaven
we might come to believe in your Word dwelling among us,
and by the Spirit's descending in the likeness of a dove
we might know that Christ your Servant
has been anointed with the oil of gladness
and sent to bring the good news to the poor.

And so, with the Powers of heaven,
we worship you constantly on earth,
and before your majesty
without end we acclaim:
Holy, Holy, Holy Lord God of hosts... *(page 35)*

● TAKING A CLOSER LOOK ●

✚ **No partiality** In the first century, personal relationships were most often strictly voluntary and so were based on the benefactor's favoritism or partiality. A wealthy or powerful person (the benefactor) could freely choose who among many potential candidates would receive his favor or gift. In religious terms, God's partiality was revealed in the free choice of Israel from among all the nations to be God's covenant partner. Peter realized that he had misunderstood God's partiality as limiting the covenant relationship only to Jews. God actually shows no partiality but invites all humanity—both Jews and Gentiles—into the new covenant.

COMMUNION ANTIPHON *(John 1:32, 34)*

Behold the One of whom John said: I have seen and testified that this is the Son of God.

PRAYER AFTER COMMUNION

Nourished with these sacred gifts,
we humbly entreat your mercy, O Lord,
that, faithfully listening to your Only Begotten Son,
we may be your children in name and in truth.
Through Christ our Lord. *Amen.*

BLESSING & DISMISSAL *(page 56)* #

• RESPONDING TO THE WORD •

At his baptism, Jesus is identified as God's beloved child.

➡ How did my baptism identify me as God's beloved child?

We are called to help God make our world a more just place.

➡ What action can I do today to help make a family or work relationship better?

At his baptism, God calls Jesus a "beloved Son."

➡ How can I thank God for making me a beloved child too?

January 19

JAN 19

We are united in baptism

Today's gospel is most appropriate as we begin a new year. Baptism is a powerful sacrament that transforms us into children of God and makes us a new creation. It is a sacrament of rebirth through which we are given the graces to embark on our journey as children of God.

When Jesus was baptized, the Spirit descended from heaven like a dove and remained on him. John testified to this by proclaiming that Jesus is the Son of God. His witness to Christ was inspired by the Holy Spirit which also opens our eyes to God's reality in the world.

We are united as Christians through baptism, and we are sealed by the Holy Spirit who protects and guides us throughout our lives. What a grace it is to be walking in the Christian faith, accompanied by the Holy Spirit! It is always a joyful occasion to welcome the newly baptized into the family of Christ.

During this Week of Prayer for Christian Unity (January 18-25), let us join the universal Church in praying for Christians everywhere, especially for those who are forced to leave their homes and countries due to persecution. We unite with them in their suffering and their witness to Christ in the world, as we are joined to them in one baptism.

▪ SARAH ESCOBAR

ENTRANCE ANTIPHON *(Psalm 66 [65]:4)*

All the earth shall bow down before you, O God, and shall sing to you, shall sing to your name, O Most High!

INTRODUCTORY RITES *(page 10)*

COLLECT

Almighty ever-living God,
who govern all things,
both in heaven and on earth,
mercifully hear the pleading of your people
and bestow your peace on our times.
Through our Lord Jesus Christ, your Son,
who lives and reigns with you in the unity of the Holy Spirit,
one God, for ever and ever. *Amen.*

FIRST READING *(Isaiah 49:3, 5-6)*

The LORD said to me: You are my **servant,**✝
Israel, through whom I show my glory.
Now the LORD has spoken
    who formed me as his servant from the womb,
that Jacob may be brought back to him
    and Israel gathered to him;
and I am made glorious in the sight of the LORD,
    and my God is now my strength!
It is too little, the LORD says, for you to be my servant,
    to raise up the tribes of Jacob,
    and restore the survivors of Israel;
I will make you a light to the nations,
    that my salvation may reach to the ends of the earth.
The word of the Lord. *Thanks be to God.*

RESPONSORIAL PSALM *(Psalm 40:2, 4, 7-8, 8-9, 10)*

℞ **Here am I, Lord; I come to do your will.**

I have waited, waited for the LORD,
    and he stooped toward me and heard my cry.
And he put a new song into my mouth,
    a hymn to our God. ℞
Sacrifice or offering you wished not,
    but ears open to obedience you gave me.
Holocausts or sin-offerings you sought not;
    then said I, "Behold I come." ℞
"In the written scroll it is prescribed for me,
to do your will, O my God, is my delight,
    and your law is within my heart!" ℞
I announced your justice in the vast assembly;
    I did not restrain my lips, as you, O Lord, know. ℞

SECOND READING *(1 Corinthians 1:1-3)*

Paul, called to be an apostle of Christ Jesus by the will of God,
and Sosthenes* our brother, to the church of God that is in
Corinth, to you who have been sanctified in Christ Jesus, called
to be holy, with all those everywhere who call upon the name
of our Lord Jesus Christ, their Lord and ours. Grace to you and
peace from God our Father and the Lord Jesus Christ.
    The word of the Lord. ***Thanks be to God.***

ALLELUIA *(John 1:14a, 12a)*

Alleluia, alleluia. The Word of God became flesh and dwelt
among us. To those who accepted him, he gave power to become
children of God. *Alleluia, alleluia.*

GOSPEL *(John 1:29–34)*

A reading from the holy Gospel according to John.

Glory to you, O Lord.

John the Baptist saw Jesus coming toward him and said, "Behold, the Lamb of God, who takes away the sin of the world. He is the one of whom I said, 'A man is coming after me who ranks ahead of me because he existed before me.' I did not know him, but the reason why I came baptizing with water was that he might be made known to Israel." John testified further, saying, "I saw the Spirit come down like a dove from heaven and remain upon him. I did not know him, but the one who sent me to baptize with water told me, 'On whomever you see the Spirit come down and remain, he is the one who will baptize with the Holy Spirit.' Now I have seen and testified that he is the Son of God."

The Gospel of the Lord. *Praise to you, Lord Jesus Christ.*

PROFESSION OF FAITH *(page 13)*

PRAYER OF THE FAITHFUL

PREPARATION OF GIFTS *(page 16)*

PRAYER OVER THE OFFERINGS
Grant us, O Lord, we pray,
that we may participate worthily in these mysteries,
for whenever the memorial of this sacrifice is celebrated
the work of our redemption is accomplished.
Through Christ our Lord. *Amen.*

PREFACE *(Sundays in Ordinary Time, pages 28–32)*

COMMUNION ANTIPHON *(Cf. Psalm 23 [22]:5)*
You have prepared a table before me, and how precious is the
chalice that quenches my thirst.

Or *(1 John 4:16)*
We have come to know and to believe in the love that God has
for us.

• TAKING A CLOSER LOOK •

✝ **Servant** The servant who is called to be a misunderstood and
ill-treated prophet to a sin-weary people is described in four famous
"Servant Songs" by Isaiah the prophet (see 42:1-4, 49:1-7, 50:4-11
[Palm Sunday] and 52:13—53:12). It is not certain whom the author
intended the servant to represent: the people of Israel (as the historical nation, as a faithful remnant or as an idealized body) or an actual
historical figure, such as the "prophet like Moses" (Deuteronomy
18:15) or even a corporate personality, that is, an individual who
would represent all the features of Israel's election and mission.
These servant songs helped Israel interpret the suffering and humili-
ation of the exile and the early Christians understand the meaning of
Jesus' suffering and resurrection.

PRAYER AFTER COMMUNION

Pour on us, O Lord, the Spirit of your love,
and in your kindness
make those you have nourished
by this one heavenly Bread
one in mind and heart.
Through Christ our Lord. *Amen.*

BLESSING & DISMISSAL *(page 56)* ✢

• RESPONDING TO THE WORD •

We are called to share in the task of bringing everyone to God.	Paul extends greetings of grace and peace to his community.	John's task is to make Jesus known to others.
➯ *What can I do today to draw someone closer to God?*	➯ *To whom might I extend a special greeting of peace today?*	➯ *How can I share my knowledge of Christ today?*

January 26

"Follow me"

We hear today the simple narrative of Jesus calling his first disciples. Simon and Andrew, James and John are invited to follow him, and they leave their nets and their boats to join Jesus in his mission. How was it possible that these mature men, responsible to their work and families, heard an invitation from a stranger and walked away from their means of livelihood, from the familiar pattern of their lives?

Perhaps they had already heard of Jesus, but Matthew gives us no indication of that. Rather we are presented with the stark immediacy of their response, which points to a remarkable and spontaneous moment of commitment. They were ready. God's grace, already at work in them, and their response to that grace, had prepared them for this moment.

The calling of these four men might seem a remarkable and unique event, but perhaps it is the same call that comes to us. Again and again Jesus says to each of us, "Follow me." By God's grace we too can respond with a complete gift of self, again and again giving our "yes" to his invitation to let ourselves be loved and to bring his love to others.

■ **KATHLEEN GIFFIN**

ENTRANCE ANTIPHON *(Cf. Psalm 96 [95]:1, 6)*

O sing a new song to the Lord; sing to the Lord, all the earth. In his presence are majesty and splendor, strength and honor in his holy place.

INTRODUCTORY RITES *(page 10)*

COLLECT

Almighty ever-living God,
direct our actions according to your good pleasure,
that in the name of your beloved Son
we may abound in good works.
Through our Lord Jesus Christ, your Son,
who lives and reigns with you in the unity of the Holy Spirit,
one God, for ever and ever. ***Amen.***

FIRST READING *(Isaiah 8:23—9:3)*

First the LORD degraded the land of Zebulun* and the land of Naphtali;* but in the end he has glorified the seaward road, the land west of the Jordan, the District of the Gentiles.

Anguish has taken wing, dispelled is darkness:
 for there is no gloom where but now there was distress.
The people who walked in darkness
 have seen a great light;
upon those who dwelt in the land of gloom
 a light has shone.
You have brought them abundant joy
 and great rejoicing,
as they rejoice before you as at the harvest,
 as people make merry when dividing spoils.
For the yoke that burdened them,
 the pole on their shoulder,

and the rod of their taskmaster
    you have smashed, as on the day of Midian.*
The word of the Lord. *Thanks be to God.*

RESPONSORIAL PSALM *(Psalm 27:1, 4, 13-14)*
℟ **The Lord is my light and my salvation.**

The LORD is my light and my salvation;
    whom should I fear?
The LORD is my life's refuge;
    of whom should I be afraid? ℟
One thing I ask of the LORD;
    this I seek:
To dwell in the house of the LORD
    all the days of my life,
that I may gaze on the loveliness of the LORD
    and contemplate his temple. ℟
I believe that I shall see the bounty of the LORD
    in the land of the living.
Wait for the LORD with courage;
    be stouthearted, and wait for the LORD. ℟

SECOND READING *(1 Corinthians 1:10-13, 17)*
I urge you, brothers and sisters, in the name of our Lord Jesus Christ, that all of you agree in what you say, and that there be no divisions among you, but that you be united in the same mind and in the same purpose. For it has been reported to me about you, my brothers and sisters, by Chloe's people, that there are rivalries among you. I mean that each of you is saying, "I belong to Paul," or "I belong to Apollos," or "I belong to Cephas,"* or "I belong to Christ." Is Christ divided? Was Paul crucified for you? Or were you baptized in the name of Paul? For Christ

did not send me to baptize but to preach the **gospel**,✝ and not with the wisdom of human eloquence, so that the cross of Christ might not be emptied of its meaning.

The word of the Lord. *Thanks be to God.*

ALLELUIA *(Matthew 4:23)*
Alleluia, alleluia. Jesus proclaimed the Gospel of the kingdom and cured every disease among the people. *Alleluia, alleluia.*

GOSPEL *(Matthew 4:12–23)*
The shorter version ends at the asterisks.

A reading from the holy Gospel according to Matthew.
Glory to you, O Lord.

When Jesus heard that John had been arrested, he withdrew to Galilee. He left Nazareth and went to live in Capernaum* by the sea, in the region of Zebulun* and Naphtali,* that what had been said through Isaiah the prophet might be fulfilled:

Land of Zebulun and land of Naphtali,
the way to the sea, beyond the Jordan,
Galilee of the Gentiles,
the people who sit in darkness have seen a great light,
on those dwelling in a land overshadowed by death
light has arisen.

From that time on, Jesus began to preach and say, "Repent, for the kingdom of heaven is at hand."

* * *

As he was walking by the Sea of Galilee, he saw two brothers, Simon who is called Peter, and his brother Andrew, casting a net into the sea; they were fishermen. He said to them, "Come after me, and I will make you fishers of men." At once they left their nets and followed him. He walked along from there and saw two other brothers, James, the son of Zebedee, and his brother John. They were in a boat, with their father Zebedee, mending their nets. He called them, and immediately they left their boat and their father and followed him. He went around all of Galilee, teaching in their synagogues, proclaiming the **gospel**✝ of the kingdom, and curing every disease and illness among the people.

The Gospel of the Lord. *Praise to you, Lord Jesus Christ.*

PROFESSION OF FAITH *(page 13)*

PRAYER OF THE FAITHFUL

PREPARATION OF GIFTS *(page 16)*

PRAYER OVER THE OFFERINGS
Accept our offerings, O Lord, we pray,
and in sanctifying them
grant that they may profit us for salvation.
Through Christ our Lord. *Amen.*

• TAKING A CLOSER LOOK •

✝ **Gospel** In everyday usage the word "gospel" (Greek: *evangelion*, Anglo-Saxon: *Godspell*), meant "good news," often about an important event such as the birthday of the emperor or a national victory in war. The Christian good news of Jesus Christ includes both his message about a new kind of community for all and his victory over the forces of evil, sin, and death by his resurrection. For the gospel writers, "gospel" became a unique Christian format for proclaiming the good news through telling Jesus' life story. Matthew's gospel is not only a life of Jesus but also a proclamation of the foundational Christian belief that Jesus is the promised Messiah who fulfills the promises of the Old Testament.

PREFACE *(Sundays in Ordinary Time, pages 28–32)*

COMMUNION ANTIPHON *(Cf. Psalm 34 [33]:6)*
Look toward the Lord and be radiant;
let your faces not be abashed.

Or *(John 8:12)*
I am the light of the world, says the Lord; whoever follows me will
not walk in darkness, but will have the light of life.

PRAYER AFTER COMMUNION
Grant, we pray, almighty God,
that, receiving the grace
by which you bring us to new life,
we may always glory in your gift.
Through Christ our Lord. *Amen.*

BLESSING & DISMISSAL *(page 56)* ❖

❖ RESPONDING TO THE WORD ❖

God's presence is often recognized in what has been overlooked or neglected.

➡ *What sources of God's presence might I not have noticed?*

Paul warns against divisions in our Christian community.

➡ *What might be a source of division that I can help resolve?*

Jesus challenges us to repent—to change our lives.

➡ *What changes might I need to make in order to follow Jesus today?*

February 2

Hunger for the Spirit

The gospel for the Feast of the Presentation is a fitting way to mark the World Day for Consecrated Life. In today's gospel, two prophets, Simeon and Anna, proclaim Jesus as the longed-for savior. Simeon, in particular, is filled with the Spirit, the Spirit through whom Jesus is "a light of revelation to the Gentiles and glory for your people Israel."

The prophetess Anna spent her life in the temple, praying and fasting. While Jesus is here presented as a sign of contradiction, so too is Anna. How her life contradicts a world indifferent to God!

Those in religious orders and other forms of consecrated life give a unique prophetic witness. Their vows (or promises) of poverty, chastity, and obedience offer a stark contrast to a world where wealth and personal autonomy are often the highest values. Religious men and women challenge us to give ourselves totally to Jesus.

Although few can spend all our days in the temple, we can live in union with the Holy Spirit in secular life. We can make time each day to sit silently in God's presence, longing for the fullness of that presence. Hunger for the Spirit is transformative of both our personal lives and our society. Lay people too can consecrate ourselves to God.

GLEN ARGAN

FIRST FORM: THE PROCESSION

A gathering takes place somewhere other than inside the church to which the procession will go. The faithful hold unlighted candles. The candles are lit while an appropriate song is sung. The priest greets the people, blesses the candles, and sprinkles the candles with holy water. The procession begins while a suitable song is sung. As the procession enters the church, the Entrance Antiphon is sung, and the Mass continues with the Gloria and Collect as usual.

SECOND FORM: THE SOLEMN ENTRANCE

When a procession cannot take place, the faithful gather in church, holding candles. Candles are lit and blessed (see above). The procession to the altar takes place while the Entrance Antiphon is sung. The Mass continues with the Gloria and Collect as usual.

ENTRANCE ANTIPHON *(Cf. Psalm 48 [47]:10-11)*

Your merciful love, O God, we have received in the midst of your temple. Your praise, O God, like your name, reaches the ends of the earth; your right hand is filled with saving justice.

INTRODUCTORY RITES *(page 10)*

COLLECT

Almighty ever-living God,
we humbly implore your majesty
that, just as your Only Begotten Son
was presented on this day in the Temple
in the substance of our flesh,
so, by your grace,
we may be presented to you with minds made pure.
Through our Lord Jesus Christ, your Son,
who lives and reigns with you in the unity of the Holy Spirit,
one God, for ever and ever. *Amen.*

FIRST READING *(Malachi 3:1-4)*

Thus says the Lord GOD:
    Lo, I am sending my messenger
to prepare the way before me;
And suddenly there will come to the temple
    the LORD whom you seek,
And the messenger of the covenant whom you desire.
    Yes, he is coming, says the LORD of hosts.
But who will endure the day of his coming?
    And who can stand when he appears?
For he is like the refiner's fire,
    or like the fuller's lye.
He will sit refining and purifying silver,
    and he will purify the sons of Levi,
Refining them like gold or like silver
    that they may offer due sacrifice to the LORD.
Then the sacrifice of Judah and Jerusalem
    will please the LORD,
    as in the days of old, as in years gone by.
The word of the Lord. ***Thanks be to God.***

RESPONSORIAL PSALM *(Psalm 24:7, 8, 9, 10)*
℟ **Who is this king of glory? It is the Lord!**

Lift up, O gates, your lintels;
    reach up, you ancient portals,
    that the king of glory may come in! ℟
Who is this king of glory?
    The LORD, strong and mighty,
    the LORD, mighty in battle. ℟
Lift up, O gates, your lintels;

reach up, you ancient portals,
that the king of glory may come in!
℟ **Who is this king of glory? It is the Lord!**
Who is this king of glory?
The LORD of hosts; he is the king of glory. ℟

SECOND READING *(Hebrews 2:14–18)*

Since the children share in blood and flesh, Jesus likewise shared in them, that through death he might destroy the one who has the power of death, that is, the Devil, and free those who through fear of death had been subject to slavery all their life. Surely he did not help angels but rather the descendants of Abraham; therefore, he had to become like his brothers and sisters in every way, that he might be a merciful and faithful high priest before God to expiate the sins of the people. Because he himself was tested through what he suffered, he is able to help those who are being tested.

The word of the Lord. *Thanks be to God.*

ALLELUIA *(Luke 2:32)*
Alleluia, alleluia. A light of revelation to the Gentiles and glory for your people Israel. *Alleluia, alleluia.*

GOSPEL *(Luke 2:22–40 or 2:22–32)*
The shorter version ends at the asterisks.

A reading from the holy Gospel according to Luke.
Glory to you, O Lord.

When the days were completed for their **purification**✝ according to the law of Moses, Mary and Joseph took Jesus up to Jerusalem to present him to the Lord, just as it is written in the law of the Lord, *Every male that opens the womb shall* *be consecrated to the Lord*, and to offer the sacrifice of *a pair of turtledoves or two young pigeons*, in accordance with the dictate in the law of the Lord.

Now there was a man in Jerusalem whose name was Simeon. This man was righteous and devout, awaiting the consolation of Israel, and the Holy Spirit was upon him. It had been revealed to him by the Holy Spirit that he should not see death before he had seen the Christ of the Lord. He came in the Spirit into the temple; and when the parents brought in the child Jesus to perform the custom of the law in regard to him, he took him into his arms and blessed God, saying:

"Now, Master, you may let your servant go
in peace, according to your word,
for my eyes have seen your salvation,
which you prepared in sight of all the peoples:
a light for revelation to the Gentiles,
and glory for your people Israel."

* * *

The child's father and mother were amazed at what was said about him; and Simeon blessed them and said to Mary his mother, "Behold, this child is destined for the fall and rise of many in Israel, and to be a sign that will be contradicted—and you yourself a sword will pierce—so that the thoughts of many hearts may be revealed." There was also a prophetess, Anna, the daughter of Phanuel, of the tribe of Asher. She was advanced in years, having lived seven years with her husband after her marriage, and then as a widow until she was eighty-four. She never left the temple, but worshiped night and day with fasting and prayer. And coming forward at that very time, she gave thanks to God and spoke about the child to all who were awaiting the redemption of Jerusalem.

When they had fulfilled all the prescriptions of the law of the Lord, they returned to Galilee, to their own town of Nazareth. The child grew and became strong, filled with wisdom; and the favor of God was upon him.

The Gospel of the Lord. *Praise to you, Lord Jesus Christ.*

PROFESSION OF FAITH *(page 13)*

PRAYER OF THE FAITHFUL

PREPARATION OF GIFTS *(page 16)*

PRAYER OVER THE OFFERINGS
May the offering made with exultation by your Church
be pleasing to you, O Lord, we pray,
for you willed that your Only Begotten Son
be offered to you for the life of the world
as the Lamb without blemish.
Who lives and reigns for ever and ever. *Amen.*

PREFACE: THE MYSTERY OF THE PRESENTATION OF THE LORD

It is truly right and just, our duty and our salvation,
always and everywhere to give you thanks,
Lord, holy Father, almighty and eternal God.

For your co-eternal Son was presented on this day in the Temple
and revealed by the Spirit
as the glory of Israel and Light of the nations.

And so, we, too, go forth, rejoicing to encounter your Salvation,
and with the Angels and Saints
praise you, as without end we acclaim:
Holy, Holy, Holy Lord God of hosts... *(page 35)*

• TAKING A CLOSER LOOK •

✚ **Purification** Like many ancient peoples, the Jews had a carefully devised system of meanings that identified and kept order in their lives. When something or someone violated that system, they were "unclean" for a specified time and could not participate in worship until a blessing or a purification rite would reinstate them to the proper relationship with the community. So a mother who gave birth to a boy was ritually "unclean" for forty days (see Leviticus 12:1-8) at which time she brought her purification gift to the priest. Luke reveals that Joseph and Mary fulfill all the ritual obligations of the Jewish law and, from their gift, that they are poor because they could not afford the usual offering of a lamb.

COMMUNION ANTIPHON *(Luke 2:30–31)*

My eyes have seen your salvation, which you prepared in the sight of all the peoples.

PRAYER AFTER COMMUNION

By these holy gifts which we have received, O Lord,
bring your grace to perfection within us,
and, as you fulfilled Simeon's expectation
that he would not see death
until he had been privileged to welcome the Christ,
so may we, going forth to meet the Lord,
obtain the gift of eternal life.
Through Christ our Lord. *Amen.*

BLESSING & DISMISSAL *(page 56)* ✠

• RESPONDING TO THE WORD •

The Lord's messenger will come like the fire that refines precious metals or the fuller's soap that cleanses cloth.

➡ *What areas of my life need purifying and cleansing?*

Because Jesus became human and suffered, he fully knows and understands life's hardships.

➡ *Whom can I tell that needs to hear this comforting message?*

Simeon was able to recognize Jesus as the promised Messiah.

➡ *Where am I able to recognize Jesus' presence in my life?*

February 9

FEB
9

Salt and light

Jesus is calling us, his disciples, to stand up and be counted, to be like salt. Hold on, I wonder, why salt? I ask "The Bride," my better half of 35 years, to remind me of the purpose of salt. Jennifer gives me one of those "you're kidding" looks, and explains that salt acts as a preservative, but also enhances texture and, most importantly, the flavor of the food.

Then our Lord calls us to be light in the world, to "shine before others." Okay, now I think I know where Jesus is going. As Christians we are called to live intentionally and differently. Our faith calls us to be in the pew on Sunday, and also much more.

Being salt and light doesn't sound difficult, but nor is it easy. It means we, who love God and follow Jesus, must make space in our busy lives for daily prayer and quiet reflection. It is here that we listen and invite the Holy Spirit to speak to our mind and heart. Then, when we feel the nudge to say hello to the stranger, help our elderly neighbor, visit the sick, and give generously to the less fortunate, we are mindful that our good deeds are because of God's loves for us and through us. We give all credit and praise to our Father in heaven.

■ HARRY MCAVOY

ENTRANCE ANTIPHON *(Psalm 95 [94]:6-7)*
O come, let us worship God and bow low before the God who
made us, for he is the Lord our God.

INTRODUCTORY RITES *(page 10)*

COLLECT
Keep your family safe, O Lord, with unfailing care,
that, relying solely on the hope of heavenly grace,
they may be defended always by your protection.
Through our Lord Jesus Christ, your Son,
who lives and reigns with you in the unity of the Holy Spirit,
one God, for ever and ever. ***Amen.***

FIRST READING *(Isaiah 58:7-10)*

Thus says the LORD:
   Share your bread with the hungry,
      shelter the oppressed and the homeless;
clothe the naked when you see them,
      and do not turn your back on your own.
Then your light shall break forth like the dawn,
      and your wound shall quickly be healed;
your vindication shall go before you,
      and the glory of the LORD shall be your rear guard.
Then you shall call, and the LORD will answer,
      you shall cry for help, and he will say: Here I am!
If you remove from your midst
      oppression, false accusation and malicious speech;
if you bestow your bread on the hungry
      and satisfy the afflicted;
then light shall rise for you in the darkness,

and the gloom shall become for you like midday.
The word of the Lord. *Thanks be to God.*

RESPONSORIAL PSALM *(Psalm 112:4-5, 6-7, 8-9)*
℞ **The just man is a light in darkness to the upright.** *Or* **Alleluia.**

Light shines through the darkness for the upright;
    he is gracious and merciful and just.
Well for the man who is gracious and lends,
    who conducts his affairs with justice. ℞
He shall never be moved;
    the just one shall be in everlasting remembrance.
An evil report he shall not fear;
    his heart is firm, trusting in the LORD. ℞
His heart is steadfast; he shall not fear.
    Lavishly he gives to the poor;
His justice shall endure forever;
    his horn shall be exalted in glory. ℞

SECOND READING *(1 Corinthians 2:1-5)*

When I came to you, brothers and sisters, proclaiming the
mystery✝ of God, I did not come with sublimity of
words or of wisdom. For I resolved to know nothing while I was
with you except Jesus Christ, and him crucified. I came to you
in weakness and fear and much trembling, and my message and
my proclamation were not with persuasive words of wisdom,
but with a demonstration of Spirit and power, so that your faith
might rest not on human wisdom but on the power of God.
    The word of the Lord. *Thanks be to God.*

ALLELUIA *(John 8:12)*
Alleluia, alleluia. I am the light of the world, says the Lord;
whoever follows me will have the light of life. *Alleluia, alleluia.*

GOSPEL *(Matthew 5:13–16)*
A reading from the holy Gospel according to Matthew.
Glory to you, O Lord.

Jesus said to his disciples: "You are the salt of the earth. But if
salt loses its taste, with what can it be seasoned? It is no longer
good for anything but to be thrown out and trampled underfoot.
You are the light of the world. A city set on a mountain cannot
be hidden. Nor do they light a lamp and then put it under a
bushel basket; it is set on a lampstand, where it gives light to all
in the house. Just so, your light must shine before others, that
they may see your good deeds and glorify your heavenly Father."

The Gospel of the Lord. *Praise to you, Lord Jesus Christ.*

PROFESSION OF FAITH *(page 13)*

PRAYER OF THE FAITHFUL

PREPARATION OF GIFTS *(page 16)*

PRAYER OVER THE OFFERINGS
O Lord our God,
who once established these created things
to sustain us in our frailty,
grant, we pray,
that they may become for us now
the Sacrament of eternal life.
Through Christ our Lord. *Amen.*

PREFACE *(Sundays in Ordinary Time, pages 28–32)*

COMMUNION ANTIPHON *(Cf. Psalm 107 [106]:8-9)*
Let them thank the Lord for his mercy, his wonders for the
children of men, for he satisfies the thirsty soul, and the hungry
he fills with good things.

Or *(Matthew 5:5-6)*
Blessed are those who mourn, for they shall be consoled. Blessed
are those who hunger and thirst for righteousness, for they shall
have their fill.

• TAKING A CLOSER LOOK •

✝ **Mystery** In the Greek world of early Christianity, mystery point-
ed to that which is hidden or secret and cannot be talked about openly.
It was most often used to describe sacred rituals which were not to be
revealed to anyone who did not belong to the religious group.

For Christians like Paul, mystery points to what is hidden and cannot be known unless God reveals it. Paul identifies this revealed mystery
as God's surprising desire to unite all humanity—both Jew and Gentile—
into one community in Christ. And this mystery of God's plan, revealed in
the life, death, and resurrection of Jesus, is one that can only be grasped
through the power of the Spirit—not through mere human wisdom.

PRAYER AFTER COMMUNION

O God, who have willed that we be partakers
in the one Bread and the one Chalice,
grant us, we pray, so to live
that, made one in Christ,
we may joyfully bear fruit
for the salvation of the world.
Through Christ our Lord. *Amen.*

BLESSING & DISMISSAL *(page 56)* ✤

• RESPONDING TO THE WORD •

God commands us to feed the hungry and satisfy the afflicted.	Under the influence of the Spirit, Paul preaches Christ crucified.	Jesus calls his disciples the salt of the earth and light for the world.
➡ *In what ways am I meeting the needs of my community?*	➡ *When have I felt the Spirit influence the way I witness to my faith?*	➡ *In what ways can I follow Jesus' teachings and be salt for the earth and light of the world?*

February 16

True freedom

In today's gospel Jesus warns us that he has not come to abolish the law, but to fulfill it.

Just because God loves us, does not mean he has to do what we want him to do. We can't manipulate God or guilt-trip God into doing what we want. It's humbling for us to realize that we are not entitled to God's favor. God chooses to help us with perfect freedom from a place of pure love. The law that God gave to us was not meant to limit us, but to ensure we use our freedom in a way that is good for us and others.

Love requires freedom, and freedom means we have to respect the other person's ability to say "no" to us. If we truly desire to be in a mature relationship with God, then we need to respect this freedom and ensure we use our freedom in a way that gives God glory, which will strengthen our relationship with God and others.

Today as we celebrate the Eucharist, a sacrifice made freely on our behalf, let us repent of the times we've trespassed against God and our neighbor, and embrace the gift of God's law and the true freedom it leads us to.

CHERIDAN SANDERS

ENTRANCE ANTIPHON *(Cf. Psalm 31 [30]:3-4)*

Be my protector, O God, a mighty stronghold to save me. For you are my rock, my stronghold! Lead me, guide me, for the sake of your name.

INTRODUCTORY RITES *(page 10)*

COLLECT

O God, who teach us that you abide
in hearts that are just and true,
grant that we may be so fashioned by your grace
as to become a dwelling pleasing to you.
Through our Lord Jesus Christ, your Son,
who lives and reigns with you in the unity of the Holy Spirit,
one God, for ever and ever. *Amen.*

FIRST READING *(Sirach 15:15-20)*

If you choose you can keep the commandments,
   they will save you;
   if you trust in God, you too shall live;
he has set before you fire and water;
   to whichever you choose, stretch forth your hand.
Before man are life and death, good and evil,
   whichever he chooses shall be given him.
Immense is the wisdom of the Lord;
   he is mighty in power, and all-seeing.
The eyes of God are on those who fear him;
   he understands man's every deed.
No one does he command to act unjustly,
   to none does he give license to sin.
The word of the Lord. *Thanks be to God.*

RESPONSORIAL PSALM *(Psalm 119:1-2, 4-5, 17-18, 33-34)*
℟ Blessed are they who follow the law of the Lord!

Blessed are they whose way is blameless,
who walk in **the law**† of the LORD.
Blessed are they who observe his decrees,
who seek him with all their heart. ℟

You have commanded that your precepts
be diligently kept.
Oh, that I might be firm in the ways
of keeping your statutes! ℟

Be good to your servant, that I may live
and keep your words.
Open my eyes, that I may consider
the wonders of your law. ℟

Instruct me, O LORD, in the way of your statutes,
that I may exactly observe them.
Give me discernment, that I may observe your law
and keep it with all my heart. ℟

SECOND READING *(1 Corinthians 2:6-10)*

Brothers and sisters: We speak a wisdom to those who are
mature, not a wisdom of this age, nor of the rulers of this
age who are passing away. Rather, we speak God's wisdom,
mysterious, hidden, which God predetermined before the ages
for our glory, and which none of the rulers of this age knew; for,
if they had known it, they would not have crucified the Lord of
glory. But as it is written:

What eye has not seen, and ear has not heard,
and what has not entered the human heart,
what God has prepared for those who love him,
this God has revealed to us through the Spirit.
For the Spirit scrutinizes everything, even the depths of God.
The word of the Lord. *Thanks be to God.*

ALLELUIA *(Matthew 11:25)*
Alleluia, alleluia. Blessed are you, Father, Lord of heaven and
earth; you have revealed to little ones the mysteries of the kingdom. *Alleluia, alleluia.*

GOSPEL *(Matthew 5:17-37)*
For the shorter version, omit the indented parts in brackets.

A reading from the holy Gospel according to Matthew.
Glory to you, O Lord.

Jesus said to his disciples:
["Do not think that I have come to abolish the law or the
prophets. I have come not to abolish but to fulfill. Amen, I say
to you, until heaven and earth pass away, not the smallest letter
or the smallest part of a letter will pass from the law, until all
things have taken place. Therefore, whoever breaks one of the
least of these commandments and teaches others to do so will
be called least in the kingdom of heaven. But whoever obeys
and teaches these commandments will be called greatest in the
kingdom of heaven.]
I tell you, unless your righteousness surpasses that of the scribes
and Pharisees, you will not enter the kingdom of heaven.
   "You have heard that it was said to your ancestors, *You shall not
kill; and whoever kills will be liable to judgment.* But I say to you,

whoever is angry with his brother will be liable to judgment;
[and whoever says to his brother, 'Raqa,' will be answerable to
the Sanhedrin; and whoever says, 'You fool,' will be liable to fiery
Gehenna. Therefore, if you bring your gift to the altar, and there
recall that your brother has anything against you, leave your gift
there at the altar, go first and be reconciled with your brother,
and then come and offer your gift. Settle with your opponent
quickly while on the way to court. Otherwise your opponent will
hand you over to the judge, and the judge will hand you over to
the guard, and you will be thrown into prison. Amen, I say to
you, you will not be released until you have paid the last penny.]

"You have heard that it was said, *You shall not commit adul-*
tery. But I say to you, everyone who looks at a woman with lust
has already committed adultery with her in his heart.

[If your right eye causes you to sin, tear it out and throw it
away. It is better for you to lose one of your members than
to have your whole body thrown into Gehenna. And if your
right hand causes you to sin, cut it off and throw it away. It is
better for you to lose one of your members than to have your
whole body go into Gehenna.

"It was also said, *Whoever divorces his wife must give her a bill*
of divorce. But I say to you, whoever divorces his wife—unless
the marriage is unlawful—causes her to commit adultery, and
whoever marries a divorced woman commits adultery.]

"Again you have heard that it was said to your ancestors, *Do*
not take a false oath, but make good to the Lord all that you vow.
But I say to you, do not swear at all;

[not by heaven, for it is God's throne; nor by the earth, for
it is his footstool; nor by Jerusalem, for it is the city of the

great King. Do not swear by your head, for you cannot make a single hair white or black.]

Let your 'Yes' mean 'Yes,' and your 'No' mean 'No.' Anything more is from the evil one."

The Gospel of the Lord. ***Praise to you, Lord Jesus Christ.***

PROFESSION OF FAITH *(page 13)*

PRAYER OF THE FAITHFUL

PREPARATION OF GIFTS *(page 16)*

PRAYER OVER THE OFFERINGS

May this oblation, O Lord, we pray,
cleanse and renew us
and may it become for those who do your will
the source of eternal reward.
Through Christ our Lord. ***Amen.***

PREFACE *(Sundays in Ordinary Time, page 28–32)*

• TAKING A CLOSER LOOK •

✠ **The law** The law (Hebrew *Torah*, "instruction") consisted of the first five books of the Old Testament (Genesis, Exodus, Leviticus, Numbers, and Deuteronomy) that tell of God's search for an appropriate covenant partner. Jewish scholars combed these books to discover all of the specific commands given by God and found 613. These became the foundation of their life in community. These laws, although difficult to keep in their entirety, were not considered a burden (as we so often think), but rather as a precious gift because the people knew what God wanted and no longer had to guess what to do in order to please God.

COMMUNION ANTIPHON *(Cf. Psalm 78 [77]:29-30)*
They ate and had their fill, and what they craved the Lord gave them; they were not disappointed in what they craved.

Or *(John 3:16)*
God so loved the world that he gave his Only Begotten Son, so that all who believe in him may not perish, but may have eternal life.

PRAYER AFTER COMMUNION
Having fed upon these heavenly delights,
we pray, O Lord,
that we may always long
for that food by which we truly live.
Through Christ our Lord. *Amen.*

BLESSING & DISMISSAL *(page 56)* ✠

• RESPONDING TO THE WORD •

Keeping God's commandments is a choice that we must make.

➲ *What helps me to keep the commandments of God?*

Paul cautions us about distinguishing worldly wisdom from God's wisdom.

➲ *How has following God's wisdom helped me in my life?*

Jesus invites us to go beyond the letter of the law.

➲ *To what might Jesus be inviting me today?*

February 23

We belong to God

How far should a Christian disciple's love extend? Are there not times when we might appropriately retaliate in response to a slight or attack? The recollection of who God is, and who we are because we belong to God—the theme of today's readings—provides a challenging response.

Christian love is meant to be limitless, extending beyond the local communities and comfort zones of disciples, and embracing even enemies and evildoers. We are not to obliterate our opponents, nor to exact revenge, even if taking only an eye for an eye, a tooth for a tooth. The extent of a disciple's obligation exceeds treating others the way we would like to be treated.

A disciple's love gives priority to the other's welfare first.

Disciples aim to emulate God's love, which is selfless, forgiving, and unconditional. Such a love has called all creation into being, is ongoing, redemptive, and life-giving. Such a love seeks the salvation of all. We can recognize all of this in the gifts of Jesus Christ, who announced the reign of God and freely gave himself up to death on a cross, and the indwelling presence of the Holy Spirit in the Church's midst. Crowned with such steadfast love and mercy, we strive to imitate the perfection—wholeness, holiness—of God with unreserved service of God and neighbor.

■ CHRISTINE MADER

ENTRANCE ANTIPHON *(Psalm 13 [12]:6)*
O Lord, I trust in your merciful love. My heart will rejoice in your salvation. I will sing to the Lord who has been bountiful with me.

INTRODUCTORY RITES *(page 10)*

COLLECT
Grant, we pray, almighty God,
that, always pondering spiritual things,
we may carry out in both word and deed
that which is pleasing to you.
Through our Lord Jesus Christ, your Son,
who lives and reigns with you in the unity of the Holy Spirit,
one God, for ever and ever. *Amen.*

FIRST READING *(Leviticus 19:1-2, 17-18)*

T he LORD said to Moses, "Speak to the whole Israelite community and tell them: Be holy, for I, the LORD, your God,
am holy.

"You shall not bear hatred for your brother or sister in your heart. Though you may have to reprove your fellow citizen, do not incur sin because of him. Take no revenge and cherish no grudge against any of your people. You shall love your neighbor as yourself. I am the LORD."

The word of the Lord. *Thanks be to God.*

RESPONSORIAL PSALM *(Psalm 103:1-2, 3-4, 8, 10, 12-13)*
R. **The Lord is kind and merciful.**

Bless the LORD, O my soul;
    and all my being, bless his holy name.
Bless the LORD, O my soul,

and forget not all his benefits.
℟ **The Lord is kind and merciful.**
He pardons all your iniquities,
 heals all your ills.
He redeems your life from destruction,
 crowns you with kindness and compassion. ℟
Merciful and gracious is the LORD,
 slow to anger and abounding in kindness.
Not according to our sins does he deal with us,
 nor does he requite us according to our crimes. ℟
As far as the east is from the west,
 so far has he put our transgressions from us.
As a father has compassion on his children,
 so the LORD has compassion on those who fear him. ℟

SECOND READING (*1 Corinthians 3:16–23*)

Brothers and sisters: Do you not know that you are the
temple of God, and that the Spirit of God dwells in you? If
anyone destroys God's temple, God will destroy that person; for
the temple of God, which you are, is holy.

Let no one deceive himself. If any one among you considers
himself wise in this age, let him become a fool, so as to become
wise. For the wisdom of this world is foolishness in the eyes of
God, for it is written:
 God catches the wise in their own ruses,
and again:
 The Lord knows the thoughts of the wise,
  that they are vain.
So let no one boast about human beings, for everything belongs
to you, Paul or Apollos or Cephas,* or the world or life or death,
or the present or the future: all belong to you, and you to Christ,

and Christ to God.

The word of the Lord. *Thanks be to God.*

ALLELUIA *(1 John 2:5)*
Alleluia, alleluia. Whoever keeps the word of Christ, the love of God is truly perfected in him. *Alleluia, alleluia.*

GOSPEL *(Matthew 5:38-48)*
A reading from the holy Gospel according to Matthew.
Glory to you, O Lord.

Jesus said to his disciples: "You have heard that it was said, *An eye for an eye and a tooth for a tooth.* But I say to you, offer no resistance to one who is evil. When someone strikes you on your right cheek, turn the other one as well. If anyone wants to go to law with you over your tunic, hand over your cloak as well. Should anyone press you into service for one mile, go for two miles. Give to the one who asks of you, and do not turn your back on one who wants to borrow.

"You have heard that it was said, *You shall love your neighbor and hate your enemy.* But I say to you, **love your enemies**✝ and pray for those who persecute you, that you may be children of your heavenly Father, for he makes his sun rise on the bad and the good, and causes rain to fall on the just and the unjust. For if you love those who love you, what recompense will you have? Do not the tax collectors do the same? And if you greet your brothers only, what is unusual about that? Do not the pagans do the same? So be perfect, just as your heavenly Father is perfect."

The Gospel of the Lord. *Praise to you, Lord Jesus Christ.*

PROFESSION OF FAITH *(page 13)*

PRAYER OF THE FAITHFUL

PREPARATION OF GIFTS *(page 16)*

PRAYER OVER THE OFFERINGS
As we celebrate your mysteries, O Lord,
with the observance that is your due,
we humbly ask you,
that what we offer to the honor of your majesty
may profit us for salvation.
Through Christ our Lord. *Amen.*

PREFACE *(Sundays in Ordinary Time, page 28–32)*

• TAKING A CLOSER LOOK •

✚ **Love your enemies** This is probably the most challenging thing Jesus demands of his followers and runs against everything they were accustomed to. In the biblical world, love and hate, friends and enemies, were strict opposites. Love was the fierce attachment to one's group, especially the family. Hate was the detachment or alienation from one's group. These attitudes were matched by actions. Love disposed one to do good for those in one's group, hatred prompted evil. A Greek proverb summed up the result: "Help a friend, harm an enemy." Nothing illustrates the demands of conversion to Jesus' values more strongly than this summons to love the persecutors whom you have every reason to hate.

COMMUNION ANTIPHON *(Psalm 9:2-3)*

I will recount all your wonders, I will rejoice in you and be glad,
and sing psalms to your name, O Most High.

Or *(John 11:27)*

Lord, I have come to believe that you are the Christ, the Son of
the living God, who is coming into this world.

PRAYER AFTER COMMUNION

Grant, we pray, almighty God,
that we may experience the effects of the salvation
which is pledged to us by these mysteries.
Through Christ our Lord. ***Amen.***

BLESSING & DISMISSAL *(page 56)* ✳

❖ RESPONDING TO THE WORD ❖

God tells us that
we are to love
our neighbor as
ourselves.

➡ *How shall I show
love toward my
neighbor this week?*

Paul reminds us
that our bodies are
temples of the Holy
Spirit.

➡ *In what ways
might I take better
care of my body?*

Jesus challenges
us to pray for
our enemies and
persecutors.

➡ *How do I respond
to those who hurt or
offend me?*

A season of joy!

We may be surprised to hear that the Church's liturgy reminds us that Lent is meant to be a joyful season.

> For by your gracious gift each year
> your faithful await the sacred paschal feasts
> with the joy of minds made pure...
> PREFACE 1 OF LENT

The season of Lent finds its meaning and origin in Easter, the annual celebration of our Lord's resurrection and our salvation. As the Church's time to prepare for the high point of the Christian year, it is the most appropriate time for persons to enter into Christ's new life through baptism. How can it not be a time of joy?

Over the centuries, Lent has become a special time for fasting, abstinence, communal and private prayer, self-discipline, serving others, study, reflection, and penance. With the whole Church we re-examine our priorities, leaving sin and self behind and intensifying our love and service of God and our neighbors.

The joy of this time of preparation is all about the surprise of new life coming from what may have appeared dead—just as fresh buds break through each spring on trees that seemed dead during the long winter.

If we use these forty days of Lent for honest examination and careful "pruning" of our lives, we will be ready to celebrate the great feast of Easter with our risen Lord and to be joyful witnesses of the power of his resurrection in our world so broken by sin.

Praying and living the Lenten season

It's a common practice to "give things up" for Lent. But when we give something up, we create an empty space into which we must then put some new form of loving behavior.

Give yourself and each household member an index card. Either divide the card into five weeks or, better, use a new card each week. Invite everyone to write on one side what they want to give up to create space for something new, and on the other side what they want to fill the space with.

For example, giving up calories by fasting creates a space for feeling a little of the hunger that haunts millions of the world's poor. The money we save from fasting can also be donated to groups that help feed the hungry. Giving up some television time as a household creates space for spending time together in conversation, prayer, or even playing games. Giving up an attitude of complaining makes space for a more cooperative approach to fixing dinners or doing chores.

When everyone is finished, take the cards and place them in the center of the dinner table or in your household Lenten prayer space. Light a candle and pray together:

God, giver of all gifts,
you have given us so much.
Now we want to give up something
so that we might experience
the emptiness that reminds us
how much we want to be filled
by your loving presence.
May our sacrifice show our willingness
to change our lives this Lent. Amen.

February 26

Letting go

Rend your hearts as our ever patient God invites us to do. Fast but do not draw attention to your fasting. There is a wonderful harmony to these paradoxes as the same tradition that teaches us to perform acts of contrition also teaches us to not despair over our sins. We are being invited to let go of our sins so that we no longer have to carry them around with us.

Have you ever had the experience of letting go of something and then receiving an unexpected gift in return? Or had a moment in which you achieved clarity of thought about a situation that had caused you many anxious moments? These experiences illustrate the benefit of being patient while waiting for the grace of God to become noticed by us in our lives. During this period of Lenten preparation there can be much value in patiently waiting for us to see the grace of God appearing in our lives. This time of preparation is a time to prepare our interior lives and reflect on those aspects of our lives we can forget, given our busy schedules.

Let us go forward today with conviction. Consider the gifts God has in store for us if only we will let go of that which is preventing us from experiencing them in our innermost self.

■ John O'Brien

*If the blessing and distribution of ashes take place
outside Mass, it is appropriate that the complete Liturgy
of the Word precede it, using texts assigned to the Mass
of Ash Wednesday.*

ENTRANCE ANTIPHON *(Wisdom 11:24, 25, 27)*
You are merciful to all, O Lord, and despise nothing that you
have made. You overlook people's sins, to bring them to repentance, and you spare them, for you are the Lord our God.

INTRODUCTORY RITES *(page 10)*

COLLECT
Grant, O Lord, that we may begin with holy fasting
this campaign of Christian service,
so that, as we take up battle against spiritual evils,
we may be armed with weapons of self-restraint.
Through our Lord Jesus Christ, your Son,
who lives and reigns with you in the unity of the Holy Spirit,
one God, for ever and ever. ***Amen.***

FIRST READING *(Joel 2:12–18)*
Even now, says the LORD,
return to me with your whole heart,
    with fasting, and weeping, and mourning;
Rend your hearts, not your garments,
    and return to the LORD, your God.
For gracious and merciful is he,
    slow to anger, rich in kindness,
    and relenting in punishment.
Perhaps he will again relent
    and leave behind him a blessing,

Offerings and libations
for the LORD, your God.

Blow the trumpet in Zion!
proclaim a fast,
call an assembly;
Gather the people,
notify the congregation;
Assemble the elders,
gather the children
and the infants at the breast;
Let the bridegroom quit his room
and the bride her chamber.
Between the porch and the altar
let the priests, the ministers of the LORD, weep,
And say, "Spare, O LORD, your people,
and make not your heritage a reproach,
with the nations ruling over them!
Why should they say among the peoples,
'Where is their God?' "

Then the LORD was stirred to concern for his land
and took pity on his people.
The word of the Lord. *Thanks be to God.*

RESPONSORIAL PSALM *(Psalm 51:3–4, 5–6ab, 12–13, 14 and 17)*
R̷ **Be merciful, O Lord, for we have sinned.**

Have mercy on me, O God, in your goodness;
in the greatness of your compassion wipe out my offense.
Thoroughly wash me from my guilt
and of my sin cleanse me. R̷

For I acknowledge my offense,
  and my sin is before me always:
"Against you only have I sinned,
  and done what is evil in your sight." ℟
A clean heart create for me, O God,
  and a steadfast spirit renew within me.
Cast me not out from your presence,
  and your Holy Spirit take not from me. ℟
Give me back the joy of your salvation,
  and a willing spirit sustain in me.
O Lord, open my lips,
    and my mouth shall proclaim your praise. ℟

SECOND READING *(2 Corinthians 5:20—6:2)*

Brothers and sisters: We are ambassadors for Christ, as if God were appealing through us. We implore you on behalf of Christ, be reconciled to God. For our sake he made him to be sin who did not know sin, so that we might become the righteousness of God in him.

Working together, then, we appeal to you not to receive the grace of God in vain. For he says:

In an acceptable time I heard you,
  and on the day of salvation I helped you.

Behold, now is a very acceptable time; behold, now is the day of salvation.

The word of the Lord. ***Thanks be to God.***

VERSE BEFORE THE GOSPEL *(See Psalm 95:8)*
Praise to you, Lord Jesus Christ, King of endless glory! If today you hear his voice, harden not your hearts. *Praise to you, Lord Jesus Christ, King of endless glory!*

GOSPEL *(Matthew 6:1-6, 16-18)*
A reading from the holy Gospel according to Matthew.
Glory to you, O Lord.

Jesus said to his disciples: "Take care not to perform righteous deeds in order that people may see them; otherwise, you will have no recompense from your heavenly Father. When you give alms, do not blow a trumpet before you, as the hypocrites do in the synagogues and in the streets to win the praise of others. Amen, I say to you, they have received their reward. But when you give alms, do not let your left hand know what your right is doing, so that your almsgiving may be secret. And your Father who sees in secret will repay you.

"When you pray, do not be like the **hypocrites**,✝ who love to stand and pray in the synagogues and on street corners so that others may see them. Amen, I say to you, they have received their reward. But when you pray, go to your inner room, close the door, and pray to your Father in secret. And your Father who sees in secret will repay you.

"When you fast, do not look gloomy like the hypocrites. They neglect their appearance, so that they may appear to others to be fasting. Amen, I say to you, they have received their reward. But when you fast, anoint your head and wash your face, so that you may not appear to be fasting, except to your Father who is hidden. And your Father who sees what is hidden will repay you."

The Gospel of the Lord. *Praise to you, Lord Jesus Christ.*

BLESSING AND DISTRIBUTION OF ASHES

After the homily, the priest says:

Dear brethren (brothers and sisters), let us humbly ask God
    our Father
that he be pleased to bless with the abundance of his grace
these ashes, which we will put on our heads in penitence.

After a brief prayer in silence he continues:

O God, who are moved by acts of humility
and respond with forgiveness to works of penance,
lend your merciful ear to our prayers
and in your kindness pour out the grace of your blessing
on your servants who are marked with these ashes,
that, as they follow the Lenten observances,
they may be worthy to come with minds made pure
to celebrate the Paschal Mystery of your Son.
Through Christ our Lord. *Amen.*

Or

O God, who desire not the death of sinners,
but their conversion,
mercifully hear our prayers
and in your kindness be pleased to bless these ashes,
which we intend to receive upon our heads,
that we, who acknowledge we are but ashes
and shall return to dust,
may, through a steadfast observance of Lent,
gain pardon for sins and newness of life
after the likeness of your Risen Son.
Who lives and reigns for ever and ever. *Amen.*

*The priest sprinkles the ashes with holy water, places ashes on the heads
of all those present who come to him, and says to each one:*

Repent, and believe in the Gospel.

Or

Remember that you are dust, and to dust you shall return.

PRAYER OF THE FAITHFUL

PREPARATION OF GIFTS *(page 16)*

PRAYER OVER THE OFFERINGS
As we solemnly offer
the annual sacrifice for the beginning of Lent,
we entreat you, O Lord,
that, through works of penance and charity,
we may turn away from harmful pleasures
and, cleansed from our sins, may become worthy
to celebrate devoutly the Passion of your Son.
Who lives and reigns for ever and ever. *Amen.*

• TAKING A CLOSER LOOK •

✢ **Hypocrites** *Hypocrite* is a Greek word that means an actor in
the theater. Since Greek plays were performed outdoors and the audience was at a distance, actors wore large stereotyped masks to identify
their characters. So in popular usage, a hypocrite was someone who pre-
tended to be something that he or she was not, and hypocrisy described
the general mismatch between one's external appearance and internal
attitudes. Just as the actor hid behind a mask, so the hypocrite hides
something behind a pleasing external appearance. To avoid being a hypocrite, we can use Lent to align our inner attitudes and our outer actions.

PREFACE (*Lent 3–4, page 22*)

COMMUNION ANTIPHON (*Cf. Psalm 1:2-3*)
He who ponders the law of the Lord day and night will yield fruit in due season.

PRAYER AFTER COMMUNION
May the Sacrament we have received sustain us, O Lord,
that our Lenten fast may be pleasing to you
and be for us a healing remedy.
Through Christ our Lord. *Amen.*

PRAYER OVER THE PEOPLE
Pour out a spirit of compunction, O God,
on those who bow before your majesty,
and by your mercy may they merit the rewards you promise
to those who do penance.
Through Christ our Lord. *Amen.*

DISMISSAL (*page 57*) ❖

• RESPONDING TO THE WORD •

Joel wants us to change on the inside and not just externally.	Paul says that now is the acceptable time to be an ambassador of Christ.	Jesus warns against hypocritical behavior.
⮑ *What change of attitude do I most want to make this Lent?*	⮑ *With whom will I share the good news of salvation today?*	⮑ *What do I need to do to match my words with my actions?*

March 1

Tested by temptation

It has been said that nothing in this world is certain except death and taxes. Surely temptation could be added as a third. Our lives are constantly fraught with urges and desires that we either succumb to or rebuff.

Having fasted for 40 days and 40 nights, Jesus was left in the most vulnerable of human conditions. Sensing weakness, Satan sprung into action and tried to tempt Jesus three times. On each occasion, the great deceiver was spurned by Jesus, who obeyed the will of God. Denying God's will didn't even enter Jesus' mind as he chided Satan for his wilderness volleys. Jesus' resolve faced a much more vigorous test in Gethsemane when he asked God if the cup of his pending crucifixion might pass him by. Even then, Jesus overcame human frailty to submit to God's will.

As was the case with our first parents in the Garden of Eden, we are offered freedom of choice and are constantly tested by temptation. Like Adam and Eve, our human infirmity renders us susceptible to Satan's seductions. As we begin Lent, let us use the practices of fasting, prayer, and almsgiving to provide us with the defense we need to fend off the advances of Satan. These practices, rooted in our belief in Jesus as our Redeemer, are the bulwarks of that resistance.

◼ FRANK CAMPBELL

Parishes engaged in the Rite of Christian Initiation of Adults (RCIA) may celebrate the Rite of Election today.

ENTRANCE ANTIPHON *(Cf. Psalm 91 [90]:15-16)*

When he calls on me, I will answer him; I will deliver him and give him glory, I will grant him length of days.

INTRODUCTORY RITES *(page 10)*

COLLECT

Grant, almighty God,
through the yearly observances of holy Lent,
that we may grow in understanding
of the riches hidden in Christ
and by worthy conduct pursue their effects.
Through our Lord Jesus Christ, your Son,
who lives and reigns with you in the unity of the Holy Spirit,
one God, for ever and ever. *Amen.*

FIRST READING *(Genesis 2:7-9; 3:1-7)*

The LORD God formed man out of the clay of the ground and blew into his nostrils the breath of life, and so man became a living being.

Then the LORD God planted a garden in Eden, in the east, and placed there the man whom he had formed. Out of the ground the LORD God made various trees grow that were delightful to look at and good for food, with the tree of life in the middle of the garden and the tree of the knowledge of good and evil.

Now the serpent was the most cunning of all the animals that the LORD God had made. The serpent asked the woman, "Did God really tell you not to eat from any of the trees in the garden?"

The woman answered the serpent: "We may eat of the fruit of the trees in the garden; it is only about the fruit of the tree in the middle of the garden that God said, 'You shall not eat it or even touch it, lest you die.' " But the serpent said to the woman: "You certainly will not die! No, God knows well that the moment you eat of it your eyes will be opened and you will be like gods who know what is good and what is evil." The woman saw that the tree was good for food, pleasing to the eyes, and desirable for gaining wisdom. So she took some of its fruit and ate it; and she also gave some to her husband, who was with her, and he ate it. Then the eyes of both of them were opened, and they realized that they were naked; so they sewed fig leaves together and made loincloths for themselves.

The word of the Lord. *Thanks be to God.*

RESPONSORIAL PSALM *(Psalm 51:3-4, 5-6, 12-13, 17)*

℟ **Be merciful, O Lord, for we have sinned.**

Have mercy on me, O God, in your goodness;
    in the greatness of your compassion wipe out my offense.
Thoroughly wash me from my guilt
    and of my sin cleanse me. ℟

For I acknowledge my offense,
    and my sin is before me always:
"Against you only have I sinned,
    and done what is evil in your sight." ℟

A clean heart create for me, O God,
    and a steadfast spirit renew within me.
Cast me not out from your presence,
    and your Holy Spirit take not from me. ℟

Give me back the joy of your salvation,
    and a willing spirit sustain in me.

O Lord, open my lips,
  and my mouth shall proclaim your praise. ℟

SECOND READING *(Romans 5:12–19)*
For the shorter version, omit the indented parts in brackets.

Brothers and sisters: Through one man sin entered the world, and through sin, death, and thus death came to all men, inasmuch as all sinned.

  [—for up to the time of the law, sin was in the world, though sin is not accounted when there is no law. But death reigned from Adam to Moses, even over those who did not sin after the pattern of the trespass of Adam, who is the type of the one who was to come.

  But the gift is not like the transgression. For if by the transgression of the one, the many died, how much more did the grace of God and the gracious gift of the one man Jesus Christ overflow for the many. And the gift is not like the result of the one who sinned. For after one sin there was the judgment that brought condemnation; but the gift, after many transgressions, brought acquittal.]

For if, by the transgression of the one, death came to reign through that one, how much more will those who receive the abundance of grace and of the gift of justification come to reign in life through the one Jesus Christ. In conclusion, just as through one transgression condemnation came upon all, so, through one righteous act, acquittal and life came to all. For just as through the disobedience of the one man the many were made sinners, so, through the obedience of the one, the many will be made righteous.

  The word of the Lord. ***Thanks be to God.***

VERSE BEFORE THE GOSPEL *(Matthew 4:4b)*
Praise to you, Lord Jesus Christ, King of endless glory! One does not live on bread alone, but on every word that comes forth from the mouth of God. ***Praise to you, Lord Jesus Christ, King of endless glory!***

GOSPEL *(Matthew 4:1-11)*
A reading from the holy Gospel according to Matthew.
Glory to you, O Lord.

At that time Jesus was led by the Spirit into the desert to be tempted by the devil. He fasted for forty days and forty nights, and afterwards he was hungry. The tempter approached and said to him, "If you are the Son of God, command that these stones become loaves of bread." He said in reply, "It is written:

One does not live on bread alone,
but on every word that comes forth
from the mouth of God."

Then the devil took him to the holy city, and made him stand on the parapet of the temple, and said to him, "If you are the Son of God, throw yourself down. For it is written:

He will command his angels concerning you
and with their hands they will support you,
lest you dash your foot against a stone."

Jesus answered him, "Again it is written,

You shall not put the Lord, your God, to the test."

Then the devil took him up to a very high mountain, and showed him all the kingdoms of the world in their magnificence, and he said to him, "All these I shall give to you, if you will prostrate yourself and worship me." At this, Jesus said to him, "Get away, **Satan!**✝ It is written:

The Lord, your God, shall you worship
and him alone shall you serve."

Then the devil left him and, behold, angels came and ministered
to him.

The Gospel of the Lord. ***Praise to you, Lord Jesus Christ.***

RITE OF ELECTION

PROFESSION OF FAITH *(page 13)*

PRAYER OF THE FAITHFUL

PREPARATION OF GIFTS *(page 16)*

PRAYER OVER THE OFFERINGS

Give us the right dispositions, O Lord, we pray,
to make these offerings,
for with them we celebrate the beginning
of this venerable and sacred time.
Through Christ our Lord. ***Amen.***

PREFACE: THE TEMPTATION OF THE LORD

It is truly right and just, our duty and our salvation,
always and everywhere to give you thanks,
Lord, holy Father, almighty and eternal God,
through Christ our Lord.

By abstaining forty long days from earthly food,
he consecrated through his fast
the pattern of our Lenten observance
and, by overturning all the snares of the ancient serpent,
taught us to cast out the leaven of malice,

so that, celebrating worthily the Paschal Mystery,
we might pass over at last to the eternal paschal feast.

And so, with the company of Angels and Saints,
we sing the hymn of your praise,
as without end we acclaim:
Holy, Holy, Holy Lord God of hosts... *(page 35)*

COMMUNION ANTIPHON *(Matthew 4:4)*
One does not live by bread alone, but by every word that comes
forth from the mouth of God.

Or *(Cf. Psalm 91 [90]:4)*
The Lord will conceal you with his pinions, and under his wings
you will trust.

PRAYER AFTER COMMUNION
Renewed now with heavenly bread,
by which faith is nourished, hope increased,

❖ TAKING A CLOSER LOOK ❖

✝ **Satan** In the earlier books of the Bible (especially Job), the "satan"
or accuser is a kind of legal prosecutor in the divine assembly who questions the sincerity of human faith. After the exile, as the Jews began to
stress God as transcendent and supremely good, they found it difficult
to account for evil in the world. Gradually, they developed the figure of
Satan as an evil spirit who is subordinate but hostile to God, struggling
with God for domination of the earth and tempting humans from following God's ways. Jesus' triumph over Satan encourages us to resist
temptations that lead us away from being sons and daughters of God.

and charity strengthened,
we pray, O Lord,
that we may learn to hunger for Christ,
the true and living Bread,
and strive to live by every word
which proceeds from your mouth.
Through Christ our Lord. *Amen.*

PRAYER OVER THE PEOPLE

May bountiful blessing, O Lord, we pray,
come down upon your people,
that hope may grow in tribulation,
virtue be strengthened in temptation,
and eternal redemption be assured.
Through Christ our Lord. *Amen.*

DISMISSAL *(page 57)* ✤

✦ RESPONDING TO THE WORD ✦

God provides everything that the first human couple needed.	Paul reminds us that we have a new chance for a sinless life as Jesus' gift to us.	Jesus uses Scripture to give him confidence in temptation.
⮕ How can I give thanks for all the gifts God has given to me?	⮕ What can I do today to imitate Jesus' generosity?	⮕ What can I do this Lent to make Scripture more important in my daily life?

March 8

Where will our heart and mind be?

Today's gospel is one of great mystery: the transfiguration. Moses and Elijah appear next to Jesus, who was completely transfigured, radiating pure light. Imagine yourself there.. The sight must have been out of this world! In the face of all this glory, Peter's first reaction is to set up three dwellings, offering them worldly comfort. How often is God right in front of us, showing us divinity and a plan for our life, and we focus on logistics and worldly preoccupations?

As a matter of fact, today during Mass, we will witness one of the greatest miracles of all time: bread and wine becoming Jesus' body and blood. The Eucharist is the sacrament where we get a glimpse of God's glory and power. For a moment, heaven and earth meet. As we witness this miracle today, where will our heart and mind be? Will we be checking the time or revelling in God's glory? Will we be thinking about the things we need to do this week or listening to God speak to our heart?

Jesus' words to the disciples are a wakeup call: "Rise, and do not be afraid." They prompt us to refocus on what's important: not worldly considerations but an attentive ear and an open heart to his ever-living word, calling us to be examples of heaven here on earth.

◼ **Myriam Dupuis**

ENTRANCE ANTIPHON *(Cf. Psalm 27 [26]:8-9)*
Of you my heart has spoken: Seek his face. It is
your face, O Lord, that I seek; hide not your face
from me.

Or *(Cf. Psalm 25 [24]:6, 2, 22)*
Remember your compassion, O Lord, and your
merciful love, for they are from of old. Let not our enemies exult
over us. Redeem us, O God of Israel, from all our distress.

INTRODUCTORY RITES *(page 10)*

COLLECT
O God, who have commanded us
to listen to your beloved Son,
be pleased, we pray,
to nourish us inwardly by your word,
that, with spiritual sight made pure,
we may rejoice to behold your glory.
Through our Lord Jesus Christ, your Son,
who lives and reigns with you in the unity of the Holy Spirit,
one God, for ever and ever. *Amen.*

FIRST READING *(Genesis 12:1-4a)*

The LORD said to Abram: "Go forth from the land of your
kinsfolk and from your father's house to a land that I will
show you.

"I will make of you a great nation,
    and I will bless you;
I will make your name great,
    so that you will be a blessing.
I will bless those who bless you

and curse those who curse you.
All the communities of the earth
    shall find blessing in you."
Abram went as the LORD directed him.
The word of the Lord. *Thanks be to God.*

RESPONSORIAL PSALM *(Psalm 33:4-5, 18-19, 20, 22)*
℟ **Lord, let your mercy be on us, as we place our trust in you.**

Upright is the word of the LORD,
    and all his works are trustworthy.
He loves justice and right;
    of the kindness of the LORD the earth is full. ℟
See, the eyes of the LORD are upon those who fear him,
    upon those who hope for his kindness,
to deliver them from death
    and preserve them in spite of famine. ℟
Our soul waits for the LORD,
    who is our help and our shield.
May your kindness, O LORD, be upon us
    who have put our hope in you. ℟

SECOND READING *(2 Timothy 1:8b-10)*

Beloved: Bear your share of hardship for the gospel with the
strength that comes from God.

He saved us and called us to a holy life, not according to our
works but according to his own design and the grace bestowed
on us in Christ Jesus before time began, but now made manifest
through the appearance of our savior Christ Jesus, who destroyed
death and brought life and immortality to light through the gospel.

The word of the Lord. *Thanks be to God.*

VERSE BEFORE THE GOSPEL *(See Matthew 17:5)*
Praise to you, Lord Jesus Christ, King of endless glory! From the shining cloud the Father's voice is heard: This is my beloved Son, listen to him. *Praise to you, Lord Jesus Christ, King of endless glory!*

GOSPEL *(Matthew 17:1-9)*
A reading from the holy Gospel according to Matthew.
Glory to you, O Lord.

Jesus took Peter, James, and John his brother, and led them up a high mountain by themselves. And he was **transfigured**✝ before them; his face shone like the sun and his clothes became white as light. And behold, Moses and Elijah appeared to them, conversing with him. Then Peter said to Jesus in reply, "Lord, it is good that we are here. If you wish, I will make three tents here, one for you, one for Moses, and one for Elijah." While he was still speaking, behold, a bright cloud cast a shadow over them, then from the cloud came a voice that said, "This is my beloved Son, with whom I am well pleased; listen to him." When the disciples heard this, they fell prostrate and were very much afraid. But Jesus came and touched them, saying, "Rise, and do not be afraid." And when the disciples raised their eyes, they saw no one else but Jesus alone.

As they were coming down from the mountain, Jesus charged them, "Do not tell the vision to anyone until the Son of Man has been raised from the dead."

The Gospel of the Lord. *Praise to you, Lord Jesus Christ.*

PROFESSION OF FAITH *(page 13)*

PRAYER OF THE FAITHFUL

PREPARATION OF GIFTS *(page 16)*

PRAYER OVER THE OFFERINGS
May this sacrifice, O Lord, we pray,
cleanse us of our faults
and sanctify your faithful in body and mind
for the celebration of the paschal festivities.
Through Christ our Lord. *Amen.*

PREFACE: THE TRANSFIGURATION OF THE LORD
It is truly right and just, our duty and our salvation,
always and everywhere to give you thanks,
Lord, holy Father, almighty and eternal God,
through Christ our Lord.

For after he had told the disciples of his coming Death,
on the holy mountain he manifested to them his glory,
to show, even by the testimony of the law and the prophets,
that the Passion leads to the glory of the Resurrection.

And so, with the Powers of heaven,
we worship you constantly on earth,
and before your majesty
without end we acclaim:
Holy, Holy, Holy Lord God of hosts... *(page 35)*

COMMUNION ANTIPHON *(Matthew 17:5)*

This is my beloved Son, with whom I am well pleased; listen to him.

PRAYER AFTER COMMUNION

As we receive these glorious mysteries,
we make thanksgiving to you, O Lord,
for allowing us while still on earth
to be partakers even now of the things of heaven.
Through Christ our Lord. ***Amen.***

• TAKING A CLOSER LOOK •

✛ **Transfigured** Although the Greek word here (*metamorphosis*) commonly described a change in form or appearance that a god might make to appear to humans, the gospel writers suggest a completely new meaning. The transfiguration is a glimpse of God's glory breaking forth from Jesus' human form. After revealing to the disciples that as Messiah he would have to suffer, Jesus' changed appearance previews the change that he will undergo at his resurrection. The dazzling light, the divine voice of approval, the support of the whole Jewish tradition represented by Moses (the Jewish Law) and Elijah (the prophets) signal that his messianic suffering is the fulfillment of God's plan for salvation.

PRAYER OVER THE PEOPLE

Bless your faithful, we pray, O Lord,
with a blessing that endures for ever,
and keep them faithful
to the Gospel of your Only Begotten Son,
so that they may always desire and at last attain
that glory whose beauty he showed in his own Body,
to the amazement of his Apostles.
Through Christ our Lord. *Amen.*

DISMISSAL *(page 57)* ✦

● RESPONDING TO THE WORD ●

Abram gave up much in order to do as the Lord commanded.	Paul reminds us that we are called to a holy life.	At the transfiguration, God approved Jesus and his mission.
➡ What must I give up this Lent to let God take up more space in my life?	➡ How can I respond more generously to this call now?	➡ With what about me and my ministry would God be most pleased?

March 15

**MAR
15**

Be transformed!

I once did a day hike in a desert-like landscape on a hot day in July. By noon, I had no water left in my water bottle. I began to experience an increasingly painful thirst. My throat was parched. My whole body was crying for water while the desert sun kept beating down on me.

The desert can be an image for a period of suffering that we experience in our lives. We can feel so drained, so tired of pain, so distressed. We thirst for some relief, for a better time. We languish.

The Samaritan woman was thirsty. Not just for water but for a better life. She meets Jesus, who offers her hope. In fact, he makes a promise to her: "Whoever drinks the water I shall give will never thirst." This sounds too good to be true. But Jesus insists by saying that he is offering her life in all its fullness. She believes in him, and her life is transformed.

Jesus invites us today to follow him more closely. As the psalm says, "Oh, that today you would hear his voice!" By listening to his infinitely merciful and caring voice, we can bring to him the parched and hurting parts of our lives and be transformed.

■ **EMMANUEL MARTEL**

Parishes engaged in the Rite of Christian Initiation of Adults (RCIA) may celebrate the First Scrutiny today (see page 216).

ENTRANCE ANTIPHON *(Cf. Psalm 25 [24]:15–16)*
My eyes are always on the Lord, for he rescues my feet from the snare. Turn to me and have mercy on me, for I am alone and poor.

Or *(Cf. Ezekiel 36:23–26)*
When I prove my holiness among you, I will gather you from all the foreign lands; and I will pour clean water upon you and cleanse you from all your impurities, and I will give you a new spirit, says the Lord.

INTRODUCTORY RITES *(page 10)*

COLLECT
O God, author of every mercy and of all goodness,
who in fasting, prayer and almsgiving
have shown us a remedy for sin,
look graciously on this confession of our lowliness,
that we, who are bowed down by our conscience,
may always be lifted up by your mercy.
Through our Lord Jesus Christ, your Son,
who lives and reigns with you in the unity of the Holy Spirit,
one God, for ever and ever. *Amen.*

FIRST READING *(Exodus 17:3–7)*
In those days, in their thirst for water, the people grumbled against Moses, saying, "Why did you ever make us leave Egypt? Was it just to have us die here of thirst with our children and our livestock?" So Moses cried out to the LORD,

"What shall I do with this people? A little more and they will stone me!" The LORD answered Moses, "Go over there in front of the people, along with some of the elders of Israel, holding in your hand, as you go, the staff with which you struck the river. I will be standing there in front of you on the rock in Horeb.* Strike the rock, and the water will flow from it for the people to drink." This Moses did, in the presence of the elders of Israel. The place was called Massah* and Meribah,* because the Israelites quarreled there and tested the LORD, saying, "Is the LORD in our midst or not?"

The word of the Lord. *Thanks be to God.*

RESPONSORIAL PSALM *(Psalm 95:1-2, 6-7, 8-9)*

R. **If today you hear his voice, harden not your hearts.**

Come, let us sing joyfully to the LORD;
  let us acclaim the Rock of our salvation.
Let us come into his presence with thanksgiving;
  let us joyfully sing psalms to him. R.
Come, let us bow down in worship;
  let us kneel before the LORD who made us.
For he is our God,
  and we are the people he shepherds, the flock he guides. R.
Oh, that today you would hear his voice:
  "Harden not your hearts as at Meribah,*
  as in the day of Massah* in the desert,
where your fathers tempted me;
  they tested me though they had seen my works." R.

SECOND READING *(Romans 5:1-2, 5-8)*

Brothers and sisters: Since we have been **justified by faith**, ✠ we have peace with God through our Lord Jesus Christ, through whom we have gained access by faith to this grace in which we stand, and we boast in hope of the glory of God.

And hope does not disappoint, because the love of God has been poured out into our hearts through the Holy Spirit who has been given to us. For Christ, while we were still helpless, died at the appointed time for the ungodly. Indeed, only with difficulty does one die for a just person, though perhaps for a good person one might even find courage to die. But God proves his love for us in that while we were still sinners Christ died for us.

The word of the Lord. *Thanks be to God.*

VERSE BEFORE THE GOSPEL *(See John 4:42, 15)*
Praise to you, Lord Jesus Christ, King of endless glory! Lord, you are truly the Savior of the world; give me living water, that I may never thirst again. *Praise to you, Lord Jesus Christ, King of endless glory!*

GOSPEL *(John 4:5–42)*
For the shorter version, omit the indented parts in brackets and add the text in parentheses.

A reading from the holy Gospel according to John.
Glory to you, O Lord.

Jesus came to a town of Samaria* called Sychar,* near the plot of land that Jacob had given to his son Joseph. Jacob's well was there. Jesus, tired from his journey, sat down there at the well. It was about noon.

A woman of Samaria came to draw water. Jesus said to her, "Give me a drink." His disciples had gone into the town to buy food. The Samaritan woman said to him, "How can you, a Jew, ask me, a Samaritan woman, for a drink?"—For Jews use nothing in common with Samaritans.—Jesus answered and said to her, "If you knew the gift of God and who is saying to you, 'Give me a drink,' you would have asked him and he would have given you living water." The woman said to him, "Sir, you do not even have a bucket and the cistern is deep; where then can you get this living water? Are you greater than our father Jacob, who gave us this cistern and drank from it himself with his children and his flocks?" Jesus answered and said to her, "Everyone who drinks this water will be thirsty again; but whoever drinks the water I shall give will never thirst; the water I shall give will become in him a spring of water welling up to eternal life." The woman said to him, "Sir, give me this water, so that I may not be thirsty or have to keep coming here to draw water."

[Jesus said to her, "Go call your husband and come back." The woman answered and said to him, "I do not have a husband." Jesus answered her, "You are right in saying, 'I do not have a husband.' For you have had five husbands, and the one you have now is not your husband. What you have said is true." The woman said to him, "Sir,] I can see that you are a prophet. Our ancestors worshiped on this mountain; but you people say that the place to worship is in Jerusalem." Jesus said to her, "Believe me, woman, the hour is coming when you will worship the Father neither on this mountain nor in Jerusalem. You people worship what you do not understand; we worship what we understand, because salvation is from the Jews. But the hour is coming, and is now

here, when true worshipers will worship the Father in Spirit
and truth; and indeed the Father seeks such people to worship
him. God is Spirit, and those who worship him must worship
in Spirit and truth." The woman said to him, "I know that the
Messiah is coming, the one called the Christ; when he comes,
he will tell us everything." Jesus said to her, "I am he, the one
(who is) speaking with you."

[At that moment his disciples returned, and were
amazed that he was talking with a woman, but still no
one said, "What are you looking for?" or "Why are you
talking with her?" The woman left her water jar and went
into the town and said to the people, "Come see a man
who told me everything I have done. Could he possibly
be the Christ?" They went out of the town and came to
him. Meanwhile, the disciples urged him, "Rabbi, eat."
But he said to them, "I have food to eat of which you do
not know." So the disciples said to one another, "Could
someone have brought him something to eat?" Jesus said
to them, "My food is to do the will of the one who sent me
and to finish his work. Do you not say, 'In four months the
harvest will be here'? I tell you, look up and see the fields
ripe for the harvest. The reaper is already receiving payment and gathering crops for eternal life, so that the sower
and reaper can rejoice together. For here the saying is veri-
fied that 'One sows and another reaps.' I sent you to reap
what you have not worked for; others have done the work,
and you are sharing the fruits of their work."]

Many of the Samaritans of that town began to believe in him
[because of the word of the woman who testified, "He told me
everything I have done."] When the Samaritans came to him,

they invited him to stay with them; and he stayed there two days.
Many more began to believe in him because of his word, and
they said to the woman, "We no longer believe because of your
word; for we have heard for ourselves, and we know that this is
truly the savior of the world."

The Gospel of the Lord. *Praise to you, Lord Jesus Christ.*

PROFESSION OF FAITH *(page 13)*

PRAYER OF THE FAITHFUL

PREPARATION OF GIFTS *(page 16)*

PRAYER OVER THE OFFERINGS
Be pleased, O Lord, with these sacrificial offerings,
and grant that we who beseech pardon for our own sins,
may take care to forgive our neighbor.
Through Christ our Lord. *Amen.*

PREFACE : THE SAMARITAN WOMAN
It is truly right and just, our duty and our salvation,
always and everywhere to give you thanks,
Lord, holy Father, almighty and eternal God,
through Christ our Lord.

For when he asked the Samaritan woman for water to drink,
he had already created the gift of faith within her
and so ardently did he thirst for her faith,
that he kindled in her the fire of divine love.

And so we, too, give you thanks
and with the Angels
praise your mighty deeds, as we acclaim:
Holy, Holy, Holy Lord God of hosts... *(page 35)*

COMMUNION ANTIPHON *(Cf. John 4:13–14)*
For anyone who drinks it, says the Lord, the water I shall give will
become in him a spring welling up to eternal life.

PRAYER AFTER COMMUNION
As we receive the pledge
of things yet hidden in heaven
and are nourished while still on earth
with the Bread that comes from on high,
we humbly entreat you, O Lord,
that what is being brought about in us in mystery
may come to true completion.
Through Christ our Lord. *Amen.*

⁘ TAKING A CLOSER LOOK ⁘

✠ **Justified by faith** For Paul, "justification" describes God's
saving action in Christ, that is, establishing the right relationship between humans and God. Paul adopts an image from the law courts,
where a judge's merciful verdict of acquittal for a guilty defendant
restores the right relationship of the acquitted to the community.
Our faith or trust in God's action sets us into right relationship. Thus,
for Paul, both Jew and Gentile, through faith and not by keeping the
Mosaic law, receive the gift of a new relationship with God and mem-
bership in God's new covenant community.

PRAYER OVER THE PEOPLE

Direct, O Lord, we pray, the hearts of your faithful,
and in your kindness grant your servants this grace:
that, abiding in the love of you and their neighbor,
they may fulfill the whole of your commands.
Through Christ our Lord. *Amen.*

DISMISSAL *(page 57)* ✠

• RESPONDING TO THE WORD •

The people grumble because they think Moses and God do not care.	Paul reminds us that God's love has been poured into our hearts.	The Samaritan woman's knowledge of Jesus grows as she talks to him.
➡ *What causes me to grumble about God's care for me?*	➡ *When have I most felt the outpouring of God's love?*	➡ *How can I increase my time in conversation with Jesus this Lent?*

MASS PRAYERS FOR
CHRISTIAN INITIATION: FIRST SCRUTINY

ENTRANCE ANTIPHON *(Ezekiel 36:23–26)*
When I prove my holiness among you, I will gather you from
all the foreign lands and I will pour clean water upon you and
cleanse you from all your impurities, and I will give you a new
spirit, says the Lord.

Or *(Cf. Isaiah 55:1)*
Come to the waters, you who are thirsty, says the Lord; you who
have no money, come and drink joyfully.

COLLECT
Grant, we pray, O Lord,
that these chosen ones may come worthily and wisely
to the confession of your praise,
so that in accordance with that first dignity
which they lost by original sin
they may be fashioned anew through your glory.
Through our Lord Jesus Christ, your Son,
who lives and reigns with you in the unity of the Holy Spirit,
one God, for ever and ever. *Amen.*

PRAYER OVER THE OFFERINGS
May your merciful grace prepare your servants, O Lord,
for the worthy celebration of these mysteries
and lead them to it by a devout way of life.
Through Christ our Lord. *Amen.*

PREFACE : THE SAMARITAN WOMAN

It is truly right and just, our duty and our salvation,
always and everywhere to give you thanks,
Lord, holy Father, almighty and eternal God,
through Christ our Lord.

For when he asked the Samaritan woman for water to drink,
he had already created the gift of faith within her
and so ardently did he thirst for her faith,
that he kindled in her the fire of divine love.

And so we, too, give you thanks
and with the Angels
praise your mighty deeds, as we acclaim:
Holy, Holy, Holy Lord God of hosts... (page 35)

COMMUNION ANTIPHON (Cf. John 4:13-14)

For anyone who drinks it, says the Lord, the water I shall give
will become in him a spring welling up to eternal life.

PRAYER AFTER COMMUNION

Give help, O Lord, we pray,
by the grace of your redemption
and be pleased to protect and prepare
those you are to initiate
through the Sacraments of eternal life.
Through Christ our Lord. *Amen.* ✢

March 22

Receive God with joy!

Today's gospel is beautifully illustrated in Franco Zeffirelli's classic film *Jesus of Nazareth*. The actor who plays the blind man is very convincing: unkempt, rather scruffy, and not on the guest list to any dinner parties of the rich. His encounter with Jesus is life-changing. By contrast, the Pharisees are presented as hostile and in darkness. Jesus reacts strongly to their ignorance of the truth. One striking aspect of the encounter is the blind man's lack of fear in answering the Pharisee's questions.

The blind man saw Jesus and accepted him as the Messiah, the Light of the World, giving us all an example of receiving God with joy and enthusiasm.

We can imagine ourselves in the person of the blind man. Placing ourselves in the gospel, we can recognize our own resistance to the truth at times as well as our profession of faith when our hearts are drawn to conversion. The deeper our relationship grows with Jesus, the more we can let go of those things in us that block the light.

When Jesus opens our eyes, we see him in all things, in our neighbor, in ourselves, and in the landscape of our path home. And in the Eucharist, we see the blind man among the communion of saints, the Mystical Body of Christ.

■ DENIS GRADY, OFS

*Parishes engaged in the Rite of Christian Initiation of Adults
(RCIA) may celebrate the Second Scrutiny today (see page 227).*

ENTRANCE ANTIPHON *(Cf. Isaiah 66:10–11)*
Rejoice, Jerusalem, and all who love her. Be joyful, all
who were in mourning; exult and be satisfied at her
consoling breast.

INTRODUCTORY RITES *(page 10)*

COLLECT
O God, who through your Word
reconcile the human race to yourself in a wonderful way,
grant, we pray,
that with prompt devotion and eager faith
the Christian people may hasten
toward the solemn celebrations to come.
Through our Lord Jesus Christ, your Son,
who lives and reigns with you in the unity of the Holy Spirit,
one God, for ever and ever. *Amen.*

FIRST READING *(1 Samuel 16:1b, 6–7, 10–13a)*
The Lord said to Samuel: "Fill your horn with oil, and be on
your way. I am sending you to Jesse of Bethlehem, for I have
chosen my king from among his sons."

As Jesse and his sons came to the sacrifice, Samuel looked at
Eliab and thought, "Surely the Lord's anointed is here before
him." But the Lord said to Samuel: "Do not judge from his
appearance or from his lofty stature, because I have rejected him.
Not as man sees does God see, because man sees the appearance but the Lord looks into the heart." In the same way Jesse
presented seven sons before Samuel, but Samuel said to Jesse,

"The LORD has not chosen any one of these." Then Samuel asked Jesse, "Are these all the sons you have?" Jesse replied, "There is still the youngest, who is tending the sheep." Samuel said to Jesse, "Send for him; we will not begin the sacrificial banquet until he arrives here." Jesse sent and had the young man brought to them. He was ruddy, a youth handsome to behold and making a splendid appearance. The LORD said, "There—anoint him, for this is the one!" Then Samuel, with the horn of oil in hand, anointed David in the presence of his brothers; and from that day on, the spirit of the LORD rushed upon David.

The word of the Lord. ***Thanks be to God.***

RESPONSORIAL PSALM *(Psalm 23:1–3a, 3b–4, 5, 6)*
℟ **The Lord is my shepherd; there is nothing I shall want.**

The LORD is my shepherd; I shall not want.
In verdant pastures he gives me repose;
beside restful waters he leads me;
he refreshes my soul. ℟
He guides me in right paths
for his name's sake.
Even though I walk in the dark valley
I fear no evil; for you are at my side
with your rod and your staff
that give me courage. ℟
You spread the table before me
in the sight of my foes;
you anoint my head with oil;
my cup overflows. ℟
Only goodness and kindness follow me
all the days of my life;

and I shall dwell in the house of the LORD
   for years to come. ℟

SECOND READING *(Ephesians 5:8-14)*

Brothers and sisters: You were once darkness, but now you are light in the Lord. Live as children of light, for light produces every kind of goodness and righteousness and truth. Try to learn what is pleasing to the Lord. Take no part in the fruitless works of darkness; rather expose them, for it is shameful even to mention the things done by them in secret; but everything exposed by the light becomes visible, for everything that becomes visible is light. Therefore, it says:

   "Awake, O sleeper,
   and arise from the dead,
   and Christ will give you light."

The word of the Lord. *Thanks be to God.*

VERSE BEFORE THE GOSPEL *(John 8:12)*
Praise to you, Lord Jesus Christ, King of endless glory! I am the light of the world, says the Lord; whoever follows me will have the light of life. *Praise to you, Lord Jesus Christ, King of endless glory!*

GOSPEL *(John 9:1-41)*
For the shorter version, omit the indented parts in brackets.

A reading from the holy Gospel according to John.
Glory to you, O Lord.

As Jesus passed by he saw a man blind from birth. [His disciples asked him, "Rabbi, who sinned, this man or his parents, that he was born blind?" Jesus answered, "Neither he nor his parents sinned; it is so that the works of God might be made visible through him. We have to do the works of the

one who sent me while it is day. Night is coming when no
one can work. While I am in the world, I am the light of the
world." When he had said this,]
he spat on the ground and made clay with the saliva, and
smeared the clay on his eyes, and said to him, "Go wash in the
Pool of Siloam*"—which means Sent—. So he went and washed,
and came back able to see.

His neighbors and those who had seen him earlier as a beggar
said, "Isn't this the one who used to sit and beg?" Some said, "It
is," but others said, "No, he just looks like him." He said, "I am."
[So they said to him, "How were your eyes opened?" He replied, "The man called Jesus made clay and anointed my eyes
and told me, 'Go to Siloam and wash.' So I went there and
washed and was able to see." And they said to him, "Where is
he?" He said, "I don't know."]
They brought the one who was once blind to the Pharisees. Now
Jesus had made clay and opened his eyes on a sabbath. So then
the Pharisees also asked him how he was able to see. He said to
them, "He put clay on my eyes, and I washed, and now I can
see." So some of the Pharisees said, "This man is not from God,
because he does not keep the sabbath." But others said, "How
can a sinful man do such signs?" And there was a division among
them. So they said to the blind man again, "What do you have
to say about him, since he opened your eyes?" He said, "He is a
prophet."

[Now the Jews did not believe that he had been blind and
gained his sight until they summoned the parents of the one
who had gained his sight. They asked them, "Is this your son,
who you say was born blind? How does he now see?" His
parents answered and said, "We know that this is our son and
that he was born blind. We do not know how he sees now,

nor do we know who opened his eyes. Ask him, he is of age; he can speak for himself." His parents said this because they were afraid of the Jews, for the Jews had already agreed that if anyone acknowledged him as the Christ, he would be expelled from the **synagogue**.☩ For this reason his parents said, "He is of age; question him."

So a second time they called the man who had been blind and said to him, "Give God the praise! We know that this man is a sinner." He replied, "If he is a sinner, I do not know. One thing I do know is that I was blind and now I see." So they said to him, "What did he do to you? How did he open your eyes?" He answered them, "I told you already and you did not listen. Why do you want to hear it again? Do you want to become his disciples, too?" They ridiculed him and said, "You are that man's disciple; we are disciples of Moses! We know that God spoke to Moses, but we do not know where this one is from." The man answered and said to them, "This is what is so amazing, that you do not know where he is from, yet he opened my eyes. We know that God does not listen to sinners, but if one is devout and does his will, he listens to him. It is unheard of that anyone ever opened the eyes of a person born blind. If this man were not from God, he would not be able to do anything."]

They answered and said to him, "You were born totally in sin, and are you trying to teach us?" Then they threw him out.

When Jesus heard that they had thrown him out, he found him and said, "Do you believe in the Son of Man?" He answered and said, "Who is he, sir, that I may believe in him?" Jesus said to him, "You have seen him, the one speaking with you is he." He said, "I do believe, Lord," and he worshiped him.

[Then Jesus said, "I came into this world for judgment, so that those who do not see might see, and those who do see might become blind."

Some of the Pharisees who were with him heard this and said to him, "Surely we are not also blind, are we?" Jesus said to them, "If you were blind, you would have no sin; but now you are saying, 'We see,' so your sin remains."]

The Gospel of the Lord. *Praise to you, Lord Jesus Christ.*

PROFESSION OF FAITH *(page 13)*

PRAYER OF THE FAITHFUL

PREPARATION OF GIFTS *(page 16)*

PRAYER OVER THE OFFERINGS

We place before you with joy these offerings,
which bring eternal remedy, O Lord,
praying that we may both faithfully revere them
and present them to you, as is fitting,
for the salvation of all the world.
Through Christ our Lord. *Amen.*

PREFACE: THE MAN BORN BLIND

It is truly right and just, our duty and our salvation,
always and everywhere to give you thanks,
Lord, holy Father, almighty and eternal God,
through Christ our Lord.

By the mystery of the Incarnation,
he has led the human race that walked in darkness
into the radiance of the faith
and has brought those born in slavery to ancient sin
through the waters of regeneration
to make them your adopted children.

Therefore, all creatures of heaven and earth
sing a new song in adoration,
and we, with all the host of Angels,
cry out, and without end acclaim:
Holy, Holy, Holy Lord God of hosts... *(page 35)*

COMMUNION ANTIPHON *(Cf. John 9:11, 38)*
The Lord anointed my eyes: I went, I washed, I saw and I
believed in God.

• TAKING A CLOSER LOOK •

✣ **Synagogue** The synagogue was not, like the Temple in Jerusalem, a place where God dwelt and where Jews worshipped and offered sacrifices. It was primarily a meeting place for community prayer and for the study and discussion of the Scriptures. Hence it was not organized and run by priests but by lay people, in particular the elders of the community. Synagogues became even more important after the Jerusalem Temple was destroyed in 70 AD by the Romans, and sacrifices ceased to be offered. Synagogues also helped affirm Jewish identity and community belonging when Jews emigrated to other nations (much like the immigrant parishes in 19th-century United States).

PRAYER AFTER COMMUNION

O God, who enlighten everyone who comes into this world,
illuminate our hearts, we pray,
with the splendor of your grace,
that we may always ponder
what is worthy and pleasing to your majesty
and love you in all sincerity.
Through Christ our Lord. *Amen.*

PRAYER OVER THE PEOPLE

Look upon those who call to you, O Lord,
and sustain the weak;
give life by your unfailing light
to those who walk in the shadow of death,
and bring those rescued by your mercy from every evil
to reach the highest good.
Through Christ our Lord. *Amen.*

DISMISSAL *(page 57)* ❖

• RESPONDING TO THE WORD •

God looks into the heart of each person.	Paul encourages us to learn what is pleasing to the Lord.	The blind man learns to recognize Jesus through faith.
➡ How can I get beyond appearances when dealing with others?	➡ What can I do today that would be most pleasing to God?	➡ What would most help me to "see" Jesus in a new way today?

MASS PRAYERS FOR
CHRISTIAN INITIATION: SECOND SCRUTINY

ENTRANCE ANTIPHON *(Cf. Psalm 25 [24]:15-16)*

My eyes are always on the Lord, for he rescues my feet from the snare. Turn to me and have mercy on me, for I am alone and poor.

COLLECT

Almighty ever-living God,
give to your Church an increase in spiritual joy,
so that those once born of earth
may be reborn as citizens of heaven.
Through our Lord Jesus Christ, your Son,
who lives and reigns with you in the unity of the Holy Spirit,
one God, for ever and ever. *Amen.*

PRAYER OVER THE OFFERINGS

We place before you with joy these offerings,
which bring eternal remedy, O Lord,
praying that we may both faithfully revere them
and present them to you, as is fitting,
for those who seek salvation.
Through Christ our Lord. *Amen.*

PREFACE: THE MAN BORN BLIND

It is truly right and just, our duty and our salvation,
always and everywhere to give you thanks,
Lord, holy Father, almighty and eternal God,
through Christ our Lord.

By the mystery of the Incarnation,
he has led the human race that walked in darkness
into the radiance of the faith
and has brought those born in slavery to ancient sin
through the waters of regeneration
to make them your adopted children.

Therefore, all creatures of heaven and earth
sing a new song in adoration,
and we, with all the host of Angels,
cry out, and without end acclaim:
Holy, Holy, Holy Lord God of hosts... *(page 35)*

COMMUNION ANTIPHON *(Cf. John 9:11, 38)*
The Lord anointed my eyes; I went, I washed,
I saw and I believed in God.

PRAYER AFTER COMMUNION
Sustain your family always in your kindness,
O Lord, we pray,
correct them, set them in order,
graciously protect them under your rule,
and in your unfailing goodness
direct them along the way of salvation.
Through Christ our Lord. *Amen.* ✴

March 29

When the time is right!

Computers! I turn mine on and then have to wait for everything to open. I press a button; I'm still waiting. But then my son comes and gently takes the time to explain things. It turns out I don't understand computers, I'm impatient, and I take them for granted.

John's story of Lazarus reminds us how important time is to understanding. Lazarus is sick, yet it takes Jesus four days to arrive in Judea. Why does it take him so long? Jesus says, "This illness is not to end in death, but is for the glory of God, that the Son of God may be glorified through it." But this is so difficult to understand.

The disciples don't seem to understand the relationship that Jesus has with his father. Some of the Jews have already taken Jesus for granted, saying that, because he cured the blind man, he could have cured Lazarus too if he'd arrived earlier.

Even Martha and Mary, who have enormous faith, have trouble understanding.

Lazarus has been dead for four days and Jesus raises him from the dead so that everyone may see the Glory of God, his father.

If there is an area in our life that causes us grief, and we walk closely with Jesus, he will help us gain a new perspective—when the time is right!

▩ LIZ SUMMERS

Parishes engaged in the Rite of Christian Initiation of Adults (RCIA) may
celebrate the Third Scrutiny today (see page 237).

ENTRANCE ANTIPHON *(Cf. Psalm 43 [42]:1-2)*

Give me justice, O God, and plead my cause against a nation that
is faithless. From the deceitful and cunning rescue me, for you,
O God, are my strength.

INTRODUCTORY RITES *(page 10)*

COLLECT

By your help, we beseech you, Lord our God,
may we walk eagerly in that same charity
with which, out of love for the world,
your Son handed himself over to death.
Through our Lord Jesus Christ, your Son,
who lives and reigns with you in the unity of the Holy Spirit,
one God, for ever and ever. *Amen.*

FIRST READING *(Ezekiel 37:12-14)*

Thus says the Lord GOD: O my people, I will open your
graves and have you rise from them, and bring you back
to the land of Israel. Then you shall know that I am the LORD,
when I open your graves and have you rise from them, O my
people! I will put my spirit in you that you may live, and I will
settle you upon your land; thus you shall know that I am the
LORD. I have promised, and I will do it, says the LORD.

The word of the Lord. *Thanks be to God.*

RESPONSORIAL PSALM *(Psalm 130:1-2, 3-4, 5-6, 7-8)*
R. **With the Lord there is mercy and fullness of redemption.**

Out of the depths I cry to you, O LORD;
  LORD, hear my voice!
Let your ears be attentive
  to my voice in supplication. R.
If you, O LORD, mark iniquities,
  LORD, who can stand?
But with you is forgiveness,
  that you may be revered. R.
I trust in the LORD;
  my soul trusts in his word.
More than sentinels wait for the dawn,
  let Israel wait for the LORD. R.
For with the LORD is kindness
  and with him is plenteous redemption;
and he will redeem Israel
  from all their iniquities. R.

SECOND READING *(Romans 8:8-11)*

Brothers and sisters: Those who are in the flesh cannot please God. But you are not in the flesh; on the contrary, you are in the spirit, if only the Spirit of God dwells in you. Whoever does not have the Spirit of Christ does not belong to him. But if Christ is in you, although the body is dead because of sin, the spirit is alive because of righteousness. If the Spirit of the One who raised Jesus from the dead dwells in you, the One who raised Christ from the dead will give life to your mortal bodies also, through his Spirit dwelling in you.

The word of the Lord. *Thanks be to God.*

VERSE BEFORE THE GOSPEL *(John 11:25, 26)*
Praise to you, Lord Jesus Christ, King of endless glory! I am the
resurrection and the life, says the Lord; whoever believes in me,
even if he dies, will never die. ***Praise to you, Lord Jesus Christ,
King of endless glory!***

GOSPEL *(John 11:1–45)*
*For the shorter version, omit the indented text in brackets and add words in
parentheses.*

A reading from the holy Gospel according to John.
Glory to you, O Lord.

[Now a man was ill, Lazarus from Bethany,* the village of
Mary and her sister Martha. Mary was the one who had
anointed the Lord with perfumed oil and dried his feet with
her hair; it was her brother Lazarus who was ill. So]
The sisters (of Lazarus) sent word to Jesus saying, "Master, the
one you love is ill." When Jesus heard this he said, "This illness
is not to end in death, but is for the glory of God, that the Son
of God may be glorified through it." Now Jesus loved Martha
and her sister and Lazarus. So when he heard that he was ill, he
remained for two days in the place where he was. Then after this
he said to his disciples, "Let us go back to Judea."

[The disciples said to him, "Rabbi, the Jews were just trying to
stone you, and you want to go back there?" Jesus answered, "Are
there not twelve hours in a day? If one walks during the day, he
does not stumble, because he sees the light of this world. But if
one walks at night, he stumbles, because the light is not in him."
He said this, and then told them, "Our friend Lazarus is asleep,
but I am going to awaken him." So the disciples said to him,
"Master, if he is asleep, he will be saved." But Jesus was talking

about his death, while they thought that he meant ordinary sleep. So then Jesus said to them clearly, "Lazarus has died. And I am glad for you that I was not there, that you may believe. Let us go to him." So Thomas, called Didymus,* said to his fellow disciples, "Let us also go to die with him."]

When Jesus arrived, he found that Lazarus had already been in the tomb for four days.

[Now Bethany was near Jerusalem, only about two miles away. And many of the Jews had come to Martha and Mary to comfort them about their brother.]

When Martha heard that Jesus was coming, she went to meet him; but Mary sat at home. Martha said to Jesus, "Lord, if you had been here, my brother would not have died. But even now I know that whatever you ask of God, God will give you." Jesus said to her, "Your brother will rise." Martha said to him, "I know he will rise, in the **resurrection**✝ on the last day." Jesus told her, "I am the resurrection and the life; whoever believes in me, even if he dies, will live, and everyone who lives and believes in me will never die. Do you believe this?" She said to him, "Yes, Lord. I have come to believe that you are the Christ, the Son of God, the one who is coming into the world."

[When she had said this, she went and called her sister Mary secretly, saying, "The teacher is here and is asking for you." As soon as she heard this, she rose quickly and went to him. For Jesus had not yet come into the village, but was still where Martha had met him. So when the Jews who were with her in the house comforting her saw Mary get up quickly and go out, they followed her, presuming that she was going to the tomb to weep there. When Mary came to where Jesus was and saw him, she fell at his feet and said to him, "Lord, if you had been here, my brother would not have died." When Jesus saw her weeping and the Jews who had come with her weeping,] He became perturbed and deeply troubled, and said, "Where have you laid him?" They said to him, "Sir, come and see." And Jesus wept. So the Jews said, "See how he loved him." But some of them said, "Could not the one who opened the eyes of the blind man have done something so that this man would not have died?"

So Jesus, perturbed again, came to the tomb. It was a cave, and a stone lay across it. Jesus said, "Take away the stone." Martha, the dead man's sister, said to him, "Lord, by now there will be a stench; he has been dead for four days." Jesus said to her, "Did I not tell you that if you believe you will see the glory of God?" So they took away the stone. And Jesus raised his eyes and said, "Father, I thank you for hearing me. I know that you always hear me; but because of the crowd here I have said this, that they may believe that you sent me." And when he had said this, he cried out in a loud voice, "Lazarus, come out!" The dead man came out, tied hand and foot with burial bands, and his face was wrapped in a cloth. So Jesus said to them, "Untie him and let him go."

Now many of the Jews who had come to Mary and seen what he had done began to believe in him.

The Gospel of the Lord. *Praise to you, Lord Jesus Christ.*

PROFESSION OF FAITH *(page 13)*

PRAYER OF THE FAITHFUL

PREPARATION OF GIFTS *(page 16)*

PRAYER OVER THE OFFERINGS

Hear us, almighty God,
and, having instilled in your servants
the teachings of the Christian faith,
graciously purify them
by the working of this sacrifice.
Through Christ our Lord. *Amen.*

PREFACE: LAZARUS

It is truly right and just, our duty and our salvation,
always and everywhere to give you thanks,
Lord, holy Father, almighty and eternal God,
through Christ our Lord.

For as true man he wept for Lazarus his friend
and as eternal God raised him from the tomb,
just as, taking pity on the human race,
he leads us by sacred mysteries to new life.

● Taking a Closer Look ●

✛ **Resurrection** What happened on Easter was a complete surprise to the disciples. The Jesus that they had known and who had died was suddenly experienced as alive again. This new life, described as resurrection, was not just a restoration of one's former life—a resuscitation from the dead. The prophets Elijah and Elisha had brought people back to this life, as had Jesus for the daughter of Jairus, the son of the widow of Nain, and Jesus' beloved friend Lazarus. Although their return from the dead left them temporarily alive, they would die again. Jesus' resurrection was a new life that would not be subject to death again. It was eternal life, permanent and undying existence in the presence of God forever.

Through him the host of Angels adores your majesty
and rejoices in your presence for ever.
May our voices, we pray, join with theirs
in one chorus of exultant praise, as we acclaim:
Holy, Holy, Holy Lord God of hosts... *(page 35)*

COMMUNION ANTIPHON *(Cf. John 11:26)*
Everyone who lives and believes in me will not die for ever, says
the Lord.

PRAYER AFTER COMMUNION
We pray, almighty God,
that we may always be counted among the members of Christ,
in whose Body and Blood we have communion.
Who lives and reigns for ever and ever. *Amen.*

PRAYER OVER THE PEOPLE
Bless, O Lord, your people,
who long for the gift of your mercy,
and grant that what, at your prompting, they desire
they may receive by your generous gift.
Through Christ our Lord. *Amen.*

DISMISSAL *(page 57)* ✣

• RESPONDING TO THE WORD •

God promises new life through the Holy Spirit.	Christ and the Holy Spirit dwell in me to give life.	Out of love, Jesus brings Lazarus back to life.
⇨ *What new spiritual life have I felt this Lent?*	⇨ *What signs of their presence have I noticed this Lent?*	⇨ *Out of love, how has Jesus been bringing me to new life this Lent?*

MASS PRAYERS FOR
CHRISTIAN INITIATION: THIRD SCRUTINY

ENTRANCE ANTIPHON *(Cf. Psalm 18 [17]:5-7)*
The waves of death rose about me; the pains of the netherworld
surrounded me. In my anguish I called to the Lord; and from his
holy temple he heard my voice.

COLLECT
Grant, O Lord, to these chosen ones
that, instructed in the holy mysteries,
they may receive new life at the font of Baptism
and be numbered among the members of your Church.
Through our Lord Jesus Christ, your Son,
who lives and reigns with you in the unity of the Holy Spirit,
one God, for ever and ever. *Amen.*

PRAYER OVER THE OFFERINGS
Hear us, almighty God,
and, having instilled in your servants
the first fruits of the Christian faith,
graciously purify them by the working of this sacrifice.
Through Christ our Lord. *Amen.*

PREFACE: LAZARUS
It is truly right and just, our duty and our salvation,
always and everywhere to give you thanks,
Lord, holy Father, almighty and eternal God,
through Christ our Lord.

For as true man he wept for Lazarus his friend
and as eternal God raised him from the tomb,
just as, taking pity on the human race,
he leads us by sacred mysteries to new life.

Through him the host of Angels adores your majesty
and rejoices in your presence for ever.
May our voices, we pray, join with theirs
in one chorus of exultant praise, as we acclaim:
Holy, Holy, Holy Lord God of hosts... *(page 35)*

COMMUNION ANTIPHON *(Cf. John 11:26)*
Everyone who lives and believes in me will not die for ever, says
the Lord.

PRAYER AFTER COMMUNION
May your people be at one, O Lord, we pray,
and in wholehearted submission to you
may they obtain this grace:
that, safe from all distress,
they may readily live out their joy at being saved
and remember in loving prayer those to be reborn.
Through Christ our Lord. *Amen.* ✤

April 5

Commit our cause to the Lord!

When the crowds see Jesus, he is on a small donkey being led by one of the Apostles. The word spreads that this is he, Jesus of Nazareth, the Messiah. Stories begin to circulate in the crowd about the wonderful things he has done: given sight to the blind, cured the sick, even raised someone from the dead. Most are eager to see him with their own eyes. The mood is festive and filled with excitement. People waving palms grow in number surrounding Jesus.

Yet Jesus is remarkably calm. He does not take advantage of the situation. He could have rallied the crowd behind him to protect himself from what was to come. He doesn't, because at this moment of seeming triumph, he knows full well what awaits him. St. Paul tells us in his letter to the Philippians what he did do: Jesus humbled himself, becoming obedient to the point of death, even death on a cross.

As Psalm 22 says, we must commit our cause to the Lord; we are in God's hands, and we must let the Lord deliver. Isaiah tells us how we must be when we face terrible situations. We must be open to hearing what the Lord asks of us. We must not turn backward but follow the path that God calls us to take.

■ JACK PANOZZO

THE COMMEMORATION OF THE LORD'S ENTRANCE INTO JERUSALEM

FIRST FORM: THE PROCESSION

INTRODUCTION

The assembly, carrying palm branches, gather in a place distinct from the church to which the procession will move. They may sing Hosanna! or another hymn.

Dear brethren (brothers and sisters),
since the beginning of Lent until now
we have prepared our hearts by penance and charitable works.
Today we gather together to herald with the whole Church
the beginning of the celebration
of our Lord's Paschal Mystery,
that is to say, of his Passion and Resurrection.
For it was to accomplish this mystery
that he entered his own city of Jerusalem.
Therefore, with all faith and devotion,
let us commemorate
the Lord's entry into the city for our salvation,
following in his footsteps,
so that, being made by his grace partakers of the Cross,
we may have a share also in his Resurrection and in his life.

Let us pray:

Almighty ever-living God,
sanctify these branches with your blessing,
that we, who follow Christ the King in exultation,

may reach the eternal Jerusalem through him.
Who lives and reigns for ever and ever. *Amen.*

Or

Increase the faith of those who place their hope in you, O God,
and graciously hear the prayers of those who call on you,
that we, who today hold high these branches
to hail Christ in his triumph,
may bear fruit for you by good works accomplished in him.
Who lives and reigns for ever and ever. *Amen.*

GOSPEL *(Matthew 21:1-11)*
A reading from the holy Gospel according to Matthew.
Glory to you, O Lord.

When Jesus and the disciples drew near Jerusalem and came to Bethphage* on the Mount of Olives, Jesus sent two disciples, saying to them, "Go into the village opposite you, and immediately you will find an ass tethered, and a colt with her. Untie them and bring them here to me. And if anyone should say anything to you, reply, 'The master has need of them.' Then he will send them at once." This happened so that what had been spoken through the prophet might be fulfilled:

Say to daughter Zion,*
"Behold, your king comes to you,
    meek and riding on an ass,
    and on a colt, the foal of a beast of burden."

The disciples went and did as Jesus had ordered them. They brought the ass and the colt and laid their cloaks over them, and he sat upon them. The very large crowd spread their cloaks on the road, while others cut branches from the trees and strewed them on the road. The crowds preceding him and those following kept crying out and saying:

"Hosanna to the Son of David;

blessed is the he who comes in the name of the Lord;

hosanna in the highest."

And when he entered Jerusalem the whole city was shaken and asked, "Who is this?" And the crowds replied, "This is Jesus the prophet, from Nazareth in Galilee."

The Gospel of the Lord. ***Praise to you, Lord Jesus Christ.***

PROCESSION

Dear brethren (brothers and sisters),

like the crowds who acclaimed Jesus in Jerusalem,

let us go forth in peace.

All process to the church singing a hymn in honor of Christ the King. Mass continues with the Collect.

SECOND FORM: THE SOLEMN ENTRANCE

The blessing of branches and proclamation of the gospel take place, as above, but in the church. After the gospel, the celebrant moves solemnly through the church to the sanctuary, while all sing. Mass continues with the Collect.

THIRD FORM: THE SIMPLE ENTRANCE

The people gather in the church as usual. While the celebrant goes to the altar, the following entrance antiphon or a suitable hymn is sung.

ENTRANCE ANTIPHON *(Cf. John 12:1, 12–13; Psalm 24 [23]:9–10)*

Six days before the Passover, when the Lord came into the city of Jerusalem, the children ran to meet him; in their hands they carried palm branches and with a loud voice cried out: Hosanna in the highest! Blessed are you, who have come in your abundant mercy!

O gates, lift high your heads; grow higher, ancient doors. Let him enter, the king of glory! Who is this king of glory? He, the Lord of hosts, he is the king of glory. Hosanna in the highest! Blessed are you, who have come in your abundant mercy!

INTRODUCTORY RITES *(page 10)*

COLLECT

Almighty ever-living God,
who as an example of humility for the human race to follow
caused our Savior to take flesh and submit to the Cross,
graciously grant that we may heed his lesson of patient suffering
and so merit a share in his Resurrection.
Who lives and reigns with you in the unity of the Holy Spirit,
one God, for ever and ever. *Amen.*

FIRST READING *(Isaiah 50:4-7)*

The Lord GOD has given me
a well-trained tongue,
that I might know how to speak to the weary
a word that will rouse them.
Morning after morning
he opens my ear that I may hear;
and I have not rebelled,
have not turned back.
I gave my back to those who beat me,
my cheeks to those who plucked my beard;
my face I did not shield

from buffets and spitting.

The Lord GOD is my help,
   therefore I am not disgraced;
I have set my face like flint,
   knowing that I shall not be put to shame.
The word of the Lord. ***Thanks be to God.***

RESPONSORIAL PSALM *(Psalm 22:8-9, 17-18, 19-20, 23-24)*
℞ **My God, my God, why have you abandoned me?**

All who see me scoff at me;
   they mock me with parted lips, they wag their heads:
"He relied on the LORD; let him deliver him,
   let him rescue him, if he loves him." ℞

Indeed, many dogs surround me,
   a pack of evildoers closes in upon me;
they have pierced my hands and my feet;
   I can count all my bones. ℞

They divide my garments among them,
   and for my vesture they cast lots.
But you, O LORD, be not far from me;
   O my help, hasten to aid me. ℞

I will proclaim your name to my brethren;
   in the midst of the assembly I will praise you:
"You who fear the LORD, praise him;
   all you descendants of Jacob, give glory to him;
   revere him, all you descendants of Israel!" ℞

SECOND READING *(Philippians 2:6-11)*

Christ Jesus, though he was in the form of God,
did not regard equality with God
  something to be grasped.
Rather, he emptied himself,
  taking the form of a slave,
  coming in human likeness;
  and found human in appearance,
  he humbled himself,
  becoming obedient to the point of death,
  even death on a cross.
Because of this, God greatly exalted him
  and bestowed on him the name
  which is above every name,
  that at the name of Jesus
  every knee should bend,
  of those in heaven and on earth and under the earth,
  and every tongue confess that
  Jesus Christ is Lord,
  to the glory of God the Father.
The word of the Lord. *Thanks be to God.*

VERSE BEFORE THE GOSPEL *(Philippians 2:8-9)*

Praise to you, Lord Jesus Christ, King of endless glory! Christ
became obedient to the point of death, even death on a cross.
Because of this, God greatly exalted him and bestowed on him
the name which is above every name. *Praise to you, Lord Jesus
Christ, King of endless glory!*

GOSPEL *(Matthew 26:14—27:66)*

Several readers may proclaim the passion narrative today. **N** *indicates the narrator,* † *the words of Jesus,* **V** *a voice, and* **C** *the crowd. The shorter version begins (page 253) and ends (page 257) at the asterisks.*

N The Passion of our Lord Jesus Christ according to Matthew.

One of the Twelve, who was called Judas Iscariot, went to the chief priests and said,

V "What are you willing to give me if I hand him over to you?"

N They paid him thirty pieces of silver, and from that time on he looked for an opportunity to hand him over.

On the first day of the **Feast of Unleavened Bread**, † the disciples approached Jesus and said,

V "Where do you want us to prepare for you to eat the **Passover**?" †

N He said,

† "Go into the city to a certain man and tell him,
'The teacher says, "My appointed time draws near; in your house I shall celebrate the Passover with my disciples." ' "

N The disciples then did as Jesus had ordered, and prepared the Passover.

When it was evening, he reclined at table with the Twelve. And while they were eating, he said,

† "Amen, I say to you, one of you will betray me."

N Deeply distressed at this, they began to say to him one after another,

V "Surely it is not I, Lord?"

N He said in reply,

✝ "He who has dipped his hand into the dish with me is the one who will betray me. The Son of Man indeed goes, as it is written of him, but woe to that man by whom the Son of Man is betrayed. It would be better for that man if he had never been born."

N Then Judas, his betrayer, said in reply,

V "Surely it is not I, Rabbi?"

N He answered,

✝ "You have said so."

N While they were eating, Jesus took bread, said the blessing, broke it, and giving it to his disciples said,

✝ "Take and eat; this is my body."

N Then he took a cup, gave thanks, and gave it to them, saying,

✝ "Drink from it, all of you, for this is my blood of the covenant, which will be shed on behalf of many for the forgiveness of sins. I tell you, from now on I shall not drink this fruit of the vine until the day when I drink it with you new in the kingdom of my Father."

N Then, after singing a hymn, they went out to the Mount of Olives.

N Then Jesus said to them,

✝ "This night all of you will have your faith in me shaken, for it is written:

> *I will strike the shepherd,*
> *and the sheep of the flock will be dispersed;*
but after I have been raised up, I shall go before you to Galilee."

N Peter said to him in reply,

V "Though all may have their faith in you shaken, mine will never be."

N Jesus said to him,

† "Amen, I say to you, this very night before the cock crows, you will deny me three times."

N Peter said to him,

V "Even though I should have to die with you, I will not deny you."

N And all the disciples spoke likewise.

Then Jesus came with them to a place called Gethsemane,* and he said to his disciples,

† "Sit here while I go over there and pray."

N He took along Peter and the two sons of Zebedee, and began to feel sorrow and distress. Then he said to them,

† "My soul is sorrowful even to death. Remain here and keep watch with me."

N He advanced a little and fell prostrate in prayer, saying,

† "My Father, if it is possible, let this cup pass from me; yet, not as I will, but as you will."

N When he returned to his disciples he found them asleep. He said to Peter,

✝ "So you could not keep watch with me for one hour? Watch and pray that you may not undergo the test. The spirit is willing, but the flesh is weak."

N Withdrawing a second time, he prayed again,

✝ "My Father, if it is not possible that this cup pass without my drinking it, your will be done!"

N Then he returned once more and found them asleep, for they could not keep their eyes open. He left them and withdrew again and prayed a third time, saying the same thing again. Then he returned to his disciples and said to them,

✝ "Are you still sleeping and taking your rest? Behold, the hour is at hand when the Son of Man is to be handed over to sinners. Get up, let us go. Look, my betrayer is at hand."

N While he was still speaking, Judas, one of the Twelve, arrived, accompanied by a large crowd, with swords and clubs, who had come from the chief priests and the elders of the people. His betrayer had arranged a sign with them, saying,

V "The man I shall kiss is the one; arrest him."

N Immediately he went over to Jesus and said,

V "Hail, Rabbi!"

N and he kissed him. Jesus answered him,

✝ "Friend, do what you have come for."

N Then stepping forward they laid hands on Jesus and arrested him. And behold, one of those who accompanied Jesus put his hand to his sword, drew it, and struck the high priest's servant, cutting off his ear. Then Jesus said to him,

✝ "Put your sword back into its sheath, for all who take the sword will perish by the sword. Do you think that I cannot call upon my Father and he will not provide me at this moment with more than twelve legions of angels? But then how would the Scriptures be fulfilled which say that it must come to pass in this way?"

N At that hour Jesus said to the crowds,

✝ "Have you come out as against a robber, with swords and clubs to seize me? Day after day I sat teaching in the temple area, yet you did not arrest me. But all this has come to pass that the writings of the prophets may be fulfilled."

N Then all the disciples left him and fled.

Those who had arrested Jesus led him away to Caiaphas the high priest, where the scribes and the elders were assembled. Peter was following him at a distance as far as the high priest's courtyard, and going inside he sat down with the servants to see the outcome. The chief priests and the entire Sanhedrin* kept trying to obtain false testimony against Jesus in order to put him to death, but they found none, though many false witnesses came forward. Finally two came forward who stated,

C "This man said, 'I can destroy the temple of God and within three days rebuild it.'"

N The high priest rose and addressed him,

V "Have you no answer? What are these men testifying against you?"

N But Jesus was silent. Then the high priest said to him,

V "I order you to tell us under oath before the living God whether you are the Christ, the Son of God."

N Jesus said to him in reply,

✝ "You have said so. But I tell you:
From now on you will see 'the Son of Man
    seated at the right hand of the Power'
    and 'coming on the clouds of heaven.'"

N Then the high priest tore his robes and said,

V "He has blasphemed! What further need have we of witnesses? You have now heard the blasphemy; what is your opinion?"

N They said in reply,

C "He deserves to die!"

N Then they spat in his face and struck him, while some slapped him, saying,

C "Prophesy for us, Christ: who is it that struck you?"

N Now Peter was sitting outside in the courtyard. One of the maids came over to him and said,

C "You too were with Jesus the Galilean."

N But he denied it in front of everyone, saying,

V "I do not know what you are talking about!"

N As he went out to the gate, another girl saw him and said to those who were there,

C "This man was with Jesus the Nazorean.*"

N Again he denied it with an oath,

V "I do not know the man!"

N A little later the bystanders came over and said to Peter,

C "Surely you too are one of them; even your speech gives you away."

N At that he began to curse and to swear,

V "I do not know the man."

N And immediately a cock crowed. Then Peter remembered the word that Jesus had spoken: "Before the cock crows you will deny me three times." He went out and began to weep bitterly.

N   When it was morning, all the chief priests and the elders of the people took counsel against Jesus to put him to death. They bound him, led him away, and handed him over to Pilate, the governor.

Then Judas, his betrayer, seeing that Jesus had been condemned, deeply regretted what he had done. He returned the thirty pieces of silver to the chief priests and elders, saying,

V "I have sinned in betraying innocent blood."

N They said,

C "What is that to us? Look to it yourself."

N Flinging the money into the temple, he departed and went off and hanged himself. The chief priests gathered up the money, but said,

C "It is not lawful to deposit this in the temple treasury, for it is the price of blood."

N After consultation, they used it to buy the potter's field as a burial place for foreigners. That is why that field even today is called the Field of Blood. Then was fulfilled what had been said through Jeremiah the prophet, *And they took the thirty pieces of silver, the value of a man with a price on his head, a price set by some of the Israelites, and they paid it out for the potter's field just as the Lord had commanded me.*

* * *

N [Now] Jesus stood before the governor (Pontius Pilate), and he questioned him,

V "Are you the king of the Jews?"

N Jesus said,

† "You say so."

N And when he was accused by the chief priests and elders, he made no answer. Then Pilate said to him,

V "Do you not hear how many things they are testifying against you?"

N But he did not answer him one word, so that the governor was greatly amazed.

Now on the occasion of the feast the governor was accustomed to release to the crowd one prisoner whom they wished. And at that time they had a notorious prisoner called

Barabbas.* So when they had assembled, Pilate said to them,

V "Which one do you want me to release to you, Barabbas, or Jesus called Christ?"

N For he knew that it was out of envy that they had handed him over. While he was still seated on the bench, his wife sent him a message, "Have nothing to do with that righteous man. I suffered much in a dream today because of him." The chief priests and the elders persuaded the crowds to ask for Barabbas but to destroy Jesus. The governor said to them in reply,

V "Which of the two do you want me to release to you?"

N They answered,

C "Barabbas!"

N Pilate said to them,

V "Then what shall I do with Jesus called Christ?"

N They all said,

C "Let him be crucified!"

N But he said,

V "Why? What evil has he done?"

N They only shouted the louder,

C "Let him be crucified!"

N When Pilate saw that he was not succeeding at all, but that a riot was breaking out instead, he took water and washed his hands in the sight of the crowd, saying,

V "I am innocent of this man's blood. Look to it yourselves."

N And the whole people said in reply,

C "His blood be upon us and upon our children."

N Then he released Barabbas to them, but after he had Jesus scourged, he handed him over to be crucified.

Then the soldiers of the governor took Jesus inside the praetorium and gathered the whole cohort around him. They stripped off his clothes and threw a scarlet military cloak about him. Weaving a crown out of thorns, they placed it on his head, and a reed in his right hand. And kneeling before him, they mocked him, saying,

C "Hail, King of the Jews!"

N They spat upon him and took the reed and kept striking him on the head. And when they had mocked him, they stripped him of the cloak, dressed him in his own clothes, and led him off to crucify him.

As they were going out, they met a Cyrenian* named Simon; this man they pressed into service to carry his cross.

And when they came to a place called Golgotha*—which means Place of the Skull—, they gave Jesus wine to drink mixed with gall. But when he had tasted it, he refused to drink. After they had crucified him, they divided his garments by casting lots; then they sat down and kept watch over him there. And they placed over his head the written charge against him: This is Jesus, the King of the Jews. Two revolutionaries were crucified with him, one on his right and the other on his left. Those passing by reviled him, shaking their heads and saying,

C "You who would destroy the temple and rebuild it in three days, save yourself, if you are the Son of God, and come down from the cross!"

N Likewise the chief priests with the scribes and elders mocked him and said,

C "He saved others; he cannot save himself. So he is the king of Israel! Let him come down from the cross now, and we will believe in him. He trusted in God; let him deliver him now if he wants him. For he said, 'I am the Son of God.'"

N The revolutionaries who were crucified with him also kept abusing him in the same way.

From noon onward, darkness came over the whole land until three in the afternoon. And about three o'clock Jesus cried out in a loud voice,

✝ *"Eli, Eli, lema sabachthani?*"*

N which means,

✝ "My God, my God, why have you forsaken me?"

N Some of the bystanders who heard it said,

C "This one is calling for Elijah."

N Immediately one of them ran to get a sponge; he soaked it in wine, and putting it on a reed, gave it to him to drink. But the rest said,

C "Wait, let us see if Elijah comes to save him."

N But Jesus cried out again in a loud voice, and gave up his spirit.

Here all kneel and pause for a short time.

N And behold, the veil of the sanctuary was torn in two from top to bottom. The earth quaked, rocks were split, tombs were opened, and the bodies of many saints who had fallen asleep were raised. And coming forth from their tombs after his resurrection, they entered the holy city and appeared to many. The centurion and the men with him who were keeping watch over Jesus feared greatly when they saw the earthquake and all that was happening, and they said,

C "Truly, this was the Son of God!"

✳ ✳ ✳

N There were many women there, looking on from a distance, who had followed Jesus from Galilee, ministering to him. Among them were Mary Magdalene and Mary the mother of James and Joseph, and the mother of the sons of Zebedee.

When it was evening, there came a rich man from Arimathea* named Joseph, who was himself a disciple of Jesus. He went to Pilate and asked for the body of Jesus; then Pilate ordered it to be handed over. Taking the body, Joseph wrapped it in clean linen and laid it in his new tomb that he had hewn in the rock. Then he rolled a huge stone across the entrance to the tomb and departed. But Mary Magdalene and the other Mary remained sitting there, facing the tomb.

The next day, the one following the day of preparation, the chief priests and the Pharisees gathered before Pilate and said,

C "Sir, we remember that this impostor while still alive said, 'After three days I will be raised up.' Give orders, then, that

the grave be secured until the third day, lest his disciples
come and steal him and say to the people, 'He has been
raised from the dead.' This last imposture would be worse
than the first."

N Pilate said to them,

V "The guard is yours; go, secure it as best you can."

N So they went and secured the tomb by fixing a seal to the stone
and setting the guard.
The Gospel of the Lord. *Praise to you, Lord Jesus Christ.*

PROFESSION OF FAITH *(page 13)*

PRAYER OF THE FAITHFUL

PREPARATION OF GIFTS *(page 16)*

PRAYER OVER THE OFFERINGS
Through the Passion of your Only Begotten Son, O Lord,
may our reconciliation with you be near at hand,
so that, though we do not merit it by our own deeds,
yet by this sacrifice made once for all,
we may feel already the effects of your mercy.
Through Christ our Lord. *Amen.*

PREFACE: THE PASSION OF THE LORD

It is truly right and just, our duty and our salvation,
always and everywhere to give you thanks,
Lord, holy Father, almighty and eternal God,
through Christ our Lord.

For, though innocent, he suffered willingly for sinners
and accepted unjust condemnation to save the guilty.
His Death has washed away our sins,
and his Resurrection has purchased our justification.

And so, with all the Angels,
we praise you, as in joyful celebration we acclaim:
Holy, Holy, Holy Lord God of hosts... *(page 35)*

● Taking a Closer Look ●

✠ Passover / Feast of Unleavened Bread

Passover (Greek, *ta pascha*) was the annual Jewish family celebration
remembering God's deliverance of Israel from Egypt. In particular,
the term recalls God's striking down of every Egyptian firstborn, both
children and animals, and "passing over" the Hebrews whose houses
were marked with lamb's blood (see Exodus 12, page 265). To this
feast was joined an eight-day period when only unleavened bread
could be eaten. Their leaven was not like our powdered yeast, but
rather a fermentation agent as is used in making sourdough bread
today. Thus leavened bread contained a corrupting agent that would
render it "unclean" for ritual use on this most sacred feast.

COMMUNION ANTIPHON *(Matthew 26:42)*
Father, if this chalice cannot pass without my drinking it, your
will be done.

PRAYER AFTER COMMUNION
Nourished with these sacred gifts,
we humbly beseech you, O Lord,
that, just as through the death of your Son
you have brought us to hope for what we believe,
so by his Resurrection
you may lead us to where you call.
Through Christ our Lord. *Amen.*

PRAYER OVER THE PEOPLE
Look, we pray, O Lord, on this your family,
for whom our Lord Jesus Christ
did not hesitate to be delivered into the hands of the wicked
and submit to the agony of the Cross.
Who lives and reigns for ever and ever. *Amen.*

DISMISSAL *(page 57)* ✢

✦ RESPONDING TO THE WORD ✦

God's servants endure much for God's sake.	Christ emptied himself for others both in life and in death.	Jesus gave himself so we might live more fully with God.
➡ *What suffering has been most challenging for me to accept recently?*	➡ *What can I do today to imitate Jesus' generosity?*	➡ *Which incident from Jesus' passion story do I want to pray about today?*

The Triduum (Latin for "three days") comes at the end of Holy Week and comprises the three-day period of prayer leading to the Easter feast, the fulfillment of the whole liturgical year.

Holy Thursday

On Holy Thursday (also called Maundy Thursday), the Church celebrates the Lord's Supper and the institution of the Eucharist. The word "Maundy" stems from the Latin word *mandatum*, meaning "commandment," and refers to the new commandment of love that Jesus gave his disciples that night.

Most parishes now observe the custom of foot-washing, recalling how Jesus washed his disciples' feet at the Last Supper (John 13:1-20). After the liturgy, the consecrated bread is transferred to a side altar and kept in the tabernacle of repose. Then the altar is stripped.

Good Friday

Good Friday is the only day of the year on which Mass is not celebrated. The altar is bare, and the liturgy consists of proclaiming John's passion account, intercessions, veneration of the cross, and a communion service.

Many churches, in addition to the liturgy of Good Friday, have a meditation on the Way of the Cross commemorating the events of Jesus' passion. Some parishes have also introduced Good Friday meditations on the seven last words of Christ on the cross taken from all four gospels.

The Great Vigil of Easter

Only the Eucharist itself is older than the liturgy of the Easter Vigil. This service re-enacts the passage from death into life. On this night, we celebrate our deliverance by Christ our Passover and look forward to the day when we shall see him face to face. During the Easter Vigil, as the Roman Missal explains, "the Church, keeping watch, awaits the Resurrection of Christ and celebrates it in the Sacraments."

The liturgy begins in a darkened church. The paschal candle is lighted as the "Light of Christ" is proclaimed and praised. In many churches, small candles held by the worshipers provide the only light for this part of the service. These candles are lighted from the paschal candle.

Then several readings from the Old Testament summarize the story of salvation, telling of God's work of creation, the calling of the Hebrews to be God's people, their deliverance in the Exodus, and God's constant care until Christ came. An air of expectancy surrounds the prayers and singing of Psalms and canticles that follow each reading.

Then the altar candles are lighted from the paschal candle, and, in a blaze of light and triumphant music, the first Easter Eucharist begins. Our risen Lord comes, in word and sacrament, into the darkness of our lives with the light of his risen life.

Baptisms follow the Scripture readings. The Easter Vigil is a traditional time for the Sacraments of Initiation: Baptism, Confirmation, and Eucharist. If there are no candidates for baptism, the congregation may join in the renewal of baptismal promises. Thus is recalled the time when we "died and were buried with Christ" and were raised with him to newness of life.

Praying and living Holy Week

When a Jewish household gathers for its Passover meal, the youngest child begins the reminiscing by asking: "Why is this night different from all other nights?" So likewise, we Christians might ask, "Why are these three days different from all other days?" The answer, of course, is that they encapsulate the deepest meaning of the story of our salvation. Through his death and resurrection, Jesus brings us all into the right relationships with God and with others.

During Holy Week and the Triduum, in order to recall the story of our salvation, individuals and family members might read the Scriptures appointed for each day or, if there are young children, read the events of Holy Week from a Bible storybook.

But knowing the story is only half the challenge. We need to connect its life-giving possibilities with our own lives. Use the following questions (based on Exodus 14:15—15:1) as a way for household members to discover the "exodus" character of their own lives.

- Tell a story of your experience of freedom and deliverance. What part did God play in this experience?

- When did you escape your own form of slavery and head for the promised land of freedom?

- When did you pass through the waters of your Red Sea and dance like Miriam on the other side?

- Tell a story of your passing over from some form of death to new life.

April 9

Following Jesus' example

In a gesture pregnant with meaning just before the highly significant Passover meal, Jesus totally disrupted the traditional expectations of his time and culture. He stunned his disciples by insisting on serving them in the most deferential of ways: washing their feet. This deepest measure of service for others is how we must also prepare ourselves for the Easter Triduum.

Pope Francis has understood Jesus' message. The Supreme Pontiff shocked the world by visiting a Roman jail on this high feast day. He then kissed the feet of young prisoners. He bent the liturgical arc of this teaching moment precisely by washing the feet of those who were never previously included in such ceremonies: two women and several Muslims.

Who are those who feel most-excluded in the Church by our cultural traditions, our religious creeds and beliefs? Whom should we kneel before and try to heal on this Holy Thursday? The acquaintance struggling with addictions? The young woman considering not bringing her pregnancy to term? The older person in pain? I wonder if such a sinner as I could follow Jesus' example and make my Easter practice the inclusion and service of the individuals most in need in my society.

■ JOE GUNN

ENTRANCE ANTIPHON *(Cf. Galatians 6:14)*

We should glory in the Cross of our Lord Jesus Christ, in whom is our salvation, life and resurrection, through whom we are saved and delivered.

INTRODUCTORY RITES *(page 10)*

COLLECT

O God, who have called us to participate
in this most sacred Supper,
in which your Only Begotten Son,
when about to hand himself over to death,
entrusted to the Church a sacrifice new for all eternity,
the banquet of his love,
grant, we pray,
that we may draw from so great a mystery,
the fullness of charity and of life.
Through our Lord Jesus Christ, your Son,
who lives and reigns with you in the unity of the Holy Spirit,
one God, for ever and ever. *Amen.*

FIRST READING *(Exodus 12:1-8, 11-14)*

The LORD said to Moses and Aaron in the land of Egypt, "This month shall stand at the head of your calendar; you shall reckon it the first month of the year. Tell the whole community of Israel: On the tenth of this month every one of your families must procure for itself a lamb, one apiece for each household. If a family is too small for a whole lamb, it shall join the nearest household in procuring one and shall share in the lamb in proportion to the number of persons who partake of it. The lamb must be a year-old male and without blemish. You may take it from either the sheep or the goats. You shall keep it until the fourteenth day of this month, and then, with the whole assembly of Israel present, it shall be slaughtered during the evening twilight. They shall take some of its blood and apply it to the two doorposts and the lintel of every house in which they partake of the lamb. That same night they shall eat its roasted flesh with unleavened bread and bitter herbs.

"This is how you are to eat it: with your loins girt, sandals on your feet and your staff in hand, you shall eat like those who are in flight. It is the Passover of the LORD. For on this same night I will go through Egypt, striking down every firstborn of the land, both man and beast, and executing judgment on all the gods of Egypt—I, the LORD! But the blood will mark the houses where you are. Seeing the blood, I will pass over you; thus, when I strike the land of Egypt, no destructive blow will come upon you.

"This day shall be a memorial feast for you, which all your generations shall celebrate with pilgrimage to the LORD, as a perpetual institution."

The word of the Lord. ***Thanks be to God.***

RESPONSORIAL PSALM *(Psalm 116:12-13, 15-16bc, 17-18)*
℟ **Our blessing-cup is a communion with the Blood of Christ.**

How shall I make a return to the LORD
    for all the good he has done for me?
The cup of salvation I will take up,
    and I will call upon the name of the LORD. ℟
Precious in the eyes of the LORD
    is the death of his faithful ones.
I am your servant, the son of your handmaid;
    you have loosed my bonds. ℟

To you will I offer sacrifice of thanksgiving,
 and I will call upon the name of the LORD.
My vows to the LORD I will pay
 in the presence of all his people. ℟

SECOND READING *(1 Corinthians 11:23-26)*

Brothers and sisters: I received from the Lord what I also handed on to you, that the Lord Jesus, on the night he was handed over, took bread, and, after he had given thanks, broke it and said, "This is my body that is for you. Do this in remembrance of me." In the same way also the cup, after supper, saying, "This cup is the new covenant in my blood. Do this, as often as you drink it, in remembrance of me." For as often as you eat this bread and drink the cup, you proclaim the death of the Lord until he comes.

 The word of the Lord. *Thanks be to God.*

VERSE BEFORE THE GOSPEL *(John 13:34)*

Glory and praise to you, Lord Jesus Christ! I give you a new commandment, says the Lord: love one another as I have loved you. *Glory and praise to you, Lord Jesus Christ!*

GOSPEL *(John 13:1-15)*

A reading from the holy Gospel according to John.
Glory to you, O Lord.

Before the feast of Passover, Jesus knew that his hour had come to pass from this world to the Father. He loved his own in the world and he loved them to the end. The devil had already induced Judas, son of Simon the Iscariot, to hand him over. So, during supper, fully aware that the Father had put everything into his power and that he had come from God and was returning to God, he rose from supper and took off his outer garments. He took a towel and tied it around his waist. Then he poured water into a basin and began to **wash the disciples' feet**✢ and dry them with the towel around his waist. He came to Simon Peter, who said to him, "Master, are you going to wash my feet?" Jesus answered and said to him, "What I am doing, you do not understand now, but you will understand later." Peter said to him, "You will never wash my feet." Jesus answered him, "Unless I wash you, you will have no inheritance with me." Simon Peter said to him, "Master, then not only my feet, but my hands and head as well." Jesus said to him, "Whoever has bathed has no need except to have his feet washed, for he is clean all over; so you are clean, but not all." For he knew who would betray him; for this reason, he said, "Not all of you are clean."

So when he had washed their feet and put his garments back on and reclined at table again, he said to them, "Do you realize what I have done for you? You call me 'teacher' and 'master,' and rightly so, for indeed I am. If I, therefore, the master and teacher, have washed your feet, you ought to wash one another's feet. I have given you a model to follow, so that as I have done for you, you should also do."

The Gospel of the Lord. ***Praise to you, Lord Jesus Christ.***

THE WASHING OF FEET

During the washing of feet, the assembly may sing an appropriate song.

PRAYER OF THE FAITHFUL

PREPARATION OF GIFTS *(page 16)*

There may be a procession of the faithful in which gifts for the poor may be presented with the bread and wine.

PRAYER OVER THE OFFERINGS

Grant us, O Lord, we pray,
that we may participate worthily in these mysteries,
for whenever the memorial of this sacrifice is celebrated
the work of our redemption is accomplished.
Through Christ our Lord. *Amen.*

PREFACE *(Most Holy Eucharist 1, page 32)*

COMMUNION ANTIPHON *(1 Corinthians 11:24–25)*

This is the Body that will be given up for you; this is the Chalice
of the new covenant in my Blood, says the Lord; do this, whenever you receive it, in memory of me.

PRAYER AFTER COMMUNION

Grant, almighty God,
that, just as we are renewed
by the Supper of your Son in this present age,
so we may enjoy his banquet for all eternity.
Who lives and reigns for ever and ever. *Amen.*

• TAKING A CLOSER LOOK •

✛ **Footwashing** Footwashing was not part of the Passover
ritual, but for John it is clearly an acting out of the deepest meaning
of Eucharist—giving oneself in loving service for others. In the biblical
world, sandals that protected the bottom of the foot did not keep the
dirt away. So a customary sign of hospitality upon entering a house was
to provide water for guests to wash their feet. This was usually the task
of a servant. So, when Jesus assumes the role of the servant instead of
the master that he is, what would normally be considered undignified
and humiliating becomes a sign of his love for his disciples.

The Blessing and Dismissal are omitted tonight.

TRANSFER OF THE MOST BLESSED SACRAMENT

The consecrated eucharistic bread is carried through the church in procession to the place of repose. During the procession, the hymn "Pange lingua" or another eucharistic song is sung.

When the procession reaches the place of repose, the celebrant incenses the eucharistic bread, while the "Tantum ergo" (stanzas 5-6 of the "Pange lingua") is sung. The tabernacle of repose is then closed.

After a few moments of silent adoration, the priests and ministers of the altar leave. The faithful are encouraged to continue adoration before the Blessed Sacrament for a suitable period of time through the evening and night, but there should be no solemn adoration after midnight. ✠

• RESPONDING TO THE WORD •

The sacrifice of the passover lamb expresses the people's dedication to God and desire to share life with God.

➡ *What sacrifice must I make to rededicate myself to God today?*

Jesus gives his blood so we can live more fully with God.

➡ *What can I do to participate more fully in the celebration of the Eucharist?*

Jesus gives himself and his life in service of others.

➡ *What can I do to be of greater service for those who are poor and in need?*

April 10

Embracing our beliefs

Good Friday leaves me with a heavy heart—a reminder of times when, like Peter, I have not stood strong in my beliefs.

I am in a profession that constantly challenges my faith. It's easy to lose sight of God when you tell a mother that you could not save her son. It's easy to feel persecuted when discussions around end of life care arise. It's easy, when asked if I am Catholic, to shy away from the question just as Peter denied knowing Jesus.

So what is it that brings me back? It's the mother that, when faced with the loss of her son, takes my hand and asks me to join her in prayer. It's the patient that, when challenged by a palliative diagnosis, tells me that he will be ready when it is on God's watch. It's the patient struggling with an addiction that asks me if I believe in forgiveness. These inspiring individuals who have clung to their faith in the darkest hours are what remind me to embrace my own beliefs.

The gospel of the Lord's passion is ultimately the narrative that defines our faith. However, for me it serves as a reminder that at times we will question our beliefs; and, like Peter, when we find our way back, we will be the rock on which our Church continues to be built.

■ **JULIANNA DEUTSCHER**

No Mass is celebrated today. The celebration of the Lord's Passion consists of three parts: the Liturgy of the Word, the Adoration of the Holy Cross, and the Reception of Holy Communion.

PRAYER

Remember your mercies, O Lord,
and with your eternal protection sanctify your servants,
for whom Christ your Son,
by the shedding of his Blood,
established the Paschal Mystery.
Who lives and reigns for ever and ever. *Amen.*

Or

O God, who by the Passion of Christ your Son, our Lord,
abolished the death inherited from ancient sin
by every succeeding generation,
grant that just as, being conformed to him,
we have borne by the law of nature
the image of the man of earth,
so by the sanctification of grace
we may bear the image of the Man of heaven.
Through Christ our Lord. *Amen.*

LITURGY OF THE WORD

FIRST READING *(Isaiah 52:13—53:12)*

See, my servant shall prosper,
he shall be raised high and greatly exalted.
Even as many were amazed at him—

so marred was his look beyond human semblance
 and his appearance beyond that of the sons of man—
so shall he startle many nations,
 because of him kings shall stand speechless;
for those who have not been told shall see,
 those who have not heard shall ponder it.

Who would believe what we have heard?
 To whom has the arm of the LORD been revealed?
He grew up like a sapling before him,
 like a shoot from the parched earth;
there was in him no stately bearing to make us look at him,
 nor appearance that would attract us to him.
He was spurned and avoided by people,
 a man of suffering, accustomed to infirmity,
one of those from whom people hide their faces,
 spurned, and we held him in no esteem.

Yet it was our infirmities that he bore,
 our sufferings that he endured,
while we thought of him as stricken,
 as one smitten by God and afflicted.
But he was pierced for our offenses,
 crushed for our sins;
upon him was the chastisement that makes us whole,
 by his stripes we were healed.
We had all gone astray like sheep,
 each following his own way;
but the LORD laid upon him
 the guilt of us all.

Though he was harshly treated, he submitted
     and opened not his mouth;
like a lamb led to the slaughter
     or a sheep before the shearers,
     he was silent and opened not his mouth.
Oppressed and condemned, he was taken away,
     and who would have thought any more of his destiny?
When he was cut off from the land of the living,
     and smitten for the sin of his people,
a grave was assigned him among the wicked
     and a burial place with evildoers,
though he had done no wrong
     nor spoken any falsehood.
But the LORD was pleased
     to crush him in infirmity.

If he gives his life as an offering for sin,
     he shall see his descendants in a long life,
     and the will of the LORD shall be accomplished through him.

Because of his affliction
     he shall see the light in fullness of days;
through his suffering, my servant shall justify many,
     and their guilt he shall bear.
Therefore I will give him his portion among the great,
     and he shall divide the spoils with the mighty,
because he surrendered himself to death
     and was counted among the wicked;
and he shall take away the sins of many,
     and win pardon for their offenses.
The word of the Lord. ***Thanks be to God.***

RESPONSORIAL PSALM *(Psalm 31:2, 6, 12-13, 15-16, 17, 25)*

℟. **Father, into your hands I commend my spirit.**

In you, O LORD, I take refuge;
    let me never be put to shame.
In your justice rescue me.
Into your hands I commend my spirit;
    you will redeem me, O LORD, O faithful God. ℟.

For all my foes I am an object of reproach,
    a laughingstock to my neighbors, and a dread to my friends;
    they who see me abroad flee from me.
I am forgotten like the unremembered dead;
    I am like a dish that is broken. ℟.

But my trust is in you, O LORD;
    I say, "You are my God.
In your hands is my destiny; rescue me
    from the clutches of my enemies and my persecutors." ℟.

Let your face shine upon your servant;
    save me in your kindness.
Take courage and be stouthearted,
    all you who hope in the Lord. ℟.

SECOND READING *(Hebrews 4:14-16; 5:7-9)*

Brothers and sisters: Since we have a great high priest who has passed through the heavens, Jesus, the Son of God, let us hold fast to our confession. For we do not have a high priest who is unable to sympathize with our weaknesses, but one who has similarly been tested in every way, yet without sin. So let us confidently approach the throne of grace to receive mercy and to find grace for timely help.

In the days when Christ was in the flesh, he offered prayers and supplications with loud cries and tears to the one who was able to save him from death, and he was heard because of his reverence. Son though he was, he learned obedience from what he suffered; and when he was made perfect, he became the source of eternal salvation for all who obey him.

The word of the Lord. *Thanks be to God.*

VERSE BEFORE THE GOSPEL *(Philippians 2:8–9)*
Glory and praise to you, Lord Jesus Christ! Christ became obedient to the point of death, even death on a cross. Because of this, God greatly exalted him and bestowed on him the name which is above every other name. *Glory and praise to you, Lord Jesus Christ!*

GOSPEL *(John 18:1—19:42)*
Several readers may proclaim the passion narrative today. **N** *indicates the narrator,* ✝ *the words of Jesus,* **V** *a voice, and* **C** *the crowd.*

N The Passion of our Lord Jesus Christ according to John.

Jesus went out with his disciples across the Kidron valley to where there was a garden, into which he and his disciples entered. Judas his betrayer also knew the place, because Jesus had often met there with his disciples. So Judas got a band of soldiers and guards from the chief priests and the Pharisees and went there with lanterns, torches, and weapons. Jesus, knowing everything that was going to happen to him, went out and said to them,

✝ "Whom are you looking for?"

N They answered him,

C "Jesus the Nazorean.*"

N He said to them,

† "I AM."

N Judas his betrayer was also with them. When he said to them, "I AM," they turned away and fell to the ground. So he again asked them,

† "Whom are you looking for?"

N They said,

C "Jesus the Nazorean."

N Jesus answered,

† "I told you that I AM. So if you are looking for me, let these men go."

N This was to fulfill what he had said, "I have not lost any of those you gave me." Then Simon Peter, who had a sword, drew it, struck the high priest's slave, and cut off his right ear. The slave's name was Malchus.* Jesus said to Peter,

† "Put your sword into its scabbard. Shall I not drink the cup that the Father gave me?"

N So the band of soldiers, the tribune, and the Jewish guards seized Jesus, bound him, and brought him to Annas first. He was the father-in-law of Caiaphas,* who was high priest that year. It was Caiaphas who had counseled the Jews that it was better that one man should die rather than the people.

Simon Peter and another disciple followed Jesus. Now the other disciple was known to the high priest, and he entered the courtyard of the high priest with Jesus. But Peter stood at the gate outside. So the other disciple, the acquaintance of the high priest, went out and spoke to the gatekeeper and brought Peter in. Then the maid who was the gatekeeper said to Peter,

C "You are not one of this man's disciples, are you?"

N He said,

V "I am not."

N Now the slaves and the guards were standing around a charcoal fire that they had made, because it was cold, and were warming themselves. Peter was also standing there keeping warm.

The high priest questioned Jesus about his disciples and about his doctrine. Jesus answered him,

† "I have spoken publicly to the world. I have always taught in a synagogue or in the temple area where all the Jews gather, and in secret I have said nothing. Why ask me? Ask those who heard me what I said to them. They know what I said."

N When he had said this, one of the temple guards standing there struck Jesus and said,

V "Is this the way you answer the high priest?"

N Jesus answered him,

† "If I have spoken wrongly, testify to the wrong; but if I have spoken rightly, why do you strike me?"

N Then Annas sent him bound to Caiaphas the high priest.

Now Simon Peter was standing there keeping warm. And they said to him,

C "You are not one of his disciples, are you?"

N He denied it and said,

V "I am not."

N One of the slaves of the high priest, a relative of the one whose ear Peter had cut off, said,

C "Didn't I see you in the garden with him?"

N Again Peter denied it. And immediately the cock crowed.
Then they brought Jesus from Caiaphas to the praetorium.*
It was morning. And they themselves did not enter the praetorium, in order not to be defiled so that they could eat the Passover. So Pilate came out to them and said,

V "What charge do you bring against this man?"

N They answered and said to him,

C "If he were not a criminal, we would not have handed him over to you."

N At this, Pilate said to them,

V "Take him yourselves, and judge him according to your law."

N The Jews answered him,

C "We do not have the right to execute anyone,"

N in order that the word of Jesus might be fulfilled that he said indicating the kind of death he would die. So Pilate went back into the praetorium and summoned Jesus and said to him,

V "Are you the King of the Jews?"

N Jesus answered,

† "Do you say this on your own or have others told you about me?"

N Pilate answered,

V "I am not a Jew, am I? Your own nation and the chief priests handed you over to me. What have you done?"

N Jesus answered,

† "My kingdom does not belong to this world. If my kingdom did belong to this world, my attendants would be fighting to keep me from being handed over to the Jews. But as it is, my kingdom is not here."

N So Pilate said to him,

V "Then you are a king?"

N Jesus answered,

† "You say I am a king. For this I was born and for this I came into the world, to testify to the truth. Everyone who belongs to the truth listens to my voice."

N Pilate said to him,

V "What is truth?"

N   When he had said this, he again went out to the Jews and said to them,

V "I find no guilt in him. But you have a custom that I release one prisoner to you at Passover. Do you want me to release to you the King of the Jews?"

N They cried out again,

C "Not this one but Barabbas!*"

N Now Barabbas was a revolutionary.

Then Pilate took Jesus and had him scourged. And the soldiers wove a crown out of thorns and placed it on his head, and clothed him in a purple cloak, and they came to him and said,

C "Hail, King of the Jews!"

N And they struck him repeatedly. Once more Pilate went out and said to them,

V "Look, I am bringing him out to you, so that you may know that I find no guilt in him."

N So Jesus came out, wearing the crown of thorns and the purple cloak. And Pilate said to them,

V "Behold, the man!"

N When the chief priests and the guards saw him they cried out,

C "Crucify him, crucify him!"✝

N Pilate said to them,

V "Take him yourselves and crucify him. I find no guilt in him."

N The Jews answered,

C "We have a law, and according to that law he ought to die, because he made himself the Son of God."

N Now when Pilate heard this statement, he became even more afraid, and went back into the praetorium and said to Jesus,

V "Where are you from?"

N Jesus did not answer him. So Pilate said to him,

V "Do you not speak to me? Do you not know that I have power to release you and I have power to crucify you?"

N Jesus answered him,

† "You would have no power over me if it had not been given to you from above. For this reason the one who handed me over to you has the greater sin."

N Consequently, Pilate tried to release him; but the Jews cried out,

C **"If you release him, you are not a Friend of Caesar.***
Everyone who makes himself a king opposes Caesar."

N   When Pilate heard these words he brought Jesus out and seated him on the judge's bench in the place called Stone Pavement, in Hebrew, Gabbatha. It was preparation day for Passover, and it was about noon. And he said to the Jews,

V "Behold, your king!"

N They cried out,

C **"Take him away, take him away! Crucify him!"**

N Pilate said to them,

V "Shall I crucify your king?"

N The chief priests answered,

C **"We have no king but Caesar."**

N Then he handed him over to them to be crucified.
   So they took Jesus, and, carrying the cross himself, he went

out to what is called the Place of the Skull, in Hebrew, Golgotha.* There they crucified him, and with him two others, one on either side, with Jesus in the middle. Pilate also had an inscription written and put on the cross. It read, "Jesus the Nazorean, the King of the Jews." Now many of the Jews read this inscription, because the place where Jesus was crucified was near the city; and it was written in Hebrew, Latin, and Greek. So the chief priests of the Jews said to Pilate,

C "Do not write 'The King of the Jews,' but that he said, 'I am the King of the Jews.'"

N Pilate answered,

V "What I have written, I have written."

N When the soldiers had crucified Jesus, they took his clothes and divided them into four shares, a share for each soldier. They also took his tunic, but the tunic was seamless, woven in one piece from the top down. So they said to one another,

C "Let's not tear it, but cast lots for it to see whose it will be,"

N in order that the passage of Scripture might be fulfilled that says:

> They divided my garments among them,
> and for my vesture they cast lots.

N This is what the soldiers did. Standing by the cross of Jesus were his mother and his mother's sister, Mary the wife of Clopas, and Mary of Magdala. When Jesus saw his mother and the disciple there whom he loved he said to his mother,

† "Woman, behold, your son."

N Then he said to the disciple,

✝ "Behold, your mother."

N And from that hour the disciple took her into his home.
　　After this, aware that everything was now finished, in order
that the Scripture might be fulfilled, Jesus said,

✝ "I thirst."

N There was a vessel filled with common wine. So they put a
sponge soaked in wine on a sprig of hyssop* and put it up to his
mouth. When Jesus had taken the wine, he said,

✝ "It is finished."

N And bowing his head, he handed over the spirit.

Here all kneel and pause for a short time.

N Now since it was preparation day, in order that the bodies
might not remain on the cross on the sabbath, for the sabbath
day of that week was a solemn one, the Jews asked Pilate that
their legs be broken and that they be taken down. So the soldiers came and broke the legs of the first and then of the other
one who was crucified with Jesus. But when they came to Jesus
and saw that he was already dead, they did not break his legs,
but one soldier thrust his lance into his side, and immediately
blood and water flowed out. An eyewitness has testified, and
his testimony is true; he knows that he is speaking the truth, so
that you also may come to believe. For this happened so that
the Scripture passage might be fulfilled:
　　Not a bone of it will be broken.

And again another passage says:

They will look upon him whom they have pierced.

After this, Joseph of Arimathea,* secretly a disciple of Jesus for fear of the Jews, asked Pilate if he could remove the body of Jesus. And Pilate permitted it. So he came and took his body. Nicodemus, the one who had first come to him at night, also came bringing a mixture of myrrh* and aloes weighing about one hundred pounds. They took the body of Jesus and bound it with burial cloths along with the spices, according to the Jewish burial custom. Now in the place where he had been crucified there was a garden, and in the garden a new tomb, in which no one had yet been buried. So they laid Jesus there because of the Jewish preparation day; for the tomb was close by. The Gospel of the Lord. *Praise to you, Lord Jesus Christ.*

PRAYER OF THE FAITHFUL
For Holy Church
Let us pray, dearly beloved, for the holy Church of God,
that our God and Lord be pleased to give her peace,
to guard her and to unite her throughout the whole world
and grant that, leading our life in tranquility and quiet,
we may glorify God the Father almighty.
(Prayer in silence.)
Almighty ever-living God,
who in Christ revealed your glory to all the nations,
watch over the works of your mercy,
that your Church, spread throughout all the world,
may persevere with steadfast faith in confessing your name.
Through Christ our Lord. *Amen.*

For the Pope

Let us pray also for our most Holy Father Pope N.,
that our God and Lord,
who chose him for the Order of Bishops,
may keep him safe and unharmed for the Lord's holy Church,
to govern the holy People of God.
(Prayer in silence.)
Almighty ever-living God,
by whose decree all things are founded,
look with favor on our prayers
and in your kindness protect the Pope chosen for us,
that, under him, the Christian people,
governed by you their maker,
may grow in merit by reason of their faith.
Through Christ our Lord. *Amen.*

For all orders and degrees of the faithful

Let us pray also for our Bishop N.,
for all Bishops, Priests, and Deacons of the Church
and for the whole of the faithful people.
(Prayer in silence.)
Almighty ever-living God,
by whose Spirit the whole body of the Church
is sanctified and governed,
hear our humble prayer for your ministers,
that, by the gift of your grace,
all may serve you faithfully.
Through Christ our Lord. *Amen.*

For catechumens

Let us pray also for (our) catechumens,
that our God and Lord
may open wide the ears of their inmost hearts
and unlock the gates of his mercy,
that, having received forgiveness of all their sins
through the waters of rebirth,
they, too, may be one with Christ Jesus our Lord.
(Prayer in silence.)
Almighty ever-living God,
who make your Church ever fruitful with new offspring,
increase the faith and understanding of (our) catechumens,
that, reborn in the font of Baptism,
they may be added to the number of your adopted children.
Through Christ our Lord. *Amen.*

For the unity of Christians

Let us pray also for all our brothers and sisters who believe in Christ,
that our God and Lord may be pleased,
as they live the truth,
to gather them together and keep them in his one Church.
(Prayer in silence.)
Almighty ever-living God,
who gather what is scattered
and keep together what you have gathered,
look kindly on the flock of your Son,
that those whom one Baptism has consecrated
may be joined together by integrity of faith
and united in the bond of charity.
Through Christ our Lord. *Amen.*

For the Jewish people

Let us pray also for the Jewish people,
to whom the Lord our God spoke first,
that he may grant them to advance in love of his name
and in faithfulness to his covenant.
(Prayer in silence.)
Almighty ever-living God,
who bestowed your promises on Abraham and his descendants,
graciously hear the prayers of your Church,
that the people you first made your own
may attain the fullness of redemption.
Through Christ our Lord. ***Amen.***

For those who do not believe in Christ

Let us pray also for those who do not believe in Christ,
that, enlightened by the Holy Spirit,
they, too, may enter on the way of salvation.
(Prayer in silence.)
Almighty ever-living God,
grant to those who do not confess Christ
that, by walking before you with a sincere heart,
they may find the truth
and that we ourselves, being constant in mutual love
and striving to understand more fully the mystery of your life,
may be made more perfect witnesses to your love in the world.
Through Christ our Lord. ***Amen.***

For those who do not believe in God

Let us pray also for those who do not acknowledge God,
that, following what is right in sincerity of heart,

they may find the way to God himself.
(Prayer in silence.)
Almighty ever-living God,
who created all people
to seek you always by desiring you
and, by finding you, come to rest,
grant, we pray,
that, despite every harmful obstacle,
all may recognize the signs of your fatherly love
and the witness of the good works
done by those who believe in you,
and so in gladness confess you,
the one true God and Father of our human race.
Through Christ our Lord. *Amen.*

For those in public office

Let us pray also for those in public office,
that our God and Lord
may direct their minds and hearts according to his will
for the true peace and freedom of all.
(Prayer in silence.)
Almighty ever-living God,
in whose hand lies every human heart
and the rights of peoples,
look with favor, we pray,
on those who govern with authority over us,
that throughout the whole world,
the prosperity of peoples,
the assurance of peace,
and freedom of religion

may through your gift be made secure.
Through Christ our Lord. *Amen.*

For those in tribulation
Let us pray, dearly beloved,
to God the Father almighty,
that he may cleanse the world of all errors,
banish disease, drive out hunger,
unlock prisons, loosen fetters,
granting to travelers safety, to pilgrims return,
health to the sick, and salvation to the dying.
(Prayer in silence.)
Almighty ever-living God,
comfort of mourners, strength of all who toil,
may the prayers of those who cry out in any tribulation
come before you,
that all may rejoice,
because in their hour of need
your mercy was at hand.
Through Christ our Lord. *Amen.*

ADORATION OF THE HOLY CROSS

Three times the celebrant invites the assembly to proclaim its faith:

Behold the wood of the Cross,
on which hung the salvation of the world.
Come, let us adore.

After each response all venerate the cross briefly in silence. After the third response, the people approach to venerate the cross. They make a simple

*genuflection or perform some other appropriate sign of reverence
according to local custom.*

*During the veneration, appropriate songs may be sung. All who have
venerated the cross return to their places and sit. Where large numbers of
people make individual veneration difficult, the celebrant may raise the
cross briefly for all to venerate in silence.*

HOLY COMMUNION

THE LORD'S PRAYER *(page 53)*

PRAYER AFTER COMMUNION
Almighty ever-living God,
who have restored us to life
by the blessed Death and Resurrection of your Christ,
preserve in us the work of your mercy,
that, by partaking of this mystery,
we may have a life unceasingly devoted to you.
Through Christ our Lord. *Amen.*

● TAKING A CLOSER LOOK ●

✠ **Crucify** Crucifixion was the most painful torture the ancient world
had devised. Besides the pain from scourging, beating, loss of blood, and
lack of vital fluids, when one's arms and legs were fixed to a cross by tying
with rope or nailing, the victim began a slow process of asphyxiation. As
the muscles of the upper body rigidly tightened in prolonged contraction,
breathing became more and more difficult and painful. The only relief was
to push oneself up by using one's legs. When the legs could no longer
lift the body up, breathing eventually stopped and the victim died. Thus
death could be hastened by breaking the victim's legs (John 19:31-32).

PRAYER OVER THE PEOPLE

May abundant blessing, O Lord, we pray,
descend upon your people,
who have honored the Death of your Son
in the hope of their resurrection:
may pardon come,
comfort be given,
holy faith increase,
and everlasting redemption be made secure.
Through Christ our Lord. *Amen.*

All depart in silence. ❖

❖ RESPONDING TO THE WORD ❖

Isaiah's suffering servant foreshadows the rejection and suffering of Jesus.	Jesus teaches us by his suffering.	John's passion story traces Jesus' victory over sin and death.
➡ What suffering is most difficult for me to deal with now in my life? Why?	➡ What have I learned from Jesus' suffering?	➡ Which event in today's gospel is most important to me right now?

April 11

APR
11

We share the same mission

The two Marys in the gospel we hear this Easter night are the first evangelists. Jewish women living under Roman occupation, they risked everything to stand nearby as Jesus was beaten, mocked, nailed to a cross, and then died. Two women alone, they came to his tomb as soon as the Sabbath was complete, even though Roman guards were posted there. They carried Jesus' instructions to Peter and the other disciples who were still in hiding.

We don't live in 33 AD in Galilee, and our world is a far different one. Yet the good news of Jesus Christ is still the best news in the world! The God who made us, who loves us, who yearns for us to enter into Divine Love and to share it with others, is the same God who called the two Marys to their mission.

Each of us receives the good news from another, someone who cares about us, walks with us, accompanies us on our journey. Each of us is to go and do likewise. Today's Christian community shares the same mission as Mary Magdalene, the other Mary, the apostles, and every follower of Jesus Christ since that day at the tomb. Our Easter mission is to "Go and tell." And when necessary, use words.

◼ **MARILYN J. SWEET**

There is no Mass celebrated during the day on Holy Saturday. But during the night, we anticipate Jesus' resurrection with one of the most ancient rites—a solemn vigil, which leads into the celebration of the fifty days of the Easter Season.

The Easter Vigil is arranged in four parts: the Service of Light (Lucernarium), the Liturgy of the Word, the Liturgy of Baptism, and the Liturgy of the Eucharist.

LUCERNARIUM

BLESSING OF THE FIRE

Dear brethren (brothers and sisters),
on this most sacred night,
in which our Lord Jesus Christ
passed over from death to life,
the Church calls upon her sons and daughters,
scattered throughout the world,
to come together to watch and pray.
If we keep the memorial
of the Lord's paschal solemnity in this way,
listening to his word and celebrating his mysteries,
then we shall have the sure hope
of sharing his triumph over death
and living with him in God.

Let us pray.

O God, who through your Son
bestowed upon the faithful the fire of your glory,

sanctify this new fire, we pray,
and grant that,
by these paschal celebrations,
we may be so inflamed with heavenly desires,
that with minds made pure
we may attain festivities of unending splendor.
Through Christ our Lord. *Amen.*

PREPARATION OF THE CANDLE

The celebrant cuts a cross in the Easter candle and traces the Greek letters
alpha (A) and omega (Ω) and the numerals 2020, saying:

Christ yesterday and today;
the Beginning and the End;
the Alpha; and the Omega.
All time belongs to him;
and all the ages.
To him be glory and power;
through every age and for ever. *Amen.*

When the marks have been made, the celebrant may insert five grains of
incense in the candle, saying:

By his holy and glorious wounds,
may Christ the Lord guard us and protect us. *Amen.*

LIGHTING OF THE CANDLE

The celebrant lights the Easter candle from the new fire, saying:

May the light of Christ rising in glory
dispel the darkness of our hearts and minds.

PROCESSION WITH THE EASTER CANDLE

The priest or deacon takes the Easter candle and, three times during the procession to the altar, lifts it high and sings alone. Then the people respond.

The Light of Christ.
Thanks be to God.

EASTER PROCLAMATION *(Exsultet)*

For the shorter version, omit the indented parts in brackets.
A lay cantor omits the parts in parentheses.

Exult, let them exult, the hosts of heaven,
exult, let Angel ministers of God exult,
let the trumpet of salvation
sound aloud our mighty King's triumph!
Be glad, let earth be glad, as glory floods her,
ablaze with light from her eternal King,
let all corners of the earth be glad,
knowing an end to gloom and darkness.
Rejoice, let Mother Church also rejoice,
arrayed with the lightning of his glory,
let this holy building shake with joy,
filled with the mighty voices of the peoples.

[[(Therefore, dearest friends,
standing in the awesome glory of this holy light,
invoke with me, I ask you,
the mercy of God almighty,
that he, who has been pleased to number me,
though unworthy, among the Levites,
may pour into me his light unshadowed,
that I may sing this candle's perfect praises).]

(The Lord be with you.
And with your spirit.)
Lift up your hearts.
We lift them up to the Lord.
Let us give thanks to the Lord our God.
It is right and just.

It is truly right and just,
with ardent love of mind and heart
and with devoted service of our voice,
to acclaim our God invisible, the almighty Father,
and Jesus Christ, our Lord, his Son, his Only Begotten.

Who for our sake paid Adam's debt to the eternal Father,
and, pouring out his own dear Blood,
wiped clean the record of our ancient sinfulness.

These then are the feasts of Passover,
in which is slain the Lamb, the one true Lamb,
whose Blood anoints the doorposts of believers.

This is the night,
when once you led our forebears, Israel's children,
from slavery in Egypt
and made them pass dry-shod through the Red Sea.

This is the night
that with a pillar of fire
banished the darkness of sin.

This is the night
that even now, throughout the world,
sets Christian believers apart from worldly vices

and from the gloom of sin,
leading them to grace
and joining them to his holy ones.

This is the night,
when Christ broke the prison-bars of death
and rose victorious from the underworld.

[Our birth would have been no gain,
had we not been redeemed.]
O wonder of your humble care for us!
O love, O charity beyond all telling,
to ransom a slave you gave away your Son!

O truly necessary sin of Adam,
destroyed completely by the Death of Christ!

O happy fault
that earned so great, so glorious a Redeemer!

[O truly blessed night,
worthy alone to know the time and hour
when Christ rose from the underworld!

This is the night
of which it is written:
The night shall be as bright as day,
dazzling is the night for me,
and full of gladness.]

The sanctifying power of this night
dispels wickedness, washes faults away,
restores innocence to the fallen, and joy to mourners,
[drives out hatred, fosters concord, and brings down the mighty.]

The longer version ending:

On this, your night of grace, O holy Father,
accept this candle, a solemn offering,
the work of bees and of your servants' hands,
an evening sacrifice of praise,
this gift from your most holy Church.

But now we know the praises of this pillar,
which glowing fire ignites for God's honor,
a fire into many flames divided,
yet never dimmed by sharing of its light,
for it is fed by melting wax,
drawn out by mother bees
to build a torch so precious.

O truly blessed night,
when things of heaven are wed to those of earth,
and divine to the human.

Therefore, O Lord,
we pray you that this candle,
hallowed to the honor of your name,
may persevere undimmed,
to overcome the darkness of this night.
Receive it as a pleasing fragrance,
and let it mingle with the lights of heaven.
May this flame be found still burning
by the Morning Star:
the one Morning Star who never sets,
Christ your Son,
who, coming back from death's domain,

has shed his peaceful light on humanity,
and lives and reigns for ever and ever. ***Amen.***

The shorter version ending:

O truly blessed night,
when things of heaven are wed to those of earth
and divine to the human.

On this, your night of grace, O holy Father,
accept this candle, a solemn offering,
the work of bees and of your servants' hands,
an evening sacrifice of praise,
this gift from your most holy Church.

Therefore, O Lord,
we pray you that this candle,
hallowed to the honor of your name,
may persevere undimmed,
to overcome the darkness of this night.
Receive it as a pleasing fragrance,
and let it mingle with the lights of heaven.
May this flame be found still burning
by the Morning Star:
the one Morning Star who never sets,
Christ your Son,
who, coming back from death's domain,
has shed his peaceful light on humanity,
and lives and reigns for ever and ever. ***Amen.***

LITURGY OF THE WORD

Dear brethren (brothers and sisters),
now that we have begun our solemn Vigil,
let us listen with quiet hearts to the Word of God.
Let us meditate on how God in times past saved his people
and in these, the last days, has sent us his Son as our Redeemer.
Let us pray that our God may complete this paschal work
   of salvation
by the fullness of redemption.

FIRST READING *(Genesis 1:1—2:2)*
For the shorter version, omit the indented parts in brackets.

In the beginning, when God created the heavens and the earth,
[the earth was a formless wasteland, and darkness covered the
abyss, while a mighty wind swept over the waters.

   Then God said, "Let there be light," and there was light. God
saw how good the light was. God then separated the light from
the darkness. God called the light "day," and the darkness he
called "night." Thus evening came, and morning followed—the
first day.

   Then God said, "Let there be a dome in the middle of the
waters, to separate one body of water from the other." And
so it happened: God made the dome, and it separated the
water above the dome from the water below it. God called
the dome "the sky." Evening came, and morning followed—
the second day.

   Then God said, "Let the water under the sky be gathered
into a single basin, so that the dry land may appear." And so
it happened: the water under the sky was gathered into its

basin, and the dry land appeared. God called the dry land "the earth," and the basin of the water he called "the sea." God saw how good it was. Then God said, "Let the earth bring forth vegetation: every kind of plant that bears seed and every kind of fruit tree on earth that bears fruit with its seed in it." And so it happened: the earth brought forth every kind of plant that bears seed and every kind of fruit tree on earth that bears fruit with its seed in it. God saw how good it was. Evening came, and morning followed—the third day.

Then God said: "Let there be lights in the dome of the sky, to separate day from night. Let them mark the fixed times, the days and the years, and serve as luminaries in the dome of the sky, to shed light upon the earth." And so it happened: God made the two great lights, the greater one to govern the day, and the lesser one to govern the night; and he made the stars. God set them in the dome of the sky, to shed light upon the earth, to govern the day and the night, and to separate the light from the darkness. God saw how good it was. Evening came, and morning followed—the fourth day.

Then God said, "Let the water teem with an abundance of living creatures, and on the earth let birds fly beneath the dome of the sky." And so it happened: God created the great sea monsters and all kinds of swimming creatures with which the water teems, and all kinds of winged birds. God saw how good it was, and God blessed them, saying, "Be fertile, multiply, and fill the water of the seas; and let the birds multiply on the earth." Evening came, and morning followed—the fifth day.

Then God said, "Let the earth bring forth all kinds of living creatures: cattle, creeping things, and wild animals of all kinds." And so it happened: God made all kinds of wild animals, all kinds of cattle, and all kinds of creeping things of the earth. God saw how good it was. Then]

God said: "Let us make man in our image, after our likeness. Let them have dominion over the fish of the sea, the birds of the air, and the cattle, and over all the wild animals and all the creatures that crawl on the ground."

God created man in his image;
> in the image of God he created him;
> male and female he created them.

God blessed them, saying: "Be fertile and multiply; fill the earth and subdue it. Have dominion over the fish of the sea, the birds of the air, and all the living things that move on the earth." God also said: "See, I give you every seed-bearing plant all over the earth and every tree that has seed-bearing fruit on it to be your food; and to all the animals of the land, all the birds of the air, and all the living creatures that crawl on the ground, I give all the green plants for food." And so it happened. God looked at everything he had made, and he found it very good.

[Evening came, and morning followed—the sixth day.

Thus the heavens and the earth and all their array were completed. Since on the seventh day God was finished with the work he had been doing, he rested on the seventh day from all the work he had undertaken.]

The word of the Lord. ***Thanks be to God.***

An alternate psalm follows.

RESPONSORIAL PSALM *(Psalm 104:1-2, 5-6, 10, 12, 13-14, 24, 35)*
R⃰ **Lord, send out your Spirit, and renew the face of the earth.**

Bless the LORD, O my soul!

O Lord, my God, you are great indeed!
You are clothed with majesty and glory,
 robed in light as with a cloak.
℟ **Lord, send out your Spirit, and renew the face of the earth.**
You fixed the earth upon its foundation,
 not to be moved forever;
with the ocean, as with a garment, you covered it;
 above the mountains the waters stood. ℟
You send forth springs into the watercourses
 that wind among the mountains.
Beside them the birds of heaven dwell;
 from among the branches they send forth their song. ℟
You water the mountains from your palace;
 the earth is replete with the fruit of your works.
You raise grass for the cattle,
 and vegetation for man's use,
producing bread from the earth. ℟
How manifold are your works, O Lord!
 In wisdom you have wrought them all—
the earth is full of your creatures.
 Bless the Lord, O my soul! ℟

OR

RESPONSORIAL PSALM *(Psalm 33:4-5, 6-7, 12-13, 20 and 22)*
℟ **The earth is full of the goodness of the Lord.**

Upright is the word of the Lord,
 and all his works are trustworthy.
He loves justice and right;
 of the kindness of the Lord the earth is full. ℟
By the word of the Lord the heavens were made;

by the breath of his mouth all their host.
He gathers the waters of the sea as in a flask;
    in cellars he confines the deep. ℟
Blessed the nation whose God is the LORD,
    the people he has chosen for his own inheritance.
From heaven the LORD looks down;
    he sees all mankind. ℟
Our soul waits for the LORD,
    who is our help and our shield.
May your kindness, O LORD, be upon us
    who have put our hope in you. ℟

PRAYER

Almighty ever-living God,
who are wonderful in the ordering of all your works,
may those you have redeemed understand
that there exists nothing more marvelous
than the world's creation in the beginning
except that, at the end of the ages,
Christ our Passover has been sacrificed.
Who lives and reigns for ever and ever. *Amen.*

Or

O God, who wonderfully created human nature
and still more wonderfully redeemed it,
grant us, we pray,
to set our minds against the enticements of sin,
that we may merit to attain eternal joys.
Through Christ our Lord. *Amen.*

SECOND READING *(Genesis 22:1–18)*
For the shorter version, omit the indented parts in brackets.

God put Abraham to the test. He called to him, "Abraham!" "Here I am," he replied. Then God said: "Take your son Isaac, your only one, whom you love, and go to the land of Moriah. There you shall offer him up as a holocaust on a height that I will point out to you."

[Early the next morning Abraham saddled his donkey, took with him his son Isaac and two of his servants as well, and with the wood that he had cut for the holocaust, set out for the place of which God had told him.

On the third day Abraham got sight of the place from afar. Then he said to his servants: "Both of you stay here with the donkey, while the boy and I go on over yonder. We will worship and then come back to you." Thereupon Abraham took the wood for the holocaust and laid it on his son Isaac's shoulders, while he himself carried the fire and the knife. As the two walked on together, Isaac spoke to his father Abraham: "Father!" Isaac said. "Yes, son," he replied. Isaac continued, "Here are the fire and the wood, but where is the sheep for the holocaust?" "Son," Abraham answered, "God himself will provide the sheep for the holocaust." Then the two continued going forward.]

When they came to the place of which God had told him, Abraham built an altar there and arranged the wood on it.

[Next he tied up his son Isaac, and put him on top of the wood on the altar.]

Then he reached out and took the knife to slaughter his son. But the LORD's messenger called to him from heaven, "Abraham, Abraham!" "Here I am," he answered. "Do not lay your hand on the boy," said the messenger. "Do not do the least thing to him.

I know now how devoted you are to God, since you did not withhold from me your own beloved son." As Abraham looked about, he spied a ram caught by its horns in the thicket. So he went and took the ram and offered it up as a holocaust in place of his son.

[Abraham named the site Yahweh-yireh;* hence people now say, "On the mountain the LORD will see."]

Again the LORD's messenger called to Abraham from heaven and said: "I swear by myself, declares the LORD, that because you acted as you did in not withholding from me your beloved son, I will bless you abundantly and make your descendants as countless as the stars of the sky and the sands of the seashore; your descendants shall take possession of the gates of their enemies, and in your descendants all the nations of the earth shall find blessing—all this because you obeyed my command."

The word of the Lord. *Thanks be to God.*

RESPONSORIAL PSALM *(Psalm 16:5, 8, 9-10, 11)*

℟ **You are my inheritance, O Lord.**

O LORD, my allotted portion and my cup,
  you it is who hold fast my lot.
I set the LORD ever before me;
  with him at my right hand I shall not be disturbed. ℟
Therefore my heart is glad and my soul rejoices,
  my body, too, abides in confidence;
because you will not abandon my soul to the netherworld,
  nor will you suffer your faithful one to undergo corruption. ℟
You will show me the path to life,
  fullness of joys in your presence,
  the delights at your right hand forever. ℟

PRAYER

O God, supreme Father of the faithful,
who increase the children of your promise
by pouring out the grace of adoption
throughout the whole world
and who through the Paschal Mystery
make your servant Abraham father of nations,
as once you swore,
grant, we pray,
that your peoples may enter worthily
into the grace to which you call them.
Through Christ our Lord. *Amen.*

THIRD READING *(Exodus 14:15—15:1)*

The LORD said to Moses, "Why are you crying out to me? Tell the Israelites to go forward. And you, lift up your staff and, with hand outstretched over the sea, split the sea in two, that the Israelites may pass through it on dry land. But I will make the Egyptians so obstinate that they will go in after them. Then I will receive glory through Pharaoh and all his army, his chariots and charioteers. The Egyptians shall know that I am the LORD, when I receive glory through Pharaoh and his chariots and charioteers."

The angel of God, who had been leading Israel's camp, now moved and went around behind them. The column of cloud also, leaving the front, took up its place behind them, so that it came between the camp of the Egyptians and that of Israel. But the cloud now became dark, and thus the night passed without the rival camps coming any closer together all night long. Then Moses stretched out his hand over the sea, and the LORD swept the sea with a strong east wind throughout the night and so turned it into dry land. When the water was thus divided, the Israelites marched into the midst of the sea on dry land, with the water like a wall to their right and to their left.

The Egyptians followed in pursuit; all Pharaoh's horses and chariots and charioteers went after them right into the midst of the sea. In the night watch just before dawn the LORD cast through the column of the fiery cloud upon the Egyptian force a glance that threw it into a panic; and he so clogged their chariot wheels that they could hardly drive. With that the Egyptians sounded the retreat before Israel, because the LORD was fighting for them against the Egyptians.

Then the LORD told Moses, "Stretch out your hand over the sea, that the water may flow back upon the Egyptians, upon their chariots and their charioteers." So Moses stretched out his hand over the sea, and at dawn the sea flowed back to its normal depth. The Egyptians were fleeing head on toward the sea, when the LORD hurled them into its midst. As the water flowed back, it covered the chariots and the charioteers of Pharaoh's whole army which had followed the Israelites into the sea. Not a single one of them escaped. But the Israelites had marched on dry land through the midst of the sea, with the water like a wall to their right and to their left. Thus the LORD saved Israel on that day from the power of the Egyptians. When Israel saw the Egyptians lying dead on the seashore and beheld the great power that the Lord had shown against the Egyptians, they feared the LORD and believed in him and in his servant Moses.

Then Moses and the Israelites sang this song to the LORD:
I will sing to the Lord, for he is gloriously triumphant;
    horse and chariot he has cast into the sea.

The word of the Lord. ***Thanks be to God.***

RESPONSORIAL CANTICLE *(Exodus 15:1-2, 3-4, 5-6, 17-18)*
℟ Let us sing to the Lord; he has covered himself in glory.

I will sing to the LORD, for he is gloriously triumphant;
    horse and chariot he has cast into the sea.
My strength and my courage is the LORD,
    and he has been my savior.
He is my God, I praise him;
    the God of my father, I extol him. ℟
The LORD is a warrior,
    LORD is his name!
Pharaoh's chariots and army he hurled into the sea;
    the elite of his officers were submerged in the Red Sea. ℟
The flood waters covered them,
    they sank into the depths like a stone.
Your right hand, O LORD, magnificent in power,
    your right hand, O LORD, has shattered the enemy. ℟
You brought in the people you redeemed
    and planted them on the mountain of your inheritance—
the place where you made your seat, O LORD,
    the sanctuary, LORD, which your hands established.
The LORD shall reign forever and ever. ℟

PRAYER
O God, whose ancient wonders
remain undimmed in splendor even in our day,
for what you once bestowed on a single people,
freeing them from Pharaoh's persecution
by the power of your right hand,
now you bring about as the salvation of the nations
through the waters of rebirth,

grant, we pray, that the whole world
may become children of Abraham
and inherit the dignity of Israel's birthright.
Through Christ our Lord. *Amen.*

Or

O God, who by the light of the New Testament
have unlocked the meaning
of wonders worked in former times,
so that the Red Sea prefigures the sacred font
and the nation delivered from slavery
foreshadows the Christian people,
grant, we pray, that all nations,
obtaining the privilege of Israel by merit of faith,
may be reborn by partaking of your Spirit.
Through Christ our Lord. *Amen.*

FOURTH READING *(Isaiah 54:5-14)*

The One who has become your husband is your Maker;
his name is the LORD of hosts;
your redeemer is the Holy One of Israel,
    called God of all the earth.
The LORD calls you back,
    like a wife forsaken and grieved in spirit,
    a wife married in youth and then cast off,
    says your God.
For a brief moment I abandoned you,
    but with great tenderness I will take you back.
In an outburst of wrath, for a moment
    I hid my face from you;
but with enduring love I take pity on you,

says the LORD, your redeemer.
This is for me like the days of Noah,
    when I swore that the waters of Noah
    should never again deluge the earth;
so I have sworn not to be angry with you,
    or to rebuke you.
Though the mountains leave their place
    and the hills be shaken,
my love shall never leave you
    nor my covenant of peace be shaken,
    says the LORD, who has mercy on you.
O afflicted one, storm-battered and unconsoled,
    I lay your pavements in carnelians,
    and your foundations in sapphires;
I will make your battlements of rubies,
    your gates of carbuncles,
    and all your walls of precious stones.
All your children shall be taught by the LORD,
    and great shall be the peace of your children.
In justice shall you be established,
    far from the fear of oppression,
    where destruction cannot come near you.
The word of the Lord. ***Thanks be to God.***

RESPONSORIAL PSALM *(Psalm 30:2, 4, 5-6, 11-12, 13)*
℟ **I will praise you, Lord, for you have rescued me.**

I will extol you, O LORD, for you drew me clear
    and did not let my enemies rejoice over me.
O LORD, you brought me up from the netherworld;
    you preserved me from among those going down into the pit. ℟

Sing praise to the LORD, you his faithful ones,
    and give thanks to his holy name.
For his anger lasts but a moment;
    a lifetime, his good will.
At nightfall, weeping enters in,
    but with the dawn, rejoicing. ℟
Hear, O LORD, and have pity on me;
    O LORD, be my helper.
You changed my mourning into dancing;
    O LORD, my God, forever will I give you thanks. ℟

PRAYER

Almighty ever-living God,
surpass, for the honor of your name,
what you pledged to the Patriarchs by reason of their faith,
and through sacred adoption increase the children of your promise,
so that what the Saints of old never doubted would come to pass
your Church may now see in great part fulfilled.
Through Christ our Lord. *Amen.*

FIFTH READING *(Isaiah 55:1-11)*

> Thus says the LORD:
>   All you who are thirsty,
>   come to the water!
> You who have no money,
>   come, receive grain and eat;
> come, without paying and without cost,
>   drink wine and milk!
> Why spend your money for what is not bread,
>   your wages for what fails to satisfy?
> Heed me, and you shall eat well,

you shall delight in rich fare.
Come to me heedfully,
    listen, that you may have life.
I will renew with you the everlasting covenant,
    the benefits assured to David.
As I made him a witness to the peoples,
    a leader and commander of nations,
so shall you summon a nation you knew not,
    and nations that knew you not shall run to you,
because of the LORD, your God,
    the Holy One of Israel, who has glorified you.

Seek the LORD while he may be found,
    call him while he is near.
Let the scoundrel forsake his way,
    and the wicked man his thoughts;
let him turn to the Lord for mercy;
    to our God, who is generous in forgiving.
For my thoughts are not your thoughts,
    nor are your ways my ways, says the LORD.
As high as the heavens are above the earth,
    so high are my ways above your ways
    and my thoughts above your thoughts.

For just as from the heavens
    the rain and snow come down
and do not return there
    till they have watered the earth,
    making it fertile and fruitful,
giving seed to the one who sows
    and bread to the one who eats,

so shall my word be
    that goes forth from my mouth;
my word shall not return to me void,
    but shall do my will,
        achieving the end for which I sent it.
The word of the Lord. *Thanks be to God.*

RESPONSORIAL CANTICLE *(Isaiah 12:2-3, 4, 5-6)*
℟ **You will draw water joyfully from the springs of salvation.**

God indeed is my savior;
    I am confident and unafraid.
My strength and my courage is the LORD,
    and he has been my savior.
With joy you will draw water
    at the fountain of salvation. ℟
Give thanks to the LORD, acclaim his name;
    among the nations make known his deeds,
    proclaim how exalted is his name. ℟
Sing praise to the LORD for his glorious achievement;
    let this be known throughout all the earth.
Shout with exultation, O city of Zion,*
    for great in your midst
        is the Holy One of Israel! ℟

PRAYER
Almighty ever-living God,
sole hope of the world,
who by the preaching of your Prophets
unveiled the mysteries of this present age,
graciously increase the longing of your people,
for only at the prompting of your grace

do the faithful progress in any kind of virtue.
Through Christ our Lord. *Amen.*

SIXTH READING *(Baruch 3:9-15, 32—4:4)*

Hear, O Israel, the commandments of life:
listen, and know prudence!
How is it, Israel,
    that you are in the land of your foes,
    grown old in a foreign land,
defiled with the dead,
    accounted with those destined for the netherworld?
You have forsaken the fountain of wisdom!
    Had you walked in the way of God,
    you would have dwelt in enduring peace.
Learn where prudence is,
    where strength, where understanding;
that you may know also
    where are length of days, and life,
    where light of the eyes, and peace.
Who has found the place of wisdom,
    who has entered into her treasuries?

The One who knows all things knows her;
    he has probed her by his knowledge—
The One who established the earth for all time,
    and filled it with four-footed beasts;
he who dismisses the light, and it departs,
    calls it, and it obeys him trembling;
before whom the stars at their posts
    shine and rejoice;
when he calls them, they answer, "Here we are!"

shining with joy for their Maker.
Such is our God;
   no other is to be compared to him:
he has traced out the whole way of understanding,
   and has given her to Jacob, his servant,
   to Israel, his beloved son.

Since then she has appeared on earth,
   and moved among people.
She is the book of the precepts of God,
   the law that endures forever;
all who cling to her will live,
   but those will die who forsake her.
Turn, O Jacob, and receive her:
   walk by her light toward splendor.
Give not your glory to another,
   your privileges to an alien race.
Blessed are we, O Israel;
   for what pleases God is known to us!
The word of the Lord. *Thanks be to God.*

RESPONSORIAL PSALM *(Psalm 19:8, 9, 10, 11)*
℟. **Lord, you have the words of everlasting life.**

The law of the LORD is perfect,
   refreshing the soul;
the decree of the LORD is trustworthy,
   giving wisdom to the simple. ℟.
The precepts of the LORD are right,
   rejoicing the heart;
the command of the LORD is clear,
   enlightening the eye. ℟.

The fear of the LORD is pure,
    enduring forever;
the ordinances of the LORD are true,
    all of them just.
℟ Lord, you have the words of everlasting life.
They are more precious than gold,
    than a heap of purest gold;
sweeter also than syrup
    or honey from the comb. ℟

PRAYER

O God, who constantly increase your Church
by your call to the nations,
graciously grant
to those you wash clean in the waters of Baptism
the assurance of your unfailing protection.
Through Christ our Lord. *Amen.*

SEVENTH READING *(Ezekiel 36:16-17a, 18-28)*

The word of the LORD came to me, saying: Son of man, when the house of Israel lived in their land, they defiled it by their conduct and deeds. Therefore I poured out my fury upon them because of the blood that they poured out on the ground, and because they defiled it with idols. I scattered them among the nations, dispersing them over foreign lands; according to their conduct and deeds I judged them. But when they came among the nations wherever they came, they served to profane my holy name, because it was said of them: "These are the people of the LORD, yet they had to leave their land." So I have relented because of my holy name which the house of Israel profaned among the nations where they came. Therefore say to the house of Israel: Thus says the Lord GOD: Not for your sakes do I act, house of Israel, but for the sake of my holy name, which you profaned among the nations to which you came. I will prove the holiness of my great name, profaned among the nations, in whose midst you have profaned it. Thus the nations shall know that I am the LORD, says the Lord GOD, when in their sight I prove my holiness through you. For I will take you away from among the nations, gather you from all the foreign lands, and bring you back to your own land. I will sprinkle clean water upon you to cleanse you from all your impurities, and from all your idols I will cleanse you. I will give you a new heart and place a new spirit within you, taking from your bodies your stony hearts and giving you natural hearts. I will put my spirit within you and make you live by my statutes, careful to observe my decrees. You shall live in the land I gave your fathers; you shall be my people, and I will be your God.

The word of the Lord. ***Thanks be to God.***

When baptism is celebrated, sing Psalm 42/43 (below); when baptism is not celebrated, sing Isaiah 12 (from after the Fifth Reading, page 315) or Psalm 51 (next page).

RESPONSORIAL PSALM *(Psalm 42:3, 5; 43:3, 4)*
℞ **Like a deer that longs for running streams,**
　　my soul longs for you, my God.

Athirst is my soul for God, the living God.
　　When shall I go and behold the face of God? ℞
I went with the throng
　　and led them in procession to the house of God,
amid loud cries of joy and thanksgiving,

with the multitude keeping festival.
℟ **Like a deer that longs for running streams,**
   my soul longs for you, my God.

Send forth your light and your fidelity;
   they shall lead me on
and bring me to your holy mountain,
   to your dwelling-place. ℟

Then will I go in to the altar of God,
   the God of my gladness and joy;
then will I give you thanks upon the harp,
   O God, my God! ℟

OR

RESPONSORIAL PSALM *(Psalm 51:12-13, 14-15, 18-19)*
℟ **Create a clean heart in me, O God.**

A clean heart create for me, O God,
   and a steadfast spirit renew within me.
Cast me not out from your presence,
   and your Holy Spirit take not from me. ℟
Give me back the joy of your salvation,
   and a willing spirit sustain in me.
I will teach transgressors your ways,
   and sinners shall return to you. ℟
For you are not pleased with sacrifices;
   should I offer a holocaust, you would not accept it.
My sacrifice, O God, is a contrite spirit;
   a heart contrite and humbled, O God, you will not spurn. ℟

PRAYER

O God of unchanging power and eternal light,
look with favor on the wondrous mystery of the whole Church
and serenely accomplish the work of human salvation,
which you planned from all eternity;
may the whole world know and see
that what was cast down is raised up,
what had become old is made new,
and all things are restored to integrity through Christ,
just as by him they came into being.
Who lives and reigns for ever and ever. *Amen.*

Or

O God, who by the pages of both Testaments
instruct and prepare us to celebrate the Paschal Mystery,
grant that we may comprehend your mercy,
so that the gifts we receive from you this night
may confirm our hope of the gifts to come.
Through Christ our Lord. *Amen.*

GLORY TO GOD *(page 12)*

COLLECT

O God, who make this most sacred night radiant
with the glory of the Lord's Resurrection,
stir up in your Church a spirit of adoption,
so that, renewed in body and mind,
we may render you undivided service.
Through our Lord Jesus Christ, your Son,
who lives and reigns with you in the unity of the Holy Spirit,
one God, for ever and ever. *Amen.*

EPISTLE *(Romans 6:3–11)*

Brothers and sisters: Are you unaware that we who were baptized✝ into Christ Jesus were baptized into his death? We were indeed buried with him through baptism into death, so that, just as Christ was raised from the dead by the glory of the Father, we too might live in newness of life.

For if we have grown into union with him through a death like his, we shall also be united with him in the resurrection. We know that our old self was crucified with him, so that our sinful body might be done away with, that we might no longer be in slavery to sin. For a dead person has been absolved from sin. If, then, we have died with Christ, we believe that we shall also live with him. We know that Christ, raised from the dead, dies no more; death no longer has power over him. As to his death, he died to sin once and for all; as to his life, he lives for God. Consequently, you too must think of yourselves as being dead to sin and living for God in Christ Jesus.

The Gospel of the Lord. *Praise to you, Lord Jesus Christ.*

RESPONSORIAL PSALM *(Psalm 118:1–2, 16–17, 22–23)*

℟ Alleluia, alleluia, alleluia.

Give thanks to the LORD, for he is good,
    for his mercy endures forever.
Let the house of Israel say,
    "His mercy endures forever." ℟
The right hand of the LORD has struck with power;
    the right hand of the LORD is exalted.
I shall not die, but live,
    and declare the works of the LORD. ℟
The stone which the builders rejected

has become the cornerstone.
By the LORD has this been done;
it is wonderful in our eyes. ℟

GOSPEL *(Matthew 28:1-10)*

A reading from the holy Gospel according to Matthew.
Glory to you, O Lord.

After the sabbath, as the first day of the week was dawning, Mary Magdalene and the other Mary came to see the tomb. And behold, there was a great earthquake; for an angel of the Lord descended from heaven, approached, rolled back the stone, and sat upon it. His appearance was like lightning and his clothing was white as snow. The guards were shaken with fear of him and became like dead men. Then the angel said to the women in reply, "Do not be afraid! I know that you are seeking Jesus the crucified. He is not here, for he has been raised just as he said. Come and see the place where he lay. Then go quickly and tell his disciples, 'He has been raised from the dead, and he is going before you to Galilee; there you will see him.' Behold, I have told you." Then they went away quickly from the tomb, fearful yet overjoyed, and ran to announce this to his disciples. And behold, Jesus met them on their way and greeted them. They approached, embraced his feet, and did him homage. Then Jesus said to them, "Do not be afraid. Go tell my brothers to go to Galilee, and there they will see me."

The Gospel of the Lord. *Praise to you, Lord Jesus Christ.*

LITURGY OF BAPTISM

·····································

INVITATION

When baptism is celebrated:

Dearly beloved,
with one heart and one soul, let us by our prayers
come to the aid of these our brothers and sisters
    in their blessed hope,
so that, as they approach the font of rebirth,
the almighty Father may bestow on them
all his merciful help.

When baptism is not celebrated, but the font is blessed:

Dearly beloved,
let us humbly invoke upon this font
the grace of God the almighty Father,
that those who from it are born anew
may be numbered among the children of adoption in Christ.

*If baptism is not celebrated and the font is not blessed, proceed to the
blessing of the water outside of baptism (page 328).*

LITANY OF SAINTS

Lord, have mercy. ***Lord, have mercy.***
Christ, have mercy. ***Christ, have mercy.***
Lord, have mercy. ***Lord, have mercy.***

Holy Mary, Mother of God, ***pray for us.***

Saint Michael,
Holy Angels of God,
Saint John the Baptist,
Saint Joseph,
Saint Peter and Saint Paul,
Saint Andrew,
Saint John,
Saint Mary Magdalene,
Saint Stephen,
Saint Ignatius of Antioch,
Saint Lawrence,
Saint Perpetua
    and Saint Felicity,
Saint Agnes,

Saint Gregory,
Saint Augustine,
Saint Athanasius,
Saint Basil,
Saint Martin,
Saint Benedict,
Saint Francis
    and Saint Dominic,
Saint Francis Xavier,
Saint John Vianney,
Saint Catherine of Siena,
Saint Teresa of Jesus,
All holy men and women,
    Saints of God,

Lord, be merciful,
Lord, deliver us, we pray.
From all evil,
From every sin,
From everlasting death,
By your Incarnation,
By your Death and Resurrection,
By the outpouring of the Holy Spirit,

Be merciful to us sinners,
Lord, we ask you, hear our prayer.

When baptism is celebrated add:

Bring these chosen ones to new birth through the grace of Baptism,
Lord, we ask you, hear our prayer.

Or, when baptism is not celebrated:

Make this font holy by your grace for the new birth of your children,
Lord, we ask you, hear our prayer.
Jesus, Son of the living God,
Lord, we ask you, hear our prayer.
Christ, hear us.
Christ, hear us.
Christ, graciously hear us.
Christ, graciously hear us.

When baptism is celebrated, the priest prays:

Almighty ever-living God,
be present by the mysteries of your great love
and send forth the spirit of adoption
to create the new peoples
brought to birth for you in the font of Baptism,
so that what is to be carried out by our humble service
may be brought to fulfillment by your mighty power.
Through Christ our Lord. **Amen.**

BLESSING OF BAPTISMAL WATER
O God, who by invisible power
accomplish a wondrous effect
through sacramental signs
and who in many ways have prepared water, your creation,
to show forth the grace of Baptism;

O God, whose Spirit
in the first moments of the world's creation
hovered over the waters,

so that the very substance of water
would even then take to itself the power to sanctify;

O God, who by the outpouring of the flood
foreshadowed regeneration,
so that from the mystery of one and the same element of water
would come an end to vice and a beginning of virtue;

O God, who caused the children of Abraham
to pass dry-shod through the Red Sea,
so that the chosen people,
set free from slavery to Pharaoh,
would prefigure the people of the baptized;

O God, whose Son,
baptized by John in the waters of the Jordan,
was anointed with the Holy Spirit,
and, as he hung upon the Cross,
gave forth water from his side along with blood,
and after his Resurrection, commanded his disciples:

"Go forth, teach all nations, baptizing them
in the name of the Father and of the Son and of the Holy Spirit,"
look now, we pray, upon the face of your Church
and graciously unseal for her the fountain of Baptism.

May this water receive by the Holy Spirit
the grace of your Only Begotten Son,
so that human nature, created in your image
and washed clean through the Sacrament of Baptism
from all the squalor of the life of old,
may be found worthy to rise to the life of newborn children
through water and the Holy Spirit.

May the power of the Holy Spirit,
O Lord, we pray,
come down through your Son
into the fullness of this font,
so that all who have been buried with Christ
by Baptism into death
may rise again to life with him.
Who lives and reigns with you in the unity of the Holy Spirit,
one God, for ever and ever. *Amen.*

Springs of water, bless the Lord;
praise and exalt him above all for ever.

Baptism is now conferred. Adults are then confirmed immediately afterward.

If there is no baptism and the font is not blessed, the priest blesses the
water and invites the assembly to renew their baptismal commitment:

THE BLESSING OF WATER (OUTSIDE OF BAPTISM)
Dear brothers and sisters,
let us humbly beseech the Lord our God
to bless this water he has created,
which will be sprinkled upon us
as a memorial of our Baptism.
May he graciously renew us,
that we may remain faithful to the Spirit
whom we have received.

Lord our God,
in your mercy be present to your people
who keep vigil on this most sacred night,
and, for us who recall the wondrous work of our creation

and the still greater work of our redemption,
graciously bless this water.
For you created water to make the fields fruitful
and to refresh and cleanse our bodies.
You also made water the instrument of your mercy:
for through water you freed your people from slavery
and quenched their thirst in the desert;
through water the Prophets proclaimed the new covenant
you were to enter upon with the human race;
and last of all,
through water, which Christ made holy in the Jordan,
you have renewed our corrupted nature
in the bath of regeneration.

Therefore, may this water be for us
a memorial of the Baptism we have received,
and grant that we may share
in the gladness of our brothers and sisters,
who at Easter have received their Baptism.
Through Christ our Lord. *Amen.*

When the Rite of Baptism (and Confirmation) has been completed or, if
this has not taken place, after the blessing of water, all stand, holding
lighted candles in their hands, and renew the promise of baptismal faith,
unless this has already been done together with those to be baptized.

RENEWAL OF BAPTISMAL PROMISES
Dear brethren (brothers and sisters), through the Paschal Mystery
we have been buried with Christ in Baptism,
so that we may walk with him in newness of life.
And so, now that our Lenten observance is concluded,

let us renew the promises of Holy Baptism,
by which we once renounced Satan and his works
and promised to serve God in the holy Catholic Church.
And so I ask you:

1 Do you renounce Satan? *I do.*
   And all his works? *I do.*
   And all his empty show? *I do.*

2 Do you renounce sin,
   so as to live in the freedom of the children of God? *I do.*
   Do you renounce the lure of evil,
   so that sin may have no mastery over you? *I do.*
   Do you renounce Satan,
   the author and prince of sin? *I do.*

PROFESSION OF FAITH

Do you believe in God, the Father almighty,
Creator of heaven and earth? *I do.*

Do you believe in Jesus Christ, his only Son, our Lord,
who was born of the Virgin Mary,
suffered death and was buried,
rose again from the dead
and is seated at the right hand of the Father? *I do.*

Do you believe in the Holy Spirit,
the holy Catholic Church,
the communion of saints,
the forgiveness of sins,
the resurrection of the body,
and life everlasting? *I do.*

And may almighty God, the Father of our Lord Jesus Christ,
who has given us new birth by water and the Holy Spirit
and bestowed on us forgiveness of our sins,
keep us by his grace,
in Christ Jesus our Lord,
for eternal life. *Amen.*

SPRINKLING WITH BAPTISMAL WATER
The Priest sprinkles all the people with the blessed baptismal water, while
an appropriate song may be sung.

PRAYER OF THE FAITHFUL

LITURGY OF THE EUCHARIST

PREPARATION OF GIFTS *(page 16)*

PRAYER OVER THE OFFERINGS
Accept, we ask, O Lord,
the prayers of your people
with the sacrificial offerings,
that what has begun in the paschal mysteries
may, by the working of your power,
bring us to the healing of eternity.
Through Christ our Lord. *Amen.*

PREFACE *(Easter 1, page 24)*

COMMUNION ANTIPHON *(1 Corinthians 5:7–8)*

Christ our Passover has been sacrificed;
therefore let us keep the feast with the unleavened bread of
purity and truth, alleluia.

PRAYER AFTER COMMUNION

Pour out on us, O Lord, the Spirit of your love,
and in your kindness make those you have nourished
by this paschal Sacrament
one in mind and heart.
Through Christ our Lord. *Amen.*

SOLEMN BLESSING: MASS OF THE EASTER VIGIL

May almighty God bless you
through today's Easter Solemnity
and, in his compassion,
defend you from every assault of sin. *Amen.*

• TAKING A CLOSER LOOK •

✝ **Baptized** Baptism means to immerse or wash in water and so becomes a natural sign for ritual purity or holiness. In Judaism, there were many ceremonial washings, either in preparation for celebrating a ritual or as part of a cleansing rite within a ritual. Thus John the Baptist uses a baptism of repentance (Matthew 3:11) to symbolize one's desire to put off sinful ways and live as God wants. But for the Christian community, going under the baptismal waters also signified a death to one's whole former life and an emergence into new life in the risen Christ.

And may he, who restores you to eternal life
in the Resurrection of his Only Begotten,
endow you with the prize of immortality. *Amen.*

Now that the days of the Lord's Passion have drawn to a close,
may you who celebrate the gladness of the Paschal Feast
come with Christ's help, and exulting in spirit,
to those feasts that are celebrated in eternal joy. *Amen.*

And may the blessing of almighty God,
the Father, and the Son, and the Holy Spirit,
come down on you and remain with you for ever. *Amen.*

DISMISSAL *(page 57)* ❖

• RESPONDING TO THE WORD •

The seven Old Testament readings tell the story of God's saving presence in our world.	Paul reminds us that with our baptism we have been united to Christ's death and resurrection.	Jesus tells his disciples not to be afraid.
⮕ Which reading was I most drawn to tonight?	⮕ What can I do to be more united to Christ today?	⮕ What fears must I overcome to witness to Christ today?

April 12

A promise fulfilled

This past year, I gave birth to a beautiful baby. He has transformed my life, bringing a sense of hope that I didn't know I was missing. Just after his birth, I went through a period of post-partum depression that laid a dark cloud over my life. As I worked my way through it, it was the joy my son brought that was the light that helped me through. Today's gospel has never resonated more than during that period in my life.

There are three phases that we have the privilege of witnessing Mary Magdalene go through: the hope that Jesus brought in his message, the loss and grief at his crucifixion, and the realization of a promise fulfilled on Easter Sunday. She is transformed—hope to grief to joy—as she meets Jesus after his resurrection, going on to become an apostle to the apostles with the good news.

It's at that intersection of hope and pain that Jesus transforms us—he walks with us on that journey. Easter Sunday is the story of our faith. This Easter, let's take the opportunity to reflect on our own journey of transformation. With Mary, we can re-live and remember those three phases of hope, grief, and joy, to truly appreciate and celebrate the transformative gift that is the resurrection of Jesus in our life.

◼ SASKIA SIVANANTHAN

ENTRANCE ANTIPHON *(Cf. Psalm 139 (138):18, 5-6)*
I have risen, and I am with you still, alleluia. You
have laid your hand upon me, alleluia. Too wonderful for me, this knowledge, alleluia, alleluia.

Or *(Luke 24:34; cf. Revelation 1:6)*
The Lord is truly risen, alleluia. To him be glory and
power for all the ages of eternity, alleluia, alleluia.

INTRODUCTORY RITES *(page 10)*

COLLECT
O God, who on this day,
through your Only Begotten Son,
have conquered death
and unlocked for us the path to eternity,
grant, we pray, that we who keep
the solemnity of the Lord's Resurrection
may, through the renewal brought by your Spirit,
rise up in the light of life.
Through our Lord Jesus Christ, your Son,
who lives and reigns with you in the unity of the Holy Spirit,
one God, for ever and ever. *Amen.*

FIRST READING *(Acts 10:34a, 37-43)*
Peter proceeded to speak and said: "You know what has happened all over Judea, beginning in Galilee after the baptism
that John preached, how God anointed Jesus of Nazareth with
the Holy Spirit and power. He went about doing good and healing all those oppressed by the devil, for God was with him. We
are witnesses of all that he did both in the country of the Jews
and in Jerusalem. They put him to death by hanging him on a

tree. This man God raised on the third day and granted that he be visible, not to all the people, but to us, the witnesses chosen by God in advance, who ate and drank with him after he rose from the dead. He commissioned us to preach to the people and testify that he is the one appointed by God as judge of the living and the dead. To him all the prophets bear witness, that everyone who believes in him will receive forgiveness of sins through his name."

The word of the Lord. *Thanks be to God.*

RESPONSORIAL PSALM *(Psalm 118:1-2, 16-17, 22-23)*
R͝ **This is the day the Lord has made; let us rejoice and be glad.**
Or **Alleluia.**

Give thanks to the Lord, for he is good,
for his mercy endures forever.
Let the house of Israel say,
"His mercy endures forever." R͝

"The right hand of the Lord has struck with power;
the right hand of the Lord is exalted.
I shall not die, but live,
and declare the works of the Lord." R͝

The stone which the builders rejected
has become the cornerstone.
By the Lord has this been done;
it is wonderful in our eyes. R͝

An alternate reading follows.

SECOND READING *(Colossians 3:1–4)*

Brothers and sisters: If then you were raised with Christ, seek what is above, where Christ is seated at the right hand of God. Think of what is above, not of what is on earth. For you have died, and your life is hidden with Christ in God. When Christ your life appears, then you too will appear with him in glory.

The word of the Lord. *Thanks be to God.*

OR

SECOND READING *(1 Corinthians 5:6b–8)*

Brothers and sisters: Do you not know that a little yeast leavens all the dough? Clear out the old yeast, so that you may become a fresh batch of dough, inasmuch as you are unleavened. For our paschal lamb, Christ, has been sacrificed. Therefore, let us celebrate the feast, not with the old yeast, the yeast of malice and wickedness, but with the unleavened bread of sincerity and truth.

The word of the Lord. *Thanks be to God.*

SEQUENCE

Christians, to the Paschal Victim
    Offer your thankful praises!
A Lamb the sheep redeems;
    Christ, who only is sinless,
    Reconciles sinners to the Father.
Death and life have contended in that combat stupendous:
    The Prince of life, who died, reigns immortal.
Speak, Mary, declaring
    What you saw, wayfaring.
"The tomb of Christ, who is living,

The glory of Jesus' resurrection;
Bright angels attesting,
    The shroud and napkin resting.
Yes, Christ my hope is arisen;
    To Galilee he goes before you."
Christ indeed from death is risen, our new life obtaining.
    Have mercy, victor King, ever reigning!
    Amen. Alleluia.

ALLELUIA *(See 1 Corinthians 5:7b–8a)*
Alleluia, alleluia. Christ, our paschal lamb, has been sacrificed;
let us then feast with joy in the Lord. *Alleluia, alleluia.*

The gospel from the Easter Vigil (Matthew 28:1-10, page 323) may be read instead. For the gospel for an afternoon or evening Mass, see next page.

GOSPEL *(John 20:1-9)*
A reading from the holy Gospel according to John.
Glory to you, O Lord

On the first day of the week, Mary of Magdala came to the tomb✝ early in the morning, while it was still dark, and saw the stone removed from the tomb. So she ran and went to Simon Peter and to the other disciple whom Jesus loved, and told them, "They have taken the Lord from the tomb, and we don't know where they put him." So Peter and the other disciple went out and came to the tomb. They both ran, but the other disciple ran faster than Peter and arrived at the tomb first; he bent down and saw the burial cloths there, but did not go in. When Simon Peter arrived after him, he went into the tomb and saw the burial cloths there, and the cloth that had covered his head, not with the burial cloths but rolled up in a separate place.

Then the other disciple also went in, the one who had arrived at the tomb first, and he saw and believed. For they did not yet understand the Scripture that he had to rise from the dead.

The Gospel of the Lord. ***Praise to you, Lord Jesus Christ.***

Alternate reading for an afternoon or evening Mass:

GOSPEL *(Luke 24:13–35)*
A reading from the holy Gospel according to Luke.
Glory to you, Lord.

That very day, the first day of the week, two of Jesus' disciples were going to a village seven miles from Jerusalem called Emmaus, and they were conversing about all the things that had occurred. And it happened that while they were conversing and debating, Jesus himself drew near and walked with them, but their eyes were prevented from recognizing him. He asked them, "What are you discussing as you walk along?" They stopped, looking downcast. One of them, named Cleopas,* said to him in reply, "Are you the only visitor to Jerusalem who does not know of the things that have taken place there in these days?" And he replied to them, "What sort of things?" They said to him, "The things that happened to Jesus the Nazarene, who was a prophet mighty in deed and word before God and all the people, how our chief priests and rulers both handed him over to a sentence of death and crucified him. But we were hoping that he would be the one to redeem Israel; and besides all this, it is now the third day since this took place. Some women from our group, however, have astounded us: they were at the tomb early in the morning and did not find his body; they came back and reported that they had indeed seen a vision of angels who announced that he was alive.

Then some of those with us went to the tomb and found things just as the women had described, but him they did not see." And he said to them, "Oh, how foolish you are! How slow of heart to believe all that the prophets spoke! Was it not necessary that the Christ should suffer these things and enter into his glory?" Then beginning with Moses and all the prophets, he interpreted to them what referred to him in all the Scriptures. As they approached the village to which they were going, he gave the impression that he was going on farther. But they urged him, "Stay with us, for it is nearly evening and the day is almost over." So he went in to stay with them. And it happened that, while he was with them at table, he took bread, said the blessing, broke it, and gave it to them. With that their eyes were opened and they recognized him, but he vanished from their sight. Then they said to each other, "Were not our hearts burning within us while he spoke to us on the way and opened the Scriptures to us?" So they set out at once and returned to Jerusalem where they found gathered together the eleven and those with them who were saying, "The Lord has truly been raised and has appeared to Simon!" Then the two recounted what had taken place on the way and how he was made known to them in the breaking of bread.

The Gospel of the Lord. ***Praise to you, Lord Jesus Christ.***

RENEWAL OF BAPTISMAL PROMISES AND PROFESSION OF FAITH
(See page 329)
In Easter Sunday Masses, the rite of the renewal of baptismal promises may take place after the homily, according to the text used at the Easter Vigil.

PRAYER OF THE FAITHFUL

PREPARATION OF GIFTS *(page 16)*

PRAYER OVER THE OFFERINGS
Exultant with paschal gladness, O Lord,
we offer the sacrifice
by which your Church
is wondrously reborn and nourished.
Through Christ our Lord. *Amen.*

PREFACE *(Easter 1, page 24)*

❖ TAKING A CLOSER LOOK ❖

✝ **The tomb** What is most apparent from the resurrection accounts in the gospels is that the meaning of the event was not immediately intelligible. The empty tomb was not a proof of the resurrection but a fact whose meaning needed to be discovered. Finding the empty tomb made Jesus' followers bewildered and confused, grasping for various possible answers to account for it. Only when the disciples experienced the risen Lord did the meaning of the empty tomb become clear. The stone was rolled back not so Jesus could get out, but so we could get in and be assured that his tomb of death will remain empty forever. He is risen!

COMMUNION ANTIPHON *(1 Corinthians 5:7-8)*

Christ our Passover has been sacrificed, alleluia; therefore let us
keep the feast with the unleavened bread
of purity and truth, alleluia, alleluia.

PRAYER AFTER COMMUNION

Look upon your Church, O God,
with unfailing love and favor,
so that, renewed by the paschal mysteries,
she may come to the glory of the resurrection.
Through Christ our Lord. *Amen.*

SOLEMN BLESSING: MASS OF THE EASTER VIGIL *(Optional, page 332)*

DISMISSAL *(page 57)* ✣

• RESPONDING TO THE WORD •

The risen Christ
sends us out to be
his witnesses.

➡ *What witness to
Jesus' words and acts
can I give today?*

Paul knows that we
will be changed by
our experience of
Christ.

➡ *How has my
experience of Christ
changed me during
the past Lent?*

The disciples found
it hard to believe
because they did
not understand the
Scriptures.

➡ *How can I use
the Scriptures to
strengthen my own
belief?*

These fifty days are like one great Sunday

The season of Easter is actually a celebration of fifty days, from Easter until Pentecost. The word "Pentecost" means "fiftieth" and is the Greek translation of the Hebrew word *Shavuot*. *Shavuot*, the Jewish Feast of Weeks, began as a harvest festival in Canaan, coming approximately seven weeks after the first day of Passover.

What Sunday is to our Christian week, the Easter season is to the whole liturgical year. The fifty days of Easter have been observed longer than any other season of the Christian year. In the early Church, it was celebrated as an "unbroken Sunday," a week of weeks (7 times 7, or 49 days) plus the eighth day of the new creation. During these fifty days of joy, we are called upon in our life and worship to proclaim the lordship of Jesus revealed through his resurrection, ascension, and the outpouring of the Holy Spirit.

This season is a time to grow in our understanding of the paschal mystery and to make it part of our lives through our renewed attentiveness to God's word that we hear each Sunday and talk about in our households, through our fuller participation in the Eucharist, and through our renewed dedication to acts of charity and justice.

As we celebrate this season, we become more deeply aware of Christ's abiding but hidden presence with us that is daily transforming us into the image of Jesus.

Praying and living the Easter season

Since the Easter season is fifty days long, it will take some effort on our part to extend its celebration for the full seven weeks until Pentecost.

As Christians we each share in the Easter experience because we have in one way or another met the risen Christ and so become connected to the community that witnesses to the good news of his resurrection.

One way to make Easter into a season of celebrations and keep its spirit alive is to adopt the daily practice of using the Collect for Sunday as the gathering prayer for a household meal.

Another practice is to connect ourselves to the long chain of Christian witnesses that have preceded us. Gather your household or faith-sharing group and explain that when Paul locates himself in the Christian tradition, he creates a chain of witnesses connecting those who experienced Christ's first Easter appearance to himself.

Invite the household to bring this chain of witnesses from Paul's time down to our present time by naming those who have been most important in handing on the living tradition (e.g., family, relatives, friends, mentors, spiritual persons you have admired, patron saints, etc.).

Write down the names to create your household's or group's unique connection to the Easter tradition. To express your solidarity, share a sign of peace with one another. Then conclude by praying the Lord's Prayer together.

April 19

APR
19

"My Lord and my God!"

"Faith is the assurance of things hoped for, the conviction of things not seen" (Hebrews 11:1). This was the challenge Thomas faced: he did not believe the apostles' report that Jesus appeared to them on Easter evening. He wanted proof. However, Thomas was with them when Jesus next appeared among them, and Jesus invited Thomas to touch him to prove that he had physically risen from the dead. Thomas did not, instead simply professing his belief in "my Lord and my God."

Still, Thomas needed to see Jesus before he believed. In contrast, Jesus commends those, like us, who believe without having seen the risen Jesus. The author then tells us that the purpose of the entire gospel was so that we would believe Jesus is the Christ and "have life in his name."

The other readings indicate two perspectives on what this should mean for us. In Acts, the believers form a community to share all aspects of their lives, while the letter of Peter celebrates our rebirth into a new life of salvation.

We celebrate Jesus' death and resurrection in every Eucharist. Each of us must decide how to also live out its effects in our daily lives.

■ JOHN L. McLAUGHLIN

ENTRANCE ANTIPHON *(1 Peter 2:2)*

Like newborn infants, you must long for the pure, spiritual milk, that in him you may grow to salvation, alleluia.

Or *(4 Esdras 2:36–37)*

Receive the joy of your glory, giving thanks to God, who has called you into the heavenly kingdom, alleluia.

INTRODUCTORY RITES *(page 10)*

COLLECT

God of everlasting mercy,
who in the very recurrence of the paschal feast
kindle the faith of the people you have made your own,
increase, we pray, the grace you have bestowed,
that all may grasp and rightly understand
in what font they have been washed,
by whose Spirit they have been reborn,
by whose Blood they have been redeemed.
Through our Lord Jesus Christ, your Son,
who lives and reigns with you in the unity of the Holy Spirit,
one God, for ever and ever. *Amen.*

FIRST READING *(Acts 2:42–47)*

They devoted themselves to the teaching of the apostles and to the communal life, to the breaking of bread and to the prayers. Awe came upon everyone, and many wonders and signs were done through the apostles. All who believed were together and had all things in common; they would sell their property and possessions and divide them among all according to each one's need. Every day they devoted themselves to meeting together in the temple area and to breaking bread in their homes. They ate their meals with exultation and sincerity of heart, praising God and enjoying favor with all the people. And every day the Lord added to their number those who were being saved.

The word of the Lord. *Thanks be to God.*

RESPONSORIAL PSALM *(Psalm 118:2–4, 13–15, 22–24)*

R. **Give thanks to the Lord for he is good, his love is everlasting.** *Or* **Alleluia.**

Let the house of Israel say,
    "His **mercy**⁺ endures forever."
Let the house of Aaron say,
    "His mercy endures forever."
Let those who fear the LORD say,
    "His mercy endures forever." R.
I was hard pressed and was falling,
    but the LORD helped me.
My strength and my courage is the LORD,
    and he has been my savior.
The joyful shout of victory
    in the tents of the just. R.
The stone which the builders rejected
    has become the cornerstone.
By the LORD has this been done;
    it is wonderful in our eyes.
This is the day the LORD has made;
    let us be glad and rejoice in it. R.

SECOND READING *(1 Peter 1:3–9)*

Blessed be the God and Father of our Lord Jesus Christ, who in his great **mercy**⁺ gave us a new birth to a living hope through the resurrection of Jesus Christ from the dead, to an inheritance that is imperishable, undefiled, and unfading, kept in heaven for you who by the power of God are safeguarded through faith, to a salvation that is ready to be revealed in the final time. In this you rejoice, although now for a little while you may have to suffer through various trials, so that the genuineness of your faith, more precious than gold that is perishable even though tested by fire, may prove to be for praise, glory, and honor at the revelation of Jesus Christ. Although you have not seen him you love him; even though you do not see him now yet believe in him, you rejoice with an indescribable and glorious joy, as you attain the goal of your faith, the salvation of your souls.

The word of the Lord. *Thanks be to God.*

ALLELUIA *(John 20:29)*
Alleluia, alleluia. You believe in me, Thomas, because you have seen me, says the Lord; blessed are they who have not seen me, but still believe! *Alleluia, alleluia.*

GOSPEL *(John 20:19–31)*
A reading from the holy Gospel according to John.
Glory to you, O Lord.

O n the evening of that first day of the week, when the doors were locked, where the disciples were, for fear of the Jews, Jesus came and stood in their midst and said to them, "Peace be with you." When he had said this, he showed them his hands and his side. The disciples rejoiced when they saw the Lord. Jesus said to them again, "Peace be with you. As the Father has sent me, so I send you." And when he had said this, he breathed on them and said to them, "Receive the Holy Spirit. Whose sins you forgive are forgiven them, and whose sins you retain are retained."

Thomas, called Didymus,* one of the Twelve, was not with them when Jesus came. So the other disciples said to him, "We have seen the Lord." But he said to them, "Unless I see the mark of the nails in his hands and put my finger into the nailmarks and put my hand into his side, I will not believe."

Now a week later his disciples were again inside and Thomas was with them. Jesus came, although the doors were locked, and stood in their midst and said, "Peace be with you." Then he said to Thomas, "Put your finger here and see my hands, and bring your hand and put it into my side, and do not be unbelieving, but believe." Thomas answered and said to him, "My Lord and my God!" Jesus said to him, "Have you come to believe because you have seen me? Blessed are those who have not seen and have believed."

Now, Jesus did many other signs in the presence of his disciples that are not written in this book. But these are written that you may come to believe that Jesus is the Christ, the Son of God, and that through this belief you may have life in his name.

The Gospel of the Lord. ***Praise to you, Lord Jesus Christ.***

PROFESSION OF FAITH *(page 13)*

PRAYER OF THE FAITHFUL

PREPARATION OF GIFTS *(page 16)*

PRAYER OVER THE OFFERINGS
Accept, O Lord, we pray,
the oblations of your people
(and of those you have brought to new birth),
that, renewed by confession of your name and by Baptism,
they may attain unending happiness.
Through Christ our Lord. ***Amen.***

PREFACE *(Easter 1, page 24)*

• TAKING A CLOSER LOOK •

✛ **Mercy** In the Old Testament, mercy (Hebrew, *hesed*) usually identifies a complex Hebrew idea that describes God's special covenant love. God's desire to be in communion with us as covenant partners reveals an attitude of divine love and faithfulness that includes loyalty, compassion, dependability, trustworthiness, and an eagerness to help when situations turn bad. And once God commits to the people in covenant fidelity, there is no question of God ever retracting that commitment. So God's covenant love will never end—hence it can aptly be described as everlasting mercy or enduring forever, as in the words of today's psalm.

COMMUNION ANTIPHON *(Cf. John 20:27)*

Bring your hand and feel the place of the nails, and do not be unbelieving but believing, alleluia.

PRAYER AFTER COMMUNION

Grant, we pray, almighty God,
that our reception of this paschal Sacrament
may have a continuing effect
in our minds and hearts.
Through Christ our Lord. *Amen.*

SOLEMN BLESSING: EASTER TIME *(Optional, page 60)*

DISMISSAL *(page 57)* ❖

• RESPONDING TO THE WORD •

The disciples used the Scriptures and prayer to deepen their community life.

➔ *What steps can I take to grow spiritually through reading and praying the Scriptures?*

God's mercy or compassion offers us new life.

➔ *How can my compassion for others give them new life?*

Thomas changes his doubts to firm faith when Jesus comes to him.

➔ *How has my faith grown through this Lent and Easter season?*

April 26

The truths in our hearts

The two disciples in our gospel today are walking from Jerusalem towards Emmaus. Their understanding is clouded by sadness and confusion and they cannot accept the joy of the resurrection.

The loss of a loved one causes deep pain in our hearts. Despite the knowledge of the resurrection, we would rather have our loved one's presence on earth. We want to run from the pain instead of experiencing it. However, the gospel reminds us of the gift of the Eucharist. When they break bread with Jesus, the disciples see beyond their grief, allowing their hearts and minds to be open to the events of the resurrection. This gives them the courage to return to Jerusalem.

As Catholics we can connect to the experience of the disciples. It is often at Mass, in the presence of the Eucharist, that we come to comprehend the truths deep in our hearts. We are reminded that our sufferings bring us closer to Christ our Savior, and we are given the space to reflect on our actions and thoughts. The breaking of bread leads to personal reflection, so we can stop walking in pain and instead embrace our human experience. In the presence of Jesus our hearts burn with love, understanding, and hope.

■ ELIZABETH CHESLEY-JEWELL

ENTRANCE ANTIPHON *(Cf. Psalm 66 [65]:1–2)*

Cry out with joy to God, all the earth; O sing to the glory of his name. O render him glorious praise, alleluia.

INTRODUCTORY RITES *(page 10)*

COLLECT

May your people exult for ever, O God,
in renewed youthfulness of spirit,
so that, rejoicing now in the restored glory of our adoption,
we may look forward in confident hope
to the rejoicing of the day of resurrection.
Through our Lord Jesus Christ, your Son,
who lives and reigns with you in the unity of the Holy Spirit,
one God, for ever and ever. ***Amen.***

FIRST READING *(Acts 2:14, 22–33)*

Then Peter stood up with the Eleven, raised his voice, and proclaimed: "You who are Jews, indeed all of you staying in Jerusalem. Let this be known to you, and listen to my words. You who are Israelites, hear these words. Jesus the Nazorean* was a man commended to you by God with mighty deeds, **wonders, and signs,**✝ which God worked through him in your midst, as you yourselves know. This man, delivered up by the set plan and foreknowledge of God, you killed, using lawless men to crucify him. But God raised him up, releasing him from the throes of death, because it was impossible for him to be held by it. For David says of him:

I saw the Lord ever before me,
    with him at my right hand I shall not be disturbed.
Therefore my heart has been glad and my tongue has exulted;

my flesh, too, will dwell in hope,
because you will not abandon my soul to the netherworld,
   nor will you suffer your holy one to see corruption.
You have made known to me the paths of life;
   you will fill me with joy in your presence.

"My brothers, one can confidently say to you about the patri-
arch David that he died and was buried, and his tomb is in our
midst to this day. But since he was a prophet and knew that God
had sworn an oath to him that he would set one of his descendants upon his throne, he foresaw and spoke of the resurrection
of the Christ, that neither was he abandoned to the netherworld
nor did his flesh see corruption. God raised this Jesus; of this we
are all witnesses. Exalted at the right hand of God, he received
the promise of the Holy Spirit from the Father and poured him
forth, as you see and hear."

The word of the Lord. ***Thanks be to God.***

RESPONSORIAL PSALM *(Psalm 16:1-2, 5, 7-8, 9-10, 11)*

℟ **Lord, you will show us the path of life.** *Or* **Alleluia.**

Keep me, O God, for in you I take refuge;
   I say to the LORD, "My Lord are you."
O LORD, my allotted portion and my cup,
   you it is who hold fast my lot. ℟
I bless the LORD who counsels me;
   even in the night my heart exhorts me.
I set the LORD ever before me;
   with him at my right hand I shall not be disturbed. ℟
Therefore my heart is glad and my soul rejoices,
   my body, too, abides in confidence;
because you will not abandon my soul to the netherworld,

nor will you suffer your faithful one to undergo corruption. ℞
You will show me the path to life,
 abounding joy in your presence,
 the delights at your right hand forever. ℞

SECOND READING *(1 Peter 1:17-21)*

Beloved: If you invoke as Father him who judges impartially according to each one's works, conduct yourselves with reverence during the time of your sojourning, realizing that you were ransomed from your futile conduct, handed on by your ancestors, not with perishable things like silver or gold but with the precious blood of Christ as of a spotless unblemished lamb.

He was known before the foundation of the world but revealed in the final time for you, who through him believe in God who raised him from the dead and gave him glory, so that your faith and hope are in God.

The word of the Lord. *Thanks be to God.*

ALLELUIA *(Luke 24:32)*

Alleluia, alleluia. Lord Jesus, open the Scriptures to us; make our hearts burn while you speak to us. *Alleluia, alleluia.*

GOSPEL *(Luke 24:13-35)*

A reading from the holy Gospel according to Luke.
Glory to you, O Lord.

That very day, the first day of the week, two of Jesus' disciples were going to a village seven miles from Jerusalem called Emmaus, and they were conversing about all the things that had occurred. And it happened that while they were conversing and debating, Jesus himself drew near and walked with them, but their eyes were prevented from recognizing him. He asked them, "What are you discussing as you walk along?" They stopped, looking downcast. One of them, named Cleopas, said to him in reply, "Are you the only visitor to Jerusalem who does not know of the things that have taken place there in these days?" And he replied to them, "What sort of things?" They said to him, "The things that happened to Jesus the Nazarene, who was a prophet mighty in deed and word before God and all the people, how our chief priests and rulers both handed him over to a sentence of death and crucified him. But we were hoping that he would be the one to redeem Israel; and besides all this, it is now the third day since this took place. Some women from our group, however, have astounded us: they were at the tomb early in the morning and did not find his body; they came back and reported that they had indeed seen a vision of angels who announced that he was alive. Then some of those with us went to the tomb and found things just as the women had described, but him they did not see." And he said to them, "Oh, how foolish you are! How slow of heart to believe all that the prophets spoke! Was it not necessary that the Christ should suffer these things and enter into his glory?" Then beginning with Moses and all the prophets, he interpreted to them what referred to him in all the Scriptures. As they approached the village to which they were going, he gave the impression that he was going on farther. But they urged him, "Stay with us, for it is nearly evening and the day is almost over." So he went in to stay with them. And it happened that, while he was with them at table, he took bread, said the blessing, broke it, and gave it to them. With that their eyes were opened and they recognized him, but he vanished from their sight. Then they said to each other, "Were not our hearts burning within us while he spoke to us on the way and opened the Scriptures to us?" So they set out at once and returned to Jerusalem where they found gathered together the eleven and those with them who were saying, "The Lord has truly been raised and has appeared to Simon!" Then the two recounted what had taken place on the way and how he was made known to them in the breaking of bread.

The Gospel of the Lord. *Praise to you, Lord Jesus Christ.*

PROFESSION OF FAITH *(page 13)*

PRAYER OF THE FAITHFUL

PREPARATION OF GIFTS *(page 16)*

PRAYER OVER THE OFFERINGS
Receive, O Lord, we pray,
these offerings of your exultant Church,
and, as you have given her cause for such great gladness,
grant also that the gifts we bring
may bear fruit in perpetual happiness.
Through Christ our Lord. *Amen.*

• TAKING A CLOSER LOOK •

✣ **Wonders and signs** Although we use the word miracles to describe these events, the biblical writers used the terms "signs" and "wonders." These are God's actions to reorder our world from the domination of Satan and evil powers that frustrate God's plan for a covenant community.

Jesus' deeds of power are directly related to his kingdom message. They are the first signs (his resurrection to new life will be the final sign) that God is reordering our world. Like Jesus' parables and meals, Jesus' cures, exorcisms, resuscitations, and nature wonders are signs of God's presence breaking into our world to change it forever.

PREFACE *(Easter 1-5, pages 24-26)*

COMMUNION ANTIPHON *(Luke 24:35)*

The disciples recognized the Lord Jesus in the breaking of the bread, alleluia.

PRAYER AFTER COMMUNION

Look with kindness upon your people, O Lord,
and grant, we pray,
that those you were pleased to renew by eternal mysteries
may attain in their flesh
the incorruptible glory of the resurrection.
Through Christ our Lord. *Amen.*

SOLEMN BLESSING: EASTER TIME *(Optional, page 60)*

DISMISSAL *(page 57)* ✢

✢ Responding to the Word ✢

Peter speaks to witness to what God has done for us through Jesus.

➨ *What can I do today to give this same kind of witness?*

Peter urges us to conduct ourselves with reverence.

➨ *What can I do to show my reverence for God and others?*

The disciples found Jesus by understanding the Scriptures and sharing the Eucharist.

➨ *What can I do to discover Christ in these same realities today?*

May 3

MAY 3

Live in hope!

As Psalm 23 never fails to remind me of funerals, I am drawn to viewing today's readings through that lens—living while suffering and living while dying, both with the hope Jesus' resurrection gives.

Our life lived in an ongoing embrace of God's will for us is also preparation for death. It brings peace and comfort to know Jesus' death and resurrection have made a way for us to be united with our Father—like our living, so our dying in the Lord will also be noticed by those around us.

In the first reading Peter says, "Save yourselves from this corrupt generation." How? Follow the Lord who has not only shown you the way but is the Way. In the second readings Peter calls Jesus "the shepherd and guardian of your souls." We follow the Lord, who has shown us the way to endure suffering.

We live in an upside-down time. The thief who comes to steal and destroy is active among us. Jesus came that we might have life and have it more abundantly. These words are also meant for those in Christ who are dying. Today, may we rest in his eucharistic presence and pray for those walking through the valley of the shadow of death. May they lack for nothing and find peace in the hope Jesus' resurrection promises.

JOHANNE BROWNRIGG

ENTRANCE ANTIPHON *(Cf. Psalm 33 [32]:5-6)*

The merciful love of the Lord fills the earth; by the word of the Lord the heavens were made, alleluia.

INTRODUCTORY RITES *(page 10)*

COLLECT

Almighty ever-living God,
lead us to a share in the joys of heaven,
so that the humble flock may reach
where the brave Shepherd has gone before.
Who lives and reigns with you in the unity of the Holy Spirit,
one God, for ever and ever. ***Amen.***

FIRST READING *(Acts 2:14a, 36–41)*

Then Peter stood up with the Eleven, raised his voice, and proclaimed: "Let the whole house of Israel know for certain that God has made both Lord and Christ, this Jesus whom you crucified."

Now when they heard this, they were cut to the heart, and they asked Peter and the other apostles, "What are we to do, my brothers?" Peter said to them, "Repent and be baptized, every one of you, in the name of Jesus Christ for the forgiveness of your sins; and you will receive the gift of the Holy Spirit. For the promise is made to you and to your children and to all those far off, whomever the Lord our God will call." He testified with many other arguments, and was exhorting them, "Save yourselves from this corrupt generation." Those who accepted his message were baptized, and about three thousand persons were added that day.

The word of the Lord. ***Thanks be to God.***

RESPONSORIAL PSALM *(Psalm 23:1–3a, 3b–4, 5, 6)*

R⫼ **The Lord is my shepherd; there is nothing I shall want.**
  Or **Alleluia.**

The LORD is my shepherd; I shall not want.
  In verdant pastures he gives me repose;
beside restful waters he leads me;
  he refreshes my soul. R⫼
He guides me in right paths
  for his name's sake.
Even though I walk in the dark valley
  I fear no evil; for you are at my side
with your rod and your staff
  that give me courage. R⫼
You spread the table before me
  in the sight of my foes;
you anoint my head with oil;
  my cup overflows. R⫼
Only goodness and kindness follow me
  all the days of my life;
and I shall dwell in the house of the LORD
  for years to come. R⫼

SECOND READING *(1 Peter 2:20b–25)*

Beloved: If you are patient when you suffer for doing what is good, this is a grace before God. For to this you have been called, because Christ also suffered for you, leaving you an example that you should follow in his footsteps. *He committed no sin, and no deceit was found in his mouth.*

  When he was insulted, he returned no insult; when he suffered, he did not threaten; instead, he handed himself over to the one who judges justly. He himself bore our sins in his body upon the cross, so that, free from sin, we might live for righteousness. By his wounds you have been healed. For you had gone astray like sheep, but you have now returned to the shepherd and guardian of your souls.

The word of the Lord. *Thanks be to God.*

ALLELUIA *(John 10:14)*
Alleluia, alleluia. I am the good shepherd, says the Lord; I know my sheep, and mine know me. *Alleluia, alleluia.*

GOSPEL *(John 10:1–10)*
A reading from the holy Gospel according to John.
Glory to you, O Lord.

Jesus said: "**Amen, amen,**✝ I say to you, whoever does not enter a sheepfold through the gate but climbs over elsewhere is a thief and a robber. But whoever enters through the gate is the shepherd of the sheep. The gatekeeper opens it for him, and the sheep hear his voice, as the shepherd calls his own sheep by name and leads them out. When he has driven out all his own, he walks ahead of them, and the sheep follow him, because they recognize his voice. But they will not follow a stranger; they will run away from him, because they do not recognize the voice of strangers." Although Jesus used this figure of speech, the Pharisees did not realize what he was trying to tell them.

So Jesus said again, "Amen, amen, I say to you, I am the gate for the sheep. All who came before me are thieves and robbers, but the sheep did not listen to them. I am the gate. Whoever enters through me will be saved, and will come in and go out and find pasture. A thief comes only to steal and slaughter and destroy; I came so that they might have life and have it more abundantly."

The Gospel of the Lord. *Praise to you, Lord Jesus Christ.*

PROFESSION OF FAITH *(page 13)*

PRAYER OF THE FAITHFUL

PREPARATION OF GIFTS *(page 16)*

PRAYER OVER THE OFFERINGS
Grant, we pray, O Lord,
that we may always find delight in these paschal mysteries,
so that the renewal constantly at work within us
may be the cause of our unending joy.
Through Christ our Lord. *Amen.*

PREFACE *(Easter 1–5, pages 24–26)*

• TAKING A CLOSER LOOK •

✛ **"Amen, amen"** *Amen* is a Hebrew word that affirms what has been said—"It is true!" It appears often throughout the Bible both in normal speech and in prayer whenever people want to signal their acceptance and affirmation. In the gospels, Jesus often begins his teaching with the phrase "Amen, I say to you" to emphasize the importance of what follows. And in John's gospel, when Jesus wants to really stress the importance of what he is about to say, he uses the curious double "Amen, amen" to invite his audience to pay close attention to his message.

COMMUNION ANTIPHON

The Good Shepherd has risen, who laid down his life for his sheep and willingly died for his flock, alleluia.

PRAYER AFTER COMMUNION

Look upon your flock, kind Shepherd,
and be pleased to settle in eternal pastures
the sheep you have redeemed
by the Precious Blood of your Son.
Who lives and reigns for ever and ever. ***Amen.***

SOLEMN BLESSING: EASTER TIME *(Optional, page 60)*

DISMISSAL *(page 57)* ✢

• RESPONDING TO THE WORD •

Personal conversion and baptism into the community are expected of new followers.	Peter uses Christ's behavior during his suffering as an example for us.	We hear the voice of Jesus our shepherd calling us by name.
➲ What changes in my life do I seek during this Easter season?	➲ Which characteristic of Christ's example do I find most difficult?	➲ When have I experienced Jesus calling me to a deeper relationship with him?

May 10

Continue Jesus' mission!

Today's gospel is the beginning of what is called Jesus' "farewell discourse" in John's gospel. He is saying goodbye, and the disciples are distressed. In response to their concern, Jesus makes some remarkable claims: that he will come back for them, that they already know the way to where he is going, that in seeing him they have seen the Father, and, finally, that they will do greater works than Jesus himself! On this last point, at least, we are often at one with the disciples. What could Jesus possibly mean? You and I are unlikely to walk on water.

Consider: Jesus healed dozens, maybe hundreds of people; the gospels tell us he fed thousands upon thousands. And how many people have received medical attention from Christ's followers since? How many have been fed? How many consoled? How many have had the good news preached to them? The answer should stun us, for it is both untold millions and not nearly enough.

In today's first reading, the resources of the early Church are challenged. The task of being Church to those in need is too big. In the face of that need new gifts are discerned, called forth, and blessed. And, as will happen again today at thousands of Masses around the world, people are fed and the gospel is preached. Let's not stop there.

■ **BRETT SALKELD**

ENTRANCE ANTIPHON *(Cf. Psalm 98 [97]:1-2)*

O sing a new song to the Lord, for he has worked wonders; in the sight of the nations he has shown his deliverance, alleluia.

INTRODUCTORY RITES *(page 10)*

COLLECT

Almighty ever-living God,
constantly accomplish the Paschal Mystery within us,
that those you were pleased to make new in Holy Baptism
may, under your protective care, bear much fruit
and come to the joys of life eternal.
Through our Lord Jesus Christ, your Son,
who lives and reigns with you in the unity of the Holy Spirit,
one God, for ever and ever. *Amen.*

FIRST READING *(Acts 6:1-7)*

As the number of disciples continued to grow, the Hellenists† complained against the Hebrews because their widows were being neglected in the daily distribution. So the Twelve called together the community of the disciples and said, "It is not right for us to neglect the word of God to serve at table. Brothers, select from among you seven reputable men, filled with the Spirit and wisdom, whom we shall appoint to this task, whereas we shall devote ourselves to prayer and to the ministry of the word." The proposal was acceptable to the whole community, so they chose Stephen, a man filled with faith and the Holy Spirit, also Philip, Prochorus, Nicanor,* Timon, Parmenas,* and Nicholas of Antioch, a convert to Judaism. They presented these men to the apostles who prayed and laid hands on them. The word of God continued to spread, and the number of the disciples in Jerusalem increased greatly; even a large group of priests were becoming obedient to the faith.

The word of the Lord. *Thanks be to God.*

RESPONSORIAL PSALM *(Psalm 33:1-2, 4-5, 18-19)*

℟. **Lord, let your mercy be on us, as we place our trust in you.**
  Or **Alleluia.**

Exult, you just, in the LORD;
  praise from the upright is fitting.
Give thanks to the LORD on the harp;
  with the ten-stringed lyre chant his praises. ℟.

Upright is the word of the LORD,
  and all his works are trustworthy.
He loves justice and right;
  of the kindness of the LORD the earth is full. ℟.

See, the eyes of the LORD are upon those who fear him,
  upon those who hope for his kindness,
To deliver them from death
  and preserve them in spite of famine. ℟.

SECOND READING *(1 Peter 2:4-9)*

Beloved: Come to him, a living stone, rejected by human beings but chosen and precious in the sight of God, and, like living stones, let yourselves be built into a spiritual house to be a holy priesthood to offer spiritual sacrifices acceptable to God through Jesus Christ. For it says in Scripture:

  Behold, I am laying a stone in Zion,*
  a cornerstone, chosen and precious,
  and whoever believes in it shall not be put to shame.

Therefore, its value is for you who have faith, but for those without faith:

> *The stone that the builders rejected*
> *has become the cornerstone,*

and

> *A stone that will make people stumble,*
> *and a rock that will make them fall.*

They stumble by disobeying the word, as is their destiny.

You are "a chosen race, a royal priesthood, a holy nation, a people of his own, so that you may announce the praises" of him who called you out of darkness into his wonderful light.

The word of the Lord. ***Thanks be to God.***

ALLELUIA *(John 14:6)*

Alleluia, alleluia. I am the way, the truth and the life, says the Lord; no one comes to the Father, except through me. ***Alleluia, alleluia.***

GOSPEL *(John 14:1-12)*

A reading from the holy Gospel according to John.
Glory to you, O Lord.

Jesus said to his disciples: "Do not let your hearts be troubled. You have faith in God; have faith also in me. In my Father's house there are many dwelling places. If there were not, would I have told you that I am going to prepare a place for you? And if I go and prepare a place for you, I will come back again and take you to myself, so that where I am you also may be. Where I am going you know the way." Thomas said to him, "Master, we do not know where you are going; how can we know the way?" Jesus said to him, "I am the way and the truth and the life. No one comes to the Father except through me. If you know me, then you will also know my Father. From now on you do know him and have seen him." Philip said to him, "Master, show us the

Father, and that will be enough for us." Jesus said to him, "Have I been with you for so long a time and you still do not know me, Philip? Whoever has seen me has seen the Father. How can you say, 'Show us the Father'? Do you not believe that I am in the Father and the Father is in me? The words that I speak to you I do not speak on my own. The Father who dwells in me is doing his works. Believe me that I am in the Father and the Father is in me, or else, believe because of the works themselves. Amen, amen, I say to you, whoever believes in me will do the works that I do, and will do greater ones than these, because I am going to the Father."

The Gospel of the Lord. *Praise to you, Lord Jesus Christ.*

PROFESSION OF FAITH *(page 13)*

PRAYER OF THE FAITHFUL

PREPARATION OF GIFTS *(page 16)*

• TAKING A CLOSER LOOK •

✛ **Hellenists** Hellenists (Greek for Greece, *Hellas*) were those from other nations who spoke Greek and were more receptive to the influence of Greek culture. Though the Romans ruled the Mediterranean nations, Greek literature and ideas formed the basis for education and the Greek language was used for international communication and business. To be educated often meant to be able to speak and read Greek (like St. Paul and the other New Testament authors who all wrote in Greek). For Jews, Hellenism posed a threat because its education was rooted in religious beliefs and social values that were not compatible with the Jewish belief that Yahweh was the one and only God (monotheism).

PRAYER OVER THE OFFERINGS

O God, who by the wonderful exchange effected in this sacrifice
have made us partakers of the one supreme Godhead,
grant, we pray,
that, as we have come to know your truth,
we may make it ours by a worthy way of life.
Through Christ our Lord. *Amen.*

PREFACE *(Easter 1–5, pages 24–26)*

COMMUNION ANTIPHON *(Cf. John 15:1, 5)*

I am the true vine and you are the branches, says the Lord.
Whoever remains in me, and I in him, bears fruit in plenty,
alleluia.

PRAYER AFTER COMMUNION

Graciously be present to your people, we pray, O Lord,
and lead those you have imbued with heavenly mysteries
to pass from former ways to newness of life.
Through Christ our Lord. *Amen.*

SOLEMN BLESSING: EASTER TIME *(Optional, page 60)*

DISMISSAL *(page 57)* ✴

● RESPONDING TO THE WORD ●

The Twelve call others to service in the community.	The rejected stone becomes useful in God's eyes.	Jesus is both the image of and the way to God.
➡ *What new service can I offer to my community?*	➡ *When did I fail to see the value of others?*	➡ *How has Jesus led me to God during this holy season?*

May 17

MAY
17

Live as people of the gospel

Soon, we will celebrate two feasts. The Ascension will close Jesus' earthly life as he is raised to the Father, while the feast of Pentecost will draw our attention to the descending Holy Spirit who comes to fulfill Jesus' promise to us: "I will not leave you orphaned... I will ask the Father, and he will give you another Advocate, to be with you always. This is the Spirit of truth."

These final movements in the Easter season prepare us to accept the great commission we hear in John's Gospel to go forth in this life to love and to serve the Lord. We become signs of God's presence by strengthening our families and friendships, respecting life, attending to our environment, keeping our bodies healthy, praying for others, consoling the sick and those in need, finding Christ in our sufferings, witnessing Christ in our lives each day, showing compassion, and promoting reconciliation.

In the Eucharist we come forward to share in the life of God as we receive the body and blood of his Son, Jesus Christ. Let us pray that we will become what we eat: the Body of Christ. Nourished with this holy food we will move with the force of the Holy Spirit and the fire of God's love to live as people of the gospel.

■ **Rev. Dr. Matthew Durham, CSB**

In those places where the Ascension of the Lord is celebrated next Sunday, the second reading and Gospel from the Seventh Sunday of Easter may be read today (see pages 385-386).

ENTRANCE ANTIPHON *(Cf. Isaiah 48:20)*

Proclaim a joyful sound and let it be heard; proclaim to the ends of the earth: The Lord has freed his people, alleluia.

INTRODUCTORY RITES *(page 10)*

COLLECT

Grant, almighty God,
that we may celebrate with heartfelt devotion these days of joy,
which we keep in honor of the risen Lord,
and that what we relive in remembrance
we may always hold to in what we do.
Through our Lord Jesus Christ, your Son,
who lives and reigns with you in the unity of the Holy Spirit,
one God, for ever and ever. *Amen.*

FIRST READING *(Acts 8:5-8, 14-17)*

Philip went down to the city of Samaria* and proclaimed the Christ to them. With one accord, the crowds paid attention to what was said by Philip when they heard it and saw the signs he was doing. For unclean spirits, crying out in a loud voice, came out of many possessed people, and many paralyzed or crippled people were cured. There was great joy in that city.

Now when the apostles in Jerusalem heard that Samaria had accepted the word of God, they sent them Peter and John, who went down and prayed for them, that they might receive the Holy Spirit, for it had not yet fallen upon any of them; they had only been baptized in the name of the Lord Jesus. Then they laid

hands on them and they received the Holy Spirit.
The word of the Lord. *Thanks be to God.*

RESPONSORIAL PSALM *(Psalm 66:1-3, 4-5, 6-7, 16, 20)*
℟ Let all the earth cry out to God with joy. *Or* Alleluia.

Shout joyfully to God, all the earth,
 sing praise to the glory of his name;
 proclaim his glorious praise.
Say to God, "How tremendous are your deeds!" ℟
"Let all on earth worship and sing praise to you,
 sing praise to your name!"
Come and see the works of God,
 his tremendous deeds among the children of Adam. ℟
He has changed the sea into dry land;
 through the river they passed on foot;
 therefore let us rejoice in him.
He rules by his might forever. ℟
Hear now, all you who fear God, while I declare
 what he has done for me.
Blessed be God who refused me not
 my prayer or his kindness! ℟

SECOND READING *(1 Peter 3:15-18)*

Beloved: Sanctify Christ as Lord in your hearts. Always be ready to give an explanation to anyone who asks you for a reason for your hope, but do it with gentleness and reverence, keeping your conscience clear, so that, when you are maligned, those who defame your good conduct in Christ may themselves be put to shame. For it is better to suffer for doing good, if that be the will of God, than for doing evil. For Christ also suffered for sins once, the righteous for the sake of the unrighteous, that he might lead you to God. Put to death in the flesh, he was brought to life in the Spirit.

The word of the Lord. *Thanks be to God.*

ALLELUIA *(John 14:23)*
Alleluia, alleluia. Whoever loves me will keep my word, says the Lord, and my Father will love him and we will come to him. *Alleluia, alleluia.*

GOSPEL *(John 14:15–21)*
A reading from the holy Gospel according to John.
Glory to you, O Lord.

Jesus said to his disciples: "If you love me, you will keep my commandments. And I will ask the Father, and he will give you another **Advocate**✝ to be with you always, the Spirit of truth, whom the world cannot accept, because it neither sees nor knows him. But you know him, because he remains with you, and will be in you. I will not leave you orphans; I will come to you. In a little while the world will no longer see me, but you will see me, because I live and you will live. On that day you will realize that I am in my Father and you are in me and I in you. Whoever has my commandments and observes them is the one who loves me. And whoever loves me will be loved by my Father, and I will love him and reveal myself to him."

The Gospel of the Lord. *Praise to you, Lord Jesus Christ.*

PROFESSION OF FAITH *(page 13)*

PRAYER OF THE FAITHFUL

PREPARATION OF GIFTS *(page 16)*

PRAYER OVER THE OFFERINGS

May our prayers rise up to you, O Lord,
together with the sacrificial offerings,
so that, purified by your graciousness,
we may be conformed to the mysteries of your mighty love.
Through Christ our Lord. *Amen.*

PREFACE *(Easter 1–5, pages 24–26)*

COMMUNION ANTIPHON *(John 14:15–16)*

If you love me, keep my commandments, says the Lord, and I
will ask the Father and he will send you another Paraclete, to
abide with you for ever, alleluia.

❖ TAKING A CLOSER LOOK ❖

✙ **Advocate** Jesus responds with the promise of an indwelling presence to those who keep his commandments. That presence is described variously as being of both the Father and Jesus, of the Holy Spirit, or that of Jesus himself. Jesus' abiding presence with the disciples after his return to the Father is accomplished in and through the Advocate (Greek, *parakletos*, Paraclete), as John usually identifies the Holy Spirit. The idea of an advocate, which is taken from the law courts, identifies the one who, like a lawyer, comes to stand by the side of the one in need and to speak in his or her defense.

PRAYER AFTER COMMUNION

Almighty ever-living God,
who restore us to eternal life in the Resurrection of Christ,
increase in us, we pray, the fruits of this paschal Sacrament
and pour into our hearts the strength of this saving food.
Through Christ our Lord. ***Amen.***

SOLEMN BLESSING: EASTER TIME *(Optional, page 60)*

DISMISSAL *(page 57)* ✣

• RESPONDING TO THE WORD •

The crowds respond with joy to the words and signs that reveal Christ.	Peter encourages us to be ready to share the reason for our hope.	Jesus reminds us that he dwells in us and will reveal himself to us.
➡ *What has caused me to rejoice during this Easter season?*	➡ *With whom might I share my hope today?*	➡ *How have I been more aware of Christ's presence in me and my life?*

May 21

MAY
21

All dioceses in the United States, except those within the ecclesiastical provinces of Boston, Hartford, New York, Newark, Philadelphia, and Omaha, transfer the celebration of the Ascension of the Lord from Thursday to this coming Sunday.

If the Ascension is celebrated on Thursday in your diocese, see the Mass for the Ascension on page 379. Then next Sunday use the Mass for the Seventh Sunday of Easter on page 384.

May 24

Always remember

As I read the Ascension Sunday readings, I kept returning to the final line of the gospel: "And behold, I am with you always, to the end of the age."

Since 2017, I have experienced memory loss, which has been initially diagnosed as mild cognitive impairment. So Jesus' urging that we remember his promise gets my attention. Memory should never be taken for granted. Since my problems began, I have done my best to remember God's love in the Eucharist, daily prayer, and the others with whom I share my life. Jesus' promise to be with us always strengthens and comforts me.

In the Act of the Apostles, before Jesus ascends into heaven, he tells his disciples they will receive power when the Holy Spirit comes upon them. God wants so much to be with us that God will find a way. We must let these great promises sink in. No matter what our circumstances, whatever difficulties we face, God is with us. We need to sit with these words, reading them slowly, again and again.

When you suffer, as we all will, remember to give God space, especially in your heart. Yours will be a powerful witness and lives will change, though you may know nothing about it. Remember Christ's words: "I am with you always."

■ HARRY MCAVOY

THE ASCENSION OF THE LORD
(MASS DURING THE DAY)

ENTRANCE ANTIPHON *(Acts 1:11)*
Men of Galilee, why gaze in wonder at the heavens?
This Jesus whom you saw ascending into heaven will return as
you saw him go, alleluia.

INTRODUCTORY RITES *(page 10)*

COLLECT
Gladden us with holy joys, almighty God,
and make us rejoice with devout thanksgiving,
for the Ascension of Christ your Son
is our exaltation,
and, where the Head has gone before in glory,
the Body is called to follow in hope.
Through our Lord Jesus Christ, your Son,
who lives and reigns with you in the unity of the Holy Spirit,
one God, for ever and ever. *Amen.*

Or

Grant, we pray, almighty God,
that we, who believe that your Only Begotten Son,
    our Redeemer,
ascended this day to the heavens,
may in spirit dwell already in heavenly realms.
Who lives and reigns with you in the unity of the Holy Spirit,
one God, for ever and ever. *Amen.*

FIRST READING *(Acts 1:1-11)*

In the first book, Theophilus, I dealt with all that Jesus did and taught until the day he was taken up, after giving instructions through the Holy Spirit to the apostles whom he had chosen. He presented himself alive to them by many proofs after he had suffered, appearing to them during forty days and speaking about the kingdom of God. While meeting with them, he enjoined them not to depart from Jerusalem, but to wait for "the promise of the Father about which you have heard me speak; for John baptized with water, but in a few days you will be **baptized with the Holy Spirit.**"✝

When they had gathered together they asked him, "Lord, are you at this time going to restore the kingdom to Israel?" He answered them, "It is not for you to know the times or seasons that the Father has established by his own authority. But you will receive power when the Holy Spirit comes upon you, and you will be my witnesses in Jerusalem, throughout Judea and Samaria,* and to the ends of the earth." When he had said this, as they were looking on, he was lifted up, and a cloud took him from their sight. While they were looking intently at the sky as he was going, suddenly two men dressed in white garments stood beside them. They said, "Men of Galilee, why are you standing there looking at the sky? This Jesus who has been taken up from you into heaven will return in the same way you have seen him going into heaven."

The word of the Lord. *Thanks be to God.*

RESPONSORIAL PSALM *(Psalm 47:2-3, 6-7, 8-9)*

R̶ **God mounts his throne to shouts of joy: a blare of trumpets for the Lord.** *Or* **Alleluia.**

All you peoples, clap your hands,
    shout to God with cries of gladness,

for the LORD, the Most High, the awesome,
   is the great king over all the earth. ℟
God mounts his throne amid shouts of joy;
   the LORD, amid trumpet blasts.
Sing praise to God, sing praise;
   sing praise to our king, sing praise. ℟
For king of all the earth is God;
   sing hymns of praise.
God reigns over the nations,
   God sits upon his holy throne. ℟

SECOND READING *(Ephesians 1:17-23)*

Brothers and sisters: May the God of our Lord Jesus Christ, the Father of glory, give you a Spirit of wisdom and revelation resulting in knowledge of him. May the eyes of your hearts be enlightened, that you may know what is the hope that belongs to his call, what are the riches of glory in his inheritance among the holy ones, and what is the surpassing greatness of his power for us who believe, in accord with the exercise of his great might, which he worked in Christ, raising him from the dead and seating him at his right hand in the heavens, far above every principality, authority, power, and dominion, and every name that is named not only in this age but also in the one to come. And he put all things beneath his feet and gave him as head over all things to the church, which is his body, the fullness of the one who fills all things in every way.

   The word of the Lord. *Thanks be to God.*

ALLELUIA *(Matthew 28:19a, 20b)*
Alleluia, alleluia. Go and teach all nations, says the Lord; I am with you always, until the end of the world. *Alleluia, alleluia.*

GOSPEL *(Matthew 28:16-20)*
A reading from the holy Gospel according to Matthew.
Glory to you, O Lord.

The eleven disciples went to Galilee, to the mountain to which Jesus had ordered them. When they saw him, they worshiped, but they doubted. Then Jesus approached and said to them, "All power in heaven and on earth has been given to me. Go, therefore, and make disciples of all nations, baptizing them in the name of the Father, and of the Son, and of the Holy Spirit, teaching them to observe all that I have commanded you. And behold, I am with you always, until the end of the age."

The Gospel of the Lord. *Praise to you, Lord Jesus Christ.*

PROFESSION OF FAITH *(page 13)*

PRAYER OF THE FAITHFUL

PREPARATION OF GIFTS *(page 16)*

PRAYER OVER THE OFFERINGS
We offer sacrifice now in supplication, O Lord,
to honor the wondrous Ascension of your Son:

• TAKING A CLOSER LOOK •

✝ **Baptized with the Holy Spirit** For the early Christians, there were two great signs of God's saving activity that would bring a new life: the resurrection of Jesus and the outpouring of God's Holy Spirit. Jesus compares this outpouring of God's Spirit (the power of life associated with breathing) to a baptismal washing that not only purifies the person but signifies one's desire to change one's ways and be more closely united with God's saving activity. Empowered by the indwelling of God's holy presence, the disciples can carry on the mission and ministry of Jesus.

grant, we pray,
that through this most holy exchange
we, too, may rise up to the heavenly realms.
Through Christ our Lord. *Amen.*

PREFACE *(Ascension of the Lord 1–2, page 27)*

COMMUNION ANTIPHON *(Matthew 28:20)*
Behold, I am with you always, even to the end of the age, alleluia.

PRAYER AFTER COMMUNION
Almighty ever-living God,
who allow those on earth to celebrate divine mysteries,
grant, we pray,
that Christian hope may draw us onward
to where our nature is united with you.
Through Christ our Lord. *Amen.*

SOLEMN BLESSING: THE ASCENSION OF THE LORD *(Optional, page 61)*

DISMISSAL *(page 57)* ⁂

⁂ RESPONDING TO THE WORD ⁂

Though Jesus departs, he promises empowerment by the Holy Spirit.

➡ When have I felt most empowered by the Holy Spirit?

Paul prays that our hearts be enlightened to know God and God's actions for us.

➡ What new insight have I had during this Easter season?

Jesus sends us to make disciples of others.

➡ What can I do to bring someone closer to Christ today?

SEVENTH SUNDAY OF EASTER

ENTRANCE ANTIPHON *(Cf. Psalm 27 [26]:7-9)*
O Lord, hear my voice, for I have called to you; of you my heart
has spoken: Seek his face; hide not your face from me, alleluia.

INTRODUCTORY RITES *(page 10)*

COLLECT
Graciously hear our supplications, O Lord,
so that we, who believe that the Savior of the human race
is with you in your glory,
may experience, as he promised,
until the end of the world,
his abiding presence among us.
Who lives and reigns with you in the unity of the Holy Spirit,
one God, for ever and ever. *Amen.*

FIRST READING *(Acts 1:12-14)*

After Jesus had been taken up to heaven the apostles returned
to Jerusalem from the mount called Olivet, which is near
Jerusalem, a sabbath day's journey away.

When they entered the city they went to the upper room
where they were staying, Peter and John and James and Andrew,
Philip and Thomas, Bartholomew and Matthew, James son of
Alphaeus,* Simon the Zealot, and Judas son of James. All these
devoted themselves with one accord to prayer, together with
some women, and Mary the mother of Jesus, and his brothers.

The word of the Lord. *Thanks be to God.*

RESPONSORIAL PSALM *(Psalm 27:1, 4, 7-8)*

℞ **I believe that I shall see the good things of the Lord
in the land of the living.** *Or* **Alleluia.**

The LORD is my light and my salvation;
  whom should I fear?
The LORD is my life's refuge;
  of whom should I be afraid? ℞

One thing I ask of the LORD;
  this I seek:
To dwell in the house of the LORD
  all the days of my life,
that I may gaze on the loveliness of the LORD
  and contemplate his temple. ℞

Hear, O LORD, the sound of my call;
  have pity on me, and answer me.
Of you my heart speaks; you my glance seeks. ℞

SECOND READING *(1 Peter 4:13-16)*

Beloved: Rejoice to the extent that you share in the sufferings of Christ, so that when his glory is revealed you may also rejoice exultantly. If you are insulted for the name of Christ, blessed are you, for the Spirit of glory and of God rests upon you. But let no one among you be made to suffer as a murderer, a thief, an evildoer, or as an intriguer. But whoever is made to suffer as a Christian should not be ashamed but glorify God because of the name.

The word of the Lord. ***Thanks be to God.***

ALLELUIA *(See John 14:18)*
Alleluia, alleluia. I will not leave you orphans, says the Lord.
I will come back to you, and your hearts will rejoice. *Alleluia,*
alleluia.

GOSPEL *(John 17:1-11a)*
A reading from the holy Gospel according to John.
Glory to you, O Lord.

Jesus raised his eyes to heaven and said, "Father, the hour has
come. Give glory to your son, so that your son may glorify
you, just as you gave him authority over all people, so that your
son may give eternal life to all you gave him. Now this is eternal
life, that they should know you, the only true God, and the
one whom you sent, Jesus Christ. I glorified you on earth by
accomplishing the work that you gave me to do. Now glorify
me, Father, with you, with the glory that I had with you before
the world✝ began.

"I revealed your name to those whom you gave me out of the
world. They belonged to you, and you gave them to me, and they
have kept your word. Now they know that everything you gave
me is from you, because the words you gave to me I have given to
them, and they accepted them and truly understood that I came
from you, and they have believed that you sent me. I pray for
them. I do not pray for the world but for the ones you have given
me, because they are yours, and everything of mine is yours and
everything of yours is mine, and I have been glorified in them.
And now I will no longer be in the world, but they are in the
world, while I am coming to you."

The Gospel of the Lord. *Praise to you, Lord Jesus Christ.*

PROFESSION OF FAITH *(page 13)*

PRAYER OF THE FAITHFUL

PREPARATION OF GIFTS *(page 16)*

PRAYER OVER THE OFFERINGS

Accept, O Lord, the prayers of your faithful
with the sacrificial offerings,
that through these acts of devotedness
we may pass over to the glory of heaven.
Through Christ our Lord. *Amen.*

PREFACE *(Easter 1-5, pages 24-26, or Ascension 1-2, page 27)*

COMMUNION ANTIPHON *(John 17: 22)*

Father, I pray that they may be one as we also are one, alleluia.

• Taking a Closer Look •

✛ **The world** As so often in John's gospel and letters, many terms have two levels of meaning. Usually "the world" (Greek, *cosmos*) would describe the ordered quality of God's creation. But since John also sees a spiritual dimension to all of our existence, he uses "the world" as a shorthand way to refer to the forces that we often experience that resist the ordering power of God and so stand in opposition to Jesus and the Christian community. Though the world is hostile to God, God is not hostile to the world but sends Jesus "into the world" for its salvation.

PRAYER AFTER COMMUNION

Hear us, O God our Savior,
and grant us confidence,
that through these sacred mysteries
there will be accomplished in the body of the whole Church
what has already come to pass in Christ her Head.
Who lives and reigns for ever and ever. *Amen.*

SOLEMN BLESSING: EASTER TIME *(Optional, page 60)*

DISMISSAL *(page 57)* ⁜

• RESPONDING TO THE WORD •

The disciples make prayer part of their life as they await the descent of the Holy Spirit.	Peter encourages us to rejoice when we suffer for Christ's sake.	Jesus offers us an example in the way that he prays for us.
➲ How might I renew my dedication to prayer this week?	➲ How can I link my sufferings to those of Christ?	➲ For whom do I wish to pray today?

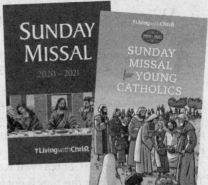

Witnesses of the good news

As the gospels show, every time the disciples experience the risen and ascended Christ, they are told to share this with others. Being a Christian can never be just a "me and Jesus" experience. We must continue the ministry and mission of Jesus in our world. Pentecost reminds us of this task and invites us to take the Easter message of Christ's resurrection and spread this good news to our world.

The remainder of the Church's year is called "ordinary time." This does not mean that this time is not important, but rather that it is "ordered" by our ever-deepening appreciation of how the mystery of our faith must be lived in our everyday lives.

During this time, Sunday by Sunday, we listen and respond to the Scripture readings and thus deepen our awareness of Jesus' life and teaching. As we better understand who he was, we also better understand who we are as his followers today.

Jesus' message was a new way to relate to God and to others, and this is what we share with our family, our friends, our fellow parishioners, and all those with whom we work and play. As individuals and communities, we begin to live right now as the kingdom community that Christ envisioned. We must dare to create communities based on justice and right relationships with one another, built on love and respect for each person as a beloved child of God.

Praying and living Pentecost all year

Find a time to pray quietly or gather the household. (You may wish to do this several times between Pentecost and the end of the liturgical year.) Pray this prayer to the Holy Spirit:

Come, Holy Spirit, fill the hearts of your faithful
and enkindle in them the fire of your love.
Send forth your Spirit and they shall be created,
and you shall renew the face of the earth.

The Holy Spirit has given each of us personal gifts to use for building the Christian community. Consider the following questions (if you are with others, reflect and share together):

• What are the Holy Spirit's gifts to me?
• What situation or event illustrates how that gift helps others?
• In what other ways might I use my gifts?

    If you are with others, invite each person to proceed around the circle, laying a hand on each person's head, while saying:

    May you use your gifts in the service of God and others.

When all have had a chance to bless and be blessed, pray:

O God, help us to use your gifts
to make the world a better place—
more filled with your presence,
more in keeping with your desires,
and more aligned with your will.
Send your Holy Spirit upon us now
so that we can recognize the gifts you have given,
more eagerly make them our own,
and more willingly share them with others.
Amen.

May 31

Mighty and mysterious

Our God is a God of contradiction. In fact, it is in these contradictions that we learn peace, a fruit of the Spirit.

In today's readings we hear two accounts of the Holy Spirit that are radically opposed. In Acts, the Spirit comes to the apostles like a mighty wind and a shower of flame. It is unexpected and frightening. It is incomprehensible to bystanders.

In the Gospel of John, Jesus comes to the disciples and breathes the Spirit onto them in person. Jesus is flesh and blood and familiar to them. He wishes them peace.

These two narratives illustrate the Holy Spirit as being at once frightening and comforting, mysterious and familiar, transcendent and immanent. This is just as it should be, because the Spirit of peace is all of these things despite apparent contradiction.

Peace, a grace given and a virtue pursued, flows from knowing the Spirit of God, God the creator of all. God is maker of fire, of venomous spiders, and of all clawed and toothed beasts inasmuch as God is the creator of the sun and the moon and the laughter of children.

To be at peace is to rest in this, which we cannot understand and which might even frighten us. It is to trust in the Lord who is mighty and mysterious, but who is good.

■ GABRIELLE JOHNSON

MASS DURING THE DAY

ENTRANCE ANTIPHON *(Wisdom 1:7)*
The Spirit of the Lord has filled the whole world and
that which contains all things understands what is
said, alleluia.

Or *(Romans 5:5; cf. 8:11)*
The love of God has been poured into our hearts through the
Spirit of God dwelling within us, alleluia.

INTRODUCTORY RITES *(page 10)*

COLLECT
O God, who by the mystery of today's great feast
sanctify your whole Church in every people and nation,
pour out, we pray, the gifts of the Holy Spirit
across the face of the earth
and, with the divine grace that was at work
when the Gospel was first proclaimed,
fill now once more the hearts of believers.
Through our Lord Jesus Christ, your Son,
who lives and reigns with you in the unity of the Holy Spirit,
one God, for ever and ever. ***Amen.***

FIRST READING *(Acts 2:1-11)*
When the time for **Pentecost**✝ was fulfilled, they were
all in one place together. And suddenly there came
from the sky a noise like a strong driving wind, and it filled
the entire house in which they were. Then there appeared to
them tongues as of fire, which parted and came to rest on each
one of them. And they were all filled with the Holy Spirit and

began to speak in different tongues, as the Spirit enabled them to proclaim.

Now there were devout Jews from every nation under heaven staying in Jerusalem. At this sound, they gathered in a large crowd, but they were confused because each one heard them speaking in his own language. They were astounded, and in amazement they asked, "Are not all these people who are speaking Galileans? Then how does each of us hear them in his native language? We are Parthians,* Medes,* and Elamites,* inhabitants of Mesopotamia,* Judea and Cappadocia,* Pontus and Asia, Phrygia* and Pamphylia,* Egypt and the districts of Libya near Cyrene, as well as travelers from Rome, both Jews and converts to Judaism, Cretans and Arabs, yet we hear them speaking in our own tongues of the mighty acts of God."

The word of the Lord. *Thanks be to God.*

RESPONSORIAL PSALM *(Psalm 104:1, 24, 29-30, 31, 34)*

℟ **Lord, send out your Spirit, and renew the face of the earth.**
　Or **Alleluia.**

Bless the LORD, O my soul!
　O LORD, my God, you are great indeed!
How manifold are your works, O LORD!
　The earth is full of your creatures. ℟
If you take away their breath, they perish
　and return to their dust.
When you send forth your spirit, they are created,
　and you renew the face of the earth. ℟
May the glory of the Lord endure forever;
　may the LORD be glad in his works!
Pleasing to him be my theme;
　I will be glad in the LORD. ℟

SECOND READING *(1 Corinthians 12:3b-7, 12-13)*

Brothers and sisters: No one can say, "Jesus is Lord," except by the Holy Spirit.

There are different kinds of spiritual gifts but the same Spirit; there are different forms of service but the same Lord; there are different workings but the same God who produces all of them in everyone. To each individual the manifestation of the Spirit is given for some benefit.

As a body is one though it has many parts, and all the parts of the body, though many, are one body, so also Christ. For in one Spirit we were all baptized into one body, whether Jews or Greeks, slaves or free persons, and we were all given to drink of one Spirit.

The word of the Lord. *Thanks be to God.*

SEQUENCE *(Veni, Sancte Spiritus)*

Come, Holy Spirit, come!
And from your celestial home
   Shed a ray of light divine!
Come, Father of the poor!
Come, source of all our store!
   Come, within our bosoms shine.
You, of comforters the best;
You, the soul's most welcome guest;
   Sweet refreshment here below;
In our labor, rest most sweet;
Grateful coolness in the heat;
   Solace in the midst of woe.
O most blessed Light divine,
Shine within these hearts of yours,
   And our inmost being fill!

Where you are not, we have naught,
Nothing good in deed or thought,
  Nothing free from taint of ill.
Heal our wounds, our strength renew;
On our dryness pour your dew;
  Wash the stains of guilt away:
Bend the stubborn heart and will;
Melt the frozen, warm the chill;
  Guide the steps that go astray.
On the faithful, who adore
And confess you, evermore
  In your sevenfold gift descend;
Give them virtue's sure reward;
Give them your salvation, Lord;
  Give them joys that never end. Amen.
  Alleluia.

ALLELUIA

Alleluia, alleluia. Come, Holy Spirit, fill the hearts of your faithful and kindle in them the fire of your love. *Alleluia, alleluia.*

GOSPEL (*John 20:19-23*)

A reading from the holy Gospel according to John.
Glory to you, O Lord.

On the evening of that first day of the week, when the doors were locked, where the disciples were, for fear of the Jews, Jesus came and stood in their midst and said to them, "Peace be with you." When he had said this, he showed them his hands and his side. The disciples rejoiced when they saw the Lord. Jesus said to them again, "Peace be with you. As the Father has sent me, so I send you." And when he had said this, he breathed on them and said to them, "Receive the Holy Spirit. Whose sins you forgive are forgiven them, and whose sins you retain are retained."

The Gospel of the Lord. *Praise to you, Lord Jesus Christ.*

PROFESSION OF FAITH (*page 13*)

PRAYER OF THE FAITHFUL

PREPARATION OF GIFTS (*page 16*)

PRAYER OVER THE OFFERINGS

Grant, we pray, O Lord,
that, as promised by your Son,
the Holy Spirit may reveal to us more abundantly
the hidden mystery of this sacrifice
and graciously lead us into all truth.
Through Christ our Lord. *Amen.*

PREFACE: THE MYSTERY OF PENTECOST

It is truly right and just, our duty and our salvation,
always and everywhere to give you thanks,
Lord, holy Father, almighty and eternal God.

For, bringing your Paschal Mystery to completion,
you bestowed the Holy Spirit today
on those you made your adopted children
by uniting them to your Only Begotten Son.
This same Spirit, as the Church came to birth,
opened to all peoples the knowledge of God
and brought together the many languages of the earth
in profession of the one faith.

Therefore, overcome with paschal joy,
every land, every people exults in your praise
and even the heavenly Powers, with the angelic hosts,
sing together the unending hymn of your glory,
as they acclaim:
Holy, Holy, Holy Lord God of hosts... *(page 35)*

• TAKING A CLOSER LOOK •

✛ **Pentecost** *Pentecost* (Greek, the "fiftieth day") was the Jewish feast (also called "Weeks" or *Shavuot*) that came fifty days after Passover. It celebrated the spring grain harvest and the offering to God of the firstfruits of the crop (Exodus 23:14-17). One of the three major Jewish feast days, over the centuries it became associated with the giving of the Law (or *Torah*) and focused more on covenant renewal. In the New Testament, this feast day echoes the Jewish themes with the descent of the Holy Spirit to form the Christian community and to harvest the firstfruits of its universal mission.

COMMUNION ANTIPHON *(Acts 2:4, 11)*

They were all filled with the Holy Spirit and spoke of the marvels of God, alleluia.

PRAYER AFTER COMMUNION

O God, who bestow heavenly gifts upon your Church,
safeguard, we pray, the grace you have given,
that the gift of the Holy Spirit poured out upon her
may retain all its force
and that this spiritual food
may gain her abundance of eternal redemption.
Through Christ our Lord. *Amen.*

SOLEMN BLESSING: THE HOLY SPIRIT *(Optional, page 62)*

DISMISSAL *(page 57)* ✢

✦ RESPONDING TO THE WORD ✦

The disciples are changed by their contact with God's Holy Spirit.	The Holy Spirit bestows gifts of service on us to build up the community.	Jesus offers peace and reconciliation to us and sends us to do the same.
⮑ *What changes has God brought about in me during this Easter season?*	⮑ *How am I using my spiritual gifts for the benefit of others?*	⮑ *How can I extend peace and reconciliation to those from whom I am estranged?*

June 7

Living in the mystery

Trinity Sunday celebrates one God, three persons, complete mystery. The readings ground us in the simplicity of who God is and what God does for us.

The story of Moses on the mountain reveals a God who meets us on the mountains of our lives, who reveals mercy and love, faithfulness and patience. When we ask God for what we need, God answers, even if the answers aren't as immediate or clear as the stone tablets. In the fullness of time, this same God reveals the plan for our salvation: Jesus is sent in human flesh to love us. By his life, death, and rising, Jesus gives us the example of how to love and then gives us the gift of the Spirit.

So much of our spiritual life is participation in a mystery that is beyond our understanding, but the second reading offers us a simple guide and blessing. Live the moments of your life seeking peace with God and one another, and allow the healing grace of Jesus, the love of the Father, and the communion of the Spirit to be poured over you and everything you do.

May it be enough for us to live right in the middle of this mystery of God working love in and through our lives. May the Father, Son, and Holy Spirit flow through us to those most in need of God's simple and saving love.

🔳 LEAH PERRAULT

ENTRANCE ANTIPHON

Blest be God the Father, and the Only Begotten Son of God, and also the Holy Spirit, for he has shown us his merciful love.

INTRODUCTORY RITES *(page 10)*

COLLECT

God our Father, who by sending into the world
the Word of truth and the Spirit of sanctification
made known to the human race your wondrous mystery,
grant us, we pray, that in professing the true faith,
we may acknowledge the Trinity of eternal glory
and adore your Unity, powerful in majesty.
Through our Lord Jesus Christ, your Son,
who lives and reigns with you in the unity of the Holy Spirit,
one God, for ever and ever. *Amen.*

FIRST READING *(Exodus 34:4b-6, 8-9)*

Early in the morning Moses went up Mount Sinai as the LORD✛ had commanded him, taking along the two stone tablets.

Having come down in a cloud, the LORD stood with Moses there and proclaimed his name, "LORD." Thus the LORD passed before him and cried out, "The LORD, the LORD, a merciful and gracious God, slow to anger and rich in kindness and fidelity." Moses at once bowed down to the ground in worship. Then he said, "If I find favor with you, O LORD, do come along in our company. This is indeed a stiff-necked people; yet pardon our wickedness and sins, and receive us as your own."

The word of the Lord. *Thanks be to God.*

RESPONSORIAL CANTICLE *(Daniel 3:52, 53, 54, 55)*
℟ **Glory and praise for ever!**

Blessed are you, O Lord, the God of our fathers,
  praiseworthy and exalted above all forever;
And blessed is your holy and glorious name,
  praiseworthy and exalted above all for all ages. ℟
Blessed are you in the temple of your holy glory,
  praiseworthy and glorious above all forever. ℟
Blessed are you on the throne of your kingdom,
  praiseworthy and exalted above all forever. ℟
Blessed are you who look into the depths
  from your throne upon the cherubim,*
  praiseworthy and exalted above all forever. ℟

SECOND READING *(2 Corinthians 13:11-13)*

Brothers and sisters, rejoice. Mend your ways, encourage one another, agree with one another, live in peace, and the God of love and peace will be with you. Greet one another with a holy kiss. All the holy ones greet you.

The grace of the Lord Jesus Christ and the love of God and the fellowship of the Holy Spirit be with all of you.

The word of the Lord. ***Thanks be to God.***

ALLELUIA *(See Revelation 1:8)*
Alleluia, alleluia. Glory to the Father, the Son, and the Holy Spirit; to God who is, who was, and who is to come. *Alleluia, alleluia.*

GOSPEL *(John 3:16–18)*

A reading from the holy Gospel according to John.

Glory to you, O Lord.

God so loved the world that he gave his only Son, so that everyone who believes in him might not perish but might have eternal life. For God did not send his Son into the world to condemn the world, but that the world might be saved through him. Whoever believes in him will not be condemned, but whoever does not believe has already been condemned, because he has not believed in the name of the only Son of God.

The Gospel of the Lord. *Praise to you, Lord Jesus Christ.*

PROFESSION OF FAITH *(page 13)*

PRAYER OF THE FAITHFUL

PREPARATION OF GIFTS *(page 16)*

PRAYER OVER THE OFFERINGS

Sanctify by the invocation of your name,
we pray, O Lord our God,
this oblation of our service,
and by it make of us an eternal offering to you.
Through Christ our Lord. *Amen.*

PREFACE: THE MYSTERY OF THE MOST HOLY TRINITY

It is truly right and just, our duty and our salvation,
always and everywhere to give you thanks,
Lord, holy Father, almighty and eternal God.

For with your Only Begotten Son and the Holy Spirit
you are one God, one Lord:
not in the unity of a single person,
but in a Trinity of one substance.

For what you have revealed to us of your glory
we believe equally of your Son
and of the Holy Spirit,
so that, in the confessing of the true and eternal Godhead,
you might be adored in what is proper to each Person,
their unity in substance,
and their equality in majesty.

• TAKING A CLOSER LOOK •

✝ **Lord** The New American translation of the Bible used for our Sunday Mass readings uses LORD in small capital letters to indicate the sacred name of God revealed to Moses and the Israelites—*Yahweh*. LORD has the same number of letters as God's sacred name: since the Hebrew language wrote only the consonants and not the vowels, God's name was written with four letters: YHWH (in English). Moreover, since God's name was and is so sacred, Jews do not speak it aloud but instead often say *Adoni*, the Hebrew word for Lord or Master. In the Bible, when God is addressed as "Lord Yahweh" (*Adoni YHWH*), God is put in the small capital letters. So when we see LORD or GOD in small capital letters in the Scripture text, we know that the original word is *Yahweh*, the unique personal name by which God wanted to be known.

For this is praised by Angels and Archangels,
Cherubim, too, and Seraphim,
who never cease to cry out each day,
as with one voice they acclaim:
Holy, holy, holy, Lord God of hosts... *(page 35)*

COMMUNION ANTIPHON *(Galatians 4:6)*
Since you are children of God, God has sent into your hearts the
Spirit of his Son, the Spirit who cries out: Abba, Father.

PRAYER AFTER COMMUNION
May receiving this Sacrament, O Lord our God,
bring us health of body and soul,
as we confess your eternal holy Trinity and undivided Unity.
Through Christ our Lord. ***Amen.***

BLESSING & DISMISSAL *(page 56)* ❖

• RESPONDING TO THE WORD •

Moses learns that God is merciful and gracious.	Paul tells us to encourage one another.	Jesus did not come to condemn us but to teach us how to love.
➡ *Who or what has taught me most about God's mercy?*	➡ *To whom might I give encouragement today?*	➡ *When am I more ready to condemn than to love? Why?*

June 14

Becoming a self-giving disciple

Today's gospel demonstrates that the incarnation and paschal mystery are essential to our understanding of Eucharist. Jesus is God incarnate, the Word made flesh. He is also the suffering servant. The underlying meaning of Eucharist is self-giving: this has implications for discipleship.

The gospel tells of manna, God's gift of daily bread that nourished the Hebrews in the desert. As the Word made flesh, Jesus is God's gift of self, freely given, to humanity. He is the eternal food, ever-present and accessible to us in the eucharistic elements of bread and wine. He is the nourishment that satisfies; he is the food that has the power to transform the individual and the world.

Through his suffering, death, and resurrection, Jesus becomes spiritual food. As the paschal mystery bodily transformed Jesus, the Body and Blood of Christ transform us. Our participation in the Eucharist indicates our willingness to be fashioned more closely into his image. We do not abide with Christ in the Eucharist solely for our own benefit. This transformation is a blessing and a responsibility.

The Body and Blood of Christ should empower us to carry the ministry of Jesus into the world. May we become food for others through our acts of mercy, compassion, and justice.

▪ **LOUISE MCEWAN**

ENTRANCE ANTIPHON *(Cf. Psalm 81 [80]:17)*
He fed them with the finest wheat and satisfied
them with honey from the rock.

INTRODUCTORY RITES *(page 10)*

COLLECT
O God, who in this wonderful Sacrament
have left us a memorial of your Passion,
grant us, we pray,
so to revere the sacred mysteries of your Body and Blood
that we may always experience in ourselves
the fruits of your redemption.
Who live and reign with God the Father
in the unity of the Holy Spirit,
one God, for ever and ever. **Amen.**

FIRST READING *(Deuteronomy 8:2–3, 14b–16a)*
Moses said to the people: "Remember how for forty years
now the LORD, your God, has directed all your journey-
ing in the desert, so as to test you by affliction and find out
whether or not it was your intention to keep his commandments. He therefore let you be afflicted with hunger, and then
fed you with manna, a food unknown to you and your fathers, in
order to show you that not by bread alone does one live, but by
every word that comes forth from the mouth of the LORD.

"Do not forget the LORD, your God, who brought you out
of the land of Egypt, that place of slavery; who guided you
through the vast and terrible desert with its saraph serpents and
scorpions, its parched and waterless ground; who brought forth
water for you from the flinty rock and fed you in the desert with

manna, a food unknown to your fathers."

The word of the Lord. ***Thanks be to God.***

RESPONSORIAL PSALM *(Psalm 147:12-13, 14-15, 19-20)*

℟ **Praise the Lord, Jerusalem.** *Or* **Alleluia.**

Glorify the LORD, O Jerusalem;
  praise your God, O Zion.*
For he has strengthened the bars of your gates;
  he has blessed your children within you. ℟

He has granted peace in your borders;
  with the best of wheat he fills you.
He sends forth his command to the earth;
  swiftly runs his word! ℟

He has proclaimed his word to Jacob,
  his statutes and his ordinances to Israel.
He has not done thus for any other nation;
  his ordinances he has not made known to them. Alleluia. ℟

SECOND READING *(1 Corinthians 10:16-17)*

Brothers and sisters: The cup of blessing that we bless, is it not a participation in the **blood**✢ of Christ? The bread that we break, is it not a participation in the body of Christ? Because the loaf of bread is one, we, though many, are one body, for we all partake of the one loaf.

The word of the Lord. ***Thanks be to God.***

SEQUENCE

The shorter version begins at the asterisks.

Laud, O Zion, your salvation,
Laud with hymns of exultation,
  Christ, your king and shepherd true:

Bring him all the praise you know,
He is more than you bestow.
  Never can you reach his due.

Special theme for glad thanksgiving
Is the quick'ning and the living
  Bread today before you set:

From his hands of old partaken,
As we know, by faith unshaken,
  Where the Twelve at supper met.

Full and clear ring out your chanting,
Joy nor sweetest grace be wanting,
  From your heart let praises burst:

For today the feast is holden,
When the institution olden
  Of that supper was rehearsed.

Here the new law's new oblation,
By the new king's revelation,
  Ends the form of ancient rite:

Now the new the old effaces,
Truth away the shadow chases,
  Light dispels the gloom of night.

What he did at supper seated,
Christ ordained to be repeated,
  His memorial ne'er to cease:

And his rule for guidance taking,
Bread and wine we hallow, making
  Thus our sacrifice of peace.

This the truth each Christian learns,
Bread into his flesh he turns,
  To his precious blood the wine:

Sight has fail'd, nor thought conceives,
But a dauntless faith believes,
  Resting on a pow'r divine.

Here beneath these signs are hidden
Priceless things to sense forbidden;
  Sign, not things are all we see:

Blood is poured and flesh is broken,
Yet in either wondrous token
  Christ entire we know to be.

Whoso of this food partakes,
Does not rend the Lord nor breaks;
  Christ is whole to all that tastes:

Thousands are, as one, receivers,
One, as thousands of believers,
  Eats of him who cannot waste.

Bad and good the feast are sharing,
Of what divers dooms preparing,
　　Endless death, or endless life.

Life to these, to those damnation,
See how like participation
　　Is with unlike issues rife.

When the sacrament is broken,
Doubt not, but believe 'tis spoken,
　　That each sever'd outward token
　　　　doth the very whole contain.

Nought the precious gift divides,
Breaking but the sign betides
　　Jesus still the same abides,
　　　　still unbroken does remain.

*　*　*

The shorter form of the sequence begins here.

Lo! the angel's food is given
To the pilgrim who has striven;
　　See the children's bread from heaven,
　　　　which on dogs may not be spent.

Truth the ancient types fulfilling,
Isaac bound, a victim willing,
　　Paschal lamb, its lifeblood spilling,
　　　　manna to the fathers sent.

Very bread, good shepherd, tend us,
Jesu, of your love befriend us,
　　You refresh us, you defend us,
　　Your eternal goodness send us
In the land of life to see.

You who all things can and know,
Who on earth such food bestow,
　　Grant us with your saints, though lowest,
　　Where the heav'nly feast you show,
Fellow heirs and guests to be. Amen. Alleluia.

ALLELUIA *(John 6:51)*
Alleluia, alleluia. I am the living bread that came down from
heaven, says the Lord; whoever eats this bread will live forever.
Alleluia, alleluia.

GOSPEL *(John 6:51–58)*
A reading from the holy Gospel according to John.
Glory to you, O Lord.

Jesus said to the Jewish crowds: "I am the living bread that
came down from heaven; whoever eats this bread will live
forever; and the bread that I will give is my flesh for the life of
the world."

　　The Jews quarreled among themselves, saying, "How can this
man give us his flesh to eat?" Jesus said to them, "Amen, amen, I
say to you, unless you eat the flesh of the Son of Man and drink
his **blood**,✝ you do not have life within you. Whoever eats my
flesh and drinks my blood has eternal life, and I will raise him
on the last day. For my flesh is true food, and my blood is true
drink. Whoever eats my flesh and drinks my blood remains
in me and I in him. Just as the living Father sent me and I have

life because of the Father, so also the one who feeds on me will have life because of me. This is the bread that came down from heaven. Unlike your ancestors who ate and still died, whoever eats this bread will live forever."

The Gospel of the Lord. *Praise to you, Lord Jesus Christ.*

PROFESSION OF FAITH *(page 13)*

PRAYER OF THE FAITHFUL

PREPARATION OF GIFTS *(page 16)*

PRAYER OVER THE OFFERINGS
Grant your Church, O Lord, we pray,
the gifts of unity and peace,
whose signs are to be seen in mystery
in the offerings we here present.
Through Christ our Lord. *Amen.*

❖ TAKING A CLOSER LOOK ❖

✠ **Blood** Blood is the carrier of life, and its power is bestowed by God, who gives life to all beings. Thus in sacrificial rituals, the animal's blood represents its life. When a covenant was ritually sealed through a sacrifice, the blood was partially sprinkled on the altar (for God) and partially on the people. This symbolized that through this covenant bond they would share a common life together. So when shared in the Eucharist, Jesus' blood bonds us into communion with him for eternal life.

PREFACE *(Most Holy Eucharist 1-2, pages 32-33)*

COMMUNION ANTIPHON *(John 6:57)*

Whoever eats my flesh and drinks my blood remains
in me and I in him, says the Lord.

PRAYER AFTER COMMUNION

Grant, O Lord, we pray,
that we may delight for all eternity
in that share in your divine life,
which is foreshadowed in the present age
by our reception of your precious Body and Blood.
Who live and reign for ever and ever. ***Amen.***

BLESSING & DISMISSAL *(page 56)* ⸭

• RESPONDING TO THE WORD •

Moses reminds us that God is directing our journey.	**Sharing in Eucharist brings us into greater communion—with God and with others.**	**Jesus offers himself as the bread that nourishes us.**
➲ *Where is God leading me today?*	➲ *How can I show my unity with others when I participate in the Eucharist?*	➲ *What can I offer to nourish the lives of others today?*

June 21

A promise for life everlasting

The theme of fear and denial seems prominent in today's gospel. It is in stark contrast to other messages presented throughout the Bible. However, perhaps the theme is actually a promise of life everlasting. Jesus is preparing his followers to spread Christianity and in describing the dangers of this journey, he also promises that their souls shall live forever.

What does this gospel mean for us today? We are faced daily with situations in which we can expose our faith or keep it hidden. I can think of many discussions in which I have not spoken up in defense of my beliefs. For this, will I be denied as the gospel describes?

Jesus also reminds us that we are so precious in God's eyes that each hair on our heads is numbered. So what will it be? Are we so loved that when we fail to proclaim our faith we will be forgiven? Then what is the denial that Jesus mentions? "Are not two sparrows sold for a small coin? Yet not one of them falls to the ground without your Father's knowledge." When we fall, we must remember that we are still in the Lord's care. We can proclaim God's love from the rooftops, as have many believers before us. We have all been promised a chance for life everlasting.

▪ **JULIANNA DEUTSCHER**

ENTRANCE ANTIPHON *(Cf. Psalm 28 [27]:8-9)*

The Lord is the strength of his people, a saving
refuge for the one he has anointed. Save your
people, Lord, and bless your heritage, and govern
them for ever.

INTRODUCTORY RITES *(page 10)*

COLLECT

Grant, O Lord,
that we may always revere and love your holy name,
for you never deprive of your guidance
those you set firm on the foundation of your love.
Through our Lord Jesus Christ, your Son,
who lives and reigns with you in the unity of the Holy Spirit,
one God, for ever and ever. *Amen.*

FIRST READING *(Jeremiah 20:10-13)*

Jeremiah said:
"I hear the whisperings of many:
    'Terror on every side!
    Denounce! Let us denounce him!'
All those who were my friends
    are on the watch for any misstep of mine.
'Perhaps he will be trapped; then we can prevail,
    and take our vengeance on him.'
But the LORD is with me, like a mighty champion:
    my persecutors will stumble, they will not triumph.
In their failure they will be put to utter shame,
    to lasting, unforgettable confusion.

O LORD of hosts, you who test the just,
    who probe mind and heart,
let me witness the vengeance you take on them,
    for to you I have entrusted my cause.
Sing to the LORD,
    praise the LORD,
for he has rescued the life of the poor
    from the power of the wicked!"
The word of the Lord. *Thanks be to God.*

RESPONSORIAL PSALM *(Psalm 69:8–10, 14, 17, 33–35)*
R᷉ **Lord, in your great love, answer me.**

For your sake I bear insult,
    and shame covers my face.
I have become an outcast to my brothers,
    a stranger to my children,
because zeal for your house consumes me,
    and the insults of those who blaspheme you fall upon me. R᷉
I pray to you, O LORD,
    for the time of your favor, O God!
In your great kindness answer me
    with your constant help.
Answer me, O LORD, for bounteous is your kindness;
    in your great mercy turn toward me. R᷉
"See, you lowly ones, and be glad;
    you who seek God, may your hearts revive!
For the LORD hears the poor,
    and his own who are in bonds he spurns not.
Let the heavens and the earth praise him,
    the seas and whatever moves in them!" R᷉

SECOND READING *(Romans 5:12-15)*

Brothers and sisters: Through one man sin entered the world, and through sin, death, and thus death came to all men, inasmuch as all sinned—for up to the time of the law, sin was in the world, though sin is not accounted when there is no law. But death reigned from Adam to Moses, even over those who did not sin after the pattern of the trespass of Adam, who is the type of the one who was to come.

But the gift is not like the transgression. For if by the transgression of the one the many died, how much more did the grace of God and the gracious gift of the one man Jesus Christ overflow for the many.

The word of the Lord. *Thanks be to God.*

ALLELUIA *(John 15:26b, 27a)*

Alleluia, alleluia. The Spirit of truth will testify to me, says the Lord; and you also will testify. *Alleluia, alleluia.*

GOSPEL *(Matthew 10:26-33)*

A reading from the holy Gospel according to Matthew.
Glory to you, O Lord.

Jesus said to the Twelve: "Fear no one. Nothing is concealed that will not be revealed, nor secret that will not be known. What I say to you in the darkness, speak in the light; what you hear whispered, proclaim on the housetops. And do not be afraid of those who kill the body but cannot kill the soul; rather, be afraid of the one who can destroy both soul and body in **Gehenna**.✝ Are not two sparrows sold for a small coin? Yet not one of them falls to the ground without your Father's knowledge. Even all the hairs of your head are counted. So do not be afraid; you are worth more than many sparrows. Everyone who acknowledges me before others I will acknowledge before my heavenly Father. But whoever denies me before others, I will deny before my heavenly Father."

The Gospel of the Lord. *Praise to you, Lord Jesus Christ.*

PROFESSION OF FAITH *(page 13)*

PRAYER OF THE FAITHFUL

PREPARATION OF GIFTS *(page 16)*

PRAYER OVER THE OFFERINGS
Receive, O Lord, the sacrifice of conciliation and praise
and grant that, cleansed by its action,
we may make offering of a heart pleasing to you.
Through Christ our Lord. *Amen.*

PREFACE *(Sundays in Ordinary Time, pages 28-32)*

❖ TAKING A CLOSER LOOK ❖

✝ **Gehenna** Located west and south of Jerusalem, Gehenna (Hebrew, valley of Hinnom) divided the tribes of Judah and Benjamin. Some of the kings of Judah used its heights for idolatrous human sacrifices and so incurred God's wrath. Jeremiah cursed it and called it a place of fire and destruction. This association soon made it a synonym for the place of God's punishment of the wicked after death—hell. It was distinguished both from heaven or paradise, where the just received their reward, and from Hades, which was either the abode of all the dead or where the wicked wait until God's final judgment.

COMMUNION ANTIPHON *(Psalm 145 [144]:15)*

The eyes of all look to you, Lord, and you give them their food in
due season.

Or *(John 10:11, 15)*

I am the Good Shepherd, and I lay down my life for my sheep,
says the Lord.

PRAYER AFTER COMMUNION

Renewed and nourished
by the Sacred Body and Precious Blood of your Son,
we ask of your mercy, O Lord,
that what we celebrate with constant devotion
may be our sure pledge of redemption.
Through Christ our Lord. *Amen.*

BLESSING & DISMISSAL *(page 56)* ✲

• RESPONDING TO THE WORD •

Jeremiah knows that God is with him in his troubles.	Jesus' death and resurrection began the overthrow of evil's power in our world.	God's care extends to the minute details of our lives.
➡ *What gives you confidence God is with you in times of trouble?*	➡ *What can I do today to increase the amount of good and lessen the amount of evil?*	➡ *In what details of my life have I experienced God's care?*

June 28

JUN 28

Find life through faithfulness

When we think about Christianity, the prophets and disciples may not be the first things that come to mind. Yet it was their bold, persevering faith that led to the spread of God's kingdom amid the persecution of Christians.

Today's readings illuminate the critical role of God's messengers, as well as the hope and renewed lives their transformative messages promised to those who welcomed them. In the gospel, Jesus reveals the great sacrifice and reward for his followers. As he instructs the disciples on their mission, he tells them to bear their crosses in order to find eternal life. Jesus in effect stresses the greatest commandment—to love God above anything else.

It's a lofty challenge for us as Christ's followers today. Yet Jesus' message is about redemption rather than perfection. Welcoming him into our lives with our little acts of love and sacrifice matters— just as those who give even a little cup of water to his messengers will be rewarded.

While it may not be realistic for us to achieve the same level of sacrifice for God as Jesus' early messengers, God's love is merciful. We offer praise for God's redeeming messages. Like the courageous prophets and disciples, we can find life through our faithfulness to God.

■ **CHRISTL DABU**

ENTRANCE ANTIPHON *(Psalm 47 [46]:2)*

All peoples, clap your hands. Cry to God with shouts of joy!

INTRODUCTORY RITES *(page 10)*

COLLECT

O God, who through the grace of adoption
chose us to be children of light,
grant, we pray,
that we may not be wrapped in the darkness of error
but always be seen to stand in the bright light of truth.
Through our Lord Jesus Christ, your Son,
who lives and reigns with you in the unity of the Holy Spirit,
one God, for ever and ever. *Amen.*

FIRST READING *(2 Kings 4:8-11, 14-16a)*

One day Elisha came to Shunem, where there was a woman of influence, who urged him to dine with her. Afterward, whenever he passed by, he used to stop there to dine. So she said to her husband, "I know that Elisha is a holy man of God. Since he visits us often, let us arrange a little room on the roof and furnish it for him with a bed, table, chair, and lamp, so that when he comes to us he can stay there." Sometime later Elisha arrived and stayed in the room overnight.

Later Elisha asked, "Can something be done for her?" His servant Gehazi answered, "Yes! She has no son, and her husband is getting on in years." Elisha said, "Call her." When the woman had been called and stood at the door, Elisha promised, "This time next year you will be fondling a baby son."

The word of the Lord. *Thanks be to God.*

RESPONSORIAL PSALM *(Psalm 89:2-3, 16-17, 18-19)*
℟ Forever I will sing the goodness of the Lord.

The promises of the LORD I will sing forever,
    through all generations my mouth shall proclaim your faithfulness.
For you have said, "My kindness is established forever";
    in heaven you have confirmed your faithfulness. ℟
Blessed the people who know the joyful shout;
    in the light of your countenance, O LORD, they walk.
At your name they rejoice all the day,
    and through your justice they are exalted. ℟
You are the splendor of their strength,
    and by your favor our horn is exalted.
For to the LORD belongs our shield,
    and to the Holy One of Israel, our king. ℟

SECOND READING *(Romans 6:3-4, 8-11)*

Brothers and sisters: Are you unaware that we who were baptized into **Christ Jesus**✢ were baptized into his death? We were indeed buried with him through baptism into death, so that, just as Christ was raised from the dead by the glory of the Father, we too might live in newness of life.

If, then, we have died with Christ, we believe that we shall also live with him. We know that Christ, raised from the dead, dies no more; death no longer has power over him. As to his death, he died to sin once and for all; as to his life, he lives for God. Consequently, you too must think of yourselves as dead to sin and living for God in Christ Jesus.

The word of the Lord. *Thanks be to God.*

ALLELUIA *(1 Peter 2:9)*
Alleluia, alleluia. You are a chosen race, a royal priesthood, a holy nation; announce the praises of him who called you out of darkness into his wonderful light. *Alleluia, alleluia.*

GOSPEL *(Matthew 10:37–42)*
A reading from the holy Gospel according to Matthew.
Glory to you, O Lord.

Jesus said to his apostles: "Whoever loves father or mother more than me is not worthy of me, and whoever loves son or daughter more than me is not worthy of me; and whoever does not take up his cross and follow after me is not worthy of me. Whoever finds his life will lose it, and whoever loses his life for my sake will find it. Whoever receives you receives me, and whoever receives me receives the one who sent me. Whoever receives a prophet because he is a prophet will receive a prophet's reward, and whoever receives a righteous man because he is a righteous man will receive a righteous man's reward. And whoever gives only a cup of cold water to one of these little ones to drink because the little one is a disciple— amen, I say to you, he will surely not lose his reward."

The Gospel of the Lord. *Praise to you, Lord Jesus Christ.*

PROFESSION OF FAITH (page 13)

PRAYER OF THE FAITHFUL

PREPARATION OF GIFTS (page 16)

PRAYER OVER THE OFFERINGS

O God, who graciously accomplish
the effects of your mysteries,
grant, we pray,
that the deeds by which we serve you
may be worthy of these sacred gifts.
Through Christ our Lord. *Amen.*

PREFACE (Sundays in Ordinary Time, pages 28–32)

• TAKING A CLOSER LOOK •

✚ **Christ Jesus** The Christ (Greek, *christos*), the messiah or anointed one, identified the agent of salvation (savior) whom God would send to deliver the people and create God's kingdom on earth. In Israel, the primary anointed figures were the priests and the kings. In the time of Jesus, the development of a messianic hope was anything but clear or well-defined. Many longed for a messiah who would be a great king who would powerfully and supernaturally rescue God's chosen people from Roman oppression, end suffering and death, and set up a kingdom that would see no end. Peter recognizes Jesus as the Messiah, but then Jesus reveals that he is not a political messiah but one who will save us through his suffering—a picture of a messiah that no one anticipated.

COMMUNION ANTIPHON *(Cf. Psalm 103 [102]:1)*
Bless the Lord, O my soul, and all within me, his holy name.

Or *(John 17:20–21)*
O Father, I pray for them, that they may be one in us, that the
world may believe that you have sent me, says the Lord.

PRAYER AFTER COMMUNION
May this divine sacrifice we have offered and received
fill us with life, O Lord, we pray,
so that, bound to you in lasting charity,
we may bear fruit that lasts for ever.
Through Christ our Lord. *Amen.*

BLESSING & DISMISSAL *(page 56)* ❖

❖ RESPONDING TO THE WORD ❖

The messianic king is a gentle ruler who brings peace.	Paul reminds us that God's spirit dwells in us.	Jesus invites us to put our burdens on him.
➡ *When have you experienced the peace of Jesus?*	➡ *When have I been most aware of the presence of the Holy Spirit in me?*	➡ *What burden do I most want to give to Jesus today?*

July 5

**JUL
5**

Christ offers us his yoke

Celebrating Mass week by week, it is easy to think that we are in communion with the God who is "out there," way back in the past and way forward into the future.

But much as Jesus walked the highways and byways of the Judean countryside 2000 years ago, Christ Jesus, the man who is God, still walks with us as we journey today. Day by day, he calls out from afar and at times comes alongside us, saying, "Come to me, all you who labor and are burdened, and I will give you rest." Who amongst us today is not carrying heaviness of some kind?

Jesus knows all too well the heaviness of heart that comes with rejection, abandonment, and even persecution. "Christ the Farmer" who is so wise to the ways of the world, the flesh, and the devil—and the faulty detours, the pitfalls, and swamps of life—offers us his yoke so that he can guide us along the path of life, like the experienced, strong master that he is.

Today as we partake of the Body and Blood of Christ, will we willingly slip into the yoke offered by the One who is gentle and humble in heart? As we do, let us learn from him and find rest for our souls.

■ **BEVERLY ILLAUQ**

ENTRANCE ANTIPHON *(Cf. Psalm 48 [47]:10-11)*
Your merciful love, O God, we have received in the midst of your
temple. Your praise, O God, like your name, reaches the ends of
the earth; your right hand is filled with saving justice.

INTRODUCTORY RITES *(page 10)*

COLLECT
O God, who in the abasement of your Son
have raised up a fallen world,
fill your faithful with holy joy,
for on those you have rescued from slavery to sin
you bestow eternal gladness.
Through our Lord Jesus Christ, your Son,
who lives and reigns with you in the unity of the Holy Spirit,
one God, for ever and ever. *Amen.*

FIRST READING *(Zechariah 9:9-10)*

Thus says the LORD:
Rejoice heartily, O daughter Zion,*
shout for joy, O daughter Jerusalem!
See, your king shall come to you;
a just savior is he,
meek, and riding on an ass,
on a colt, the foal of an ass.
He shall banish the chariot from Ephraim,*
and the horse from Jerusalem;
the warrior's bow shall be banished,
and he shall proclaim peace to the nations.
His dominion shall be from sea to sea,
and from the River to the ends of the earth.
The word of the Lord. *Thanks be to God.*

RESPONSORIAL PSALM *(145:1-2, 8-9, 10-11, 13-14)*

R̶ **I will praise your name forever, my king and my God.**
Or **Alleluia.**

I will extol you, O my God and King,
   and I will bless your name forever and ever.
Every day will I bless you,
   and I will praise your name forever and ever. R̶

The Lᴏʀᴅ is gracious and merciful,
   slow to anger and of great kindness.
The Lᴏʀᴅ is good to all
   and compassionate toward all his works. R̶

Let all your works give you thanks, O Lᴏʀᴅ,
   and let your faithful ones bless you.
Let them discourse of the glory of your kingdom
   and speak of your might. R̶

The Lᴏʀᴅ is faithful in all his words
   and **holy**✝ in all his works.
The Lᴏʀᴅ lifts up all who are falling
   and raises up all who are bowed down. R̶

SECOND READING *(Romans 8:9, 11-13)*

Brothers and sisters: You are not in the flesh; on the contrary,
you are in the spirit, if only the Spirit of God dwells in you.
Whoever does not have the Spirit of Christ does not belong
to him. If the Spirit of the one who raised Jesus from the dead
dwells in you, the one who raised Christ from the dead will give
life to your mortal bodies also, through his Spirit that dwells in
you. Consequently, brothers and sisters, we are not debtors to
the flesh, to live according to the flesh. For if you live according
to the flesh, you will die, but if by the Spirit you put to death the

deeds of the body, you will live.

The word of the Lord. *Thanks be to God.*

ALLELUIA *(Matthew 11:25)*
Alleluia, alleluia. Blessed are you, Father, Lord of heaven and earth; you have revealed to little ones the mysteries of the kingdom. *Alleluia, alleluia.*

GOSPEL *(Matthew 11:25—30)*
A reading from the holy Gospel according to Matthew.
Glory to you, O Lord.

At that time Jesus exclaimed: "I give praise to you, Father, Lord of heaven and earth, for although you have hidden these things from the wise and the learned you have revealed them to little ones. Yes, Father, such has been your gracious will. All things have been handed over to me by my Father. No one knows the Son except the Father, and no one knows the Father except the Son and anyone to whom the Son wishes to reveal him.

"Come to me, all you who labor and are burdened, and I will give you rest. Take my yoke upon you and learn from me, for I am meek and humble of heart; and you will find rest for yourselves. For my yoke is easy, and my burden light."

The Gospel of the Lord. *Praise to you, Lord Jesus Christ.*

PROFESSION OF FAITH *(page 13)*

PRAYER OF THE FAITHFUL

PREPARATION OF GIFTS *(page 16)*

PRAYER OVER THE OFFERINGS
May this oblation dedicated to your name
purify us, O Lord,
and day by day bring our conduct
closer to the life of heaven.
Through Christ our Lord. ***Amen.***

PREFACE *(Sundays in Ordinary Time, pages 28–32)*

• TAKING A CLOSER LOOK •

✣ **Holy** Holiness describes the unique quality that makes God to be divine and thus wholly other or separate from all created realities. Strictly speaking, human persons like priests or the community of Israel and created objects like the Jerusalem Temple or altars or sacrificial offerings only become holy through contact with God. God's presence transforms the person or place or thing into something sacred. As Isaiah demonstrates, this quality of holiness demands reverent fear, for to come into contact with God is supremely dangerous because it changes whatever is touched.

COMMUNION ANTIPHON *(Psalm 34 [33]:9)*

Taste and see that the Lord is good; blessed the man who seeks refuge in him.

Or *(Matthew 11:28)*

Come to me, all who labor and are burdened, and I will refresh you, says the Lord.

PRAYER AFTER COMMUNION

Grant, we pray, O Lord,
that, having been replenished by such great gifts,
we may gain the prize of salvation
and never cease to praise you.
Through Christ our Lord. *Amen.*

BLESSING & DISMISSAL *(page 56)* ❖

❖ RESPONDING TO THE WORD ❖

The messianic king is a gentle ruler who brings peace.	Paul reminds us that God's Spirit dwells in us.	Jesus invites us to put our burdens on him.
➡ *When have I experienced the peace of Jesus recently?*	➡ *When have I been most aware of the presence of the Holy Spirit in me?*	➡ *What burden do I most want to give to Jesus today?*

IT'S TIME TO ORDER YOUR 2020-2021 SUNDAY MISSAL

Take Advantage Of Our PREPUBLICATION SPECIAL PRICING

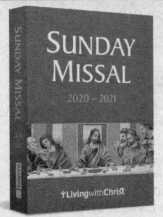

This inspirational Sunday Missal includes all Sunday readings for Year B (American Lectionary), complete Order of Mass, Sunday prayers and reflections, and much more right at your fingertips!

The Sunday Missal is the ideal gift for parish staff, volunteers, and friends!

2020-2021
Sunday Missal for Young Catholics

(recommended for ages 7 and up)

Prepare ■ Participate ■ Reflect

LSM19P1-PVB

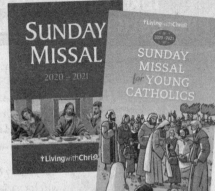

July 12

Defying all logic

A brilliant orange flower is growing on, or rather, in our front porch. It appears to be rooted in pavement. Its stem leans alongside a fracture of a small cement retaining wall. While improbable, there is no denying that seed fell and that it is now blooming and bright with color. It seems incredible, yet my eyes have seen it and I cannot but believe it possible.

The biological determination of a flower to grow in circumstances defying logic and probability has me think about the still deeper power of the word of God that is scattered on different terrains. I pray that my heart be good soil, be a place where I listen and understand so that the word takes hold and pushes through to fullness and beauty—knowing that sometimes my heart is also a terrain that defies logic and probability.

Do I look at the world with that same desire and faith in the power of God's word? Do I see neighbor, stranger, the familiar and the distinct, as places where this seed might well thrive? As people who strive to understand with the heart, we have no idea in which places the word and its beauty will take hold. May the word take hold wildly and freely in this fractured world so that something extraordinary blooms.. by grace, rather than logic or probability.

■ SR. KIMBERLY M. KING, RSCJ

ENTRANCE ANTIPHON *(Cf. Psalm 17 [16]:15)*
As for me, in justice I shall behold your face; I shall be filled with
the vision of your glory.

INTRODUCTORY RITES *(page 10)*

COLLECT
O God, who show the light of your truth
to those who go astray,
so that they may return to the right path,
give all who for the faith they profess
are accounted Christians
the grace to reject whatever is contrary to the name of Christ
and to strive after all that does it honor.
Through our Lord Jesus Christ, your Son,
who lives and reigns with you in the unity of the Holy Spirit,
one God, for ever and ever. *Amen.*

FIRST READING *(Isaiah 55:10–11)*

Thus says the LORD:
Just as from the **heavens**✛
 the rain and snow come down
and do not return there
 till they have watered the earth,
 making it fertile and fruitful,
giving seed to the one who sows
 and bread to the one who eats,
so shall my word be
 that goes forth from my mouth;
my word shall not return to me void,
 but shall do my will,

achieving the end for which I sent it.
The word of the Lord. *Thanks be to God.*

RESPONSORIAL PSALM *(Psalm 65:10, 11, 12-13, 14)*

R. **The seed that falls on good ground will yield a
fruitful harvest.**

You have visited the land and watered it;
    greatly have you enriched it.
God's watercourses are filled;
    you have prepared the grain. R.
Thus have you prepared the land: drenching its furrows,
    breaking up its clods,
Softening it with showers,
    blessing its yield. R.
You have crowned the year with your bounty,
    and your paths overflow with a rich harvest;
The untilled meadows overflow with it,
    and rejoicing clothes the hills. R.
The fields are garmented with flocks
    and the valleys blanketed with grain.
    They shout and sing for joy. R.

SECOND READING *(Romans 8:18-23)*

Brothers and sisters: I consider that the sufferings of this
present time are as nothing compared with the glory to be
revealed for us. For creation awaits with eager expectation the
revelation of the children of God; for creation was made subject
to futility, not of its own accord but because of the one who
subjected it, in hope that creation itself would be set free from
slavery to corruption and share in the glorious freedom of the
children of God. We know that all creation is groaning in labor

pains even until now; and not only that, but we ourselves, who have the firstfruits of the Spirit, we also groan within ourselves as we wait for adoption, the redemption of our bodies.

The word of the Lord. *Thanks be to God.*

ALLELUIA

Alleluia, allelùia. The seed is the word of God, Christ is the sower. All who come to him will have life forever. *Alleluia, alleluia.*

GOSPEL *(Matthew 13:1–23)*
The shorter version ends at the asterisks.

A reading from the holy Gospel according to Matthew.
Glory to you, O Lord.

On that day, Jesus went out of the house and sat down by the sea. Such large crowds gathered around him that he got into a boat and sat down, and the whole crowd stood along the shore. And he spoke to them at length in parables, saying: "A sower went out to sow. And as he sowed, some seed fell on the path, and birds came and ate it up. Some fell on rocky ground, where it had little soil. It sprang up at once because the soil was not deep, and when the sun rose it was scorched, and it withered for lack of roots. Some seed fell among thorns, and the thorns grew up and choked it. But some seed fell on rich soil, and produced fruit, a hundred or sixty or thirtyfold. Whoever has ears ought to hear."

* * *

The disciples approached him and said, "Why do you speak to them in parables?" He said to them in reply, "Because knowledge of the mysteries of the kingdom of heaven has been granted to you, but to them it has not been granted. To anyone who has, more will be given and he will grow rich; from anyone who has not, even what he has will be taken away. This is why I speak to them in parables, because *they look but do not see and hear but do not listen or understand.* Isaiah's prophecy is fulfilled in them, which says:

> *You shall indeed hear but not understand,*
>> *you shall indeed look but never see.*
> *Gross is the heart of this people,*
>> *they will hardly hear with their ears,*
>> *they have closed their eyes,*
>> *lest they see with their eyes*
>> *and hear with their ears*
> *and understand with their hearts and be converted,*
>> *and I heal them.*

"But blessed are your eyes, because they see, and your ears, because they hear. Amen, I say to you, many prophets and righteous people longed to see what you see but did not see it, and to hear what you hear but did not hear it.

"Hear then the parable of the sower. The seed sown on the path is the one who hears the word of the kingdom without understanding it, and the evil one comes and steals away what was sown in his heart. The seed sown on rocky ground is the one who hears the word and receives it at once with joy. But he has no root and lasts only for a time. When some tribulation or persecution comes because of the word, he immediately falls away. The seed sown among thorns is the one who hears the word, but then worldly anxiety and the lure of riches choke the word and it bears no fruit. But the seed sown on rich soil is the one who hears the word and understands it, who indeed bears fruit and yields a hundred or sixty or thirtyfold."

The Gospel of the Lord. ***Praise to you, Lord Jesus Christ.***

PROFESSION OF FAITH *(page 13)*

PRAYER OF THE FAITHFUL

PREPARATION OF GIFTS *(page 16)*

PRAYER OVER THE OFFERINGS

Look upon the offerings of the Church, O Lord,
as she makes her prayer to you,
and grant that, when consumed by those who believe,
they may bring ever greater holiness.
Through Christ our Lord. *Amen.*

PREFACE *(Sundays in Ordinary Time, pages 28–32)*

• TAKING A CLOSER LOOK •

✝ **The heavens** In the ancient universe, the heavens are imagined as a great vault or dome (the sky) that covers the earth and divides the heavenly waters above it from those below (Genesis 1:6-7). God's original creative activity is to divide these waters by creating this vault and thus allowing the earth to have dry land. A kind of thinly beaten metallic plate or bowl (the "firmament") keeps the waters above the heavens from inundating the earth except through doors that, when opened (Genesis 7:11), allow the wind, rain, snow, and hail stored in heaven (Job 37:9, 38:22, 37) to descend to earth.

COMMUNION ANTIPHON *(Cf. Psalm 84 [83]:4-5)*

The sparrow finds a home, and the swallow a nest for her young:
by your altars, O Lord of hosts, my King and my God. Blessed
are they who dwell in your house, for ever singing your praise.

Or *(John 6:57)*

Whoever eats my flesh and drinks my blood remains in me and I
in him, says the Lord.

PRAYER AFTER COMMUNION

Having consumed these gifts, we pray, O Lord,
that, by our participation in this mystery,
its saving effects upon us may grow.
Through Christ our Lord. *Amen.*

BLESSING & DISMISSAL *(page 56)* ✦

● RESPONDING TO THE WORD ●

God's word changes
our world.

➡ *What changes
have I experienced
due to my attention
to Scripture?*

Paul says that we,
along with all creation,
are in the process of
being transformed by
God's grace.

➡ *What transforma-
tion would I most like
God to bring about?*

Jesus teaches in
parables to make us
think more deeply
about his message.

➡ *What can I do this
week to "see" more
clearly what Jesus
wants from me?*

July 19

Trust God's justice

One of the great laments of the psalms is, "O Lord, why do the wicked prosper?" All people—like children at play—have an instinctive desire for justice. And when we see injustice seemingly rewarded by prosperity, we begin to question God's oversight of the world.

In response to this concern, there are two good reflections in today's gospel parable of the weeds and the wheat. First, we may not understand why somebody sows weeds among the wheat, but we do experience the reality of the two growing together. Thus, the parable invites us to trust that God's justice, despite what we see, will ultimately be exercised. Meanwhile, there is something important about the wheat—good people—accepting the presence of the weeds and continuing to be faithful despite them.

Then, a second thought arises. Do we not all have within us both wheat and weeds? Why do they grow together within us? And what will happen to our weeds? Such a thought, I would hope, should help us not to judge others whom we consider "weeds," while overlooking our own faults. Perhaps we also need to accommodate ourselves, without giving in, to our own weeds. For the concluding phrase of the first reading gives us hope: "You gave your children good ground for hope that you would permit repentance for their sins."

■ FR. MARK MILLER, CSsR

ENTRANCE ANTIPHON *(Psalm 54 [53]:6, 8)*

See, I have God for my help. The Lord sustains my soul. I will sacrifice to you with willing heart, and praise your name, O Lord, for it is good.

INTRODUCTORY RITES *(page 10)*

COLLECT

Show favor, O Lord, to your servants
and mercifully increase the gifts of your grace,
that, made fervent in hope, faith and charity,
they may be ever watchful in keeping your commands.
Through our Lord Jesus Christ, your Son,
who lives and reigns with you in the unity of the Holy Spirit,
one God, for ever and ever. *Amen.*

FIRST READING *(Wisdom 12:13, 16–19)*

There is no god besides you who have the care of all,
　　that you need show you have not unjustly condemned.
For your might is the source of justice;
　　your mastery over all things makes you lenient to all.
For you show your might when the perfection of
　　　your power is disbelieved;
　　and in those who know you, you rebuke temerity.
But though you are master of might, you judge with clemency,
　　and with much lenience you govern us;
　　for power, whenever you will, attends you.
And you taught your people, by these deeds,
　　that those who are just must be kind;
and you gave your children good ground for hope
　　that you would permit repentance for their sins.
The word of the Lord. *Thanks be to God.*

RESPONSORIAL PSALM *(Psalm 86:5-6, 9-10, 15-16)*

℟ **Lord, you are good and forgiving.**

You, O LORD, are good and forgiving,
  abounding in kindness to all who call upon you.
Hearken, O LORD, to my prayer
  and attend to the sound of my pleading. ℟

All the nations you have made shall come
  and worship you, O LORD,
  and glorify your name.
For you are great, and you do wondrous deeds;
  you alone are God. ℟

You, O LORD, are a God merciful and gracious,
  slow to anger, abounding in kindness and fidelity.
Turn toward me, and have pity on me;
  give your strength to your servant. ℟

SECOND READING *(Romans 8:26-27)*

Brothers and sisters: The Spirit comes to the aid of our weakness; for we do not know how to pray as we ought, but the Spirit himself intercedes with inexpressible groanings. And the one who searches hearts knows what is the intention of the Spirit, because he intercedes for the holy ones according to God's will.

The word of the Lord. *Thanks be to God.*

ALLELUIA *(See Matthew 11:25)*

Alleluia, alleluia. Blessed are you, Father, Lord of heaven and earth; you have revealed to little ones the mysteries of the kingdom. *Alleluia, alleluia.*

GOSPEL *(Matthew 13:24–43)*
The shorter version ends at the asterisks.

A reading from the holy Gospel according to Matthew.
Glory to you, O Lord.

Jesus proposed another **parable**✝ to the crowds, saying: "The kingdom of heaven may be likened to a man who sowed good seed in his field. While everyone was asleep his enemy came and sowed weeds all through the wheat, and then went off. When the crop grew and bore fruit, the weeds appeared as well. The slaves of the householder came to him and said, 'Master, did you not sow good seed in your field? Where have the weeds come from?' He answered, 'An enemy has done this.' His slaves said to him, 'Do you want us to go and pull them up?' He replied, 'No, if you pull up the weeds you might uproot the wheat along with them. Let them grow together until harvest; then at harvest time I will say to the harvesters, "First collect the weeds and tie them in bundles for burning; but gather the wheat into my barn." ' "

* * *

He proposed another parable to them. "The kingdom of heaven is like a mustard seed that a person took and sowed in a field. It is the smallest of all the seeds, yet when full-grown it is the largest of plants. It becomes a large bush, and the 'birds of the sky come and dwell in its branches.' "

He spoke to them another parable. "The kingdom of heaven is like yeast that a woman took and mixed with three measures of wheat flour until the whole batch was leavened."

All these things Jesus spoke to the crowds in parables. He spoke to them only in parables, to fulfill what had been said through the prophet:

> *I will open my mouth in parables,*
> *I will announce what has lain hidden*
> *from the foundation of the world.*

Then, dismissing the crowds, he went into the house. His disciples approached him and said, "Explain to us the parable of the weeds in the field." He said in reply, "He who sows good seed is the Son of Man, the field is the world, the good seed the children of the kingdom. The weeds are the children of the evil one, and the enemy who sows them is the devil. The harvest is the end of the age, and the harvesters are angels. Just as weeds are collected and burned up with fire, so will it be at the end of the age. The Son of Man will send his angels, and they will collect out of his kingdom all who cause others to sin and all evildoers. They will throw them into the fiery furnace, where there will be wailing and grinding of teeth. Then the righteous will shine like the sun in the kingdom of their Father. Whoever has ears ought to hear."

The Gospel of the Lord. *Praise to you, Lord Jesus Christ.*

PROFESSION OF FAITH *(page 13)*

PRAYER OF THE FAITHFUL

PREPARATION OF GIFTS *(page 16)*

PRAYER OVER THE OFFERINGS

O God, who in the one perfect sacrifice
brought to completion varied offerings of the law,
accept, we pray, this sacrifice from your faithful servants
and make it holy, as you blessed the gifts of Abel,
so that what each has offered to the honor of your majesty
may benefit the salvation of all.
Through Christ our Lord. *Amen.*

PREFACE *(Sundays in Ordinary Time, pages 28–32)*

❖ Taking a Closer Look ❖

✛ **Parable** A parable (from the Greek word *parabole*, to "throw together" things for comparison or illustration) is a short realistic story intended to encourage reflection by connecting the parable to our own life. Since one can connect the parable to various aspects of one's life or that of one's family or community, parables are open-ended in their application.

Parables were a common teaching device of the Jewish rabbis and important to Jesus in his teaching, because the only way we have to talk about what is unfamiliar to us (God's ruling presence or "kingdom") is in terms that are familiar to us (our everyday life and world). Thus, parables challenge the hearers to think about their meaning and change their lives because of what they discover.

COMMUNION ANTIPHON *(Psalm 111 [110]:4-5)*

The Lord, the gracious, the merciful,
has made a memorial of his wonders; he gives food to those
who fear him.

Or *(Revelation 3:20)*

Behold, I stand at the door and knock, says the Lord. If anyone
hears my voice and opens the door to me, I will enter his house
and dine with him, and he with me.

PRAYER AFTER COMMUNION

Graciously be present to your people, we pray, O Lord,
and lead those you have imbued with heavenly mysteries
to pass from former ways to newness of life.
Through Christ our Lord. *Amen.*

BLESSING & DISMISSAL *(page 56)* ❖

❖ RESPONDING TO THE WORD ❖

God's example tells us that we must have both justice and compassion.	The Holy Spirit helps us to pray when we don't know how.	Jesus tells us that God's presence (kingdom) often starts out very small but can grow very large.
➡ *What might I do today to be more just and compassionate toward others?*	➡ *For what help with my prayer do I ask the Holy Spirit today?*	➡ *How has my awareness of God grown recently?*

July 26

JUL 26

God's perfect justice

The world often feels more random than fair. Sometimes good people seem to be rewarded. Just as often though, there seems to be no rhyme or reason behind who succeeds or fails.

In today's gospel, Jesus harkens on simplistic analogies to help our understanding. Humans gravitate towards wealth, so he compares God's kingdom to a fortune waiting to be found in a field or a pearl of immeasurable value.

His final depiction, as foreign as it may be to anyone who doesn't work in the fishing industry, is perhaps the most powerful. We can picture the profitable fish being separated from the muck and imagine what it will be like when good and evil are literally partitioned from each other in our world. Victims no longer tormented by perpetrators; the vulnerable no longer attacked by predators; the kind-hearted no longer manipulated by the spiteful. Instead, all people will answer for their actions.

It is perhaps the greatest of all images Jesus gives us of God's kingdom. Perfect justice distributed to all peoples. In God's kingdom—unlike in our world—no one will be the victim of random actions, but rather, moral integrity and personal prosperity will always be the rule.

■ **ANDREW HUME**

ENTRANCE ANTIPHON *(Cf. Psalm 68 [67]:6-7, 36)*

God is in his holy place, God who unites those who dwell in his
house; he himself gives might and strength to his people.

INTRODUCTORY RITES *(page 10)*

COLLECT

O God, protector of those who hope in you,
without whom nothing has firm foundation, nothing is holy,
bestow in abundance your mercy upon us
and grant that, with you as our ruler and guide,
we may use the good things that pass
in such a way as to hold fast even now
to those that ever endure.
Through our Lord Jesus Christ, your Son,
who lives and reigns with you in the unity of the Holy Spirit,
one God, for ever and ever. *Amen.*

FIRST READING *(1 Kings 3:5, 7-12)*

The LORD appeared to Solomon in a dream at night. God
said, "Ask something of me and I will give it to you."
Solomon answered: "O LORD, my God, you have made me, your
servant, king to succeed my father David; but I am a mere youth,
not knowing at all how to act. I serve you in the midst of the
people whom you have chosen, a people so vast that it cannot be
numbered or counted. Give your servant, therefore, an understanding **heart**+ to judge your people and to distinguish right
from wrong. For who is able to govern this vast people of yours?"

The LORD was pleased that Solomon made this request. So
God said to him: "Because you have asked for this—not for a long
life for yourself, nor for riches, nor for the life of your enemies,
but for understanding so that you may know what is right—I do

as you requested. I give you a **heart**✝ so wise and understanding that there has never been anyone like you up to now, and after you there will come no one to equal you."

The word of the Lord. ***Thanks be to God.***

RESPONSORIAL PSALM *(Psalm 119:57, 72, 76-77, 127-128, 129-130)*

℟ **Lord, I love your commands.**

I have said, O LORD, that my part
  is to keep your words.
The law of your mouth is to me more precious
  than thousands of gold and silver pieces. ℟

Let your kindness comfort me
  according to your promise to your servants.
Let your compassion come to me that I may live,
  for your law is my delight. ℟

For I love your commands
  more than gold, however fine.
For in all your precepts I go forward;
  every false way I hate. ℟

Wonderful are your decrees;
  therefore I observe them.
The revelation of your words sheds light,
  giving understanding to the simple. ℟

SECOND READING *(Romans 8:28-30)*

Brothers and sisters: We know that all things work for good for those who love God, who are called according to his purpose. For those he foreknew he also predestined to be conformed to the image of his Son, so that he might be the firstborn among many brothers and sisters. And those he predestined he also called; and those he called he also justified; and those he justified he also glorified.

The word of the Lord. ***Thanks be to God.***

ALLELUIA *(Matthew 11:25)*
Alleluia, alleluia. Blessed are you, Father, Lord of heaven and earth; you have revealed to little ones the mysteries of the kingdom. *Alleluia, alleluia.*

GOSPEL *(Matthew 13:44–52)*
For the shorter version, omit the indented parts in brackets.

A reading from the holy Gospel according to Matthew.
Glory to you, O Lord.

J esus said to his disciples: "The kingdom of heaven is like a treasure buried in a field, which a person finds and hides again, and out of joy goes and sells all that he has and buys that field. Again, the kingdom of heaven is like a merchant searching for fine pearls. When he finds a pearl of great price, he goes and sells all that he has and buys it.

[Again, the kingdom of heaven is like a net thrown into the sea, which collects fish of every kind. When it is full they haul it ashore and sit down to put what is good into buckets. What is bad they throw away. Thus it will be at the end of the age. The angels will go out and separate the wicked from the righteous and throw them into the fiery furnace, where there will be wailing and grinding of teeth.

"Do you understand all these things?" They answered, "Yes." And he replied, "Then every scribe who has been instructed in the kingdom of heaven is like the head of a household who brings from his storeroom both the new and the old."]

The Gospel of the Lord. ***Praise to you, Lord Jesus Christ.***

PROFESSION OF FAITH *(page 13)*

PRAYER OF THE FAITHFUL

PREPARATION OF GIFTS *(page 16)*

PRAYER OVER THE OFFERINGS
Accept, O Lord, we pray, the offerings
which we bring from the abundance of your gifts,
that through the powerful working of your grace
these most sacred mysteries may sanctify our present way of life
and lead us to eternal gladness.
Through Christ our Lord. *Amen.*

PREFACE *(Sundays in Ordinary Time, pages 28-32)*

• TAKING A CLOSER LOOK •

✝ **Heart** For biblical people, the heart did not just identify the physical organ but rather the psychological activity associated with it. Since the heart was associated with emotional changes (speeding up when we are excited) and physical life (ceasing to beat when we die), "heart" becomes a general word to identify the location of the distinctively human activities of feeling, thinking, and deciding. Today we might describe this as the "self." So Solomon's request is not for wealth and power, but rather for the understanding and discernment he will need to be a wise king.

COMMUNION ANTIPHON *(Psalm 103 [102]: 2)*

Bless the Lord, O my soul, and never forget all his benefits.

Or *(Matthew 5:7-8)*

Blessed are the merciful, for they shall receive mercy. Blessed are the clean of heart, for they shall see God.

PRAYER AFTER COMMUNION

We have consumed, O Lord, this divine Sacrament,
the perpetual memorial of the Passion of your Son;
grant, we pray, that this gift,
which he himself gave us with love beyond all telling,
may profit us for salvation.
Through Christ our Lord. *Amen.*

BLESSING & DISMISSAL *(page 56)* ❖

❖ RESPONDING TO THE WORD ❖

Solomon asks God for an understanding heart.

➡ *What would I ask God for?*

Paul reminds us that all things work together for good when God is present.

➡ *When have I experienced this kind of surprising harmony in the events of my life?*

Jesus tells us that to gain God's kingdom we have to sacrifice what we now have.

➡ *What must I give up to have God more fully in my life?*

August 2

Miracles await us!

Living in todays "instant" world, it is often difficult to strike a balance. We are rushing everywhere and demands are weighing on our shoulders. It can make us weak: we forget the love that Jesus taught us and sometimes our weaknesses prevail. Living by the example of Jesus—being loving, slow to anger, without acting hastily—requires us to dramatically slow down in this fast-paced world, to contemplate, and to pray. As a reward, God's abundant blessings will rain on us in the form of spiritual food and nourishment. We need to find the time, make the commitment to prayer, and deepen our relationship with God.

Prayer is the food that we need in order to be nourished spiritually and consequently to conquer all that our earthly lives demand from us. No sickness or hardship, no sorrow will distance us from the love of God. With God's help, we can rise above every adversity or hardship. And through God we find the way and strength to do good for others.

The miracle of feeding the 5,000 with five loaves and two fish is a miracle indeed. If Jesus was able to satisfy their physical hunger in such a radical way, we can only imagine the miracles that await us when we ask him to feed our very souls.

▪ ILDIKO O'DACRE

ENTRANCE ANTIPHON *(Psalm 70 [69]:2, 6)*

O God, come to my assistance; O Lord, make haste to help me!
You are my rescuer, my help; O Lord, do not delay.

INTRODUCTORY RITES *(page 10)*

COLLECT

Draw near to your servants, O Lord,
and answer their prayers with unceasing kindness,
that, for those who glory in you as their Creator and guide,
you may restore what you have created
and keep safe what you have restored.
Through our Lord Jesus Christ, your Son,
who lives and reigns with you in the unity of the Holy Spirit,
one God, for ever and ever. ***Amen.***

FIRST READING *(Isaiah 55:1-3)*

Thus says the LORD:
All you who are thirsty,
 come to the water!
You who have no money,
 come, receive grain and eat;
Come, without paying and without cost,
 drink wine and milk!
Why spend your money for what is not bread;
 your wages for what fails to satisfy?
Heed me, and you shall eat well,
 you shall delight in rich fare.
Come to me heedfully,
 listen, that you may have life.

I will renew with you the everlasting covenant,
    the benefits assured to David.
The word of the Lord. *Thanks be to God.*

RESPONSORIAL PSALM *(Psalm 145:8-9, 15-16, 17-18)*
R̷ **The hand of the Lord feeds us; he answers all our needs.**

The LORD is gracious and merciful,
    slow to anger and of great kindness.
The LORD is good to all
    and compassionate toward all his works. R̷
The eyes of all look hopefully to you,
    and you give them their food in due season;
you open your hand
    and satisfy the desire of every living thing. R̷
The LORD is just in all his ways
    and holy in all his works.
The LORD is near to all who call upon him,
    to all who call upon him in truth. R̷

SECOND READING *(Romans 8:35, 37-39)*

Brothers and sisters: What will separate us from the love of Christ? Will anguish, or distress, or persecution, or famine, or nakedness, or peril, or the sword? No, in all these things we conquer overwhelmingly through him who loved us. For I am convinced that neither death, nor life, nor angels, nor principalities, nor present things, nor future things, nor powers, nor height, nor depth, nor any other creature will be able to separate us from the love of God in Christ Jesus our Lord.
    The word of the Lord. *Thanks be to God.*

ALLELUIA *(Matthew 4:4b)*

Alleluia, alleluia. One does not live on bread alone, but on every word that comes forth from the mouth of God. *Alleluia, alleluia.*

GOSPEL *(Matthew 14:13–21)*

A reading from the holy Gospel according to Matthew.
Glory to you, O Lord.

When Jesus heard of the death of John the Baptist, he withdrew in a boat to a deserted place by himself. The crowds heard of this and followed him on foot from their towns. When he disembarked and saw the vast crowd, his heart was moved with **pity**✝ for them, and he cured their sick. When it was evening, the disciples approached him and said, "This is a deserted place and it is already late; dismiss the crowds so that they can go to the villages and buy food for themselves." Jesus said to them, "There is no need for them to go away; give them some food yourselves." But they said to him, "Five loaves and two fish are all we have here." Then he said, "Bring them here to me," and he ordered the crowds to sit down on the grass. Taking the five loaves and the two fish, and looking up to heaven, he said the blessing, broke the loaves, and gave them to the disciples, who in turn gave them to the crowds. They all ate and were satisfied, and they picked up the fragments left over—twelve wicker baskets full. Those who ate were about five thousand men, not counting women and children.

The Gospel of the Lord. *Praise to you, Lord Jesus Christ.*

PROFESSION OF FAITH *(page 13)*

PRAYER OF THE FAITHFUL

PREPARATION OF GIFTS *(page 16)*

PRAYER OVER THE OFFERINGS
Graciously sanctify these gifts, O Lord, we pray,
and, accepting the oblation of this spiritual sacrifice,
make of us an eternal offering to you.
Through Christ our Lord. *Amen.*

PREFACE *(Sundays in Ordinary Time, pages 28–32)*

COMMUNION ANTIPHON *(Wisdom 16:20)*
You have given us, O Lord, bread from heaven, endowed with all
delights and sweetness in every taste.

Or *(John 6:35)*
I am the bread of life, says the Lord; whoever comes to me will not
hunger and whoever believes in me will not thirst.

• TAKING A CLOSER LOOK •

✛ **Pity** Pity, in its common modern sense of "to feel sorry for someone," is not a very good translation of what Jesus feels here. The Greek word is much closer to our sense of compassion, that is, a strong emotional reaction that is felt deep within (as we would say in our "gut") in response to someone else's difficulty or suffering. This strong sense of compassion is the springboard that launches Jesus into action. Thus it echoes the divine compassion that prompted God to come down to deliver the people from their Egyptian oppressors (Exodus 3:7).

PRAYER AFTER COMMUNION

Accompany with constant protection, O Lord,
those you renew with these heavenly gifts
and, in your never-failing care for them,
make them worthy of eternal redemption.
Through Christ our Lord. *Amen.*

BLESSING & DISMISSAL *(page 56)* ✛

• RESPONDING TO THE WORD •

Isaiah invites us to be nourished with new life by God's gifts.	Paul thinks that nothing can separate us from the love of God.	When the disciples cannot feed the crowd, Jesus takes their food and does.
➡ *When have I felt the gift of God's new life in recent weeks?*	➡ *What has felt like a barrier separating me from God's love?*	➡ *What "food" am I offering so that others can be nourished today?*

August 9

AUG
9

The promise of God's presence

I have never been called to go and stand on a mountain, like Elijah was. I have never been invited to walk to Jesus on water, like Peter was. I got a job offer—a summer job, teaching basic reading and math in a men's prison. Everything about this was scary, but it was my only job offer and I needed the money. Like Peter, I cried out, "Lord, save me." Knowing that God was with me, I broke through the fear, got the job, and that wonderful prison experience has colored my life to this day.

We have all taken steps out in faith. In scary moments, when we are faced with a life-changing, faith-testing decision—the new job, the new relationship, the new life path—faith in God is all we have. Our faith emboldens us to call out to the One who says, "Take heart, it is I; do not be afraid." Things might not always turn out the way we want them to, but God remains with us to see us through it.

In today's liturgy, we celebrate God's promise of presence: in each other, in the Word, in the sacrament, and in the world we are called to serve. Let us give thanks for God's presence and for our calling, as we step forth in faith to answer that call.

■ MARGARET BICK

ENTRANCE ANTIPHON *(Cf. Psalm 74 [73]:20, 19, 22, 23)*

Look to your covenant, O Lord, and forget not the life of your poor ones for ever. Arise, O God, and defend your cause, and forget not the cries of those who seek you.

INTRODUCTORY RITES *(page 10)*

COLLECT

Almighty ever-living God,
whom, taught by the Holy Spirit,
we dare to call our Father,
bring, we pray, to perfection in our hearts
the spirit of adoption as your sons and daughters,
that we may merit to enter into the inheritance
which you have promised.
Through our Lord Jesus Christ, your Son,
who lives and reigns with you in the unity of the Holy Spirit,
one God, for ever and ever. *Amen.*

FIRST READING *(1 Kings 19:9a, 11–13a)*

At the mountain of God, Horeb,* Elijah came to a cave where he took shelter. Then the LORD said to him, "Go outside and stand on the mountain before the LORD; the LORD will be passing by." A strong and heavy wind was rending the mountains and crushing rocks before the LORD—but the LORD was not in the wind. After the wind there was an earthquake—but the LORD was not in the earthquake. After the earthquake there was fire—but the LORD was not in the fire. After the fire there was a tiny whispering sound. When he heard this, Elijah hid his face in his cloak and went and stood at the entrance of the cave.

The word of the Lord. *Thanks be to God.*

RESPONSORIAL PSALM *(Psalm 85:9, 10, 11-12, 13-14)*
R̴ **Lord, let us see your kindness and grant us your salvation.**

I will hear what God proclaims;
  the LORD—for he proclaims peace.
Near indeed is his salvation to those who fear him,
  glory dwelling in our land. R̴
Kindness and truth shall meet;
  justice and peace shall kiss.
Truth shall spring out of the earth,
  and justice shall look down from heaven. R̴
The LORD himself will give his benefits;
  our land shall yield its increase.
Justice shall walk before him,
  and prepare the way of his steps. R̴

SECOND READING *(Romans 9:1-5)*

Brothers and sisters: I speak the truth in Christ, I do not lie;
my conscience joins with the Holy Spirit in bearing me witness that I have great sorrow and constant anguish in my heart.
For I could wish that I myself were accursed and cut off from
Christ for the sake of my own people, my kindred according to
the flesh. They are Israelites; theirs the adoption, the glory, the
covenants, the giving of the law, the worship, and the promises;
theirs the patriarchs, and from them, according to the flesh, is
the Christ, who is over all, God blessed forever. Amen.
  The word of the Lord. *Thanks be to God.*

ALLELUIA *(Psalm 130:5)*
Alleluia, alleluia. I wait for the Lord; my soul waits for his
word. *Alleluia, alleluia.*

GOSPEL *(Matthew 14:22–33)*

A reading from the holy Gospel according to Matthew.
Glory to you, O Lord.

After he had fed the people, Jesus made the disciples get into a boat and precede him to the other side, while he dismissed the crowds. After doing so, he went up on the mountain by himself to pray. When it was evening he was there alone. Meanwhile the boat, already a few miles offshore, was being tossed about by the waves, for the wind was against it. During the fourth watch of the night, he came toward them walking on the sea. When the disciples saw him walking on the sea they were terrified. "It is a ghost," they said, and they cried out in fear. At once Jesus spoke to them, "Take courage, it is I; do not be afraid." Peter said to him in reply, "Lord, if it is you, command me to come to you on the water." He said, "Come." Peter got out of the boat and began to walk on the water toward Jesus. But when he saw how strong the wind was he became frightened; and, beginning to sink, he cried out, "Lord, save me!" Immediately Jesus stretched out his hand and caught Peter, and said to him, "O you of **little faith**,✝ why did you doubt?" After they got into the boat, the wind died down. Those who were in the boat did him homage, saying, "Truly, you are the Son of God."

The Gospel of the Lord. *Praise to you, Lord Jesus Christ.*

PROFESSION OF FAITH *(page 13)*

PRAYER OF THE FAITHFUL

PREPARATION OF GIFTS *(page 16)*

PRAYER OVER THE OFFERINGS
Be pleased, O Lord, to accept the offerings of your Church,
for in your mercy you have given them to be offered
and by your power you transform them
into the mystery of our salvation.
Through Christ our Lord. *Amen.*

PREFACE *(Sundays in Ordinary Time, pages 28–32)*

❖ TAKING A CLOSER LOOK ❖

✛ **"Little faith"** Although today we tend to identify "faith" as an intellectual assent in relation to doctrines, in Jesus' time it was not so narrowly understood. Faith describes the basic trust on which a relationship can be built. It recognizes that the other person is trustworthy and dependable and so can be relied on with confidence. So, those who trust in Jesus accept him for what he claims to be and expect him to do what he promises—both heal and forgive sins. In the gospels, this basic faith is often contrasted with its opposite, fear, which keeps a relationship from being established or continuing. Matthew emphasizes that disciples grow from their "little faith" (see 6:30, 8:26, 14:31, 16:8, 17:20) by responding to the teaching and example of Jesus the Teacher (8:19, 9:11, 10:24, 10:25, 12:38, 17:24, 19:16, 22:16, 22:24, 22:36, 23:8, 26:18).

COMMUNION ANTIPHON *(Psalm 147:12, 14)*

O Jerusalem, glorify the Lord, who gives you your fill of finest wheat.

Or *(Cf. John 6:51)*

The bread that I will give, says the Lord, is my flesh for the life of the world.

PRAYER AFTER COMMUNION

May the communion in your Sacrament
that we have consumed, save us, O Lord,
and confirm us in the light of your truth.
Through Christ our Lord. *Amen.*

BLESSING & DISMISSAL *(page 56)* ❖

• RESPONDING TO THE WORD •

Elijah hears God only in the faint, whispering sound.	Paul would do anything to help others come to Christ.	Peter begins to sink when he turns his attention away from Jesus.
➡ *What tiny whispers from God have I noticed recently?*	➡ *What can I do today to draw someone closer to Christ?*	➡ *When have I turned away from Jesus and felt like I was sinking?*

August 15

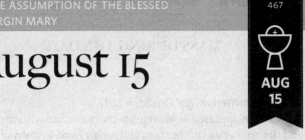

AUG
15

A promise of transformation

Both Mary and Elizabeth were in peculiar situations. Neither should be with child, according to the wisdom of this world. But they welcomed these unexpected events as gifts from God. Their greetings were exuberant. Mary, unwed and pregnant, came to assist her older cousin Elizabeth during the final months. From this young woman comes a hymn of praise for a God whose promises are great.

We read the Magnificat on the feast of the Assumption of Mary. The song reminds us that we do not wait for death to enter into God's presence.

We belong to God already. God is not distant, but moves through our lives in the most personal of ways. God also speaks to the world in words far from neutral or detached. The broken and forgotten are lifted up. Those secure in their own sufficiency are strangely empty. The power that seems ultimate collapses before God's truth.

God, Mary and Elizabeth— young and old—trusted you. Help me to believe that this promise of transformation and justice includes me and our world today.

■ **JEANNE SCHULER**

MASS DURING THE DAY

ENTRANCE ANTIPHON *(Cf. Revelation 12:1)*
A great sign appeared in heaven: a woman clothed with the sun,
and the moon beneath her feet, and on her head a crown of
twelve stars.

Or

Let us all rejoice in the Lord, as we celebrate the feast day in hon-
or of the Virgin Mary, at whose Assumption the Angels rejoice
and praise the Son of God.

INTRODUCTORY RITES *(page 10)*

COLLECT
Almighty ever-living God,
who assumed the Immaculate Virgin Mary, the Mother of your Son,
body and soul into heavenly glory,
grant, we pray,
that, always attentive to the things that are above,
we may merit to be sharers of her glory.
Through our Lord Jesus Christ, your Son,
who lives and reigns with you in the unity of the Holy Spirit,
one God, for ever and ever. *Amen.*

FIRST READING *(Revelation 11:19a; 12:1-6a, 10ab)*
God's temple in heaven was opened, and the ark of his covenant could be seen in the temple.

A great sign appeared in the sky, **a woman clothed with the
sun,** ☩ with the moon under her feet, and on her head a crown of
twelve stars. She was with child and wailed aloud in pain as she

labored to give birth. Then another sign appeared in the sky; it was a huge red dragon, with seven heads and ten horns, and on its heads were seven diadems. Its tail swept away a third of the stars in the sky and hurled them down to the earth. Then the dragon stood before the woman about to give birth, to devour her child when she gave birth. She gave birth to a son, a male child, destined to rule all the nations with an iron rod. Her child was caught up to God and his throne. The woman herself fled into the desert where she had a place prepared by God.

Then I heard a loud voice in heaven say:

"Now have salvation and power come,
    and the Kingdom of our God
    and the authority of his Anointed One."
The word of the Lord. *Thanks be to God.*

RESPONSORIAL PSALM *(Psalm 45:10, 11, 12, 16)*
℟ **The queen stands at your right hand, arrayed in gold.**

The queen takes her place at your right hand in gold of Ophir. ℟
Hear, O daughter, and see; turn your ear,
    forget your people and your father's house. ℟
So shall the king desire your beauty;
    for he is your lord. ℟
They are borne in with gladness and joy;
    they enter the palace of the king. ℟

SECOND READING *(1 Corinthians 15:20–27)*

Brothers and sisters: Christ has been raised from the dead, the firstfruits of those who have fallen asleep. For since death came through man, the resurrection of the dead came also through man. For just as in Adam all die, so too in Christ shall all be brought to life, but each one in proper order: Christ the firstfruits;

then, at his coming, those who belong to Christ; then comes the end, when he hands over the Kingdom to his God and Father, when he has destroyed every sovereignty and every authority and power. For he must reign until he has put all his enemies under his feet. The last enemy to be destroyed is death, for "he subjected everything under his feet."

The word of the Lord. *Thanks be to God.*

ALLELUIA

Alleluia, alleluia. Mary is taken up to heaven; a chorus of angels exults. *Alleluia, alleluia.*

GOSPEL *(Luke 1:39–56)*

A reading from the holy Gospel according to Luke.

Glory to you, O Lord.

Mary set out and traveled to the hill country in haste to a town of Judah, where she entered the house of Zechariah* and greeted Elizabeth. When Elizabeth heard Mary's greeting, the infant leaped in her womb, and Elizabeth, filled with the Holy Spirit, cried out in a loud voice and said, "Blessed are you among women, and blessed is the fruit of your womb. And how does this happen to me, that the mother of my Lord should come to me? For at the moment the sound of your greeting reached my ears, the infant in my womb leaped for joy. Blessed are you who believed that what was spoken to you by the Lord would be fulfilled."

And Mary said:

"My soul proclaims the greatness of the Lord;
    my spirit rejoices in God my Savior
    for he has looked with favor on his lowly servant.
From this day all generations will call me blessed:

the Almighty has done great things for me
and holy is his Name.
He has mercy on those who fear him
in every generation.
He has shown the strength of his arm,
and has scattered the proud in their conceit.
He has cast down the mighty from their thrones,
and has lifted up the lowly.
He has filled the hungry with good things,
and the rich he has sent away empty.
He has come to the help of his servant Israel
for he has remembered his promise of mercy,
the promise he made to our fathers,
to Abraham and his children forever."

Mary remained with her about three months and then returned
to her home.

The Gospel of the Lord. ***Praise to you, Lord Jesus Christ.***

PROFESSION OF FAITH *(page 13)*

PRAYER OF THE FAITHFUL

PREPARATION OF GIFTS *(page 16)*

PRAYER OVER THE OFFERINGS
May this oblation, our tribute of homage,
rise up to you, O Lord,
and, through the intercession of the most Blessed Virgin Mary,
whom you assumed into heaven,
may our hearts, aflame with the fire of love,
constantly long for you.
Through Christ our Lord. ***Amen.***

PREFACE: THE GLORY OF MARY ASSUMED INTO HEAVEN

It is truly right and just, our duty and our salvation,
always and everywhere to give you thanks,
Lord, holy Father, almighty and eternal God,
through Christ our Lord.

For today the Virgin Mother of God
was assumed into heaven
as the beginning and image
of your Church's coming to perfection
and a sign of sure hope and comfort to your pilgrim people;
rightly you would not allow her
to see the corruption of the tomb
since from her own body she marvelously brought forth
your incarnate Son, the Author of all life.

And so, in company with the choirs of Angels,
we praise you, and with joy we proclaim:
Holy, Holy, Holy Lord God of hosts... (page 35)

● TAKING A CLOSER LOOK ●

✟ **A woman clothed with the sun** Today's first reading portrays the conflict between Christ and the power of evil (Satan) through the symbolic conflict of a huge red dragon and a celestial woman clothed with the sun, the moon, and twelve stars. The woman could represent God's people—either as Israel giving birth to the Messiah or as the Church being persecuted by Satan—or Mary, enduring the pain of birth for a son, "destined to rule all the nations." In the vision, the evil intentions of the dragon are foiled, the child is taken up to God, and the woman flees to a place of safety prepared by God.

COMMUNION ANTIPHON *(Luke 1:48–49)*

All generations will call me blessed, for he who is mighty has done great things for me.

PRAYER AFTER COMMUNION

Having received the Sacrament of salvation,
we ask you to grant, O Lord,
that, through the intercession of the Blessed Virgin Mary,
whom you assumed into heaven,
we may be brought to the glory of the resurrection.
Through Christ our Lord. *Amen.*

SOLEMN BLESSING: THE BLESSED VIRGIN MARY *(Optional, page 62)*

DISMISSAL *(page 57)* ❖

• RESPONDING TO THE WORD •

God takes care of the mother and child in their danger.	Christ is our guarantee that death is not the end but a transition to new life.	Mary recognizes that God's design for the world will reverse the way we have set things up.
➲ What can I do today to help mothers and children who are at risk?	➲ How does this truth give me hope when thinking of my death?	➲ Which of these reversals do I look forward to the most?

August 16

A prayer of abandonment

The silent adoration of the infant Jesus by the Magi is one of the purest prayers in the New Testament. These men put aside everything in their lives to travel across the desert to kneel down and pay homage to Jesus. They bring him precious gifts and ask nothing for themselves.

In contrast stands the disruptive Canaanite woman in today's gospel who comes to Jesus shouting and demanding that he cast out the demon which oppresses her daughter. Jesus says nothing.

The woman's tune changes upon hearing Jesus say that he was sent only to the lost sheep of Israel. She kneels before him and says a prayer of abandonment: "Lord, help me." Now she no longer demands favors from a wonder-worker Jesus, but places herself at his feet. It is a moment of vulnerability and conversion.

What does this mean for us? Like the foreign woman and the foreign wise men, we can come to Jesus, not to make him hop to our agenda, but rather to bow before him. We are puny; Jesus is awesome. Praise and worship are the stance of faith. Our right relationship with Jesus is to pay him homage and to humbly beg, "Jesus, help me."

■ **GLEN ARGAN**

ENTRANCE ANTIPHON *(Psalm 84 [83]:10-11)*
Turn your eyes, O God, our shield; and look on
the face of your anointed one; one day within your
courts is better than a thousand elsewhere.

INTRODUCTORY RITES *(page 10)*

COLLECT
O God, who have prepared for those who love you
good things which no eye can see,
fill our hearts, we pray, with the warmth of your love,
so that, loving you in all things and above all things,
we may attain your promises,
which surpass every human desire.
Through our Lord Jesus Christ, your Son,
who lives and reigns with you in the unity of the Holy Spirit,
one God, for ever and ever. *Amen.*

FIRST READING *(Isaiah 56:1, 6-7)*

Thus says the LORD:
Observe what is right, do what is just;
for my salvation is about to come,
my justice, about to be revealed.

The foreigners who join themselves to the LORD,
ministering to him,
loving the name of the LORD,
and becoming his servants—
all who keep the sabbath free from profanation
and hold to my **covenant**, ✝
them I will bring to my holy mountain
and make joyful in my house of prayer;

their burnt offerings and sacrifices
    will be acceptable on my altar,
for my house shall be called
    a house of prayer for all peoples.
The word of the Lord. *Thanks be to God.*

RESPONSORIAL PSALM *(Psalm 67:2–3, 5, 6, 8)*
℟ **O God, let all the nations praise you!**

May God have pity on us and bless us;
    may he let his face shine upon us.
So may your way be known upon earth;
    among all nations, your salvation. ℟
May the nations be glad and exult
    because you rule the peoples in equity;
    the nations on the earth you guide. ℟
May the peoples praise you, O God;
    may all the peoples praise you!
May God bless us,
    and may all the ends of the earth fear him! ℟

SECOND READING *(Romans 11:13–15, 29–32)*

Brothers and sisters: I am speaking to you Gentiles. Inasmuch
as I am the apostle to the Gentiles, I glory in my ministry in
order to make my race jealous and thus save some of them. For if
their rejection is the reconciliation of the world, what will their
acceptance be but life from the dead?

For the gifts and the call of God are irrevocable. Just as you
once disobeyed God but have now received mercy because of
their disobedience, so they have now disobeyed in order that,
by virtue of the mercy shown to you, they too may now receive

mercy. For God delivered all to disobedience, that he might have mercy upon all.

The word of the Lord. *Thanks be to God.*

ALLELUIA *(Matthew 4:23)*

Alleluia, alleluia. Jesus proclaimed the Gospel of the kingdom and cured every disease among the people. *Alleluia, alleluia.*

GOSPEL *(Matthew 15:21–28)*

A reading from the holy Gospel according to Matthew.

Glory to you, O Lord.

At that time, Jesus withdrew to the region of Tyre* and Sidon.* And behold, a Canaanite woman of that district came and called out, "Have pity on me, Lord, Son of David! My daughter is tormented by a demon." But Jesus did not say a word in answer to her. Jesus' disciples came and asked him, "Send her away, for she keeps calling out after us." He said in reply, "I was sent only to the lost sheep of the house of Israel." But the woman came and did Jesus homage, saying, "Lord, help me." He said in reply, "It is not right to take the food of the children and throw it to the dogs." She said, "Please, Lord, for even the dogs eat the scraps that fall from the table of their masters." Then Jesus said to her in reply, "O woman, great is your faith! Let it be done for you as you wish." And the woman's daughter was healed from that hour.

The Gospel of the Lord. *Praise to you, Lord Jesus Christ.*

PROFESSION OF FAITH *(page 13)*

PRAYER OF THE FAITHFUL

PREPARATION OF GIFTS *(page 16)*

PRAYER OVER THE OFFERINGS
Receive our oblation, O Lord,
by which is brought about a glorious exchange,
that, by offering what you have given,
we may merit to receive your very self.
Through Christ our Lord. *Amen.*

PREFACE *(Sundays in Ordinary Time, pages 28–32)*

❖ TAKING A CLOSER LOOK ❖

✛ **Covenant** A covenant is a formal agreement between two persons or parties that spells out the obligations of their relationship. In the biblical world, the general expectations were modeled on the customs that guided relationships between persons of unequal honor, status, and wealth. These relationships were freely entered into and were not required by law. The covenant bound the parties in mutual and reciprocal obligations. The "patron" or more powerful person (like God) promised to provide for and protect the less powerful "clients" (from the Latin word for dependents). In return, to enhance the honor and reputation of the patron, the clients offered respect, praise, gratitude, and other favors when requested.

COMMUNION ANTIPHON *(Psalm 130 [129]:7)*
With the Lord there is mercy; in him is plentiful redemption.

Or *(John 6:51–52)*
I am the living bread that came down from heaven, says the
Lord. Whoever eats of this bread will live for ever.

PRAYER AFTER COMMUNION
Made partakers of Christ through these Sacraments,
we humbly implore your mercy, Lord,
that, conformed to his image on earth,
we may merit also to be his coheirs in heaven.
Who lives and reigns for ever and ever. *Amen.*

BLESSING & DISMISSAL *(page 56)* ❖

• RESPONDING TO THE WORD •

Isaiah reminds us that God wants the temple to be a house of prayer for all persons.

➡ *What can I do to make my household more prayerful?*

Paul believes that God's call and gifts to the Jews have not been taken back.

➡ *How can I show greater respect for the path to God that non-Christians are following?*

The persistent woman will accept no excuse from Jesus about why he will not heal her daughter.

➡ *For what am I continually asking Jesus in my prayer?*

August 23

Reflecting on our relationship with Christ

My attention is riveted by today's gospel and Jesus' poignant questions to his disciples: "Who do people say that the Son of Man is?" and "Who do you say that I am?" Peter's quick reply to the latter was, "You are the Christ." Did he know what he was saying? In the same situation, I would have been at a loss for an answer. Now, 2000 years later, I ponder that second question and I can come up with varied answers. Jesus said, "I am the good shepherd... I am the gate... I am the light... I am the true vine.."

A retreat I attended some months ago was based on this Scripture passage and provided me with a new perspective. We spent our time for meditation and prayer focusing on reverse questioning. Who am I? How do I see myself? How does Jesus see me? How do I want Jesus to see me?

Reflecting on my relationship with Jesus offered me new insights and a heartfelt desire to follow him more closely. I often take for granted the fact that he is a constant in my life—always present to me, whether or not I acknowledge him. Today's psalm proclaims, "I will give thanks to you, O Lord, with all my heart....Your kindness, O Lord, endures forever." How blessed are we!

❖ BARBARA K. D'ARTOIS

ENTRANCE ANTIPHON *(Cf. Psalm 86 [85]:1-3)*
Turn your ear, O Lord, and answer me; save the
servant who trusts in you, my God. Have mercy on
me, O Lord, for I cry to you all the day long.

INTRODUCTORY RITES *(page 10)*

COLLECT
O God, who cause the minds of the faithful
to unite in a single purpose,
grant your people to love what you command
and to desire what you promise,
that, amid the uncertainties of this world,
our hearts may be fixed on that place
where true gladness is found.
Through our Lord Jesus Christ, your Son,
who lives and reigns with you in the unity of the Holy Spirit,
one God, for ever and ever. *Amen.*

FIRST READING *(Isaiah 22:19-23)*

Thus says the LORD to Shebna, master of the palace:
"I will thrust you from your office
and pull you down from your station.
On that day I will summon my servant
Eliakim,* son of Hilkiah;*
I will clothe him with your robe,
and gird him with your sash,
and give over to him your authority.
He shall be a father to the inhabitants of Jerusalem,
and to the house of Judah.
I will place the key of the House of David on Eliakim's shoulder;

> when he opens, no one shall shut
> when he shuts, no one shall open.
> I will fix him like a peg in a sure spot,
> to be a place of honor for his family."

The word of the Lord. *Thanks be to God.*

RESPONSORIAL PSALM *(Psalm 138:1-2, 2-3, 6, 8)*

R⁀ **Lord, your love is eternal; do not forsake the work of your hands.**

I will give thanks to you, O LORD, with all my heart,
  for you have heard the words of my mouth;
in the presence of the angels I will sing your praise;
  I will worship at your holy temple. R⁀

I will give thanks to your name,
  because of your kindness and your truth:
When I called, you answered me;
  you built up strength within me. R⁀

The LORD is exalted, yet the lowly he sees,
  and the proud he knows from afar.
Your kindness, O LORD, endures forever;
  forsake not the work of your hands. R⁀

SECOND READING *(Romans 11:33-36)*

Oh, the depth of the riches and wisdom and knowledge of God! How inscrutable are his judgments and how unsearchable his ways!

> *For who has known the mind of the Lord*
>   *or who has been his counselor?*
> *Or who has given the Lord anything*
>   *that he may be repaid?*

For from him and through him and for him are all things. To him be glory forever. Amen.

The word of the Lord. ***Thanks be to God.***

ALLELUIA *(Matthew 16:18)*
Alleluia, alleluia. You are Peter and upon this rock I will build my Church and the gates of the netherworld shall not prevail against it. *Alleluia, alleluia.*

GOSPEL *(Matthew 16:13–20)*
A reading from the holy Gospel according to Matthew.
Glory to you, O Lord.

Jesus went into the region of Caesarea* Philippi and he asked his disciples, "Who do people say that the Son of Man is?" They replied, "Some say John the Baptist, others Elijah, still others Jeremiah or one of the prophets." He said to them, "But who do you say that I am?" Simon Peter said in reply, "You are the Christ, the Son of the living God." Jesus said to him in reply, "Blessed are you, Simon son of Jonah. For flesh and blood has not revealed this to you, but my heavenly Father. And so I say to you, you are Peter, and upon this rock I will build my church, and the gates of the netherworld shall not prevail against it. I will give you the keys to the **kingdom of heaven.** ☩ Whatever you bind on earth shall be bound in heaven; and whatever you loose on earth shall be loosed in heaven." Then he strictly ordered his disciples to tell no one that he was the Christ.

The Gospel of the Lord. ***Praise to you, Lord Jesus Christ.***

PROFESSION OF FAITH *(page 13)*

PRAYER OF THE FAITHFUL

PREPARATION OF GIFTS *(page 16)*

PRAYER OVER THE OFFERINGS

O Lord, who gained for yourself a people by adoption
through the one sacrifice offered once for all,
bestow graciously on us, we pray,
the gifts of unity and peace in your Church.
Through Christ our Lord. *Amen.*

PREFACE *(Sundays in Ordinary Time, pages 28–32)*

• TAKING A CLOSER LOOK •

✚ **Kingdom of heaven** In his teaching and preaching, Jesus
identifies God's ideal community as the kingdom of God, or as Matthew
often calls it, the "kingdom of heaven." This community is to be characterized by a new way of living together that includes everyone (both Jew
and Gentile), who as brothers and sisters will relate to God as Father and
a king whose benevolent rule over them guides every moment of their
lives. The kingdom is inaugurated by Jesus and continues today in the
Christian community that daily strives to make God's ideal community
a reality.

COMMUNION ANTIPHON *(Cf. Psalm 104 [103]:13-15)*

The earth is replete with the fruits of your work, O Lord; you bring forth bread from the earth and wine to cheer the heart.

Or *(Cf. John 6:54)*

Whoever eats my flesh and drinks my blood has eternal life, says the Lord, and I will raise him up on the last day.

PRAYER AFTER COMMUNION

Complete within us, O Lord, we pray,
the healing work of your mercy
and graciously perfect and sustain us,
so that in all things we may please you.
Through Christ our Lord. *Amen.*

BLESSING & DISMISSAL *(page 56)* ❖

❖ RESPONDING TO THE WORD ❖

God's doorkeeper must not abuse his authority but care for those under his authority.

➡ *How might I care more for those under my authority?*

Paul tells us that God's ways are often not clear to us.

➡ *What has made me most aware that God's ways are not necessarily my ways?*

Jesus demands that his disciples understand who he is.

➡ *Today, how do I answer Jesus' question: "Who do you say that I am?"*

August 30

We belong to God

We all want to belong. Today's readings are about belonging to God. How do we belong to God? To belong to God is to love. Jesus shows us that love is at the very heart of those who belong to God.

Jeremiah is a reluctant prophet who cannot ignore God's call "like fire burning in my heart, imprisoned in my bones." His only answer is "yes," and he belongs to God.

Jesus belongs to God. He is firm in his mission to serve the poor, the rejected, and the voiceless, even to the point of losing his life. There were followers of Jesus who sought to stop him because they were afraid of losing their lives. Fear is the opposite of love.

Fear is exclusive. Belonging is inclusive.

Jesus was single-minded in his purpose to love and create belonging. He berated those who sought to stop him. Our culture claims that we can protect ourselves by excluding others. Our culture promotes fear and exclusion as the way to preserve life.

In today's gospel, Jesus challenges us to belong to God by letting go of fear. What fears do we have to leave behind to belong to God? Are we willing to allow God to entice us and change our behavior? In today's Eucharist, let us pray that our way of life is an imitation of God, who is love.

■ ANTHONY CHEZZI

ENTRANCE ANTIPHON *(Cf. Psalm 86 [85]:3, 5)*

Have mercy on me, O Lord, for I cry to you all the
day long. O Lord, you are good and forgiving, full of
mercy to all who call to you.

INTRODUCTORY RITES *(page 10)*

COLLECT

God of might, giver of every good gift,
put into our hearts the love of your name,
so that, by deepening our sense of reverence,
you may nurture in us what is good
and, by your watchful care,
keep safe what you have nurtured.
Through our Lord Jesus Christ, your Son,
who lives and reigns with you in the unity of the Holy Spirit,
one God, for ever and ever. *Amen.*

FIRST READING *(Jeremiah 20:7-9)*

You duped me, O Lord, and I let myself be duped;
   you were too strong for me, and you triumphed.
All the day I am an object of laughter;
   everyone mocks me.

Whenever I speak, I must cry out,
   violence and outrage is my message;
the word of the Lord has brought me
   derision and reproach all the day.

I say to myself, I will not mention him,
   I will speak in his name no more.
But then it becomes like fire burning in my heart,

imprisoned in my bones;
I grow weary holding it in, I cannot endure it.
The word of the Lord. *Thanks be to God.*

RESPONSORIAL PSALM *(Psalm 63:2, 3-4, 5-6, 8-9)*
R My soul is thirsting for you, O Lord my God.

O God, you are my God whom I seek;
    for you my flesh pines and my soul thirsts
    like the earth, parched, lifeless and without water. R
Thus have I gazed toward you in the sanctuary
    to see your power and your glory,
for your kindness is a greater good than life;
    my lips shall glorify you. R
Thus will I bless you while I live;
    lifting up my hands, I will call upon your name.
As with the riches of a banquet shall my soul be satisfied,
    and with exultant lips my mouth shall praise you. R
You are my help,
    and in the shadow of your wings I shout for joy.
My soul clings fast to you;
    your right hand upholds me. R

SECOND READING *(Romans 12:1-2)*
I urge you, brothers and sisters, by the mercies of God, to offer
your bodies as a living sacrifice, holy and pleasing to God, your
spiritual worship. Do not conform yourselves to this age but be
transformed by the renewal of your mind, that you may discern
what is the will of God, what is good and pleasing and perfect.
    The word of the Lord. *Thanks be to God.*

ALLELUIA *(Cf. Ephesians 1:17-18)*
Alleluia, alleluia. May the Father of our Lord Jesus Christ enlighten the eyes of our hearts, that we may know what is the hope that belongs to our call. *Alleluia, alleluia.*

GOSPEL *(Matthew 16:21-27)*
A reading from the holy Gospel according to Matthew.
Glory to you, O Lord.

Jesus began to show his disciples that he must go to Jerusalem and suffer greatly from the elders, the chief priests, and the scribes, and be killed and on the third day be raised. Then Peter took Jesus aside and began to rebuke him, "God forbid, Lord! No such thing shall ever happen to you." He turned and said to Peter, "Get behind me, Satan! You are an obstacle to me. You are thinking not as God does, but as human beings do."

Then Jesus said to his disciples, "Whoever wishes to come after me must deny himself, take up his cross, and follow me. For whoever wishes to save his life will lose it, but whoever loses his life for my sake will find it. What profit would there be for one to gain the whole world and forfeit his life? Or what can one give in exchange for his life? For the **Son of Man** ✝ will come with his angels in his Father's glory, and then he will repay all according to his conduct."

The Gospel of the Lord. *Praise to you, Lord Jesus Christ.*

PROFESSION OF FAITH *(page 13)*

PRAYER OF THE FAITHFUL

PREPARATION OF GIFTS *(page 16)*

PRAYER OVER THE OFFERINGS

May this sacred offering, O Lord,
confer on us always the blessing of salvation,
that what it celebrates in mystery
it may accomplish in power.
Through Christ our Lord. *Amen.*

PREFACE *(Sundays in Ordinary Time, pages 28–32)*

COMMUNION ANTIPHON *(Psalm 31 [30]:20)*

How great is the goodness, Lord, that you keep for those who
fear you.

Or *(Matthew 5:9-10)*

Blessed are the peacemakers, for they shall be called children
of God. Blessed are they who are persecuted for the sake of
righteousness, for theirs is the Kingdom of Heaven.

❖ TAKING A CLOSER LOOK ❖

✠ **Son of Man** In Semitic languages, when connected to a col-
lective noun, "son of" designates the individual member belonging
to a group. Thus a son of man means a human person, especially in
contrast to God. But this title also takes on a particularly important
meaning for Christians because the prophet Daniel (7:13) describes
God's final agent, to whom all power is given to accomplish God's rule
in the world, as a "son of man." Jesus also adds further meanings by
connecting the Son of Man with the suffering that is part of his messianic task and with the forgiveness of sins, which only God could do.
Thus the title could point to him as just another human person, or as
the suffering, sin-forgiving savior or, finally, as God's final triumphant
figure brandishing the power of God for the kingdom.

PRAYER AFTER COMMUNION
Renewed by this bread from the heavenly table,
we beseech you, Lord,
that, being the food of charity,
it may confirm our hearts
and stir us to serve you in our neighbor.
Through Christ our Lord. *Amen.*

BLESSING & DISMISSAL *(page 56)* ❖

❖ RESPONDING TO THE WORD ❖

Jeremiah feels God's word like a burning fire that he cannot keep hidden.	Paul encourages us to be transformed so we know what is good and pleasing to God.	Jesus tells us that we must take up our cross and follow him.
➡ *When have I burned to tell someone of God's message of love?*	➡ *What do I most need to change in my life to be more pleasing to God?*	➡ *What cross do I wish I didn't have to carry in my life now?*

September 6

Let love be our guide

Today's gospel touches on one of the seven spiritual works of mercy: admonishing sinners. People often find that this has a negative connotation, as it brings to mind the judgmental hypocrisy and Pharisaism of which Christians have all to often been guilty. Therefore, let us take the time to understand Jesus' words today.

Our Lord is very clear that we must not judge others. Yet today he provides guidelines on how to correct one another. How can we correct our brothers and sisters without being judgmental?

There is a tremendous difference between Christian correction and rash judgment. Being judgmental seeks and takes pleasure in the faults of others. Although Christians can and do slip into this, it is a very un-Christian thing.

The Christian admonishment of sinners comes from a place of love. Love motivates us to desire the sanctification of others. Therefore, when people behave inappropriately or sinfully, charity may call on us to address it with them, in a compassionate way. The goal is not to put them down but to help them grow. This truly differentiates Christian correction from rash judgment.

May the Holy Spirit rid our hearts of all forms of rash judgment. When necessary, may God also give us the compassion and fortitude to mercifully admonish sinners.

■ **CONNOR BROWNRIGG**

ENTRANCE ANTIPHON *(Psalm 119 [118]:137, 124)*
You are just, O Lord, and your judgment is right;
treat your servant in accord with your merciful love.

INTRODUCTORY RITES *(page 10)*

COLLECT
O God, by whom we are redeemed and receive adoption,
look graciously upon your beloved sons and daughters,
that those who believe in Christ
may receive true freedom
and an everlasting inheritance.
Through our Lord Jesus Christ, your Son,
who lives and reigns with you in the unity of the Holy Spirit,
one God, for ever and ever. *Amen.*

FIRST READING *(Ezekiel 33:7-9)*

Thus says the LORD: You, son of man, I have appointed watchman for the house of Israel; when you hear me say anything,
you shall warn them for me. If I tell the wicked, "O wicked one,
you shall surely die," and you do not speak out to dissuade the
wicked from his way, the wicked shall die for his guilt, but I will
hold you responsible for his death. But if you warn the wicked, trying to turn him from his way, and he refuses to turn from his way,
he shall die for his guilt, but you shall save yourself.

   The word of the Lord. *Thanks be to God.*

RESPONSORIAL PSALM *(Psalm 95:1-2, 6-7, 8-9)*
R⁄ If today you hear his voice, harden not your hearts.

Come, let us sing joyfully to the LORD;
    let us acclaim the rock of our salvation.
Let us come into his presence with thanksgiving;

let us joyfully sing psalms to him.
℟ **If today you hear his voice, harden not your hearts.**
Come, let us bow down in worship;
    let us kneel before the LORD who made us.
For he is our God,
    and we are the people he shepherds, the flock he guides. ℟
Oh, that today you would hear his voice:
    "Harden not your hearts as at Meribah,*
    as in the day of Massah* in the desert,
where your fathers tempted me;
    they tested me though they had seen my works." ℟

SECOND READING *(Romans 13:8-10)*

Brothers and sisters: Owe nothing to anyone, except to love one another; for the one who loves another has fulfilled the law. The commandments, "You shall not commit adultery; you shall not kill; you shall not steal; you shall not covet," and whatever other commandment there may be, are summed up in this saying, namely, "You shall love your neighbor as yourself." Love does no evil to the neighbor; hence, love is the fulfillment of the law.

The word of the Lord. *Thanks be to God.*

ALLELUIA *(2 Corinthians 5:19)*
Alleluia, alleluia. God was reconciling the world to himself in Christ and entrusting to us the message of reconciliation. *Alleluia, alleluia.*

GOSPEL *(Matthew 18:15–20)*
A reading from the holy Gospel according to Matthew.
Glory to you, O Lord.

Jesus said to his disciples: "If your brother sins against you, go and tell him his fault between you and him alone. If he listens to you, you have won over your brother. If he does not listen, take one or two others along with you, so that 'every fact may be established on the testimony of two or three witnesses.' If he refuses to listen to them, tell the church. If he refuses to listen even to the church, then treat him as you would a Gentile or a **tax collector**. ✢ Amen, I say to you, whatever you bind on earth shall be bound in heaven, and whatever you loose on earth shall be loosed in heaven. Again, amen, I say to you, if two of you agree on earth about anything for which they are to pray, it shall be granted to them by my heavenly Father. For where two or three are gathered together in my name, there am I in the midst of them."

The Gospel of the Lord. *Praise to you, Lord Jesus Christ.*

PROFESSION OF FAITH *(page 13)*

PRAYER OF THE FAITHFUL

PREPARATION OF GIFTS *(page 16)*

PRAYER OVER THE OFFERINGS
O God, who give us the gift of true prayer and of peace,
graciously grant that, through this offering,
we may do fitting homage to your divine majesty
and, by partaking of the sacred mystery,
we may be faithfully united in mind and heart.
Through Christ our Lord. *Amen.*

PREFACE *(Sundays in Ordinary Time, pages 28–32)*

• TAKING A CLOSER LOOK •

✝ **Tax Collector** In Jesus' times, Rome set the amount of revenue to be raised by a district and then sold the right to collect taxes to the highest bidder, who could charge whatever he wished in order to make a profit. The tax collector was thus viewed as an extortioner and traitor and so was an outcast to his fellow Jews. He was considered a "sinner" because his occupation was considered sure to lead him into immorality. Jesus' advice here is paradoxical for readers of Matthew since at first we might assume that it would mean Matthew's own exclusion. However, from Jesus' own example, tax collectors are included among his disciples (Matthew 9:1, 10:3), and he eats with them to try to convert them (Matthew 18:17, 5:46, 9:10, 9:11, 11:19, 21:31, 21:32).

COMMUNION ANTIPHON *(Cf. Psalm 42 [41]:2–3)*

Like the deer that yearns for running streams, so my soul is yearning for you, my God; my soul is thirsting for God, the living God.

Or *(John 8:12)*

I am the light of the world, says the Lord; whoever follows me will not walk in darkness, but will have the light of life.

PRAYER AFTER COMMUNION

Grant that your faithful, O Lord,
whom you nourish and endow with life
through the food of your Word and heavenly Sacrament,
may so benefit from your beloved Son's great gifts
that we may merit an eternal share in his life.
Who lives and reigns for ever and ever. ***Amen.***

BLESSING & DISMISSAL *(page 56)* ⁑

• RESPONDING TO THE WORD •

Ezekiel is appointed a watchman to warn the people about what God wants.

➡ *About what would I want to warn people today?*

Paul declares that loving one another is what God requires.

➡ *What might I do to show my love for others today?*

Jesus encourages us to find a practical way toward reconciliation.

➡ *With whom might I need to reconcile today?*

September 13

Reflecting Jesus' love and mercy

Today's readings all carry reference to the central theme of forgiveness and the importance of showing God's mercy to others in order to receive it ourselves.

In the gospel, Jesus uses the parable of the unforgiving servant to teach of the need to always forgive our neighbor. We hear today about a man who pleads for forgiveness but is unwavering in his refusal to grant the same. This ironic tale showing the hypocrisy of society aptly presents both the power and difficulty of forgiveness. As recited in the Lord's Prayer and detailed in the readings of today's Mass, we are challenged to demonstrate our desire for God's unconditional love and compassion through our practice of the Golden Rule each day.

We are reminded in today's gospel how new life through forgiveness far outweighs the cost of any debt owed. Yet, just as the king's remission of the servant's debt shows God's redemption from our sin by his invaluable and boundless grace, we, too, must never overlook our calling and responsibility to model the same to each of our brothers and sisters in Christ.

For as we will one day be judged based on our life's body of work as testament of our faith, let us always seek to reflect Jesus' love by modelling his forgiving mercy in both words and deeds.

■ **MATT CHARBONNEAU**

ENTRANCE ANTIPHON *(Cf. Sirach 36:18)*

Give peace, O Lord, to those who wait for you, that
your prophets be found true. Hear the prayers of
your servant, and of your people Israel.

INTRODUCTORY RITES *(page 10)*

COLLECT

Look upon us, O God,
Creator and ruler of all things,
and, that we may feel the working of your mercy,
grant that we may serve you with all our heart.
Through our Lord Jesus Christ, your Son,
who lives and reigns with you in the unity of the Holy Spirit,
one God, for ever and ever. *Amen.*

FIRST READING *(Sirach 27:30—28:7)*

Wrath and anger are hateful things,
   yet the sinner hugs them tight.
The vengeful will suffer the LORD's vengeance,
      for he remembers their sins in detail.
Forgive your neighbor's injustice;
      then when you pray, your own sins will be forgiven.
Could anyone nourish anger against another
      and expect healing from the LORD?
Could anyone refuse mercy to another like himself,
      can he seek pardon for his own sins?
If one who is but flesh cherishes wrath,
      who will forgive his sins?
Remember your last days, set enmity aside;
      remember death and decay, and cease from sin!

Think of the commandments, hate not your neighbor;
  remember the Most High's covenant, and overlook faults.
The word of the Lord. ***Thanks be to God.***

RESPONSORIAL PSALM *(Psalm 103:1-2, 3-4, 9-10, 11-12)*
℟ **The Lord is kind and merciful, slow to anger, and rich in compassion.**

Bless the LORD, O my soul;
  and all my being, bless his holy name.
Bless the LORD, O my soul,
  and forget not all his benefits. ℟
He pardons all your iniquities,
  heals all your ills.
He redeems your life from destruction,
  crowns you with kindness and **compassion**.✝ ℟
He will not always chide,
  nor does he keep his wrath forever.
Not according to our sins does he deal with us,
  nor does he requite us according to our crimes. ℟
For as the heavens are high above the earth,
  so surpassing is his kindness toward those who fear him.
As far as the east is from the west,
  so far has he put our transgressions from us. ℟

SECOND READING *(Romans 14:7-9)*

Brothers and sisters: None of us lives for oneself, and no one dies for oneself. For if we live, we live for the Lord, and if we die, we die for the Lord; so then, whether we live or die, we are the Lord's. For this is why Christ died and came to life, that he might be Lord of both the dead and the living.
The word of the Lord. ***Thanks be to God.***

ALLELUIA *(John 13:34)*
Alleluia, alleluia. I give you a new commandment, says the Lord; love one another as I have loved you. *Alleluia, alleluia.*

GOSPEL *(Matthew 18:21–35)*
A reading from the holy Gospel according to Matthew.
Glory to you, O Lord.

Peter approached Jesus and asked him, "Lord, if my brother sins against me, how often must I forgive? As many as seven times?" Jesus answered, "I say to you, not seven times but seventy-seven times. That is why the kingdom of heaven may be likened to a king who decided to settle accounts with his servants. When he began the accounting, a debtor was brought before him who owed him a huge amount. Since he had no way of paying it back, his master ordered him to be sold, along with his wife, his children, and all his property, in payment of the debt. At that, the servant fell down, did him homage, and said, 'Be patient with me, and I will pay you back in full.' Moved with **compassion**✠ the master of that servant let him go and forgave him the loan. When that servant had left, he found one of his fellow servants who owed him a much smaller amount. He seized him and started to choke him, demanding, 'Pay back what you owe.' Falling to his knees, his fellow servant begged him, 'Be patient with me, and I will pay you back.' But he refused. Instead, he had the fellow servant put in prison until he paid back the debt. Now when his fellow servants saw what had happened, they were deeply disturbed, and went to their master and reported the whole affair. His master summoned him and said to him, 'You wicked servant! I forgave you your entire debt because you begged me to. Should you not have had pity on your fellow servant, as I had pity on you?' Then in anger his master handed him over to the torturers until he should pay back the whole debt. So will my heavenly Father do to you, unless each of you forgives your brother from your heart."

The Gospel of the Lord. *Praise to you, Lord Jesus Christ.*

PROFESSION OF FAITH *(page 13)*

PRAYER OF THE FAITHFUL

PREPARATION OF GIFTS *(page 16)*

PRAYER OVER THE OFFERINGS
Look with favor on our supplications, O Lord,
and in your kindness accept these, your servants' offerings,
that what each has offered to the honor of your name
may serve the salvation of all.
Through Christ our Lord. *Amen.*

PREFACE *(Sundays in Ordinary Time, pages 28–32)*

• Taking a Closer Look •

✢ **Compassion** The Greek word used here is the same one that is used when the gospels describe Jesus as being "moved with compassion" (e.g., Matthew 14:14; Mark 1:41, 6:34, 8:2; Luke 7:13). It is a strong emotional reaction felt deep within the person (literally, in one's inward parts, one's entrails, or, as we would say, one's "guts"—or the seat of emotion, the heart) in response to someone else's difficulty or suffering. Jesus extends the duty of compassionate forgiveness to his disciples and to each of us.

COMMUNION ANTIPHON *(Cf. Psalm 36 [35]:8)*
How precious is your mercy, O God! The children of men seek shelter in the shadow of your wings.

Or *(Cf. 1 Corinthians 10:16)*
The chalice of blessing that we bless is a communion in the Blood of Christ; and the bread that we break is a sharing in the Body of the Lord.

PRAYER AFTER COMMUNION
May the working of this heavenly gift, O Lord, we pray,
take possession of our minds and bodies,
so that its effects, and not our own desires,
may always prevail in us.
Through Christ our Lord. ***Amen.***

BLESSING & DISMISSAL *(page 56)* ❖

❖ RESPONDING TO THE WORD ❖

The Book of Sirach tells us that sinners hold onto their anger and seek vengeance.

➡ *Is there something or someone that remains unforgiven in my own heart? What might I do about it?*

Paul reminds the Romans that we are meant to live and die for the Lord.

➡ *Is there an area in my life where I live more for myself than the Lord? What one change can I make this week?*

Jesus invites us to extend compassion to our brothers and sisters.

➡ *Who is in need of my compassion this week?*

September 20

Rejoice in God's infinite compassion!

It's just not fair! Like children who bemoan being denied something that has been afforded another, we all intermittently rail against God for not getting our just desserts. Why did this faithful, God-loving and generous person get struck with cancer, lose a job, or get rear-ended in traffic while another who appears completely arrogant, inconsiderate, and self-absorbed is spared life's misfortunes?

Like the laborers in the vineyard, we challenge God about the perceived inequity of our situation. It's hard to accept that living a long life of loving and faithful service can net the same eternal reward as an eleventh-hour conversion and repentance that follows a lifetime of depravity. It's like a get-into-heaven-free card for a Johnny-come-lately who previously had not demonstrated a smidgen of love, compassion, or care for God or neighbor.

We think and judge with the limited human understanding provided us. God sees all and judges with infinite knowledge. The get-into-heaven-free card can only be played if the holder has had a true conversion and comes to know Jesus personally as their Savior. We ought to rejoice that God's infinite compassion and forgiveness can offer us the eternal reward promised for a life well-lived instead of fretting that someone else may not have merited the same benefit.

■ FRANK CAMPBELL

ENTRANCE ANTIPHON

I am the salvation of the people, says the Lord. Should
they cry to me in any distress, I will hear them, and I
will be their Lord for ever.

INTRODUCTORY RITES *(page 10)*

COLLECT

O God, who founded all the commands of your sacred Law
upon love of you and of our neighbor,
grant that, by keeping your precepts,
we may merit to attain eternal life.
Through our Lord Jesus Christ, your Son,
who lives and reigns with you in the unity of the Holy Spirit,
one God, for ever and ever. *Amen.*

FIRST READING *(Isaiah 55:6–9)*

Seek the Lord while he may be found,
      call him while he is near.
Let the scoundrel forsake his way,
      and the wicked his thoughts;
let him turn to the Lord for mercy;
      to our God, who is generous in forgiving.
For my thoughts are not your thoughts,
      nor are your ways my ways, says the Lord.
As high as the heavens are above the earth,
      so high are my ways above your ways
      and my thoughts above your thoughts.
The word of the Lord. *Thanks be to God.*

RESPONSORIAL PSALM *(Psalm 145:2-3, 8-9, 17-18)*

R. The Lord is near to all who call upon him.

Every day will I bless you,
　　and I will praise your name forever and ever.
Great is the LORD and highly to be praised;
　　his greatness is unsearchable. R.
The LORD is gracious and merciful,✝
　　slow to anger and of great kindness.
The LORD is good to all
　　and compassionate toward all his works. R.
The LORD is just in all his ways
　　and holy in all his works.
The LORD is near to all who call upon him,
　　to all who call upon him in truth. R.

SECOND READING *(Philippians 1:20c-24, 27a)*

Brothers and sisters: Christ will be magnified in my body, whether by life or by death. For to me life is Christ, and death is gain. If I go on living in the flesh, that means fruitful labor for me. And I do not know which I shall choose. I am caught between the two. I long to depart this life and be with Christ, for that is far better. Yet that I remain in the flesh is more necessary for your benefit.

　　Only, conduct yourselves in a way worthy of the gospel of Christ.

　　The word of the Lord. *Thanks be to God.*

ALLELUIA *(Acts 16:14b)*

Alleluia, alleluia. Open our hearts, O Lord, to listen to the words of your Son. *Alleluia, alleluia.*

GOSPEL *(Matthew 20:1-16a)*

A reading from the holy Gospel according to Matthew.
Glory to you, O Lord.

Jesus told his disciples this parable: "The kingdom of heaven is like a landowner who went out at dawn to hire laborers for his vineyard. After agreeing with them for the usual daily wage, he sent them into his vineyard. Going out about nine o'clock, the landowner saw others standing idle in the marketplace, and he said to them, 'You too go into my vineyard, and I will give you what is just.' So they went off. And he went out again around noon, and around three o'clock, and did likewise. Going out about five o'clock, the landowner found others standing around, and said to them, 'Why do you stand here idle all day?' They answered, 'Because no one has hired us.' He said to them, 'You too go into my vineyard.' When it was evening the owner of the vineyard said to his foreman, 'Summon the laborers and give them their pay, beginning with the last and ending with the first.' When those who had started about five o'clock came, each received the usual daily wage. So when the first came, they thought that they would receive more, but each of them also got the usual wage. And on receiving it they grumbled against the landowner, saying, 'These last ones worked only one hour, and you have made them equal to us, who bore the day's burden and the heat.' He said to one of them in reply, 'My friend, I am not cheating you. Did you not agree with me for the usual daily wage? Take what is yours and go. What if I wish to give this last one the same as you? Or am I not free to do as I wish with my own money? Are you envious because I am generous?' Thus, the last will be first, and the first will be last."

The Gospel of the Lord. *Praise to you, Lord Jesus Christ.*

PROFESSION OF FAITH *(page 13)*

PRAYER OF THE FAITHFUL

PREPARATION OF GIFTS *(page 16)*

PRAYER OVER THE OFFERINGS
Receive with favor, O Lord, we pray,
the offerings of your people,
that what they profess with devotion and faith
may be theirs through these heavenly mysteries.
Through Christ our Lord. *Amen.*

PREFACE *(Sundays in Ordinary Time, pages 28-32)*

● TAKING A CLOSER LOOK ●

✚ **The Lord is gracious and merciful** In the Old Testament, "gracious" and "merciful" were characteristics of God's special covenant love (Hebrew, *hesed*) that binds God to us. God's attitude of love or attachment to the covenant community includes aspects of loyalty, dependability, trustworthiness, and an eagerness to help when situations turn bad.

Like a father or patron of a family, God is an especially generous benefactor who lavishes gifts on the people. These are not distributed because of their merits, but strictly out of God's favor or mercy. Mercy is not just the response felt toward those who are suffering, but even more the fierce attachment of God to be with us and save us.

COMMUNION ANTIPHON *(Psalm 119 [118]:4-5)*

You have laid down your precepts to be carefully kept; may my ways be firm in keeping your statutes.

Or *(John 10:14)*

I am the Good Shepherd, says the Lord; I know my sheep, and mine know me.

PRAYER AFTER COMMUNION

Graciously raise up, O Lord,
those you renew with this Sacrament,
that we may come to possess your redemption
both in mystery and in the manner of our life.
Through Christ our Lord. *Amen.*

BLESSING & DISMISSAL *(page 56)* ❖

❖ RESPONDING TO THE WORD ❖

Isaiah encourages us to seek God who is already near us.

➡ *What can I do this week to draw closer to God?*

Paul encourages us to conduct ourselves in a way worthy of the gospel.

➡ *What can I do today to offer an example of gospel living?*

In Jesus' parable, the workers grumble about the landowner's generosity.

➡ *How might I imitate God's generosity in my dealings with others today?*

September 27

SEP 27

Let us open our hearts!

Jesus explains today that our love for God is revealed especially through our actions. We can profess our faith with words and make lofty promises, but if we fail to keep these promises they have no value.

In today's gospel, both sons disappoint their father, one by his refusal to work in the vineyard and the other by his empty promises. Yet the rebellious son has a complete change of heart; he repents and does his father's will. The unrighteous tax collectors and prostitutes were open to Jesus' teaching and call to conversion. They recognized their need for forgiveness and responded with concrete faith. God asks us to be compassionate and genu-inely concerned to help others. St. Paul offers us examples of how true followers of Jesus should behave. He invites us to place the well-being of others before our own, and to follow Christ's example of humility and selfless love.

Although we hope to always say yes to the Father and to be faithful to these promises, at times we stumble. God is infinitely patient and always offers us the opportunity to repent and receive loving mercy. Let us open our hearts to the Lord today and allow God to transform our lives. Let us ask for guidance to faithfully respond to everyday events with patience, generosity, and love.

■ **NADA MAZZEI**

ENTRANCE ANTIPHON *(Daniel 3:31, 29, 30, 43, 42)*
All that you have done to us, O Lord, you have done with true judgment, for we have sinned against you and not obeyed your commandments. But give glory to your name and deal with us according to the bounty of your mercy.

INTRODUCTORY RITES *(page 10)*

COLLECT
O God, who manifest your almighty power
above all by pardoning and showing mercy,
bestow, we pray, your grace abundantly upon us
and make those hastening to attain your promises
heirs to the treasures of heaven.
Through our Lord Jesus Christ, your Son,
who lives and reigns with you in the unity of the Holy Spirit,
one God, for ever and ever. *Amen.*

FIRST READING *(Ezekiel 18:25-28)*

Thus says the LORD: You say, "The LORD's way is not fair!" Hear now, house of Israel: Is it my way that is unfair, or rather, are not your ways unfair? When someone virtuous turns away from virtue to commit iniquity, and dies, it is because of the iniquity he committed that he must die. But if he turns from the wickedness he has committed, he does what is right and just, he shall preserve his life; since he has turned away from all the sins that he has committed, he shall surely live, he shall not die.

The word of the Lord. *Thanks be to God.*

RESPONSORIAL PSALM *(Psalm 25:4-5, 6-7, 8-9)*

R. **Remember your mercies, O Lord.**

Your ways, O LORD, make known to me;
    teach me your paths,
guide me in your truth and teach me,
    for you are **God my savior.** + R.

Remember that your compassion, O LORD,
    and your love are from of old.
The sins of my youth and my frailties remember not;
    in your kindness remember me,
    because of your goodness, O LORD. R.

Good and upright is the LORD;
    thus he shows sinners the way.
He guides the humble to justice,
    and he teaches the humble his way. R.

SECOND READING *(Philippians 2:1-11)*

For the shorter version, omit the indented parts in brackets.

Brothers and sisters: If there is any encouragement in Christ, any solace in love, any participation in the Spirit, any compassion and mercy, complete my joy by being of the same mind, with the same love, united in heart, thinking one thing. Do nothing out of selfishness or out of vainglory; rather, humbly regard others as more important than yourselves, each looking out not for his own interests, but also for those of others.

    Have in you the same attitude that is also in Christ Jesus.
[Who, though he was in the form of God,
    did not regard equality with God
    something to be grasped.

Rather, he emptied himself,
  taking the form of a slave,
  coming in human likeness;
  and found human in appearance,
  he humbled himself,
  becoming obedient to the point of death,
  even death on a cross.
Because of this, God greatly exalted him
  and bestowed on him the name
  which is above every name,
  that at the name of Jesus
  every knee should bend,
  of those in heaven and on earth and under the earth,
  and every tongue confess that
  Jesus Christ is Lord,
  to the glory of God the Father.]
The word of the Lord. ***Thanks be to God.***

ALLELUIA *(John 10:27)*
Alleluia, alleluia. My sheep hear my voice, says the Lord;
I know them, and they follow me. *Alleluia, alleluia.*

GOSPEL *(Matthew 21:28-32)*
A reading from the holy Gospel according to Matthew.
Glory to you, O Lord.
Jesus said to the chief priests and elders of the people: "What is
your opinion? A man had two sons. He came to the first and said,
'Son, go out and work in the vineyard today.' He said in reply, 'I will
not,' but afterwards changed his mind and went. The man came to
the other son and gave the same order. He said in reply, 'Yes, sir,' but
did not go. Which of the two did his father's will?" They answered,

"The first." Jesus said to them, "Amen, I say to you, tax collectors and prostitutes are entering the kingdom of God before you. When John came to you in the way of righteousness, you did not believe him; but tax collectors and prostitutes did. Yet even when you saw that, you did not later change your minds and believe him."

The Gospel of the Lord. *Praise to you, Lord Jesus Christ.*

PROFESSION OF FAITH *(page 13)*

PRAYER OF THE FAITHFUL

PREPARATION OF GIFTS *(page 16)*

PRAYER OVER THE OFFERINGS
Grant us, O merciful God,
that this our offering may find acceptance with you
and that through it the wellspring of all blessing
may be laid open before us.
Through Christ our Lord. *Amen.*

PREFACE *(Sundays in Ordinary Time, pages 28–32)*

• TAKING A CLOSER LOOK •

✝ **God my savior** Before it became a theological term, savior meant one who rescued someone from a difficult situation. Thus it was commonly attributed to the king or emperor or general who saved the nation by winning a war. For the Jews, God was their primary Savior because God rescued them from their oppression in Egypt. For Christians, Jesus is the Savior because he rescued us from our broken relationship with God and offered us a new relationship under God's rule, a new "way of righteousness" as Matthew calls it in today's gospel.

COMMUNION ANTIPHON *(Cf. Psalm 119 [118]:49-50)*

Remember your word to your servant, O Lord, by which you have given me hope. This is my comfort when I am brought low.

Or *(1 John 3:16)*

By this we came to know the love of God: that Christ laid down his life for us; so we ought to lay down our lives for one another.

PRAYER AFTER COMMUNION

May this heavenly mystery, O Lord,
restore us in mind and body,
that we may be coheirs in glory with Christ,
to whose suffering we are united
whenever we proclaim his Death.
Who lives and reigns for ever and ever. ***Amen.***

BLESSING & DISMISSAL *(page 56)* ✦

✦ RESPONDING TO THE WORD ✦

The people complain that God's way "is not fair."	Paul offers ways that we can improve our relationships with others.	Jesus' parable describes the contrasting attitudes of two sons.
➡ *What has made me think that God's ways are not fair?*	➡ *Which of his suggestions might I do today?*	➡ *Which of the two sons have I been like this week?*

October 4

Be rooted in Christ!

What does it mean to be, as today's gospel mentions, a people that produce the fruits of the kingdom? Jesus demands two things. Just as trees are fed from their roots, we must be rooted in Jesus; and, just as they grow toward the sky, we must have heaven in mind.

The tenants in the parable are the Pharisees, who persecuted God's prophets and killed his son. They had God, in the person of Jesus, living among them, teaching them, eating with them, performing miracles before their eyes. Yet they were so sure that they knew who God was that they did not recognize God. Their faith had become about their status and their laws, not about God. We must remember that our faith is not only a series of truths or practices. It is a relationship with Jesus. We must have open eyes, ears, and hearts to recognize his presence in our midst. We must talk to, listen to, and spend time with him in prayer, Mass, and adoration.

We must also remember that God has a much greater gift in mind for us than anything on earth. The tenants were so set on short-term gain that they lost their eternal reward. Let us not forget or fail to recognize God's gifts.

KATE LARSON

ENTRANCE ANTIPHON *(Cf. Esther 4:17)*

Within your will, O Lord, all things are established, and there
is none that can resist your will. For you have made all things,
the heaven and the earth, and all that is held within the circle of
heaven; you are the Lord of all.

INTRODUCTORY RITES *(page 10)*

COLLECT

Almighty ever-living God,
who in the abundance of your kindness
surpass the merits and the desires of those who entreat you,
pour out your mercy upon us
to pardon what conscience dreads
and to give what prayer does not dare to ask.
Through our Lord Jesus Christ, your Son,
who lives and reigns with you in the unity of the Holy Spirit,
one God, for ever and ever. *Amen.*

FIRST READING *(Isaiah 5:1-7)*

Let me now sing of my friend,
my friend's song concerning his vineyard.
My friend had a vineyard
on a fertile hillside;
he spaded it, cleared it of stones,
and planted the choicest vines;
within it he built a watchtower,
and hewed out a wine press.
Then he looked for the crop of grapes,
but what it yielded was wild grapes.

Now, inhabitants of Jerusalem and people of Judah,
    judge between me and my vineyard:
What more was there to do for my vineyard
    that I had not done?
Why, when I looked for the crop of grapes,
    did it bring forth wild grapes?
Now, I will let you know
    what I mean to do with my vineyard:
take away its hedge, give it to grazing,
    break through its wall, let it be trampled!
Yes, I will make it a ruin:
    it shall not be pruned or hoed,
    but overgrown with thorns and briers;
I will command the clouds
    not to send rain upon it.
The vineyard of the LORD of hosts is the house of Israel,
    and the people of Judah are his cherished plant;
he looked for judgment, but see, bloodshed!
    for justice, but hark, the outcry!
The word of the Lord. ***Thanks be to God.***

RESPONSORIAL PSALM *(Psalm 80:9, 12, 13-14, 15-16, 19-20)*
℟ **The vineyard of the Lord is the house of Israel.**

A vine from Egypt you transplanted;
    you drove away the nations and planted it.
It put forth its foliage to the Sea,
    its shoots as far as the River. ℟
Why have you broken down its walls,
    so that every passer-by plucks its fruit,
the boar from the forest lays it waste,

and the beasts of the field feed upon it?
℟ **The vineyard of the Lord is the house of Israel.**
Once again, O LORD of hosts,
    look down from heaven, and see;
take care of this vine,
    and protect what your right hand has planted,
    the son of man whom you yourself made strong. ℟
Then we will no more withdraw from you;
    give us new life, and we will call upon your name.
O LORD, God of hosts, restore us;
    if your face shine upon us, then we shall be saved. ℟

SECOND READING (*Philippians 4:6-9*)

Brothers and sisters: Have no anxiety at all, but in everything, by prayer and petition, with thanksgiving, make your requests known to God. Then the **peace**✝ of God that surpasses all understanding will guard your hearts and minds in Christ Jesus.

Finally, brothers and sisters, whatever is true, whatever is honorable, whatever is just, whatever is pure, whatever is lovely, whatever is gracious, if there is any excellence and if there is anything worthy of praise, think about these things. Keep on doing what you have learned and received and heard and seen in me. Then the God of peace will be with you.

The word of the Lord. *Thanks be to God.*

ALLELUIA (*John 15:16*)

Alleluia, alleluia. I have chosen you from the world, says the Lord, to go and bear fruit that will remain. *Alleluia, alleluia.*

GOSPEL *(Matthew 21:33–43)*

A reading from the holy Gospel according to Matthew.
Glory to you, O Lord.

Jesus said to the chief priests and the elders of the people:
"Hear another parable. There was a landowner who planted a vineyard, put a hedge around it, dug a wine press in it, and built a tower. Then he leased it to tenants and went on a journey. When vintage time drew near, he sent his servants to the tenants to obtain his produce. But the tenants seized the servants and one they beat, another they killed, and a third they stoned. Again he sent other servants, more numerous than the first ones, but they treated them in the same way. Finally, he sent his son to them, thinking, 'They will respect my son.' But when the tenants saw the son, they said to one another, 'This is the heir. Come, let us kill him and acquire his inheritance.' They seized him, threw him out of the vineyard, and killed him. What will the owner of the vineyard do to those tenants when he comes?" They answered him, "He will put those wretched men to a wretched death and lease his vineyard to other tenants who will give him the produce at the proper times." Jesus said to them, "Did you never read in the Scriptures:

The stone that the builders rejected
   has become the cornerstone;
by the Lord has this been done,
   and it is wonderful in our eyes?

Therefore, I say to you, the kingdom of God will be taken away from you and given to a people that will produce its fruit."

The Gospel of the Lord. ***Praise to you, Lord Jesus Christ.***

PROFESSION OF FAITH *(page 13)*

PRAYER OF THE FAITHFUL

PREPARATION OF GIFTS *(page 16)*

PRAYER OVER THE OFFERINGS
Accept, O Lord, we pray,
the sacrifices instituted by your commands
and, through the sacred mysteries,
which we celebrate with dutiful service,
graciously complete the sanctifying work
by which you are pleased to redeem us.
Through Christ our Lord. *Amen.*

PREFACE *(Sundays in Ordinary Time, pages 28–32)*

• TAKING A CLOSER LOOK •

✣ **Peace** Peace (Hebrew, *shalom*) describes the experience of fullness or completeness—lacking nothing that one needs for a full and happy life. Peace is a gift that comes with God's presence. Thus it is also the goal for the life of the covenant community. The way to peace is justice—establishing and maintaining rightly ordered relationships for the covenant community according to God's guidelines. As a greeting, peace is a wish for the fullness of life, for union with God, and for harmony with others leading to happiness for all.

COMMUNION ANTIPHON *(Lamentations 3:25)*

The Lord is good to those who hope in him, to the soul that seeks him.

Or *(Cf. 1 Corinthians 10:17)*

Though many, we are one bread, one body, for we all partake of the one Bread and one Chalice.

PRAYER AFTER COMMUNION

Grant us, almighty God,
that we may be refreshed and nourished
by the Sacrament which we have received,
so as to be transformed into what we consume.
Through Christ our Lord. *Amen.*

BLESSING & DISMISSAL *(page 56)* ⁘

⁘ Responding to the Word ⁘

God tends to us like a vineyard owner working to make sure that he will have a good crop.	Paul urges us to let go of our anxieties and turn in prayer to God.	God expects much from us who have been entrusted with God's gifts.
▣ How have I experienced God's workings in me this week?	▣ What anxieties make it hard for me to pray right now?	▣ What can I do today to become a more trusted steward of God's gifts?

October 11

All are called to the banquet

For Matthew, the kingdom of God—the relationship between God and humanity—is fulfilled in Jesus the Christ. Traditional aspects of feasting, of gathering in community to celebrate the intimate life-giving relationship of marriage, are allusions to oneness with Christ through the Eucharist. The physical banquet evokes a spiritual experience.

However, other aspects of today's gospel parable are shocking. Celebration and violence are interwoven. The host responds with harshness and intolerance—even banishing one who arrives unprepared to perpetual suffering. How are we to understand these images in relation to the kingdom of God?

We are reminded that each of the gospels is distinct and that the authors bring something of themselves into the narratives which they relate. Written at least 50 years after Jesus' death and resurrection, Matthew's gospel focuses on Jesus as the anticipated Messiah. Frustrated with those who disagree, perhaps Matthew used the chilling image of isolation in darkness to shock his contemporaries into rethinking their unbelief.

In Matthew's gospel, all are called to the banquet. All have the power to choose the peace and fulfillment of the kingdom of God. In doing so, all commit to celebrate Christ's transformative love through their relationships with God, self, and community.

■ ELLA ALLEN

ENTRANCE ANTIPHON *(Psalm 130 [129]:3–4)*
If you, O Lord, should mark iniquities, Lord, who
could stand? But with you is found forgiveness,
O God of Israel.

INTRODUCTORY RITES *(page 10)*

COLLECT
May your grace, O Lord, we pray,
at all times go before us and follow after
and make us always determined
to carry out good works.
Through our Lord Jesus Christ, your Son,
who lives and reigns with you in the unity of the Holy Spirit,
one God, for ever and ever. *Amen.*

FIRST READING *(Isaiah 25:6–10a)*
On this mountain the LORD of hosts
 will provide for all peoples
a feast of rich food and choice wines,
 juicy, rich food and pure, choice wines.
On this mountain he will destroy
 the veil that veils all peoples,
the web that is woven over all nations;
 he will destroy death forever.
The Lord GOD will wipe away
 the tears from every face;
the reproach of his people he will remove
 from the whole earth; for the LORD has spoken.
 On that day it will be said:
"Behold our God, to whom we looked to save us!
 This is the LORD for whom we looked;

let us rejoice and be glad that he has saved us!"
For the hand of the LORD will rest on this mountain.
The word of the Lord. *Thanks be to God.*

RESPONSORIAL PSALM *(Psalm 23:1–3a, 3b–4, 5, 6)*
℟ **I shall live in the house of the Lord all the days of my life.**

The LORD is my shepherd; I shall not want.
In verdant pastures he gives me repose;
beside restful waters he leads me;
he refreshes my soul. ℟

He guides me in right paths
for his name's sake.
Even though I walk in the dark valley
I fear no evil; for you are at my side
with your rod and your staff
that give me courage. ℟

You spread the table before me
in the sight of my foes;
you anoint my head with oil;
my cup overflows. ℟

Only goodness and kindness follow me
all the days of my life;
and I shall dwell in the house of the LORD
for years to come. ℟

SECOND READING *(Philippians 4:12-14, 19-20)*

Brothers and sisters: I know how to live in humble circumstances; I know also how to live with abundance. In every circumstance and in all things I have learned the secret of being well fed and of going hungry, of living in abundance and of being in need. I can do all things in him who strengthens me. Still, it was kind of you to share in my distress.

My God will fully supply whatever you need, in accord with his glorious riches in Christ Jesus. To our God and Father, glory forever and ever. Amen.

The word of the Lord. *Thanks be to God.*

ALLELUIA *(Ephesians 1:17-18)*
Alleluia, alleluia. May the Father of our Lord Jesus Christ enlighten the eyes of our hearts, so that we may know what is the hope that belongs to our call. *Alleluia, alleluia.*

GOSPEL *(Matthew 22:1-14)*
For the shorter version, omit the indented parts in brackets.

A reading from the holy Gospel according to Matthew.
Glory to you, O Lord.

Jesus again in reply spoke to the chief priests and elders of the people in parables, saying, "The kingdom of heaven may be likened to a king who gave a wedding feast for his son. He dispatched his servants to summon the invited guests to the feast, but they refused to come. A second time he sent other servants, saying, 'Tell those invited: "Behold, I have prepared my **banquet**,✝ my calves and fattened cattle are killed, and everything is ready; come to the feast."' Some ignored the invitation and went away, one to his farm, another to his business. The rest laid hold of his servants, mistreated them, and killed them. The king was enraged and sent his troops, destroyed those murderers, and burned their city. Then he said to his servants, 'The feast is ready, but those who were invited were not worthy to come. Go out, therefore, into the main roads and invite to the feast whomever you find.' The servants went out into the streets and gathered all they found, bad and good alike, and the hall was filled with guests.

[But when the king came in to meet the guests, he saw a man there not dressed in a wedding garment. The king said to him, 'My friend, how is it that you came in here without a wedding garment?' But he was reduced to silence. Then the king said to his attendants, 'Bind his hands and feet, and cast him into the darkness outside, where there will be wailing and grinding of teeth.' Many are invited, but few are chosen."]

The Gospel of the Lord. ***Praise to you, Lord Jesus Christ.***

PROFESSION OF FAITH *(page 13)*

PRAYER OF THE FAITHFUL

PREPARATION OF GIFTS *(page 16)*

PRAYER OVER THE OFFERINGS
Accept, O Lord, the prayers of your faithful
with the sacrificial offerings,
that, through these acts of devotedness,
we may pass over to the glory of heaven.
Through Christ our Lord. ***Amen.***

• TAKING A CLOSER LOOK •

✛ **Banquet** Jesus' parable about a banquet challenges his audience to respond to his invitation to join the new kingdom community. He describes the practice of using meals to make a public statement about one's social status. When invited guests (like the Jewish leaders in his audience) dishonor the host (God) and refuse his invitation and mistreat his messengers (Moses and the prophets), he is angry and shows his contempt for those who refused by inviting those Jesus' audience thinks of as the dregs of society (non-Jews). Matthew adds that those who are invited (non-Jews) can still be thrown out if they are not prepared with the proper behavior.

PREFACE *(Sundays in Ordinary Time, pages 28–32)*

COMMUNION ANTIPHON *(Cf. Psalm 34 [33]:11)*
The rich suffer want and go hungry, but those who seek the Lord
lack no blessing.

Or *(1 John 3:2)*
When the Lord appears, we shall be like him, for we shall see
him as he is.

PRAYER AFTER COMMUNION
We entreat your majesty most humbly, O Lord,
that, as you feed us with the nourishment
which comes from the most holy Body and Blood of your Son,
so you may make us sharers of his divine nature.
Who lives and reigns for ever and ever. *Amen.*

BLESSING & DISMISSAL *(page 56)* ❖

❖ RESPONDING TO THE WORD ❖

Isaiah encourages us to rejoice and be glad, for God has saved us.	Paul trusts that God will supply what he needs to live.	God invites us to the banquet, but we must be responsible for how we act.
▶ How can I offer my thanks today for all God has done for me?	▶ When has God surprised me by responding to my needs?	▶ What can I do today to be more generous in my response to God's call?

October 18

Clearing away the obstacles

What is our heart's loyalty? In today's gospel, the Pharisees attempt to trap Jesus by asking about the obligation of paying taxes to the emperor. They know that if Jesus says that taxes should be paid, he would show a loyalty to another authority over their religious authority. But Jesus does not answer as they expect.

"Repay... to God what belongs to God." Jesus' answer helps us reflect on loyalties in a new light. What are the things that are God's? Our hearts are made to seek and to glorify God. Our lives are God's! The path of faith is to discover what things we are giving priority to in our lives and to intentionally set God ahead of all of them. We put obstacles in our spiritual path whenever we set *anything* above seeking God in the heart of the gospel and placing God first in our hearts,

So how do we clear away the obstacles from our path? We acknowledge that "what belongs to God" is *all* things. We owe God our very hearts, first and foremost, uncluttered by other attachments. When something else comes first before God, we have placed ourselves as the first priority. Seeking to discover how our priorities are not first rooted in trust and gratitude for God helps to loosen their hold on us.

■ **KELLY BOURKE**

ENTRANCE ANTIPHON *(Cf. Psalm 17 [16]:6, 8)*
To you I call; for you will surely heed me, O God;
turn your ear to me; hear my words. Guard me as
the apple of your eye; in the shadow of your wings
protect me.

INTRODUCTORY RITES *(page 10)*

COLLECT
Almighty ever-living God,
grant that we may always conform our will to yours
and serve your majesty in sincerity of heart.
Through our Lord Jesus Christ, your Son,
who lives and reigns with you in the unity of the Holy Spirit,
one God, for ever and ever. *Amen.*

FIRST READING *(Isaiah 45:1, 4-6)*

Thus says the LORD to his anointed, Cyrus,
   whose right hand I grasp,
subduing nations before him,
   and making kings run in his service,
opening doors before him
   and leaving the gates unbarred:
For the sake of Jacob, my servant,
   of Israel, my chosen one,
I have called you by your **name**,✝
   giving you a title, though you knew me not.
I am the LORD and there is no other,
   there is no God besides me.
It is I who arm you, though you know me not,
   so that toward the rising and the setting of the sun

people may know that there is none besides me.
I am the LORD, there is no other.
The word of the Lord. *Thanks be to God.*

RESPONSORIAL PSALM *(Psalm 96:1, 3, 4-5, 7-8, 9-10)*
℟ **Give the Lord glory and honor.**

Sing to the LORD a new song;
   sing to the LORD, all you lands.
Tell his glory among the nations;
   among all peoples, his wondrous deeds. ℟
For great is the LORD and highly to be praised;
   awesome is he, beyond all gods.
For all the gods of the nations are things of nought,
   but the LORD made the heavens. ℟
Give to the LORD, you families of nations,
   give to the LORD glory and praise;
   give to the LORD the glory due his name!
Bring gifts, and enter his courts. ℟
Worship the LORD, in holy attire;
   tremble before him, all the earth;
say among the nations: The LORD is king,
   he governs the peoples with equity. ℟

SECOND READING *(1 Thessalonians 1:1-5b)*

Paul, Silvanus,* and Timothy to the church of the
Thessalonians in God the Father and the Lord Jesus Christ:
grace to you and peace. We give thanks to God always for all
of you, remembering you in our prayers, unceasingly calling to
mind your work of faith and labor of love and endurance in hope
of our Lord Jesus Christ, before our God and Father, knowing,

brothers and sisters loved by God, how you were chosen. For our gospel did not come to you in word alone, but also in power and in the Holy Spirit and with much conviction.

The word of the Lord. *Thanks be to God.*

ALLELUIA *(Philippians 2:15d, 16a)*
Alleluia, alleluia. Shine like lights in the world as you hold on to the word of life. *Alleluia, alleluia.*

GOSPEL *(Matthew 22:15-21)*
A reading from the holy Gospel according to Matthew.
Glory to you, O Lord.

The Pharisees went off and plotted how they might entrap Jesus in speech. They sent their disciples to him, with the Herodians, saying, "Teacher, we know that you are a truthful man and that you teach the way of God in accordance with the truth. And you are not concerned with anyone's opinion, for you do not regard a person's status. Tell us, then, what is your opinion: Is it lawful to pay the census tax to Caesar* or not?" Knowing their malice, Jesus said, "Why are you testing me, you hypocrites? Show me the coin that pays the census tax." Then they handed him the Roman coin. He said to them, "Whose image is this and whose inscription?" They replied, "Caesar's." At that he said to them, "Then repay to Caesar what belongs to Caesar and to God what belongs to God."

The Gospel of the Lord. *Praise to you, Lord Jesus Christ.*

PROFESSION OF FAITH *(page 13)*

PRAYER OF THE FAITHFUL

PREPARATION OF GIFTS *(page 16)*

PRAYER OVER THE OFFERINGS
Grant us, Lord, we pray,
a sincere respect for your gifts,
that, through the purifying action of your grace,
we may be cleansed by the very mysteries we serve.
Through Christ our Lord. *Amen.*

PREFACE *(Sundays in Ordinary Time, pages 28-32)*

⁘ **TAKING A CLOSER LOOK** ⁘

✝ **Name** In ancient societies, one's name revealed the nature and the essence of the person named. To name someone was a way of defining the person's identity and potential, the person's main characteristic. This was the kind of definition that Moses sought from God at the burning bush (Exodus 3:13), when he asked for a Divine Name that would signify the existence of God's benevolent nature and protection, a "name" that would assure the Hebrews of their salvation.

God calls Cyrus by name and announces his royal enthronement by calling him "anointed," the only foreigner in the Old Testament given that title of honor by God.

COMMUNION ANTIPHON *(Cf. Psalm 33 [32]:18-19)*
Behold, the eyes of the Lord are on those who fear him, who hope in his merciful love, to rescue their souls from death, to keep them alive in famine.

Or *(Mark 10:45)*
The Son of Man has come to give his life as a ransom for many.

PRAYER AFTER COMMUNION
Grant, O Lord, we pray,
that, benefiting from participation in heavenly things,
we may be helped by what you give in this present age
and prepared for the gifts that are eternal.
Through Christ our Lord. *Amen.*

BLESSING & DISMISSAL *(page 56)* ❖

• RESPONDING TO THE WORD •

God governs political events even though political rulers do not know it.

❯ *Where do I detect God's presence in political events today?*

Paul remembers the Thessalonians' "work of faith and labor of love."

❯ *For whose faith and love am I most thankful today?*

Jesus tells us to give back to God what belongs to God.

❯ *What will I offer back to God today?*

October 25

Return to the source of all love!

In today's gospel Jesus makes clear that all of divine law is summed up in a love which embraces the totality of our relationship with God, self, and neighbor. Serving our neighbor draws us more fully into the heart of God, and knowing ourselves loved by God propels us to love our neighbor. There are no limitations or boundaries to love: it is not a minimum expectation but a maximum commitment of ourselves to God, through imitation of the Son, Jesus Christ, who gave himself for the world.

Loving our neighbor, as the first reading tells us, extends to caring for the aliens in our land, the widows and orphans, and the poor. Early in our marriage, our faith was enlivened by hours of volunteering as we sought to be in solidarity with those on the margins. Our youthful faith was challenged as our family grew, and our available time and energy shrunk. It called us to enter more deeply into the complexity of the great commandment and to spend more time in prayer.

Returning to the source of all love helps us to discern how we can be in solidarity with our neighbor in new ways. May God's grace help us, like the Thessalonians, to receive the word with joy, seeking continuously to be people of justice, living our faith in a way that makes love known.

■ **VANESSA AND MICHAEL NICHOLAS-SCHMIDT**

ENTRANCE ANTIPHON *(Cf. Psalm 105 [104]:3–4)*
Let the hearts that seek the Lord rejoice; turn to the
Lord and his strength; constantly seek his face.

INTRODUCTORY RITES *(page 10)*

COLLECT
Almighty ever-living God,
increase our faith, hope and charity,
and make us love what you command,
so that we may merit what you promise.
Through our Lord Jesus Christ, your Son,
who lives and reigns with you in the unity of the Holy Spirit,
one God, for ever and ever. ***Amen.***

FIRST READING *(Exodus 22:20–26)*

Thus says the LORD: "You shall not molest or oppress an
alien, for you were once aliens yourselves in the land of
Egypt. You shall not wrong any **widow or orphan.** ✝ If ever you
wrong them and they cry out to me, I will surely hear their cry.
My wrath will flare up, and I will kill you with the sword; then
your own wives will be widows, and your children orphans.

"If you lend money to one of your poor neighbors among
my people, you shall not act like an extortioner toward him by
demanding interest from him. If you take your neighbor's cloak
as a pledge, you shall return it to him before sunset; for this
cloak of his is the only covering he has for his body. What else
has he to sleep in? If he cries out to me, I will hear him; for I am
compassionate."

The word of the Lord. ***Thanks be to God.***

RESPONSORIAL PSALM *(Psalm 18:2-3, 3-4, 47, 51)*

R. I love you, Lord, my strength.

I love you, O LORD, my strength,
    O LORD, my rock, my fortress, my deliverer. R.
My God, my rock of refuge,
    my shield, the horn of my salvation, my stronghold!
Praised be the LORD, I exclaim,
    and I am safe from my enemies. R.
The LORD lives and blessed be my rock!
    Extolled be God my savior.
You who gave great victories to your king
    and showed kindness to your anointed. R.

SECOND READING *(1 Thessalonians 1:5c-10)*

Brothers and sisters: You know what sort of people we were among you for your sake. And you became imitators of us and of the Lord, receiving the word in great affliction, with joy from the Holy Spirit, so that you became a model for all the believers in Macedonia and in Achaia. For from you the word of the Lord has sounded forth not only in Macedonia and in Achaia, but in every place your faith in God has gone forth, so that we have no need to say anything. For they themselves openly declare about us what sort of reception we had among you, and how you turned to God from idols to serve the living and true God and to await his Son from heaven, whom he raised from the dead, Jesus, who delivers us from the coming wrath.

The word of the Lord. ***Thanks be to God.***

ALLELUIA *(John 14:23)*
Alleluia, alleluia. Whoever loves me will keep my word, says the Lord and my Father will love him and we will come to him. *Alleluia, alleluia.*

GOSPEL *(Matthew 22:34–40)*
A reading from the holy Gospel according to Matthew.
Glory to you, O Lord.

When the Pharisees heard that Jesus had silenced the Sadducees, they gathered together, and one of them, a scholar of the law, tested him by asking, "Teacher, which commandment in the law is the greatest?" He said to him, "You shall love the Lord, your God, with all your heart, with all your soul, and with all your mind. This is the greatest and the first commandment. The second is like it: You shall love your neighbor as yourself. The whole law and the prophets depend on these two commandments."

The Gospel of the Lord. *Praise to you, Lord Jesus Christ.*

PROFESSION OF FAITH *(page 13)*

PRAYER OF THE FAITHFUL

PREPARATION OF GIFTS *(page 16)*

PRAYER OVER THE OFFERINGS
Look, we pray, O Lord,
on the offerings we make to your majesty,
that whatever is done by us in your service
may be directed above all to your glory.
Through Christ our Lord. ***Amen.***

PREFACE *(Sundays in Ordinary Time, pages 28–32)*

● TAKING A CLOSER LOOK ●

✚ **Widow or orphan** In the rigidly structured society of biblical times, families had to rely on themselves and their relatives for
protection and sustenance rather than on the legal system. Women
and children were socially "located" beneath the head of the household (the father, husband, or master). Those such as widows, orphans, and foreigners residing in the land who were not connected
to a household were thus "dislocated" and vulnerable because they
lacked a protective male. In Israel, God assumed the role of protector
of widows and orphans and promised to take vengeance on those who
would seek to exploit these vulnerable ones.

COMMUNION ANTIPHON *(Cf. Psalm 20 [19]:6)*
We will ring out our joy at your saving help and exult in the
name of our God.

Or *(Ephesians 5:2)*
Christ loved us and gave himself up for us, as a fragrant offering
to God.

PRAYER AFTER COMMUNION
May your Sacraments, O Lord, we pray,
perfect in us what lies within them,
that what we now celebrate in signs
we may one day possess in truth.
Through Christ our Lord. *Amen.*

BLESSING & DISMISSAL *(page 56)* ❖

• RESPONDING TO THE WORD •

God's special compassion is for those most vulnerable who are liable to be victimized by others.	Christianity is spread by good example more than words.	Jesus summarizes the whole law as loving God and others.
⇨ What can I do to help someone who is vulnerable?	⇨ Whose example has been most influential in making me a better Christian?	⇨ Which of these loves needs more attention in my life now?

November 1

Called to be saints

Today we celebrate and give thanks for the witness and companionship of those we call the saints. The communion of saints includes, in its broadest sense, not only those formally recognized by the Church but also the exemplary people of faith whom we encounter in our communities and our families. The saints—both those who have gone before us and those who walk among us still—are icons of holiness, windows through which we glimpse the face of God.

All of us are called to holiness, to a life shaped by gospel values. Today's reading of the beatitudes offers us some guidelines. Bombarded by the lures of consumerism, we are called to be poor in spirit. In a world beset by war and violence, we are called to be peacemakers. In a society that prioritizes competitiveness and ruthless individuality, we are called to be humble. Where grief and discouragement prevail, we are called to be merciful. In the face of injustice, we are invited to "hunger and thirst for righteousness."

Today we pray for the grace to recognize that we are all called to be saints. In the words of the psalm, may we live with hands that are sinless and hearts that are clean as we look forward in hope to sharing in the light of eternal life.

■ **KRYSTYNA HIGGINS**

ENTRANCE ANTIPHON

Let us all rejoice in the Lord, as we celebrate the feast day in honor of all the Saints, at whose festival the Angels rejoice and praise the Son of God.

INTRODUCTORY RITES *(page 10)*

COLLECT

Almighty ever-living God,
by whose gift we venerate in one celebration
the merits of all the Saints,
bestow on us, we pray,
through the prayers of so many intercessors,
an abundance of the reconciliation with you
for which we earnestly long.
Through our Lord Jesus Christ, your Son,
who lives and reigns with you in the unity of the Holy Spirit,
one God, for ever and ever. *Amen.*

FIRST READING *(Revelation 7:2-4, 9-14)*

I, John, saw another angel come up from the East, holding the seal of the living God. He cried out in a loud voice to the four angels who were given power to damage the land and the sea, "Do not damage the land or the sea or the trees until we put the seal on the foreheads of the servants of our God." I heard the number of those who had been marked with the seal, **one hundred and forty-four thousand**✝ marked from every tribe of the children of Israel.

After this I had a vision of a great multitude, which no one could count, from every nation, race, people, and tongue. They stood before the throne and before the Lamb, wearing white robes and holding palm branches in their hands. They cried out in a loud voice:

"Salvation comes from our God, who is seated on the throne, and from the Lamb."

All the angels stood around the throne and around the elders and the four living creatures. They prostrated themselves before the throne, worshiped God, and exclaimed:

"Amen. Blessing and glory, wisdom and thanksgiving,
honor, power, and might
be to our God forever and ever. Amen."

Then one of the elders spoke up and said to me, "Who are these wearing white robes, and where did they come from?" I said to him, "My lord, you are the one who knows." He said to me, "These are the ones who have survived the time of great distress; they have washed their robes and made them white in the Blood of the Lamb."

The word of the Lord. ***Thanks be to God.***

RESPONSORIAL PSALM (*Psalm 24:1bc-2, 3-4ab, 5-6*)
R. **Lord, this is the people that longs to see your face.**

The LORD's are the earth and its fullness;
the world and those who dwell in it.
For he founded it upon the seas
and established it upon the rivers. R.

Who can ascend the mountain of the LORD?
or who may stand in his holy place?
One whose hands are sinless, whose heart is clean,
who desires not what is vain. R.

He shall receive a blessing from the LORD,
a reward from God his savior.

Such is the race that seeks him,
that seeks the face of the God of Jacob. ℟

SECOND READING *(1 John 3:1–3)*

Beloved: See what love the Father has bestowed on us that we may be called the children of God. Yet so we are. The reason the world does not know us is that it did not know him. Beloved, we are God's children now; what we shall be has not yet been revealed. We do know that when it is revealed we shall be like him, for we shall see him as he is. Everyone who has this hope based on him makes himself pure, as he is pure.

The word of the Lord. *Thanks be to God.*

ALLELUIA *(Matthew 11:28)*

Alleluia, alleluia. Come to me, all you who labor and are burdened, and I will give you rest, says the Lord. *Alleluia, alleluia.*

GOSPEL *(Matthew 5:1–12a)*

A reading from the holy Gospel according to Matthew.
Glory to you, O Lord.

When Jesus saw the crowds, he went up the mountain, and after he had sat down, his disciples came to him. He began to teach them, saying:

"Blessed are the poor in spirit,
for theirs is the Kingdom of heaven.
Blessed are they who mourn,
for they will be comforted.
Blessed are the meek,
for they will inherit the land.
Blessed are they who hunger and thirst for righteousness,
for they will be satisfied.

Blessed are the merciful,
> for they will be shown mercy.

Blessed are the clean of heart,
> for they will see God.

Blessed are the peacemakers,
> for they will be called children of God.

Blessed are they who are persecuted for the sake of righteousness,
> for theirs is the Kingdom of heaven.

Blessed are you when they insult you and persecute you and utter
every kind of evil against you falsely because of me. Rejoice and
be glad, for your reward will be great in heaven."

The Gospel of the Lord. ***Praise to you, Lord Jesus Christ.***

PROFESSION OF FAITH *(page 13)*

PRAYER OF THE FAITHFUL

PREPARATION OF GIFTS *(page 16)*

PRAYER OVER THE OFFERINGS

May these offerings we bring in honor of all the Saints
be pleasing to you, O Lord,
and grant that, just as we believe the Saints
to be already assured of immortality,
so we may experience their concern for our salvation.
Through Christ our Lord. ***Amen.***

PREFACE: THE GLORY OF JERUSALEM, OUR MOTHER

It is truly right and just, our duty and our salvation,
always and everywhere to give you thanks,
Lord, holy Father, almighty and eternal God.

For today by your gift we celebrate the festival of your city,
the heavenly Jerusalem, our mother,
where the great array of our brothers and sisters
already gives you eternal praise.

Towards her, we eagerly hasten as pilgrims advancing by faith,
rejoicing in the glory bestowed upon those exalted members
    of the Church
through whom you give us, in our frailty, both strength
    and good example.

And so, we glorify you with the multitude of Saints and Angels,
as with one voice of praise we acclaim:
Holy, Holy, Holy Lord God of hosts... *(page 35)*

❖ TAKING A CLOSER LOOK ❖

✦ **One hundred and forty-four thousand**

Although some Christian groups have taken this number as the actual count of those saved, it is evident both from the general way large numbers are used in the Bible and from what follows that this is a symbolic number. For people without sophisticated mathematics, large numbers are almost always symbolic, the way we say "million" or "zillion" for emphasis. In everyday life, counting to 144,000 of anything would be a major chore. The number means that an incredibly large number of Jews are saved. But this is not all the saved because there is an additional "great multitude" of non-Jews. This is John's way of saying that the number of those saved is innumerable.

COMMUNION ANTIPHON *(Matthew 5:8-10)*
Blessed are the clean of heart, for they shall see God. Blessed are the peacemakers, for they shall be called children of God. Blessed are they who are persecuted for the sake of righteousness, for theirs is the Kingdom of Heaven.

PRAYER AFTER COMMUNION
As we adore you, O God, who alone are holy
and wonderful in all your Saints,
we implore your grace,
so that, coming to perfect holiness in the fullness of your love,
we may pass from this pilgrim table
to the banquet of our heavenly homeland.
Through Christ our Lord. *Amen.*

SOLEMN BLESSING: ALL SAINTS *(Optional, page 63)*

DISMISSAL *(page 57)* ✣

• RESPONDING TO THE WORD •

Those in heaven give praise and thanks to God.

➡ For what do I most want to give praise and thanks to God today?

Our hope is to see God directly and to be like God.

➡ How have I grown this year to be more like Jesus?

Jesus' beatitudes outline a new way of living.

➡ Which beatitude most needs my attention today?

November 8

**NOV
8**

Stay awake!

Have you ever stayed up late waiting for an important call or for a child to come home? You struggle to keep your eyes open but you are aching to rest. In these darkening days of November, Jesus warns us to fight that urge to give in to sleep because to slumber comes with a cost.

The canny bridesmaids are shrewd and their ability to plan ahead allows them to fully experience the presence of the bridegroom, or God, at the feast. It seems unfair to us that the disorganized and thoughtless bridesmaids miss being with the bridegroom. It is actually the wise ones who send them away and we are puzzled, wondering what Jesus could actually be warning us about.

Perhaps the bridesmaids are a metaphor: the wise ones of this world are already making time to be with God in their everyday lives, keeping the night watches like the psalmist and allowing God's love to fill their oil jars so they always experience God's presence. And the foolish ones are unprepared and unaware. They are not ready and do not realize that God, in fact, is actually waiting for them.

What distractions do we need to lay aside, keeping our lamps lit as we stay aware of God's presence in all things?

■ **MAUREEN WICKEN**

ENTRANCE ANTIPHON *(Cf. Psalm 88 [87]:3)*

Let my prayer come into your presence. Incline
your ear to my cry for help, O Lord.

INTRODUCTORY RITES *(page 10)*

COLLECT

Almighty and merciful God,
graciously keep from us all adversity,
so that, unhindered in mind and body alike,
we may pursue in freedom of heart
the things that are yours.
Through our Lord Jesus Christ, your Son,
who lives and reigns with you in the unity of the Holy Spirit,
one God, for ever and ever. *Amen.*

FIRST READING *(Wisdom 6:12-16)*

Resplendent and unfading is **wisdom,**✝
and she is readily perceived by those who love her,
    and found by those who seek her.
She hastens to make herself known in anticipation of their desire;
    whoever watches for her at dawn shall not be disappointed,
    for he shall find her sitting by his gate.
For taking thought of wisdom is the perfection of prudence,
    and whoever for her sake keeps vigil
    shall quickly be free from care;
because she makes her own rounds, seeking those worthy of her,
    and graciously appears to them in the ways,
    and meets them with all solicitude.
The word of the Lord. *Thanks be to God.*

RESPONSORIAL PSALM *(Psalm 63:2, 3-4, 5-6, 7-8)*
℟ My soul is thirsting for you, O Lord my God.

O God, you are my God whom I seek;
  for you my flesh pines and my soul thirsts
  like the earth, parched, lifeless and without water. ℟
Thus have I gazed toward you in the sanctuary
  to see your power and your glory,
for your kindness is a greater good than life;
  my lips shall glorify you. ℟
Thus will I bless you while I live;
  lifting up my hands, I will call upon your name.
As with the riches of a banquet shall my soul be satisfied,
  and with exultant lips my mouth shall praise you. ℟
I will remember you upon my couch,
  and through the night-watches I will meditate on you:
you are my help,
  and in the shadow of your wings I shout for joy. ℟

SECOND READING *(1 Thessalonians 4:13-18)*
The shorter version ends at the asterisks.

We do not want you to be unaware, brothers and sisters, about those who have fallen asleep, so that you may not grieve like the rest, who have no hope. For if we believe that Jesus died and rose, so too will God, through Jesus, bring with him those who have fallen asleep.

* * *

Indeed, we tell you this, on the word of the Lord, that we who are alive, who are left until the coming of the Lord, will surely not precede those who have fallen asleep. For the Lord himself, with a word of command, with the voice of an archangel and with the trumpet of God, will come down from heaven, and the dead in Christ will rise first. Then we who are alive, who are left, will be caught up together with them in the clouds to meet the Lord in the air. Thus we shall always be with the Lord. Therefore, console one another with these words.

The word of the Lord. *Thanks be to God.*

ALLELUIA *(Matthew 24:42a, 44)*
Alleluia, alleluia. Stay awake and be ready! For you do not know on what day your Lord will come. *Alleluia, alleluia.*

GOSPEL *(Matthew 25:1-13)*
A reading from the holy Gospel according to Matthew.
Glory to you, O Lord.

Jesus told his disciples this parable: "The kingdom of heaven will be like ten virgins who took their lamps and went out to meet the bridegroom. Five of them were foolish and five were wise. The foolish ones, when taking their lamps, brought no oil with them, but the wise brought flasks of oil with their lamps. Since the bridegroom was long delayed, they all became drowsy and fell asleep. At midnight, there was a cry, 'Behold, the bridegroom! Come out to meet him!' Then all those virgins got up and trimmed their lamps. The foolish ones said to the wise, 'Give us some of your oil, for our lamps are going out.' But the wise ones replied, 'No, for there may not be enough for us and you. Go instead to the merchants and buy some for yourselves.' While they went off to buy it, the bridegroom came and those who were ready went into the wedding feast with him. Then the door was locked. Afterwards the other virgins came and said, 'Lord, Lord, open the door for us!' But he said in reply, 'Amen, I say to you, I do not know you.' Therefore, stay awake, for you know neither the day nor the hour."

The Gospel of the Lord. *Praise to you, Lord Jesus Christ.*

PROFESSION OF FAITH *(page 13)*

PRAYER OF THE FAITHFUL

PREPARATION OF GIFTS *(page 16)*

PRAYER OVER THE OFFERINGS
Look with favor, we pray, O Lord,
upon the sacrificial gifts offered here,
that, celebrating in mystery the Passion of your Son,
we may honor it with loving devotion.
Through Christ our Lord. *Amen.*

❖ TAKING A CLOSER LOOK ❖

✦ **Wisdom** For the Jews, wisdom was the practical understanding of how the world and society worked, and so it helped people cope with the complexities of everyday life, especially sickness and suffering, death and disaster. Since wisdom did not rely on divine revelation but rather on practical human experience and observation of nature, it summarized the most helpful advice for responsible living which the Jews shared with many ancient Near Eastern peoples. The Jews, though, sought to merge this secular tradition with the religious guidelines of their covenant instruction (*Torah*). Thus wisdom joined the pursuit of knowledge to the ordering of life in relation to God.

PREFACE *(Sundays in Ordinary Time, pages 28–32)*

COMMUNION ANTIPHON *(Cf. Psalm 23 [22]:1-2)*

The Lord is my shepherd; there is nothing I shall want. Fresh and green are the pastures where he gives me repose, near restful waters he leads me.

Or *(Cf. Luke 24:35)*

The disciples recognized the Lord Jesus in the breaking of bread.

PRAYER AFTER COMMUNION

Nourished by this sacred gift, O Lord,
we give you thanks and beseech your mercy,
that, by the pouring forth of your Spirit,
the grace of integrity may endure
in those your heavenly power has entered.
Through Christ our Lord. *Amen.*

BLESSING & DISMISSAL *(page 56)*

• RESPONDING TO THE WORD •

Wisdom is found by those who seek her.

➡ *Where have I found wisdom in my life? Where do I look for wisdom?*

Paul tells us to console those who are grieving with the hope of resurrection in Christ.

➡ *How might I reach out to support someone who is now grieving at the death of a loved one?*

Jesus reminds us of the need to be vigilant because he will come when we least expect him.

➡ *What has helped me to be more attentive to Jesus' voice in my life?*

November 15

**NOV
15**

Thank God for your gifts!

Today's gospel challenges us to think about what we bring to life's table. It's time to take stock: *What are my gifts? How will I contribute? If life is a potluck, what will I bring?*

This may be difficult for some of us. Instead of seeing what we do have, we obsess over the many ingredients we lack. We peer inside, dismayed to realize: *I'm not inspiring like Cheryl. I'm not creative, like Graham. I can't lead, like Sean.*

Don't bother, doubt says when we think we can make something of our gifts, *it'll never be enough. Besides, someone more capable is probably bringing it already.* We convince ourselves that we have nothing worth sharing and so we don't contribute. Like that talent-burying servant, we are talked out of trying by fear and laziness. We hoard and bury; we close ourselves off. In doing so, we mooch from life's table. By taking and failing to give, we feast on the gifts of others yet leave them hungry for what we hoard. Perhaps that is why the master was so upset.

God has equipped us with exact ingredients. Don't let them expire. Today, take stock and thank God for your gifts. Ask for God's help to get cooking with them, because the world craves what only you can bring to the table.

■ CAROLINE PIGNAT

ENTRANCE ANTIPHON *(Jeremiah 29:11, 12, 14)*
The Lord said: I think thoughts of peace and not of affliction.
You will call upon me, and I will answer you, and I will lead back
your captives from every place.

INTRODUCTORY RITES *(page 10)*

COLLECT
Grant us, we pray, O Lord our God,
the constant gladness of being devoted to you,
for it is full and lasting happiness
to serve with constancy
the author of all that is good.
Through our Lord Jesus Christ, your Son,
who lives and reigns with you in the unity of the Holy Spirit,
one God, for ever and ever. *Amen.*

FIRST READING *(Proverbs 31:10-13, 19-20, 30-31)*

When one finds a worthy wife,
   her value is far beyond pearls.
Her husband, entrusting his heart to her,
   has an unfailing prize.
She brings him good, and not evil,
   all the days of her life.
She obtains wool and flax
   and works with loving hands.
She puts her hands to the distaff,
   and her fingers ply the spindle.
She reaches out her hands to the poor,
   and extends her arms to the needy.
Charm is deceptive and beauty fleeting;

the woman who fears the LORD is to be praised.
Give her a reward for her labors,
  and let her works praise her at the city gates.
The word of the Lord. *Thanks be to God.*

RESPONSORIAL PSALM *(Psalm 128:1-2, 3, 4-5)*

R̸ **Blessed are those who fear the Lord.**

Blessed are you who **fear the LORD,**✝
  who walk in his ways!
For you shall eat the fruit of your handiwork;
  blessed shall you be, and favored. R̸
Your wife shall be like a fruitful vine
  in the recesses of your home;
Your children like olive plants
  around your table. R̸
Behold, thus is the man blessed
  who fears the LORD.
The LORD bless you from Zion:*
  may you see the prosperity of Jerusalem
  all the days of your life. R̸

SECOND READING *(1 Thessalonians 5:1-6)*

Concerning times and seasons, brothers and sisters, you have
no need for anything to be written to you. For you yourselves know very well that the day of the Lord will come like
a thief at night. When people are saying, "Peace and security,"
then sudden disaster comes upon them, like labor pains upon a
pregnant woman, and they will not escape.

But you, brothers and sisters, are not in darkness, for that day
to overtake you like a thief. For all of you are children of the
light and children of the day. We are not of the night or of dark-

ness. Therefore, let us not sleep as the rest do, but let us stay alert and sober.

The word of the Lord. ***Thanks be to God.***

ALLELUIA *(John 15:4a, 5b)*
Alleluia, alleluia. Remain in me as I remain in you, says the Lord. Whoever remains in me bears much fruit. *Alleluia, alleluia.*

GOSPEL *(Matthew 25:14–30)*
For the shorter version, omit the indented parts in brackets.

A reading from the holy Gospel according to Matthew.
Glory to you, O Lord.

Jesus told his disciples this parable: "A man going on a journey called in his servants and entrusted his possessions to them. To one he gave five talents; to another, two; to a third, one—to each according to his ability. Then he went away.

[Immediately the one who received five talents went and traded with them, and made another five. Likewise, the one who received two made another two. But the man who received one went off and dug a hole in the ground and buried his master's money.]

"After a long time the master of those servants came back and settled accounts with them. The one who had received five talents came forward bringing the additional five. He said, 'Master, you gave me five talents. See, I have made five more.' His master said to him, 'Well done, my good and faithful servant. Since you were faithful in small matters, I will give you great responsibilities. Come, share your master's joy.'

[Then the one who had received two talents also came forward and said, 'Master, you gave me two talents. See, I have

made two more.' His master said to him, 'Well done, my good
and faithful servant. Since you were faithful in small matters, I will give you great responsibilities. Come, share your
master's joy.' Then the one who had received the one talent
came forward and said, 'Master, I knew you were a demanding person, harvesting where you did not plant and gathering
where you did not scatter; so out of fear I went off and buried
your talent in the ground. Here it is back.' His master said to
him in reply, 'You wicked, lazy servant! So you knew that I
harvest where I did not plant and gather where I did not scatter? Should you not then have put my money in the bank so
that I could have got it back with interest on my return? Now
then! Take the talent from him and give it to the one with ten.
For to everyone who has, more will be given and he will grow
rich; but from the one who has not, even what he has will be
taken away. And throw this useless servant into the darkness
outside, where there will be wailing and grinding of teeth.']"
The Gospel of the Lord. ***Praise to you, Lord Jesus Christ.***

PROFESSION OF FAITH *(page 13)*

PRAYER OF THE FAITHFUL

PREPARATION OF GIFTS *(page 16)*

PRAYER OVER THE OFFERINGS
Grant, O Lord, we pray,
that what we offer in the sight of your majesty
may obtain for us the grace of being devoted to you
and gain us the prize of everlasting happiness.
Through Christ our Lord. *Amen.*

PREFACE *(Sundays in Ordinary Time, pages 28–32)*

COMMUNION ANTIPHON *(Psalm 73 [72]:28)*
To be near God is my happiness, to place my hope in God the
Lord.

Or *(Mark 11:23–24)*
Amen, I say to you: Whatever you ask in prayer, believe that you
will receive, and it shall be given to you, says the Lord.

• TAKING A CLOSER LOOK •

+ **Fear the Lord** "Fear of the Lord" describes the reverent respect
or awe that a person must have before God. Since God is so utterly different from anything created, coming into God's presence creates ap-
prehension about what might happen. Thus God often counsels us: "Do
not be afraid." Fear in God's presence thus changes to adoration. But it almost always carries an overtone of judgment because, when confronted
by God's holiness, humans cannot help but recognize their distance from
God (sinfulness). Fear of the Lord is also the beginning of wisdom, for it
is the experience of one's humble place in relation to God.

PRAYER AFTER COMMUNION

We have partaken of the gifts of this sacred mystery,
humbly imploring, O Lord,
that what your Son commanded us to do
in memory of him
may bring us growth in charity.
Through Christ our Lord. *Amen.*

BLESSING & DISMISSAL *(page 56)* ✢

⟡ RESPONDING TO THE WORD ⟡

The woman "works with loving hands" for the poor and needy.

➥ What can I do today to be of help to others?

Paul warns that Jesus' coming will always be a surprise.

➥ When has Jesus surprised me with an unexpected coming?

In Jesus' parable, the servants are accountable for the talents they are given.

➥ How am I using the talents that God has given me?

November 22

God remains the center of our story

Look up at the night sky. Remember that we live on a small planet spinning around our sun. It sits on a spiral arm of our 150,000-plus-light-year-wide Milky Way galaxy. Our galactic home holds an estimated 200 billion other stars. Recent calculations place the number of galaxies in the known universe at two trillion. Each of these could contain billions of stars, together totaling more than all grains of sand on earth. And each star likely hosts a planetary system. The sheer vastness of creation staggers the mind. Yet this presents just the tiniest inkling of the majesty of God.

Today's feast ends our liturgical year. From Ezekiel through Paul to Matthew, Jesus is characterized as king and shepherd, glorious and humble at the same time. While today these regal and agrarian images seem distant, even alienating, they are certainly far less challenging than the cosmic reality that science opens our eyes to. Whatever images we chose for our triune deity—the Alpha and Omega, the prime mover of all creation—God remains the center of our cosmic story. And the grandeur of the universe is linked directly to how we behave towards one another. "Just as you did it to one of the least brothers and sisters of mine, you did to me."

▪ **MICHAEL DOUGHERTY**

ENTRANCE ANTIPHON *(Revelation 5:12; 1:6)*

How worthy is the Lamb who was slain, to receive power and divinity, and wisdom and strength and honor. To him belong glory and power for ever and ever.

INTRODUCTORY RITES *(page 10)*

COLLECT

Almighty ever-living God,
whose will is to restore all things
in your beloved Son, the King of the universe,
grant, we pray,
that the whole creation, set free from slavery,
may render your majesty service
and ceaselessly proclaim your praise.
Through our Lord Jesus Christ, your Son,
who lives and reigns with you in the unity of the Holy Spirit,
one God, for ever and ever. ***Amen.***

FIRST READING *(Ezekiel 34:11-12, 15-17)*

Thus says the Lord GOD: I myself will look after and tend my sheep. As a shepherd tends his flock when he finds himself among his scattered sheep, so will I tend my sheep. I will rescue them from every place where they were scattered when it was cloudy and dark. I myself will pasture my sheep; I myself will give them rest, says the Lord GOD. The lost I will seek out, the strayed I will bring back, the injured I will bind up, the sick I will heal, but the sleek and the strong I will destroy, shepherding them rightly.

As for you, my sheep, says the Lord GOD, I will judge between one sheep and another, between rams and goats.

The word of the Lord. ***Thanks be to God.***

RESPONSORIAL PSALM *(Psalm 23:1-2, 2-3, 5-6)*

℟ The Lord is my shepherd; there is nothing I shall want.

The LORD is my shepherd; I shall not want.
In verdant pastures he gives me repose. ℟
Beside restful waters he leads me;
he refreshes my soul.
He guides me in right paths
for his name's sake. ℟
You spread the table before me
in the sight of my foes;
you anoint my head with oil;
my cup overflows. ℟
Only goodness and kindness follow me
all the days of my life;
and I shall dwell in the house of the LORD
for years to come. ℟

SECOND READING *(1 Corinthians 15:20-26, 28)*

Brothers and sisters: Christ has been raised from the dead, the **firstfruits**✝ of those who have fallen asleep. For since death came through man, the resurrection of the dead came also through man. For just as in Adam all die, so too in Christ shall all be brought to life, but each one in proper order: Christ the firstfruits; then, at his coming, those who belong to Christ; then comes the end, when he hands over the kingdom to his God and Father, when he has destroyed every sovereignty and every authority and power. For he must reign until he has put all his enemies under his feet. The last enemy to be destroyed is death. When everything is subjected to him, then the Son himself will also be subjected to the one who subjected everything to him, so that God may be all in all.

The word of the Lord. ***Thanks be to God.***

ALLELUIA *(Mark 11:9, 10)*
Alleluia, alleluia. Blessed is he who comes in the name of the Lord! Blessed is the kingdom of our father David that is to come! *Alleluia, alleluia.*

GOSPEL *(Matthew 25:31–46)*
A reading from the holy Gospel according to Matthew.
Glory to you, O Lord.

Jesus said to his disciples: "When the Son of Man comes in his glory, and all the angels with him, he will sit upon his glorious throne, and all the nations will be assembled before him. And he will separate them one from another, as a shepherd separates the sheep from the goats. He will place the sheep on his right and the goats on his left. Then the king will say to those on his right, 'Come, you who are blessed by my Father. Inherit the kingdom prepared for you from the foundation of the world. For I was hungry and you gave me food, I was thirsty and you gave me drink, a stranger and you welcomed me, naked and you clothed me, ill and you cared for me, in prison and you visited me.' Then the righteous will answer him and say, 'Lord, when did we see you hungry and feed you, or thirsty and give you drink? When did we see you a stranger and welcome you, or naked and clothe you? When did we see you ill or in prison, and visit you?' And the king will say to them in reply, 'Amen, I say to you, whatever you did for one of the least brothers of mine, you did for me.' Then he will say to those on his left, 'Depart from me, you ac-cursed, into the eternal fire prepared for the devil and his angels. For I was hungry and you gave me no food, I was thirsty and you gave me no drink, a stranger and you gave me no welcome, naked and you gave me no clothing, ill and in prison, and you did not care for me.' Then they will answer and say, 'Lord, when did we see you hungry or thirsty or a stranger or naked or ill or in prison, and not minister to your needs?' He will answer them, 'Amen, I say to you, what you did not do for one of these least ones, you did not do for me.' And these will go off to eternal punishment, but the righteous to eternal life."

The Gospel of the Lord. *Praise to you, Lord Jesus Christ.*

PROFESSION OF FAITH *(page 13)*

PRAYER OF THE FAITHFUL

PREPARATION OF GIFTS *(page 16)*

PRAYER OVER THE OFFERINGS
As we offer you, O Lord, the sacrifice
by which the human race is reconciled to you,
we humbly pray
that your Son himself may bestow on all nations
the gifts of unity and peace.
Through Christ our Lord. *Amen.*

PREFACE: CHRIST, KING OF THE UNIVERSE
It is truly right and just, our duty and our salvation,
always and everywhere to give you thanks,
Lord, holy Father, almighty and eternal God.

For you anointed your Only Begotten Son,
our Lord Jesus Christ, with the oil of gladness
as eternal Priest and King of all creation,
so that, by offering himself on the altar of the Cross

as a spotless sacrifice to bring us peace,
he might accomplish the mysteries of human redemption
and, making all created things subject to his rule,
he might present to the immensity of your majesty
an eternal and universal kingdom,
a kingdom of truth and life,
a kingdom of holiness and grace,
a kingdom of justice, love and peace.

And so, with Angels and Archangels,
with Thrones and Dominions,
and with all the hosts and Powers of heaven,
we sing the hymn of your glory,
as without end we acclaim:
Holy, Holy, Holy Lord God of hosts... (page 35)

⁑ TAKING A CLOSER LOOK ⁑

✝ **Firstfruits** The firstfruits are the initial agricultural products and so represent the rest of the harvest. Like the firstborn son and first offspring of animals, they were considered sacred to God, the source of all good. The reason for their sacred character is not clearly indicated, but perhaps it was associated with the idea that in them God continued the process of creating new life, or perhaps they were a token of the people's need to thank God for the continuation of life. So if Christ is the firstfruits of the resurrection, then the new life that first appears in him will also be found in all those who share his life.

COMMUNION ANTIPHON *(Psalm 29 [28]:10–11)*
The Lord sits as King for ever. The Lord will bless his people with peace.

PRAYER AFTER COMMUNION
Having received the food of immortality,
we ask, O Lord,
that, glorying in obedience
to the commands of Christ, the King of the universe,
we may live with him eternally in his heavenly Kingdom.
Who lives and reigns for ever and ever. ***Amen.***

BLESSING & DISMISSAL *(page 56)* ❉

❉ RESPONDING TO THE WORD ❉

God promises to be our shepherd.

➡ *Which actions of God the shepherd are most important in my life now?*

Our hope for new life means belonging fully to Christ now.

➡ *What can I do to offer myself completely to Christ and his people?*

Jesus tells us that he will be present in others so that when we do good to them, we do it to him.

➡ *What acts of kindness and service to others can I do today?*

Praying
and Living
the Eucharist

Praying with the Scriptures

The Bible's message is that God desires to be with us in our world for a relationship. God invites us into a relationship that will not end with death but will go on forever. Building and nurturing this relationship is what living with Christ is all about.

Each week our Sunday Scripture readings help us to deepen our relationship with Jesus. Through Scripture, we learn who God is and who we are. We also discover ways to grow in our relationship with God and with others. By reading, reflecting, and discussing the meaning of these readings, we find keys to imitating Jesus' example, making his vision and values our own and discovering what a relationship with God demands.

A EUCHARISTIC FORMAT: PATTERN FOR OUR SPIRITUALITY

In our Eucharist and also in our preparation for the Eucharist, we imitate Jesus' actions at the Last Supper—*take, bless, break, share*. Jesus' command to *do this in his memory* characterizes not just our worship but our very lives and mission as Christians.

Participating in the eucharistic liturgy and living eucharistic lives is our way of thanking Jesus and of celebrating and nurturing his continual presence with us, not only in church but in all the moments and situations of our daily lives. Through our deepening experience of Christ in word and sacrament, we announce and celebrate the good news of God's presence among us.

The elements of the simple eucharistic format—*take, bless, break, share*—provide a pattern that can assist us in our goal of praying and living the Eucharist.

■ **TAKE** To "take" is to accept the reality of the moment, to open our-selves to God's presence and God's gifts as they present themselves to us. We take a few moments of quiet to become centered, prayerful, and attentive to God's presence.

■ **BLESS** To "bless" is to acknowledge God's role in something—as in the biblical acclamation, *Bless the Lord, O my soul!* When we think of God's creation, how can we not give thanks and praise? The word "eu-charist" actually comes from the Greek *eucharistia* ("thanksgiving").

■ **BREAK** To "break" the bread of our lives is to be willing to break through to the deeper meaning of our experience. To do that, we explore Sacred Scripture, we think about the ways that God is speaking to us in the events of our lives, we reflect on the words of Jesus, we listen to the wisdom of the Church's teachings—we open ourselves to the voice of God as it whispers to us in our daily experiences. And we discover God's love and forgiveness in the midst of our own brokenness.

■ **SHARE** Christian spirituality is not a narrowly focused "God and me" affair. Christians discover that "I" is never alone; "I" is always an "I *in Christ*." And as one realizes his or her identity as a member of Christ's body, one discovers that the true "I" is really a "we."

We have been called into communion with God and with one an-other. Our own experience of Jesus leads us to ministry, to share the gifts that God has given us, and to bring the fruits of our prayer to others and to our world.

SAMPLE FORMAT FOR PERSONAL REFLECTION

≫ **TAKE** Find a quiet spot where you can read, reflect, and pray. If you wish to record your thoughts and experiences, have your prayer journal handy. Take a few moments of quiet to become prayerful and centered.

≫ **BLESS** Begin your reflection time with a prayer. You may wish to use a spontaneous prayer, the Collect for the coming Sunday, or one from *A Treasury of Prayers* (page 587).

≫ **BREAK**
- *Read:* Read the Scripture readings from the coming Sunday. Pause in silence to be attentive to God's message for you today.
- *Reflect:* Read the Sunday reflection found at the start of the coming Sunday.
- *Respond:* To explore the meaning of the readings, consider first the questions in the *Responding to the Word* at the end of each Sunday. If you wish to explore the readings further, choose one or more of the *Basic Questions for Exploring Scripture* (page 573).

After reflecting on the questions and writing down your answers in your prayer journal, if you wish, take some time to be quiet and attentive to Christ's presence with you—where he wants to dwell right now.

≫ **SHARE** Close with a spontaneous prayer, one chosen from the Mass for the coming Sunday, or one from *A Treasury of Prayers* (page 587).

Now you are better prepared to share the good news with others in the coming week!

Basic Questions for Exploring Scripture

There are several basic questions and some follow-up questions that we can use to explore any biblical reading. *(Note that not all of these questions are equally answered in every passage.)*

What does this text tell me about God? about Jesus? about the Holy Spirit?

● Does this confirm what I already know? ● Is there something new here that I had not noticed before? ● What does God want me to know or do?

What does God/Jesus/the Holy Spirit do in relation to us and our world?

● How is the divine presence and power revealed? ● Why does God come to us? ● What is required of us to do or not do?

What does this text tell me about myself?

● How am I like the person(s) in Scripture? ● How would I respond if this happened to me? ● How would I be changed if I did what the text says? ● What challenged me to live out my faith more fully?
● What surprised me the most about this passage? ● What puzzled me the most? ● What made me most comfortable? Why?
● What made me most uncomfortable? Why?

What do I learn about the community that God desires?

● What does this text tell me about how to love God? ● What does this text tell me about how to love others? ● What guidelines for better community living does the passage offer?

The Practice of Lectio Divina

Lectio divina ("sacred reading") is a contemplative way of reading Sacred Scripture that has been part of the Christian tradition since the third century.

We may find it helpful to think of it as involving three "moments" or stages: reading, meditating, and praying.

READING

This *first moment* consists in our reading a short Scripture passage slowly, attentively, repeatedly—and aloud whenever possible. We may wish to choose the gospel reading for the coming Sunday and read it from the previous Monday all through the week.

Paying close attention to the story, and especially to the words themselves, we let ourselves *enjoy* the story and even grow to *love* the story and the very words in which it is told. When a word or phrase catches our attention, we may jot it down or simply stay with it for awhile to savor its message, allowing its fullness to penetrate our being.

MEDITATION

Reading leads us naturally to the *second moment*: meditation. Having settled on one section, phrase, or even a single word, we let its meaning unfold in our hearts.

Our meditation can take place as we sit in quiet prayer or as we perform the simple activities of our day. It may last an hour, a day, or over the course of a week.

During meditation, we may find ourselves focusing on the present: what does this text have to say about what is happening in my life or in the world around me now? Something in the text may jog a memory of an experience from our own lives. Or we may find that, when we return to our daily activities, some event or situation will unexpectedly bring us back to the text. In either case, the Holy Spirit may be trying to open up a dialogue with us!

PRAYER

Prayer, the *third moment*, also occurs naturally. This is not an intellectual exercise, but a dialogue with God. We respond authentically and spontaneously—as we would in a conversation with a close friend.

Our prayer may take four different forms:

- *Thanksgiving:* When the text reminds us of blessings and good things we have known, we praise and thank God.
- *Repentance:* When we become aware of wrong we have done or good we have failed to do, we humbly ask for forgiveness.
- *Petition:* When the text reminds us of our own needs or of the needs of others, we ask God for guidance and assistance.
- *Contemplation:* By grace, we may be led to a deeper moment of prayer in which we are no longer thanking or repenting or asking, but simply joyfully resting in God's presence, trustfully leaving ourselves in God's hands. This is called contemplative prayer.

I would like to recall and recommend the ancient tradition of **lectio divina***: the diligent reading of Sacred Scripture accompanied by prayer brings about that intimate dialogue in which the person reading hears God who is speaking, and in praying, responds to God with trusting openness of heart. If it is effectively promoted, this practice will bring to the Church— I am convinced of it—a new spiritual springtime."*

POPE BENEDICT XVI

The Liturgical Calendar:
UNFOLDING THE MYSTERY OF CHRIST

One way the Church tells the story of God's saving activity is by its calendar. "Within the cycle of a year, she unfolds the whole mystery of Christ. Recalling thus the mysteries of redemption, the Church opens to the faithful the riches of her Lord's powers and mercies, so that they are in some way made present at all times, and the faithful are enabled to lay hold of them and become filled with saving grace" (Vatican II, *Constitution on the Sacred Liturgy*, #102). During this yearly cycle, we remember our story and deepen our understanding of its meaning for us.

The Church year is anchored by two segments: **Advent–Christmas–Epiphany** and **Lent–Holy Week–Easter**. **Pentecost** and the **Sundays in Ordinary Time** fill out the rest of the year. The overall pattern highlights the transitions from darkness to light to manifestation, and from promise to fulfillment to proclamation.

ADVENT, CHRISTMAS, AND EPIPHANY

Advent, the time of preparation for Christmas, begins on the fourth Sunday before Christmas. As December's darkness and short days permeate our lives, the Church proclaims that Christ comes as the light of the world. Christmas celebrates the mystery of God's incarnation—God-with-us as one of us in human flesh.

Christmas is followed by the Epiphany, celebrating the visit of the magi who traveled from afar to worship the babe in Bethlehem. They represent all the nations of the world searching for their savior. The revelation of God's light and the fulfillment of God's promise in Jesus lead to the proclamation of this good news. In the season after Epiphany, we share the news that God's love is available for every person, for all of creation!

LENT, HOLY WEEK, AND EASTER

The Church's greatest feast and most important rites were celebrated on Easter—the time of initiation, when new members would be baptized and emerge into a new life of fellowship. Today, the seasons of Lent and Easter retain this baptismal focus. Vatican II has renewed the ancient practice of initiation in its Rite of Christian Initiation for Adults (RCIA).

The forty days (excluding Sundays) of Lent recall Jesus' forty days in the wilderness prior to his public ministry. Lent is a time of inwardness, of spiritual discipline, and of growth. During Lent we seek out the shadows in our souls, inviting Christ's light to illumine them.

Lent concludes with Holy Week when we recall the last events of Jesus' life, beginning with his entry into Jerusalem (Passion or Palm Sunday). Then the most sacred Three Days (the Triduum) recall Jesus' Last Supper (Holy Thursday), his crucifixion and death (Good Friday), and his resurrection (Easter Vigil and Easter Day). Then, for fifty days, we bask in the joy of the resurrection and the promise of new life with God forever.

PENTECOST AND ORDINARY TIME

Witnesses are needed to guide others to discover the transforming presence of God. At Pentecost, the Holy Spirit descends on the disciples, uniting them as a community and giving them new tongues to proclaim the good news of God's triumph over death to the ends of the earth.

After Pentecost, we continue with Ordinary Time. It is "ordinary" not because it is common but because the Sundays are counted (they are "in order"). Each Sunday we follow Jesus and have the opportunity to move ever more deeply into sharing in his life, death, and resurrection.

As we attune ourselves to the rhythms of the Church's liturgical year, the mysteries of the Lord's life are made present, and our lives are sanctified by our participation.

Understanding the Lectionary

Since its beginning, the Church has gathered faithfully every Sunday to listen carefully to God's word. The Lectionary for Mass is the selection of the most important Bible readings for use at Mass. Through them the Church remembers and renews its relationship with God.

THE LECTIONARY'S ARRANGEMENT

The lectionary is not a chronological approach to reading the Bible, nor is it a book-by-book approach. Each week the gospel readings are closely linked to the seasons of the Church's life cycle, its liturgical calendar. In the first half of the Church year, we follow the major events of the life of Jesus, including his birth, death, resurrection, and the birth of the Church, and in the second half we study Jesus' actions and teachings.

In addition, the lectionary provides an opportunity to remember great persons in Church history on saints' days and to celebrate special events in the life of a parish, such as confirmation. Throughout the year, Scriptures have been chosen for their appropriateness for the occasions on which they are read.

THE EVOLUTION OF THE CURRENT LECTIONARY

From the time of the Council of Trent (1545-63), when the liturgy was fixed in the form that was familiar to all Catholics before Vatican II, the selection of lectionary readings consisted simply of a one-year cycle that included two Sunday readings, one from a New Testament letter or epistle and another from one of the gospels. The gospel readings were taken mostly from Matthew and Luke, with very few from Mark or John. The Old Testament was read only on Epiphany and during Holy Week.

The liturgical renewal of Vatican Council II (1962-65) directed that the "treasures of Scripture" be made more available so that the faithful would be fed on this richer fare. This momentous change reversed the previous limitation of Scripture by adding an additional reading that, for the first time in centuries, opened the riches of the Old Testament to the weekly Christian gathering (and the Acts of the Apostles during the Easter Season).

The new lectionary includes the following features:

- **Three-year Cycle of Readings:** The Sunday lectionary covers the most significant parts of the Old and New Testaments every three years. The three years, designated A, B, and C, always begin on the First Sunday of Advent. Each of the cycles focuses on one of the synoptic gospels. In Year A, Matthew is read; Year B, Mark; Year C, Luke. The Gospel of John is used during all three years on certain feast days, during Holy Week, and during the Easter season. Since the Gospel of Mark is so brief, the sixth chapter of John's gospel (on the Bread of Life) is read for five weeks of Year B.

- **Four Readings Every Sunday:** Each Sunday, four Scripture passages are assigned to be read: the first reading from the Old Testament (except during the Easter season), chosen to coincide thematically with the gospel; a responsorial psalm relating to the first reading or to the liturgical season; the second reading from the letters or other New Testament writings; and finally the gospel reading.

- **The selected readings are about:**
  - **Christ,** so as to unfold the mystery of Christ's person and teachings over the cycle of the year (see Vatican II, *Constitution on the Sacred Liturgy* [CSL], #102)
  - **Salvation history,** in order to show the place of Christ in God's plan of salvation, thus connecting God's work with Israel (Old Testament) to God's work in Christ (New Testament) (CSL, #5)
  - **"The guiding principles of the Christian life"** (CSL, #52), to help people understand the Christian message and live it more fully in their everyday lives.

This Year's Scriptures:
THE GOSPEL OF MATTHEW

Throughout the centuries, the gospel according to Matthew has played a central part in the life and worship of the Church. As the primary gospel for the Sunday lectionary readings of this year (Lectionary Year A), it launches the new liturgical cycle of seasons as Advent begins.

MATTHEW'S CHALLENGE

Matthew's gospel was composed about 85-90 AD. As more and more Gentiles streamed into the Christian communities after Paul's missionary success, Christians faced a crucial decision about their relationship to Judaism. The fall of Jerusalem in 70 AD and the destruction of its temple forced the decision.

Judaism had to decide how to be Jewish without a temple. This meant thinking seriously about how the community ought to live out its covenant relation to God. Two major options were then available.

The Pharisees advocated a holiness agenda: God was holy and so Jews should become a holy people in a holy land by observing completely the Mosaic law. They demanded a separatist attitude distinguished by practices like circumcision, Sabbath observance, and kosher food regulations that set them apart from everyone else.

The other major option was that of Christianity, which was still viewed as a form of messianic Judaism. Christians, following the "Way" of Jesus, offered an alternative vision for life in the covenant community. Christianity advocated a mercy agenda: God is merciful or compassionate, generously bestowing benefits on everyone and asking for "mercy not sacrifice." So Jesus' kingdom community was open to everyone—Jews and Gentiles.

By about 85 AD, when Matthew was writing, the Pharisees had won the battle over how Judaism would develop, and Christians were no longer welcome in the synagogues. Christians needed to take their heritage and move on.

MATTHEW'S GOSPEL

Matthew's thorough knowledge of Pharisaic Judaism and its teachings allowed him to teach Christians how their way of life, like Jesus himself, was rooted in their Jewish traditions. But he also knew that their old Jewish way of life was no longer possible and, as God's new covenant people, they needed a new way of life and a new mission to bring all the nations into God's kingdom community.

Matthew depends on the gospel of Mark (written about 70 AD) for much of his content and for the outline for his life of Jesus. But Matthew reshaped Mark's gospel and added new material (many more of Jesus' sayings and the accounts of his infancy and of his resurrection appearances) to present the gospel message to meet his community's needs.

Matthew revised Mark's gospel to teach his community to embrace their Jewish tradition because it was the foundation for their Christian way of life. But he also stressed that their future task was participation in the Church's evangelizing mission to the Gentiles.

By portraying Jesus both as the fulfillment of the hopes of Judaism and as the inaugurator of the new Christian way of relating to God, Matthew's gospel serves as a powerful tool for conversion and an invitation to be the new people of God with a mission.

TEACHING HIS COMMUNITY

Matthew revised Mark's gospel because it no longer answered the new problems facing his community in the mid-eighties of the first century. Matthew's primarily Jewish community was facing marginalization in a Church that was fast becoming almost exclusively non-Jewish.

He realized that his community would not be able to continue unless they could find a place in the increasingly Gentile-Christian community. How could he affirm their Jewish tradition and yet urge them to participate in the growing worldwide mission? His gospel is his answer.

JESUS: THE COMPASSIONATE HEALER

Matthew presents Jesus as the Master, a teacher and compassionate healer who guides us step by step through a process of Christian discipleship. The disciples are learners, which is the primary meaning of the Greek word for disciple. Matthew's Jesus often characterizes the disciples as having "little faith" (6:30, 8:26, 14:31, 16:8, 17:20).

They respond to the call of Jesus and then tag along with him—listening to his words and observing his actions. Like us, they grow in faith as they learn about Jesus and his challenging demands for discipleship. Becoming a disciple means not just knowing about what Jesus said and did, but putting his demands into action (7:21).

PETER: A DISCIPLE TO LEARN FROM

Peter serves as Matthew's example of both the positive and negative possibilities of our discipleship. The first to be called (4:18-22), Peter responds eagerly and becomes the leader of the disciples (10:2, 15:15, 17:1-8, 24-27). He responds so correctly to Jesus' question about his identity that Jesus recognizes that Peter's profession of faith is the kind on which a Church can be built (16:13-20).

But despite this great privilege, Peter is still a person of "little faith" who needs to grow. He can be the founding rock or a stumbling block. He is challenged to have faith enough to follow Jesus across water (14:20-33), to avoid being an obstacle to the passion (16:21-23), and to be a leader whose forgiveness is unlimited (18:21-35). Even Peter's failure during the passion does not keep him from being a leader.

Peter shows the ups and downs of the discipleship challenge. Always a learner, he can be a model for us who know that we are far from perfect in our following of Jesus.

THE MISSION OF DISCIPLES

The risen Christ tells the disciples that their task in the world is to "make disciples of all nations" (28:19-20). To help do this, they can use Matthew's gospel to teach the way of discipleship as Jesus had taught it to them.

For Matthew, being a disciple means carrying on the mission of Jesus, becoming a master of the Christian Way, and sharing it so that others can also become Jesus' followers. Taking up this challenge is the daily work that we do as his disciples today.

Liturgical and Devotional Prayer:
WHAT'S THE DIFFERENCE?

There are real differences between liturgical and devotional prayer, but they are linked; we need both, and both have the same goal: to help us grow in our life as Catholic disciples of our Lord. But just what are the major differences between these types of prayer? Here are a few central elements:

Liturgical prayer—officially, the celebration of the seven sacraments and the Liturgy of the Hours—is always primary. These celebrations are primary because these are the privileged ways we enter into Christ's paschal mystery (his life, death, and resurrection that bring life to the world) and learn to live this mystery in our own lives. While we are meant to pray these prayers in a deeply personal way, they are also always intended to link us to the whole Church at prayer. They belong to everybody, which is why the Church insists that individuals may not change them. Liturgical prayer *shapes us* into being ever more perfect members of the Body of Christ.

Devotional prayers, in the words of Vatican II's *Constitution on the Sacred Liturgy,* "should be so drawn up that they harmonize with the liturgical seasons, accord with the sacred liturgy, are in some fashion derived from it, and lead people to it, since the liturgy by its very nature far surpasses any of them" (#13). Devotions are meant to be prayed in a deeply personal way, and may or may not have a communal dimension. *We shape* these prayers to meet our personal prayer needs and encounter God in our daily lives, which in turn helps make us ready for full, conscious, and active participation in the liturgy. There are no required forms of devotional prayer—individuals are free to create or adopt and pray them as meets their needs, within the guidelines set by the Church.

What kind of guidelines? Along with the quote from the *Constitution on the Sacred Liturgy* given above, the Church advises, for example, that these devotions not be overly sentimental. They should not lead one into superstition or be based solely on legendary tales. They should not be added to the liturgy or preferred to liturgical prayer. People are free to pray them or not. They should help us relate emotionally—with the heart and not just the intellect—to the central mysteries of our faith. They should increase our yearning for liturgical prayer and help us pray the Mass deeply and reverently. And their ultimate aim should be the same as that of the liturgy: to say with St. Paul, "I live now, not I, but Christ lives in me" (Galatians 2:20).

Mass and Eucharistic Adoration provide an example of the difference between liturgical and devotional prayer. The Mass is the weekly or daily way we join ourselves to the dying and rising of the Lord. We gather through, with, and in Christ to offer thanks and praise to the Father and to be transformed by the Holy Spirit into the body and blood of Christ in our world—and to eat and drink of Christ's body and blood that we are, and are becoming.

Eucharistic Adoration (in the form of prayer before the tabernacle), on the other hand, is a wonderful way to pause in our busy lives, to step into the presence of God, and to marvel at the great mystery of love celebrated in the Eucharist, to thank God for it, and to pray about what it means to share in Christ's Body and Blood and be his disciples in the world around us.

Of the two, the Mass is always primary, because it is the action of our entering into the paschal mystery. Adoration is meant to strengthen our desire to participate in the Mass and to pray it more deeply, with our heart, mind, and soul. Because Adoration is derived from the eucharistic liturgy and meant to lead us back to the eucharistic liturgy, it has the same goal as the liturgy: to praise and thank God and to help us lead more Christ-like lives in all that we do.

*Prayer is the source and origin of every
upward journey toward God. Let us each,
then, turn to prayer and say to our Lord
God: "Lead me, O Lord, on your path,
that I may walk in your truth."*

— St. Bonaventure

A Treasury
of Prayers

PRAYERS FROM THE BIBLE

The Lord's Prayer: found in Matthew 6:9-13 and in Luke 11:2-4, it is also used in our eucharistic liturgy (page 53)

Song of Moses: from Exodus 15 (page 310)

Paul's Prayers: from Ephesians 1 (page 381) and Romans 15 (page 76)

Canticle of Zechariah (Benedictus): *Luke 1:68-79*
Blessed be the Lord, the God of Israel;
    he has come to his people and set them free.
He has raised up for us a mighty savior,
    born of the house of his servant David.
Through his prophets he promised of old
    that he would save us from our enemies,
    from the hands of all who hate us.
He promised to show mercy to our fathers
    and to remember his holy covenant.
This was the oath he swore
    to our father Abraham: to set us free from the hands of our enemies,
    free to worship him without fear,
    holy and righteous in his sight all the days of our life.
You, my child, shall be called the prophet of the Most High,
    for you will go before the Lord to prepare his way,
    to give his people knowledge of salvation
    by the forgiveness of their sins.
In the tender compassion of our God
    the dawn from on high shall break upon us,
    to shine on those who dwell in darkness and the shadow of death,
    and to guide our feet into the way of peace.

Canticle of Mary (Magnificat): *Luke 1:46-55*

My soul proclaims the greatness of the Lord,
    my spirit rejoices in God my Savior
    for he has looked with favor upon his lowly servant.
From this day all generations will call me blessed:
    the Almighty has done great things for me,
    and holy is his Name.
He has mercy on those who fear him in every generation.
He has shown the strength of his arm,
    and has scattered the proud in their conceit.
He has cast down the mighty from their thrones,
    and has lifted up the lowly.
He has filled the hungry with good things,
    and the rich he has sent away empty.
He has come to the help of his servant Israel
    for he has remembered his promise of mercy,
    the promise he made to our fathers,
    to Abraham and his children for ever.

The Song of Simeon: *Luke 2:29-32*

Lord, now let your servant go in peace;
    your word has been fulfilled:
my own eyes have seen the salvation
    which you have prepared in the sight of every people:
a light to reveal you to the nations
    and the glory of your people Israel.

Paul's Blessing: *Ephesians 3:16-21*
May you be strengthened with power
through God's Spirit in your inner self.
May Christ dwell in your hearts through faith;
so that you, rooted and grounded in love, may have
strength to comprehend with all the holy ones
what is the breadth and length and height and depth,
and to know the love of Christ
that surpasses knowledge, so that you may be filled
with all the fullness of God.
Now to God, who by the power at work within us is able
to accomplish far more than all we ask or imagine,
be glory in the church and in Christ Jesus
to all generations, forever and ever. Amen.

TRADITIONAL PRAYERS FOR EUCHARISTIC ADORATION

The Divine Praises
Blessed be God.
Blessed be his holy name.
Blessed be Jesus Christ, true God and true man.
Blessed be the name of Jesus.
Blessed be his most Sacred Heart.
Blessed be his most Precious Blood.
Blessed be Jesus in the most holy sacrament of the altar.
Blessed be the Holy Spirit, the Paraclete.
Blessed be the great Mother of God, Mary most holy.
Blessed be her holy and immaculate conception.
Blessed be her glorious assumption.

Blessed be the name of Mary, Virgin and Mother.
Blessed be St. Joseph, her most chaste spouse.
Blessed be God in his angels and in his saints.

O Saving Host (O Salutaris Hostia) *By St. Thomas Aquinas*

O saving Victim, opening wide
The gate of Heaven to us below;
Our foes press hard on every side;
Your aid supply; Your strength bestow.
To your great name be endless praise,
Immortal Godhead, One in Three.
O grant us endless length of days,
In our true native land with thee.
Amen.

Latin Text:

O salutaris Hostia,
Quae cæli pandis ostium:
Bella premunt hostilia,
Da robur, fer auxilium.
Uni trinoque Domino
Sit sempiterna gloria,
Qui vitam sine termino
Nobis donet in patria.
Amen.

Sing My Tongue (Pange Lingua Gloriosi)

Latin text by St. Thomas Aquinas, English translation by E. Caswall (1849)

Sing, my tongue, the Savior's glory,
of his flesh the mystery sing;
of the blood, all price exceeding,
shed by our immortal King,
destined, for the world's redemption,
from a noble womb to spring.

Of a pure and spotless Virgin
born for us on earth below,
He, as Man, with us conversing,
stayed, the seeds of truth to sow;
then he closed in solemn order
wond'rously his Life of woe.

On the night of that Last Supper,
seated with his chosen band,
He, the Paschal Victim eating,
first fulfills the Law's command;
then as Food to his Apostles
gives himself with his own hand.

Word-made-Flesh, the bread of nature
by his Word to Flesh he turns;
wine into his Blood he changes;
what though sense no change discerns?
Only be the heart in earnest,
faith her lesson quickly learns.

Down in adoration falling,
This great Sacrament we hail,
O'er ancient forms of worship
Newer rites of grace prevail;
Faith will tell us Christ is present,
When our human senses fail.

To the Everlasting Father,
And the Son who made us free
And the Spirit, God proceeding
From them each eternally,
Be salvation, honor, blessing,
Might and endless majesty.
Amen. Alleluia.

Latin Text:
Pange, lingua, gloriosi
Corporis mysterium,
Sanguinisque pretiosi,
quem in mundi pretium
fructus ventris generosi
Rex effudit Gentium.

Nobis datus, nobis natus
ex intacta Virgine,
et in mundo conversatus,
sparso verbi semine,
sui moras incolatus
miro clausit ordine.

In supremae nocte coenae
recumbens cum fratribus
observata lege plene
cibis in legalibus,
cibum turbae duodenae
se dat suis manibus.

Verbum caro, panem verum
verbo carnem efficit:
fitque sanguis Christi merum,
et si sensus deficit,
ad firmandum cor sincerum
sola fides sufficit.

Tantum ergo Sacramentum
veneremur cernui:
et antiquum documentum
novo cedat ritui:
praestet fides supplementum
sensuum defectui.

Genitori, Genitoque
laus et jubilatio,
salus, honor, virtus quoque
sit et benedictio:
Procedenti ab utroque
compar sit laudatio.
Amen. Alleluja.

PRAYERS FROM THE CHRISTIAN TRADITION

Glory be to the Father

Glory be to the Father,
    and to the Son,
    and to the Holy Spirit.
As it was in the beginning, is now,
    and ever shall be, world without end. Amen.

The Hail Mary

Hail Mary, full of grace, the Lord is with thee.
Blessed art thou among women
and blessed is the fruit of thy womb, Jesus.
Holy Mary, Mother of God, pray for us sinners,
now and at the hour of our death. Amen.

Hail, Holy Queen (Salve Regina)

Hail, holy Queen, mother of mercy,
our life, our sweetness and our hope.
To you do we cry, poor banished children of Eve;
to you do we send up our sighs,
mourning and weeping in this valley of tears.
Turn then, most gracious advocate,
your eyes of mercy toward us,
and after this, our exile, show unto us
the blessed fruit of your womb, Jesus.
O clement, O loving, O sweet Virgin Mary.

Anima Christi

Soul of Christ, be my sanctification;
Body of Christ, be my salvation;
Blood of Christ, fill all my veins;
Water of Christ's side, wash out my stains;
Passion of Christ, my comfort be;
O good Jesu, listen to me;
In Thy wounds I fain would hide;
Ne'er to be parted from Thy side;
Guard me, should the foe assail me;
Call me when my life shall fail me;
Bid me come to Thee above,
With Thy saints to sing Thy love,
World without end. Amen.
(Translation by St. John Henry Cardinal Newman)

The Memorare

Remember, most gracious Virgin Mary,
that never was it known that anyone
who fled to your protection, implored your help,
and sought your intercession, was left unaided.
Inspired with this confidence, I fly to you,
O Virgin of virgins, my mother.
To you do I come; before you I stand,
sinful and sorrowful.
Mother of the Word Incarnate,
despise not my petitions
but in your mercy hear and answer me. Amen.

Regina Caeli (Queen of Heaven)
O Queen of heaven, rejoice, alleluia!
    For he whom you chose to bear, alleluia!
Is risen as he said, alleluia!
    Pray for us to God, alleluia!
Rejoice and be glad, O Virgin Mary, alleluia!
    For the Lord is truly risen, alleluia!

O God, by the resurrection of your Son, our Lord,
You were pleased to make glad the whole world;
grant, we beseech you, that through
the intercession of the Virgin Mary, his mother,
we may attain the joys of everlasting life,
through the same Christ our Lord. Amen.

Act of Contrition
My God, I am sorry for my sins with all my heart.
In choosing to do wrong and failing to do good,
I have sinned against you
whom I should love above all things.
I firmly intend, with your help,
to do penance,
to sin no more,
and to avoid whatever leads me to sin.
Our Savior Jesus Christ suffered and died for us.
In his name, my God, have mercy. Amen.

The Angelus

The angel of the Lord declared unto Mary,
    and she conceived of the Holy Spirit. *Hail Mary...*
Behold, the handmaid of the Lord;
    be it done to me according to your word. *Hail Mary...*
And the word was made flesh,
    and dwelt among us. *Hail Mary...*

Pray for us, O holy Mother of God;
    that we may be made worthy of the promises of Christ.

Pour forth, we beseech you, O Lord,
your grace into our hearts
that we, to whom the incarnation of your Son
was made known by the message of an angel,
may by his passion and cross
be brought to the glory of his resurrection.
We ask this through the same Christ, our Lord. Amen.

THE ROSARY

Like the prayer beads that are used in many religious traditions, the rosary keeps our hands moving while our minds and hearts are meditating on the mysteries of Jesus' life, death, and resurrection. While using the rosary, we focus on twenty events or mysteries in the life and death of Jesus and reflect on how we share with Mary in the saving work of Christ today. Reading a related passage from the Bible helps to deepen meditation on a particular mystery. The Scripture citations given here are not exhaustive. Many other biblical texts are also be suitable for your prayerful reflection.

To pray the rosary:

- Begin the rosary at the crucifix, making the Sign of the Cross and praying the **Apostles' Creed**
- At the first large bead say the **Our Father**, then for the three beads pray the **Hail Mary** for each of the gifts of faith, hope, and love, then **Glory be to the Father.**
- For each mystery, begin with the **Our Father** (the single bead), then recite the **Hail Mary** ten times, and end with **Glory be to the Father**

The Five Joyful Mysteries

The Annunciation (Luke 1:26-38)
The Visitation (Luke 1:39-56)
The Nativity (Luke 2:1-20)
The Presentation (Luke 2:22-38)
The Finding in the Temple (Luke 2:41-52)

The Five Mysteries of Light
The Baptism in the Jordan (Matthew 3:13-17)
The Wedding at Cana (John 2:1-12)
The Proclamation of the Kingdom (Mark 1:14-15)
The Transfiguration (Luke 9:28-36)
The First Eucharist (Matthew 26:26-29)

The Five Sorrowful Mysteries
The Agony in the Garden (Matthew 26:36-56)
The Scourging at the Pillar (Matthew 27:20-26)
The Crowning with Thorns (Matthew 27:27-30)
The Carrying of the Cross (Matthew 27:31-33)
The Crucifixion (Matthew 27:34-60)

The Five Glorious Mysteries
The Resurrection (John 20:1-18)
The Ascension (Acts 1:9-11)
The Descent of the Holy Spirit (John 20:19-23)
The Assumption of Mary (John 11:26)
The Crowning of Mary (Philippians 2:1-11)

PRAYERS FROM THE SAINTS

May the angel of peace watch over us

May God the Father, who made us, bless us.
May God the Son send his healing among us.
May God the Holy Spirit move within us
and give us eyes to see with, ears to hear with,
and hands that your work might be done.
May we walk and preach the word of God to all.
May the angel of peace watch over us
and lead us at last by God's grace to the kingdom. Amen.

● St. Dominic (1170-1221)

O Love

O Love Almighty, in your love confirm me.
O Love most wise, give me wisdom in the love of you.
O Love most valuable, grant that I may live only for you.
O Love most faithful, in all my tribulations comfort me.
O Love always with me, work all my works in me.
O Love victorious, grant that I may persevere in you. Amen.

● St. Gertrude the great (1256-1302)

To be like Jesus

O God, make us more like Jesus.
Help us to bear difficulty, pain, disappointment, sorrow,
knowing that in your perfect working and design
you can use such bitter experiences to shape our characters
and make us more like our Lord.
We look with hope for that day when we shall be wholly like Christ,
because we shall see him as he is. Amen.

● St. Ignatius of Antioch (35-108)

Lord, make me an instrument of your peace

Lord, make me an instrument of your peace.
Where there is hatred, let me sow love;
where there is injury, pardon;
where there is doubt, faith;
where there is despair, hope;
where there is darkness, light;
and where there is sadness, joy.
Divine Master, grant that I may not so much seek
to be consoled as to console,
to be understood as to understand,
to be loved as to love.
For it is in giving that we receive,
in pardoning that we are pardoned,
and in dying that we are born to eternal life. Amen.

● INSPIRED BY ST. FRANCIS OF ASSISI (1181/82-1226)

May we serve others

Make us worthy, Lord, to serve others throughout the world
who live and die in poverty and hunger.
Give them, through our hands, this day their daily bread.
And by our understanding love, give peace and joy. Amen.

● ST. TERESA OF CALCUTTA (1910-1997)

Help me to seek you

Grant me, O Lord my God, a mind to know you, a heart to seek you,
wisdom to find you, conduct pleasing to you,
faithful perseverance in waiting for you,
and a hope of finally embracing you. Amen.

● ST. THOMAS AQUINAS (1225-1274)

Thankful is the life I live

Christ, O Creator, hear my cry,
I am all yours, your call I hear,
My Savior, Love, yours am I,
My heart to yours be ever near.
Whether in life or death's last hour,
If sickness, pain, or health you give,
Or shame or honor, weakness, power,
Thankful is the life I live. Amen.

● St. Teresa of Ávila (1515-1582)

Day by day

Thanks be to you, my Lord Jesus Christ,
for all the benefits that you have won for us,
for all the pains and insults that you have borne for us.
O most merciful Redeemer, Friend, and Brother,
may we know you more clearly, love you more dearly,
and follow you more nearly, day by day. Amen.

● St. Richard de Wyche, Bishop of Chichester (1197-1253)

O Heart of Love

O my God, fill my soul with holy joy,
courage and strength to serve you.
Enkindle your love in me and then walk with me
along the next stretch of road before me.
I do not see very far ahead, but when I have arrived
where the horizon now closes down,
a new prospect will open before me,
and I shall meet it with peace. Amen.

● St. Teresa Benedicta of the Cross [Edith Stein] (1891-1942)

MORNING PRAYERS

Grant us grace
Christ Jesus, we ask not that you would spare us affliction,
but that you will not abandon us in it.
When we encounter affliction,
teach us to see you in it as our sole comforter.
Let affliction strengthen our faith, fortify our hope, and purify our love.
Grant us the grace to see how we can use our affliction to your glory,
and to desire no other comforter but you,
our Savior, Strengthener, and Friend. Amen.
● St. Bernadette Soubirous (1844-1879)

I give you this day
My God, I give you this day.
I offer you, now, all of the good that I shall do
and I promise to accept, for love of you,
all of the difficulty that I shall meet.
Help me to conduct myself during this day in a way that pleases you.
● St. Francis de Sales (1567-1622)

Help us to follow your will
O Father, the first rule of our Savior's life was to do your will.
Let his will of the present moment
be the first rule of our daily life and work,
with no other desire
but for its most full and complete accomplishment.
Help us to follow it faithfully,
so that in doing what you wish
we will be pleasing to you. Amen.
● St. Elizabeth Ann Seton (1774-1821)

EVENING PRAYERS

O Lord, draw near
We bring before you, O Lord,
the troubles and perils of people and nations,
the sighing of prisoners and captives,
the sorrows of the bereaved,
the necessities of strangers,
the helplessness of the weak,
the despondency of the weary,
the failing powers of the aged.
O Lord, draw near to each,
for the sake of Jesus Christ our Lord. Amen.
• St. Anselm of Canterbury (1033-1109)

You are the One
Spirit of truth, you are the reward to the saints,
the comforter of souls, light in the darkness, riches to the poor,
treasure to lovers, food for the hungry, comfort to the wanderer.
To sum up, you are the One in whom all treasures are contained.
• St. Mary Magdalene de'Pazzi (1566-1607)

Be with us
Watch, dear Lord,
with those who wake, or watch, or weep tonight,
and give your angels charge over those who sleep.
Tend your sick ones, O Lord Jesus Christ.
Rest your weary ones. Bless your dying ones.
Soothe your suffering ones. Pity your afflicted ones.
Shield your joyous ones. And all for your love's sake. Amen.
• St. Augustine of Hippo (354-430)

LITANY OF THE MOST HOLY NAME OF JESUS

Lord, have mercy	*Lord, have mercy*
Christ, have mercy	*Christ, have mercy*
Lord, have mercy	*Lord, have mercy*
God our Father in heaven	*Have mercy on us*
God the Son, Redeemer of the world	*Have mercy on us*
God the Holy Spirit	*Have mercy on us*
Holy Trinity, one God	*Have mercy on us*
Jesus, Son of the living God	*Have mercy on us*
Jesus, splendor of the Father	*Have mercy on us*
Jesus, brightness of everlasting light	*Have mercy on us*
Jesus, king of glory	*Have mercy on us*
Jesus, dawn of justice	*Have mercy on us*
Jesus, Son of the Virgin Mary	*Have mercy on us*
Jesus, worthy of our love	*Have mercy on us*
Jesus, worthy of our wonder	*Have mercy on us*
Jesus, mighty God	*Have mercy on us*
Jesus, father of the world to come	*Have mercy on us*
Jesus, prince of peace	*Have mercy on us*
Jesus, all-powerful	*Have mercy on us*
Jesus, pattern of patience	*Have mercy on us*
Jesus, model of obedience	*Have mercy on us*
Jesus, gentle and humble of heart	*Have mercy on us*
Jesus, lover of chastity	*Have mercy on us*
Jesus, lover of us all	*Have mercy on us*
Jesus, God of peace	*Have mercy on us*
Jesus, author of life	*Have mercy on us*
Jesus, model of goodness	*Have mercy on us*

Jesus, seeker of souls	*Have mercy on us*
Jesus, our God	*Have mercy on us*
Jesus, our refuge	*Have mercy on us*
Jesus, father of the poor	*Have mercy on us*
Jesus, treasure of the faithful	*Have mercy on us*
Jesus, Good Shepherd	*Have mercy on us*
Jesus, the true light	*Have mercy on us*
Jesus, eternal wisdom	*Have mercy on us*
Jesus, infinite goodness	*Have mercy on us*
Jesus, our way and our life	*Have mercy on us*
Jesus, joy of angels	*Have mercy on us*
Jesus, king of patriarchs	*Have mercy on us*
Jesus, teacher of apostles	*Have mercy on us*
Jesus, master of evangelists	*Have mercy on us*
Jesus, courage of martyrs	*Have mercy on us*
Jesus, light of confessors	*Have mercy on us*
Jesus, purity of virgins	*Have mercy on us*
Jesus, crown of all saints	*Have mercy on us*
Lord, be merciful	*Jesus, save your people*
From all evil	*Jesus, save your people*
From every sin	*Jesus, save your people*
From the snares of the devil	*Jesus, save your people*
From your anger	*Jesus, save your people*
From the spirit of infidelity	*Jesus, save your people*
From everlasting death	*Jesus, save your people*
From neglect of your Holy Spirit	*Jesus, save your people*
By the mystery of your incarnation	*Jesus, save your people*
By your birth	*Jesus, save your people*
By your childhood	*Jesus, save your people*

By your hidden life	*Jesus, save your people*
By your public ministry	*Jesus, save your people*
By your agony and crucifixion	*Jesus, save your people*
By your abandonment	*Jesus, save your people*
By your grief and sorrow	*Jesus, save your people*
By your death and burial	*Jesus, save your people*
By your rising to new life	*Jesus, save your people*
By your return in glory to the Father	*Jesus, save your people*
By your gift of the holy Eucharist	*Jesus, save your people*
By your joy and glory	*Jesus, save your people*

Christ, hear us	*Christ, hear us*
Lord Jesus, hear our prayer	*Lord Jesus, hear our prayer*
Lamb of God, you take away the sins of the world	*Have mercy on us*
Lamb of God, you take away the sins of the world	*Have mercy on us*
Lamb of God, you take away the sins of the world	*Have mercy on us*

Let us pray.

Lord, may we who honor the holy name of Jesus
enjoy his friendship in this life
and be filled with eternal joy
in the kingdom where he lives and reigns
for ever and ever. Amen.

RECEIVING COMMUNION OUTSIDE MASS

In the celebration of the Eucharist we recognize the presence of Christ in the priest, in the word proclaimed, in the prayer and song of the assembly, and above all in the consecrated elements. Our eucharistic communion with Christ and one another is the living sign of our belonging to Jesus' kingdom community. So from its beginning, the Christian community has always made provision for those who are unable to be present to celebrate this eucharistic communion with Christ. The communion ritual outside of Mass mirrors the same four parts that give the Mass its structure: an introductory rite, a liturgy of the word, a liturgy of the Eucharist, and a concluding rite. You may wish to begin with the following prayers of preparation:

For the extraordinary minister of Holy Communion

O loving God, may your healing and nurturing presence be clearly evident in my whole being today: in my speaking and listening, in my attitude of compassion and understanding. Help me to communicate to those who are homebound the love and care of Christ and of our Christian community from whom I am sent. Let all that is in my mind, all that comes from my lips and from within my heart, reflect the greatness of your love. Amen.

For the communicant

This prayer may be said by the communicant, a family or household member, or the minister.

O loving and faithful God, you invite us to share in the eucharistic food, a sign of your commitment to be with us each day of our life's journey. Despite our personal limitations, you love us completely and nourish us with your divine life. Give us the strength we need to meet whatever challenges that we are now experiencing. Amen.

INTRODUCTORY RITE

May the blessing of God, the love of Christ,
the power of the Holy Spirit,
and the good wishes of our parish community be with you.
And with your spirit.

Use the Collect from any Sunday or from Holy Thursday (page 265).

LITURGY OF THE WORD

Jesus' words offer comfort in our time of need
and invite us to continue to be like Jesus
even in the difficult times of our lives.

*Read aloud one of the Sunday Scripture readings from this missal or a
reading from the suggestions below. After some time for quiet reflection,
pray the Responsorial Psalm together and/or share one or two thoughts
about the reading.*

*The following readings from this missal are also especially appropriate
for a communion service.*

> Holy Thursday: Mass of the Lord's Supper, page 265
> Feast of the Most Holy Body and Blood of Christ, page 407
> The Last Supper in Matthew's gospel, page 246
> Come to me (Matthew 11:25-30), page 430
> A spirit of wisdom (Ephesians 1:17-23), page 381
> The Holy Spirit is given to us (Romans 5:1-2, 5-8), page 210
> God so loved the world (John 3:16-18), page 403

RECEPTION OF THE EUCHARIST

The Lord's Prayer
Hearing God's word has drawn us together, and now we deepen our communion by sharing the body of Christ. To prepare ourselves for his coming, let us pray as he taught us: *Our Father...*

Invitation to communion
This bread that we share is the body of Christ,
the sign of his endless love and the gift of himself
so that we may live with God now and forever.
Take and eat this bread with confidence that Jesus' presence in it
will nourish you, heal and strengthen you, and transform you from within.

As the bread is given, the minister says:
The Body of Christ. *Amen.*

CONCLUDING RITE

After communion, allow time for quiet reflection to attend to Jesus' presence. You may wish to say a prayer such as the Anima Christi (page 596) or Psalm 23 (page 220).

Prayer after communion
Pray this prayer after communion or one from a Sunday:
Gracious God, you have nourished us with the bread that makes us one in Christ. Fill us with your Spirit, make us one in peace and love, and help us to bring your salvation and joy to those we meet today. We ask this through Christ our Lord. *Amen.*

Conclude by sharing a sign of peace with one another.

Keep God at the Center of Your Daily Life

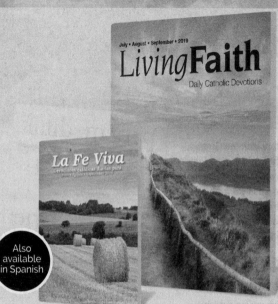

Living Faith **helps you develop the habit of daily prayer with simple and faith-filled devotions.**

Each devotion is a personal reflection on a Scripture passage from one of the day's Mass readings.

Timely, inexpensive and easy to use, *Living Faith* will become a cherished part of your daily prayer life.

POCKET 4" X 5" — **$15** per year

LARGE PRINT 5" X 8" — **$16** per year

SPANISH 4" X 5" — **$15** per year

bayard   Published by Creative Communications for the Parish, a division of Bayard, Inc.

Pronunciation Guide
for Biblical Words

*Many biblical personal and place names are familiar to us and so offer little problem with their pronunciation. The following lists only unfamiliar names that might be difficult to pronounce. Words marked with an asterisk (*) in the readings are found in this pronunciation guide. The **bold syllable** indicates the accent for the word.*

Ahaz (**ay**-haz)

Alphaeus (**al**-fee-uhs)

Arimathea
    (ahr-uh-muh-**thee**-uh)

Barabbas (buh-**rab**-uhs)

Bethany (**beth**-uh-nee)

Bethphage (beth-**fuh**-dzhee)

Caesar (**see**-zer)

Caesarea (ses-uh-**ree**-uh)

Caiaphas (**keye**-a-fas)

Capernaum (ka-**per**-nah-um)

Cephas (**see**-fahs)

Cappadocia (kap-uha-**doh**-shuh)

cherubim (**cher**-uh-bim)

Cleopas (**klee**-oh-puhs)

Cyrenian (sahy-**ree**-nee-uhn)

Didymus (**did**-ee-muhs)

Elamites (**ee**-luh-mahyts)

Eliakim (eh-**lye**-uh-kim)

Ephah (**ef**-ah)

Ephraim (**ee**-frah-im)

Gabbatha (**gab**-uh-thuh)

Gethsemane (geth-**sem**-uh-nee)

Gehenna (geh-**hen**-uh)

Golgotha (**gahl**-guh-thuh)

Hilkiah (hel-**kye**-uh)

Horeb (**hohr**-eb)

hyssop (**his**-uhp)

lema sabachthani
    (**lah**-mah sah-bahk-**tah**-nee)

Malchus (**mal**-kuhs)

Massah (**mah**-suh)

Medes (**meeds**)

Meribah (**mehr**-ih-bah)

Mesopotamia
    (mes-uh-puh-**tey**-mee-uh)

Midian (**mid**-ee-uhn)

myrrh (**mur**)

Naphtali (**naf**-tuh-lye)

Nazorean (naz-uh-**ree**-uhn)

Nicanor (nai-**kay**-nawr)

Pamphylia (pam-**fil**-ee-uh)

Parthians (**pahr**-thee-uhns)

Parmenas (**pahr**-mee-nahs)

Phrygia (**frij**-ee-uh)

praetorium (pray-**tahr**-ee-uhm)

Quirinius (kwih-**rihn**-ee-uhs)

Samaria (suh-**mair**-ee-uh)

Sanhedrin (san-**hee**-drin)

Seba (**see**-buh)

Sheba (**shee**-buh)

Sidon (**sahyd**-n)

Siloam (sih-**lo**-uhm)

Silvanus (sihl-**vay**-nuhs)

Sosthenes (**sahs**-thuh-neez)

Sychar (**sahy**-kar)

Tarshish (**tahr**-shish)

Tyre (**tai**-er)

Yahweh-yireh
    (**yah**-weh-**yeer**-eh)

Zebulun (**zeb**-yuh-luhn)

Zechariah (zek-uh-**rahy**-uh)

Zion (**zahy**-uhn)